I0126264

EARLY MARRIAGES IN BATH COUNTY, KENTUCKY

Bonds 1811-1850
AND
Returns 1811-1852

Paul McClure

HERITAGE BOOKS
2015

HERITAGE BOOKS

AN IMPRINT OF HERITAGE BOOKS, INC.

Books, CDs, and more—Worldwide

For our listing of thousands of titles see our website
at
www.HeritageBooks.com

Published 2015 by
HERITAGE BOOKS, INC.
Publishing Division
5810 Ruatan Street
Berwyn Heights, Md. 20740

Copyright © 1994 Paul McClure

All rights reserved. No part of this book may be reproduced or transmitted in any form or by any means, electronic or mechanical, including photocopying, recording or by any information storage and retrieval system without written permission from the author, except for the inclusion of brief quotations in a review.

International Standard Book Numbers
Paperbound: 978-1-55613-952-9
Clothbound: 978-0-7884-6101-9

Contents

Introduction

This volume brings together, for the first time, the two types of records which exist for early marriages in Bath County, Kentucky: marriage bonds and marriage returns.

Marriage bonds, in early Kentucky, were roughly equivalent to the modern-day marriage license. They constituted a legally binding contract of marriage, with at least two parties—usually the groom and a male relative of the bride—agreeing to pay a fine if the wedding did not take place. The bond was supposed to be sent to the county clerk before the wedding, though actual practice was more flexible, at least in Bath County. With the bond there came the neccessary statements of parental consent, particularly if the bondsman was not a parent or guardian of the bride. Widows, and perhaps some older single women (spinsters, as they were called), could give consent for themselves. Younger men— apparently those under twenty-one—also needed a parent's consent to marry, though this appears to have been another flexible requirement.

In the early days, after Bath County was formed from Montgomery in January 1811, there was no standard form for marriage bonds and parental consent, so that the records preserved and microfilmed at the Kentucky State Archives are the individual slips of paper that families sent to the county clerk. Hence a few of the bonds that survive offer some unusual information. For example, when Nathaniel W. Ralls gave consent for his daughter Marian to wed Samuel Jones in April 1814, he included a social invitation to the county clerk on the same piece of paper: "Major Fletcher & family are requested to dine with me on Thursday next. N. W. R." In days when so few people were literate, however, it must generally have been the case that professional scribes were employed to write out the bonds and statements of consent—all but the X that served as a signature.

Marriage returns, on the other hand, were sent to the county clerk after the wedding, by the person who had performed the ceremony. They were then entered into the marriage book at the county courthouse. Though clergymen and justices of the peace were expected to report all marriages, they in fact did this only periodically—just once a year, in most cases. As a result, some early marriages may have been forgotten, and some of the people performing weddings may never have established the habit of keeping and sending in records. At the clerk's office there would be another delay, until a scribe was able to copy the returns into the permanent register. It is clear from the second Bath County marriage book, the oldest of these volumes to survive, that some of the loose returns were lost before they could be copied out: we encounter a minister's statement that his marriages for a given year are "enclosed," but the marriages themselves do not follow.

It is important to recognize, therefore, that the present volume can only be as complete as its sources. For some Bath County marriages our only record is earlier transcriptions, since some marriage bonds appear to have disappeared or disintegrated before the Kentucky State Archives could microfilm them, and the first Bath County marriage book, for the period 1811 to 1826, is missing. It is because we must rely in some cases on earlier transcriptions that the present volume juxtaposes all available records for each individual marriage. In some cases, one transcriber may have made an error in reading the original, whereas another did not. Most errors involve the spelling of names; but dates also pose problems, since marriage returns often include the date on which the minister wrote to the county clerk as well the date of the wedding itself. Where one date for a given marriage is months after another, it must often be the case that the later one is the date of the marriage return, not the day the marriage took place.

On the other hand, since the spelling of many surnames and given names was by no means fixed prior to 1850, perfectly accurate transcriptions of both the marriage bond and marriage return may make the same individuals' names look very different. Even when the parties themselves were literate, these marriage records may tell us more about how the scribes at the courthouse spelled particular names than about the preferences of the early families. Some names seem to have had interchangeable forms, such as "Goodpasture" and "Goodpaster." In other cases, however, we may find clues to an earlier pronunciation or spelling: "Darnell," for example, is standard at a later date, whereas in these early Bath County records we more often see "Darnal / Darnall" or "Darnold."

Some specific sources of error:
— Single initials are especially difficult to decipher (full names at least provide a context for deciphering an unclear capital letter). The most common problems: S. vs. L.; T. vs. F.; M. (or Mc / M') vs. W.
— Lower case letters: r's, n's, m's, u's, v's, and w's can all look alike; undotted i looks like e; a often looks like o.
— Titles are occasionally included, and can cause confusion: Mrs. or Miss may look like the initial M., or the first name Mary.

As in the earlier transcriptions of Annie Walker Burns, Julia Ardery, and John Sharp, every effort has been made here to preserve the spelling of the original records, including the abbreviations of first names.

Thanks to the following, and others, for help with the genealogical research that has led to this volume: Mrs. Farris Roschi; Joy S. Adams; Mrs. Mildred Wonn; Mrs. Phyllis Hart Leedom; Mrs. Barbara H. Sundermeyer; Mrs. Earnestine Harned; my brother, Matthew K. McClure; most of all my parents, M. Kenneth and Noma P. McClure, whose energy and patience has made it possible for me to compile this book from so far away.

This book is dedicated in memory of Mrs. Farris Hendrix Roschi of Bath County, Kentucky.

Paul McClure
Ithaca, New York

Sources for Bath County, Kentucky, marriage records

[AB]   Annie Walker Burns, "Record of Marriages of Bath County, Kentucky, copied from the marriage bonds, which gives names of parents and bondsman" (1811-1850), Washington, DC, 1937. Unpublished typescript on file at the Kentucky Historical Society Library, Frankfort, KY. Includes some early bonds which are missing from the microfilms at the state archives. Where bonds do survive, Burns's transcription is quite accurate, though some bonds offer more information than Burns copied down.

[KM]   Kentucky State Archives, microfilms of Bath County, KY, marriage bonds.

[JA]   Mrs. W. B. (Julia) Ardery, "Bath County Marriages" (1811-1817), in *Kentucky Records, Volume II*, Lexington, 1932. Includes the statement: "The following marriages, copied from the marriage book of certificates returned by the clergy, contain many names difficult to decipher and many misspelled names. The spelling of all names in the following list is given as it appears in the original."

[S1]   John L. Sharp, "Bath County, Kentucky, Marriage Records, 1811-1826," Morehead, KY, 1975. A transcription of the first book of Bath County marriage returns, which has been lost from the courthouse in Owingsville. States that "many names . . . were misspelled in the original record." For some marriages 1817-1826, Sharp's transcription is our only source.

[S2]   John L. Sharp, "Bath County, Kentucky, Marriages, Volume Two, 1826-1866," Kuttawa, KY, 1977. Transcriptions of the second and third Bath County marriage books, 1826-52 and 1852-66, respectively. My transcription of the 1826-52 volume [B2] has been checked thoroughly against Sharp's.

[B2]   Second volume of Bath County marriage returns, 1826-52, Owingsville, KY.

[RS]   Robert Stuart Sanders, "An Historical Sketch of Springfield Presbyterian Church, Bath County, Kentucky," Frankfort, KY, 1954: includes a transcription of the marriage book kept by Rev. Joseph P. Howe, 1795-1826. (See Appendix.)

[TP]   Anonymous typescript of J. P. Howe's marriages, bound at Ky. Historical Society Library with Burns's Bath Co. marriage bonds, no date. Includes the statement: "Copied from photostats made from the original manuscript in the Presbyterian Historical Society, Philadelphia, Pa." (See Appendix.)

Persons performing marriages in Bath County, Kentucky, 1811-1852:

(MG or PG: Minister / Preacher of the Gospel; JP: Justice of the Peace)

WDA	Abbott, MG (Methodist Episcopal Church South)
JAn	J. Anderson
BBv	Bazell Bivin / Bivins
JBn	James Blain
EBr	Elisha Bradley
ABr	A. [?]Brinddws
CBw	Cummens Brown, MG
ODB	O. D. Buckner
DBk	Daniel S. Burksdale
GWB	G. W. Bush, minister (Methodist Episcopal Church South)
GBu	George Butler, elder & teacher of gospel (Church of Christ)
RFC	R. F. Caldwell, Sharpsburg
LCb	Lewis Campbell, MG (Baptist)
PCy	Peter Cassity / Cassety / Casady
TWC	T. W. Chandler, TE[?]
ACs	Amos Cleares, Rector (M. Peter[?] Church, Paris)
JCm	John Clement / Clements
BCs	Bohannon Collins
JCr	John Creary
TCp	Thos. Cropper
JCC	Jas. C. Crow
EAD	E. A. Daniel, elder, [?]WB
TDm	Thos. Demoss
DDt	Danl. Dillon / Ditton, elder (Church of Christ)
JDh	John Donohew
JDy	John Doyle, MG
HSD	Henry S. Ducks
HEv	Henry J. Evans, MG
JEv	John Evans / Evins, MG
TEv	Thomas Evins
WFg	Wm. Fagg
GFs	Geo. Foster
JFs	Jeremiah Foster

SYG	Saml. Y. Garrison, [?]VDM
RGd	Reuben Gidders
GGd	G[ilbert?] Gordon
MGs	Mathias Gosset / Gossett
AGg	Allen Gudgell, JP
CHp	Charles Harper, minister (Baptist)
BHr	Bishop Harris, MG
JCH	John C. Harrison
GHk	George Haskell, MG (Baptist)
SLH	S. L. ?Heclem
JHg	John H. Hedges, elder (Church of Christ)
JHe	John Hensley / Hencely, MG
LGH	Lewis Garnes Hicks, MG
WHm	W. Holman, elder (Methodist Episcopal)
JHn	John Hon, MG (Baptist)
PHn	Peter Hon
SHo	Solomon Hosteller, elder (Church of Christ)
EHw	Eli Howard
JPH	Joseph Price Howe, minister (Presbyterian)
JHH	John H. Hughes
AHu	Absulum Hunt
BHu	Bazel Hunt
JHu	Jeremiah Hunt
TIs	Thomas Iles, JP
SJk	Samuel Jackson
MJm	Milton Jamison
EJo	Elkanah Johnson, MG
SJo	Samuel Johnson
JJn	James Jones
SJn	Samuel Jones
AKe	Allen Kendrick, MG
SKc	Samuel Kincaid / Kincade / Kingcade, MG
WBL	William B. Landrum, MG
TDL	Thomas D. Lea
JGL	James G. Leach
SVL	S. V. Lee, MG
IGL	Israel G. Lewis, MG
SPL	S. Percival Little
JLk	J. ?A. Locke
ALy	Andrew Lynam, MG

TLy	Thomas Lynam, PG
GMr	George Marshall, MG (Baptist)
WMt	William Martin
MFM	M. F. Maury
AMx	Asa Maxey, elder (Church of Christ)
RMx	Raney Maxey, MG
HMy	Hugh Mayne, Pastor (Associate Reformed Congregation of Christ)
RWM	Reubin W. McCormick
SMc	Samuel N. McCormick, elder (Church of Christ)
JMc	James McVey, elder, PG (Church of Christ)
WMc	Wilson McMurry
GWM	Geo. W. Merritt, MG
TMy	Thomas [?]Mewzry
SKM	S. K. Milton, MG
JMh	Joel Morehead, MG
FBN	F. B. Nash (Methodist Episcopal)
BNc	Benjamin Northcott
HCN	H. C. Northcutt
JPk	Joel Parker
TRk	Thomas Rankin, PG (Methodist Episcopal Church South)
JRa	John Rash
SAR	S. A. Rathburn, MG (Methodist Episcopal)
JWR	John W. (or M.?) Riggen / Riggin
JRg	John Rogers
SRg	Samuel Rogers, MG, elder (Church of Christ)
WRg	William Rogers
ASd	Aaron Sanders / Saunders
WSd	William W. Saddler
OSx	Obadiah Sexton
WSh	Walter Shearson, minister (Methodist Episcopal Church South)
ISh	Isack Shockly
ASh	Abraham Shrout
JnSm	John Smith
JtSm	Jonathan Smith
JSt	J. B. Stamper, MG (Methodist Episcopal)
JDS	James D. Stoops
WCS	William C. Stribling
GSz	George Switzer
WBT	William B. Taylor

JWT	J. W. B. Tazor, PG
RTh	Richard Thomas, MG
DST	David S. Tod
ATd	Andrew Todd
LTu	Leonard Turley, minister (Baptist)
RTy	Richard Tydings (Methodist Episcopal)
JVc	John Vice, Sr., MG
WMV	William M. Vize
JWc	Joseph W. Wallace, minister (Presbyterian)
SGW	S. G. Ward (Presbyterian)
JRW	John R. White
WWh	William White
DWh	Dewey Whitney / Davies Whiting, MG (Presbyterian)
TJW	Thornton J. Will
AGW	A. G. Williams, PG
JWW	J. W. Williams
JGW	Joseph G. Williams, MG (Methodist Episcopal)
TWn	Thos. Wilson
WWn	William Wilson
JFY	John F. Young

The following persons performed marriages and sent in returns which are mentioned but
not copied out in Bath County, KY, Marriage Book 2 (1826-1852):

Bazell Bivin / Bivins

Geo. Fagg

John H. Hedges, ECC

John Hencely / Hensley

Eli Howard

Jeremiah Hunt

George Marshall, MG

S. N. McCormick

D. R. ?Nosely

J. W. (or M.) Riggin

G. N. Robison

A. D. Scriggs, MG

Obadiah Sexton

Abbreviations

f/b, f/g	father of the bride, father of the groom
m/b, m/g	mother of the bride, mother of the groom
guardian/b, /g	guardian of the bride, or groom
consent/b, /g	consent from an individual whose relationship is not specified
bdsm	bondsman

[   ]   Brackets indicate the compiler's additions and/or corrections to a given entry. Where marriages are alphabetized according to a corrected form of the surname, this is clearly indicated.

[sic]   This phrase follows material that is accurately copied from a given source, but which the compiler knows to be contradicted by other surviving records.

(   )   Parentheses indicate the compiler's educated guesses, particularly where one or more letters are apparently missing from a given source. In a few cases, where a given name is recorded in two forms with one minor difference, parentheses indicate the variation: e.g., "Sall(e)y."

?   ?   Question marks indicate all material about which there is any doubt, including whether the original record is accurate. Note, however, that this doubt attaches to the words or numbers directly adjacent to the question mark, never to the entire name, date, or record.

CAPS   All capital letters indicate the surnames of brides and grooms, and all significant variants of these individuals' surnames among different records of a single marriage. A few exceptions are made where these variants seem especially improbable, or are known to be mistakes.
NOTE: The surnames of parents and bondsmen do not appear in all capital letters. However, these often present further variations in spelling, and should be taken into account whenever there is doubt about the spelling of a bride or groom's surname.

ABBOTT, Henry, & Malilda[?] BYROM, 21 Sept. 18(50?). (SKc) [B2]
ADAIR, William A., & Ane Elisa DUCKWORTH, 2 Sept. 1852. (LGH) [B2]
ADAMS, Aaron, & Polly HUNT, bond 2 Sept. 1829;
    f/b: John Hunt; bdsm: Thomas Hunt. [AB]
    Aaron Adams & Polly HART, 24 Sept. 1829. (JEv) [B2]
ADAMS, Fethegil, & Miranda YOUNG, bond 14 May 1838;
    bdsm: Benj. F. Sudouth. [AB]
    Fothergal Adams & Miranda You(n)g, 15 May 1838. (JnSm) [B2]
ADAMS, James, & Elizabeth GRAY, bond 30 Aug. 1814;
    bdsm: James Adams, Joseph Gray. [AB]
    James Adams & Elizabeth Gray, 10 Feb. 1814. [JA,S1]
ADAMS, James W., & Mary SNEDEGAR, bond 22 March 1847;
    bdsm: Isaac Snedegar. [AB]
    James Adams & Mary SNEDIGER, 28 March 1847. (SKc) [B2]
ADAMS, Jefferson, & Matilda TRAYLOR, 8 Aug. 1837. (PCy) [B2]
ADAMS, John, & Polly PAINTER, bond 3 June 1815;
    ?bdsm: Thomas Adams. [AB]
    John Adams & Polly Painter, 6 June 1815. [JA,S1]
ADAMS, Richard, & Peggy RICHARDS, bond 10 June 1820;
    bdsm: Fielding Green. [AB]
    Richard Adams & Peggy Richards, 13 June 1820. [S1]
ADAMS, Samuel W., & Susan W. ADAMS, 4 Oct. 1827. (RTy) [B2]
ADAMS, Thomas, & Dolly HOWELL, bond 24 Dec. 1830;
    bdsm: Samuel Williams. [AB]
ADAMS, Thomas, & Jane WHITECRAFT, bond 14 Dec. 1842;
    bdsm: W. S. Sudouth. [AB]
ADAMS, Wm., & Lucy BAILEY, bond 25 Nov. 1858;
    bdsm: Wm. Bailey. [AB]
    William ?Adams & Lucy Bailey or Bonley, 26 Nov. 1828. (JVc) [B2]
ADDAMS, Samuel, & Rebecca [?]LEDINGZ, bond 3 Dec. 1827;
    bdsm: T. J. Rogens. [AB]
AITKIN or Atkin?, George, & Jane N. DUTY, bond 23 Jan. 1849;
    bdsm: David (D.?) Duty. [AB]
ALEXANDER, Benj., & Catharine SMALL, bond 20 Aug. 1822;
    bdsm: Thomas Small. [AB]
    Benjamin Alexander & Catharine Small, 29 Aug. 1822. [S1]
ALEXANDER, Daniel, & Nancy BARNETT, 19 Nov. 1835. (GSz) [B2]
ALEXANDER, John, & Polly SMITH, bond 17 June. 1815;
    bdsm: James Woodland; Polly Smith gives own consent. [KM]

1

ALEXANDER, John L., & Mary SIMPSON, bond 3 Feb. 1820;
    bdsm: Asa Canterbury.   [AB]
    John Alexander & Mary Simpson, 4 Feb. 1820.   [S1]
ALEXANDER, Joseph, & Mary THOMPSON, bond 11 Dec. 1838;
    f/g: John Alexander; m/b: Jane Thompson; bdsm: Lewis Fortune.   [AB]
    Joseph Alexander & Mary Thompson, 18 Feb. 1838. (SMc)   [B2]
ALFREY, Absolum, & Patsy HOWELL, bond 29 March 1820;
    f/b: Wm. Howell; bdsm: Abram Alfrey.   [AB]
    Absolem Alfrey & Patsey HOOD, 1 Apr. 1820.   [S1]
ALFREY, Fielding, & Patsey JOHNSON, bond 3 Aug. 1831;
    f/b: James Johnson; bdsm: Anderson Johnson.   [AB]
ALFREY, George, & Louisa LANCASTER, bond 10 Sept. 1829;
    f/g: John Alfrey; bdsm: Adam Alfrey.   [AB]
    Geo. Alfrey & Louisa Lancaster / Luesa Lankerster, 10 Sept. 1829. (SJk)   [B2]
ALFREY, James, & Magerne PEBLER, 22 March 1815.   [S1]
ALFREY, Moses, & Ann BANTA, bond 17 Oct. 1825;
    bdsm: Anderson Johnson.   [AB]
    Moses Alfrey & Ann BONTY., 17 Oct. 1825.   [S1]
ALFREY, Samuel, & Rachel CASSITY, bond 13 March 1811;
    f/g: John Alfrey; f/b: John Cassity; bdsm: Jonathan Cassity, Samuel Alfrey.   [AB]
ALLEN, Churchill, & Mary ANDERSON, bond 10 Aug. 1822;
    bdsm: Alexander Hughes.   [AB]
    Churchhill Allen & Mary Anderson, 10 Aug. 1838. (JnSm)   [B2]
ALLEN, Daniel, & Nancy HUGHES, bond 27 Feb. 1822;
    bdsm: Alexander Hughes.   [AB]
ALLEN, D. W., & Narcissa PERGRAM, bond 21 Nov. 1848;
    f/b: James Pergram; bdsm: Solomon Rothwell.   [AB]
    Daniel? W. Allen & Narcissa PURGRON, 23 Nov. 1848. (RWM)   [B2]
ALLEN, Francis W., & Mariah HERNDON or Herendon, bond 19 May 1836;
    bdsm: B. F. Sudduth.   [AB]
    Francis W. Allen & Maria Herndon, 19 May 1836. (JnSm)   [B2]
ALLEN, James, & Sally SMITH, bond 27 Dec. 1816;
    bdsm: James Allen, [?]Sou Hassie or Soue Hes.   [AB]
ALLEN, James F., & Sarah A. TRUMBO, bond 16 June 1846;
    bdsm: M. A. Trumbo.   [AB]
    James F. Allen & Sarah A. Trumbo, 18 June 1846. (TRk)   [B2]
ALLEN, John, & George Ann BOTTS, bond 5 Aug. 1833;
    f/b: Wm. Botts.   [AB]
    John Allen & George Ann Botts, 10 Aug. 1833. (JHn)   [B2]

ALLEN, Wm. P., & Pheby PEARSAL, bond 27 Sept. 1830;
    bdsm: Jesse P. Nelson. [AB]
ALLEY, Jackson, & Elizabeth CASSITY, bond 21 July 1846;
    f/b: Henry Cassity; bdsm: John B. Hardin. [AB]
    John J. Alley & Elizabeth Cassity, 23 July 1846. (JGW) [B2]
ALLEY, James, & Delilah SAILOR, bond 28 Sept. 1820;
    f/b: John Sailor; bdsm: Adam Caleb [Caleb Adams?]. [AB]
    James Alley & Delila Sailor, 28 Sept. 1820. [S1]
ALLEY, John, & Rachell HARMON, bond 18 May 1833;
    bdsm: Michael Harmon. [AB]
    John G. Alley & Racheal ?HANNON, 25 ?March 1833. (JGW) [B2]
AMOS, William, & Emily HARDIN, bond 11 March 1829;
    f/b: Joseph Hardin; bdsm: Nicely Hardin. [AB]
    Wm. M. Amos & Emily Hardin, 12 March 1829. (DWh) [B2]
ANDERSON, Colbert, & Jane ELLIS, bond 8 Dec. 1832;
    bdsm [f/b]: Owen Ellis. [AB]
    Colbert Anderson & Jane Ellis, 9 Jan. 1833. (SJn) [B2]
ANDERSON, Culbert, & Sarah ANDERSON, bond 28 Sept. 1837;
    bdsm: Lewis Hunt. [AB]
ANDERSON, Richard, & Lyra HUNT, bond 16 July 1834;
    bdsm: Foster Hunt. [AB]
ANDERSON, Sanford, & Susannah CONYERS, bond 14 Feb. 1825;
    bdsm: Isaac Conyers. [AB]
    Sanford Anderson & Susannah Conyers, 15 Feb. 1825. [S1]
ANDERSON, Laifro[?], & Ann WOODARD, bond 26 Jan. 1846;
    bdsm: Cobert(?) Anderson. [AB]
    Talifero Anderson & Ann Woodard, 24 Dec. 1846. (LCb) [B2]
ANDERSON, Wm., & Sarah TOMLINSON, 20 Aug. 1824;
    bdsm: Archibald Tomlinson. [AB]
    William Anderson & Sally Tomlinson, 31 Aug. 1824. [S1]
ANDERSON, Wm., & Fanny GRAHAM, bond 30 Oct. 1827;
    bdsm: Robert Crooks. [AB]
    William Anderson & Fanny Graham, 30 Oct. 1827. (DWh) [B2]
ARCHER, Franklin, & Kesiah ROBERTSON, bond 10 Jan. 1832;
    f/b: L. R. Robertson; bdsm: W. M. Sudduth. [AB]
    Franklin Archer & Kesiah ROBERTION, Jan. 1832:
    "the day after the Second Saturday." (JMh) [B2]
ARGO, Edmin, & Elizabeth VICE, 16 May 1837. (JVc) [B2]
ARGO, James, & Sally PRATHER, 15 Jan. 1835. (PHn) [B2]
ARMINTAGE, James, & Lucretia BENSON, 18 Feb. 1839. (JGW) [B2]

ARMSTRONG, John, & Lucy ALLEN, bond 12 Feb. 1838;
    bdsm: John Allen. [AB]
    John Armstrong & Lucy Allen, 13 Feb. 1838. (JWR) [B2]
ARMSTRONG, John, & Vira KINDER, bond 13 Apr. 1850;
    bdsm: Geo. Aullick. [AB]
ARMSTRONG, Robert, & Ruth RAMEY, 24 Jan. 1824. (PCy) [S1]
ARNETT, Abijah, & Permelia EVINS, bond 20 May 1822;
    bdsm: Francis Evins. [AB]
    Alijah Arnett & Permelia EWINS, 23 May 1822. [S1]
AR[NETT?], Cleanthus, & Margarett DEAN, 12 Oct. 1826. (PHn) [B2]
ARNETT, David, & Isabel PAINTER, bond 24 Sept. 1836;
    bdsm: Solomon Painter. [AB]
    David ARNET & Isabele PANTHER, 25 Sept. 1836. (PHn) [B2]
ARNETT, Robert, & Matilda FOUCH, bond 12 March 1837;
    f/b: Wm. Fouch; bdsm: John F. Trumbo. [AB]
    Robert ARNET & Matilda FOUTCH, 10 March 1838. (EBr) [B2]
ARNOLD, David B., & Maranda McHENRY, bond 7 Oct. 1847;
    bdsm: John D. Young. [AB]
ARNOLD, James H., & Artaniss PARKS, bond 17 June 1842;
    bdsm: Geo. Parkes. [AB]
ARNOLD, John, & Keziah HORNBACK, bond 16 July 1831;
    bdsm: David Hornback. [AB]
    John Arnold & Keseah Hornback, 19 June 1831. (MGs) [B2]
ARNOLD, Joseph, & Margaret WARNER, 18 June 1851. (SMc) [B2]
ARNOLD, Thomas, & Betsey HUGHES, bond 15 Apr. 1816;
    bdsm: Reuben Hughes. [AB]
    W. Thomas Arnold & Betsy Hughes, 18 Apr. 1816. [S1]
    Thos. Arnold & Betsy Hugh(e)s (listed twice) [JA]
ARRASMITH, Massey, & Lucia MORGAN, 10 Sept. 1826. (JtSm) [B2]
ARRASMITH, Wesley, & Katharine BUTLER, bond 27 Aug. 1831;
    bdsm [f/b]: Nathan Butler. [AB]
ARROSMITH, John & Sarah JONES, bond 27 March 1832;
    bdsm: Charles Pierce. [AB]
    John ARRASMITH & Sarah Jones, 29 March 1832. (SJn) [B2]
ARROSMITH, Joseph, & Sharlah GREGORY, bond 10 Feb. 1834;
    bdsm: Wm. Gregory. [AB]
ARROWSMITH, Massey, & Elizabeth KERNS, bond 24 June 1823;
    f/b: Tilmon Kerns; bdsm: Charles Pierce, Lucindah Kerns. [KM]
    ARRASMITH, Mossey, & Elizabeth Kevins [sic], 29 June 1823. [S1]

ARROWSMITH, Thomas, & Mary Jane AMOS, 5 Sept. 1850. (GHk)   [B2]
ASHLEY, Wm., & Elizabeth BAILEY, bond 9 Sept. 1830;
   bdsm: James Martin.   [AB]
    William Ashley & Elizabeth Bailey, 9 Sept. 1830. (JHH)   [B2]
ASHLEY, Wm., & Emily WRIGHT, bond 9 Dec. 1840;
   f/b: Samuel C. Gill; bdsm: Travis Daniel.   [AB]
ATCHISON, Elijah, & Polly ROGERS, bond 11 May 1814;
   bdsm: Elijah Atchison, James Rogers.   [AB]
    Elijah Atchison & Pol(l)y Rogers, 12 May 1814.   [JA,S1]
ATCHISON, F., & Polly BAILEY, bond 12 Jan. 1829;
   bdsm: Thos. Fles [Iles?].   [AB]
    Jesse T. Atchison & Polly Bailey, 15 Jan. 1829. (JHH)   [B2]
[ATCHISON] Atchisin, Henry, & Aby MOORE, bond 1 Apr. 1834;
   bdsm: David Moore.   [AB]
    William P. ATCHISON & Abergail MOOR, 7 Apr. 1834. (TIs)   [B2]
ATCHISON, James, & Margaret MARKLAND, bond 19 Sept. 1832;
   bdsm: Fourtlan [?]Macklan.   [AB]
    James J.Atchison & Margaret Markland, 20 Sept. 1832. (JVc)   [B2]
ATCHISON, Jas. W., & Melvina CLAYTON, bond 5 Aug. 1840;
   f/b & bdsm: Charles Clayton.   [AB]
ATCHISON, Jene, & Charlotte PIERCE, bond 17 Aug. 1829;
   bdsm: Peter Pierce.   [AB]
    Jesse Atchison & Charlotte Pierce, 20 Aug. 1829. (JHH)   [B2]
[ATCHISON] Atckison, John, & Margaret HEDRICK, bond 27 May 1839;
   f/b: John Hedrick; bdsm: John Clark.   [AB]
    John ATCHISON & Margaret Hedrick, 30 June 1839. (SMc)   [B2]
ATCHISON, Joshua O., & Mary Jane TRUMBO, 2 Dec. 1851. (SMc)   [B2]
[ATCHISON] Atchinson, Samuel C., & Lucretia CLAYTON, bond 23 Jan. 1840;
   bdsm: Chas. Clayton.   [AB]
    Samuel O. or C. ATCHISON & Lawrence CLATON, 25 Jan. 1840. (EBr)   [B2]
ATCHISON, Silas, & Sally DO_____ [ditto?], 21 Feb. 1826. (RGd)   [B2]
ATCHISON, Theophilus, & Martha HENDRIX, bond 16 Aug. 1834;
   bdsm: Thomas Atchison.   [AB]
ATCHISON, Thomas, & Matilda BARNS, bond 1 Sept. 1834;
   bdsm: Jesse Atchison.   [AB]
ATCHISON, Thomas J., & Elizabeth Carolina ?MEXES, 22 Jan. 1852. (JJn)   [B2]
ATCHISON, Wm. B., & Eliza ADAMS, bond 14 July 1830;
   f/g: Silas Atchison; bdsm: Jesse Atchison.   [AB]
    Wm. Atchison & Elizabeth Adams, 15 July 1830. (JHH)   [B2]
ATCHISON, William J., & Nancy JOHNSON, 3 May 1844. (SMc)   [B2]

ATHA, John A., & Delila Ann BRAMELL, bond 19 Oct. 1846;
    bdsm: Cadmun Freeman.   [AB]
    John ATHY & Delila BRAMBLET, 9 Oct. 1846. (BCs)   [B2]
ATHA, Samuel, & Arnolds CUTRIGHT, bond 10 March 1845;
    bdsm: Walter Atha.   [AB]
ATHE, John, & Selah ROGERS, 15 Sept. 1835. (SRg)   [B2]
ATKINSON, James, & Sally KING, bond 17 May 1823;
    bdsm: Jesse King.   [AB]
    James Atkinson & Sally King, 22 May 1823.   [S1]
ATKINSON, John, & Sarah COSHOW, bond 10 Aug. 1812;
    bdsm: John Atkinson, John Coshaw.   [AB]
    John Atkinson & Sarah Coshow, 13 Aug. 1812.   [JA,S1]
ATKINSON or Atchison?, John, & Lucy PHILIPS, bond 18 Oct. 1847;
    bdsm: Wm. Philips.   [AB]
ATKINSON, William, & Lucy COSHAW, bond 2 Nov. 1820;
    bdsm: John Coshaw.   [AB]
    William Atkinson & Lucy Coshaw, 23 Nov. 1820.   [S1]
BACK, Frederick, & Rebecca ?FENTON, bond 17 July 1821;
    bdsm: Wm. Selton.   [AB]
    Frederick BOOK & Rebecca SEXTON, 19 July 1821.   [S1]
BADGER, Robert, & Eliza WHEELER, bond 19 Aug. 1822;
    bdsm: Wm. Lane.   [AB]
    Robert M. Badger & Eliza Wheeler, 20 Aug. 1822.   [S1]
BADGER, Robert N., & Eliza BADGER, bond 31 Oct. 1837;
    bdsm: James Sudduth.   [AB]
BAILEY, Charles, & Martha ENGLAND, bond 18 July 1821;
    bdsm: Jesse England.   [AB]
    Charles Bailey & Martha England, 22 July 1821.   [S1]
BAILEY, David, & Gehazi ROE, bond 23 Aug. 1824;
    bdsm: James Noe [Roe?].   [AB]
    David Bailey & Jahazah Roe, 24 Aug. 1824.   [S1]
BAILEY, Edward, & Lucy RUDDER, bond 22 June 1831;
    bdsm: Absolom Bailey.   [AB]
BAILEY, Isaac, & Martha WARREN, bond 19 Oct. 1847;
    bdsm: Wm. Warren.   [AB]
    Isaac ?Bailey & Martha WARNER or Warren, 20 Oct. 1847. (SKc)   [B2]
BAIL(E)Y, Jefferson, & Harriet? R. JONES, 3 July 1835. (SJn)   [B2]
BAILEY, Jesse, & Caty EUIN, bond 23 Nov. 1816;
    bdsm: Evin Fouch;   [AB]

Jesse BAILY or Bailey & Caty EVANS, 23 Nov. 1816. [JA,S1]
BAILEY, John, & Nancy RUDDER, bond 18 Feb. 1832;
   bdsm: Ed Rudder. [AB]
BAILEY, Roberts, & James[?] VICE, bond 14 Jan. 1827;
   bdsm: David Bailey. [AB]
BAILEY, Warren, & Elizabeth BOYD, bond 21 Feb. 1832;
   bdsm: Alson Bailey. [AB]
BAILEY, Warren, & Milly Jane WILLSON, bond 7 March 1848;
   bdsm: Geo. Wilson. [AB]
   Warren BAILY & Milly Jane Willson, 9 March 1848. (SJn) [B2]
BAILEY, Wm., & Trinnelly SWETNAM, bond 21 Feb. 1832;
   bdsm: John Swetnam. [AB]
   William Bailey & Trinvilla SWEATNAM, 23 Feb. 1832. (SJn) [B2]
[BAILEY] Baley, Wm., & Polly ENGLAND, bond 23 June 1833;
   bdsm: David England. [AB]
   William BAILEY & Polly England, 23 June 1833. (ALy) [B2]
BAIRD, Arch B., & Emily I. COON, bond 12 Dec. 1847;
   f/g: H. Baird; f/b: Thomas Coon; bdsm: Samuel Mitchell. [AB]
   Bouls BEARD & Emily COONS, 14 Oct. 1847. (PHn) [B2]
BAIRD, Archibald, & Catharine Ann MOORE, bond 11 Dec. 1848;
   bdsm: Richard Moore. [AB]
   Archibald Baird & Catharine Ann ?Moore, 14 Dec. 1848. (PHn) [B2]
BAIRD or Bairds, Caleb, & Hester A. R. WILLIAMS, 26 Dec. 1844. (RFC) [B2]
BAIRD, Geo. W., & Ann STONE, bond 6 May 1848;
   bdsm: Sam Stone. [AB]
   George W. Baird & Ann Stone, 10 May 1848. (ABr) [B2]
BAIRD, H. I., & Maria L. STONE, bond 26 Sept. 1840;
   bdsm: Samuel Stone. [AB]
   H. L. Baird & Maria S. Stone, 12 Oct. 1840. (MGs) [B2]
BAIRD, Hardiman, & Jane HARDIN, 19 March 1835. (PHn) [B2]
BAIRD, Joseph C., & Eliza Ann JONES, 29 May 1850. (SJn) [B2]
BAIRD, Richard, & Mariah EVANS, bond 18 Jan. 1847;
   bdsm: Dan Evans. [AB]
   Richard S. Baird & Mariah M. Evans, 26 Jan. 1847. (WWn) [B2]
BAIRD, Samuel, & Elizabeth MORGAN, bond 9 Oct. 1834;
   bdsm: Wm. Amos. [AB]
   Samuel D. Baird & Elizabeth Morgan, 14 Aug. 1834. (JMh) [B2]
BAKER, James, & Nancy SQUIRES, 1813. (LTu) [KM]
BAKER, Thomas, & Sally DELAY, 16 Apr. 1818. [S1]
BALDWIN, James, & Betsey THOMPSON, bond 2 Dec. 1820;

bdsm: Joseph M. Thompson. [AB]

BALLARD, David, & Pattsy COOPER, bond 3 Apr. 1840;
    bdsm: James Stull. [AB]
    David Ballard & Patsey HOOPER, 8 Apr. 1845. (JHn) [B2]

BALLARD, Garrard, & Rachel INGRAM, bond 5 Nov. 1828;
    bdsm: Tom Ferguson. [AB]
    Garret BALLERD & Rocher INGHAM, 20 Nov. 1828. (JPk) [B2]

BAL(L)ARD, Thomas, & Margaret ROTHWELL, 12 Aug. 1852. (JHn) [B2]

BARBEE, Lewis, & Elizabeth HENDRIX, 21 Oct. 1841. (JVc) [B2]

BARBER, Daniel, & Katharine FILAND, bond 19 May 1845;
    bdsm: Geo. Feland. [AB]
    Daniel Barber & Chtarine FOLAND, 19 May 1845. (SKc) [B2]

BARBER, Jesse, & Nancy ABBET, 18 Nov. 1839. (EBr) [B2]

BARBER, Joseph, & Nancy TACKETT, bond 24 June 1831;
    f/b: Wm. Tackett; bdsm: Wm. Gregory. [AB]

BARBER, Landon, & Sarah ATCHISON, bond 29 Aug. 1829;
    bdsm: Ed Barber. [AB]

BARBER [Barbee?], Robert, & Lydia RICHARDT, bond 27 Feb. 1812;
    f/b: James Richardt; bdsm: Samuel Manley. [AB]
    Robt. Barber or BARBES & Lidia RICHART, 2 March 1815. [JA,S1]

BARBER, Robert, & Nancy HUGHES, bond 27 Feb. 1832;
    bdsm: Thos. Arnold. [AB]

BARBOUR, Thomas, & Peggy RICE, bond 29 July 1811;
    bdsm: Thos. Barbour, Jackin Thomas. [AB]

BARCLAY or Barday?, James, & Polly MUNS or Muir, bond 5 May 1824;
    bdsm: John Munns. [AB]
    James BANDAY & Polly Muns, 13 May 1824. [S1]

BARKER, Silas, & Fransis FERGUSON, bond 12 Jan. 1825;
    bdsm: V. Ferguson. [AB]
    Silas Barker & Frances Ferguson, 13 Jan. 1825. [S1]

BARKLEY, Edward, & Polly S(H)ANKLIN, bond 4 May 1821;
    f/b: Andrew Shanklin; bdsm: John Henseley. [AB]
    Edward BARCLEY or Barclay & Polly Shanklin, 10 May 1821. (JPH) [TP,RS]

BARKLEY, Joseph, & Mary Elizabeth KIMBROUGH, bond 1 May 1849;
    f/b: W. Kimbrough; bdsm: Jas. Ginins. [AB]
    Dr. Joseph BARKLY & Elizabeth Kimbrough, 1 May 1849. (RFC) [B2]

BARKLEY, Silas, & Ann LOVE, bond 13 Sept. 1847;
    f/b: W. N. Love; bdsm: W. N. [?]Levi. [AB]

BARNABY, Elias W., & ?E. J. J. HUNT, 21 Jan. 1851. (JDy) [B2]

BARNES, F., & Elizabeth COGER or Cager?, bond 30 Aug. 1819;
  bdsm: John Smith.   [AB]
    Firsheatha Barnes & Elizabeth COOGTO, 2 Sept. 1819.   [S1]
BARNES, G. A., & Margaret MOORE, bond 9 March 1846;
  bdsm: Wm. Moore.   [AB]
    Grandison Barnes & Margret Moore, 10 March 1846. (BBv)   [B2]
BARNES, George, & Nancy BURCH, bond 17 Jan. 1842;
  bdsm: John Burch.   [AB]
BARNES, Greenup A., & Betsey GINTER, bond 3 Jan. 1831;
  bdsm: John Ginter.   [AB]
BARNES, John, & Polly BRACKEN or Brocken, bond 11 Nov. 1822;
  bdsm: James Bracken.   [AB]
    John BARNER & Polly Bracken, 12 Nov. 1822.   [S1]
BARNES, John E., & Martha SELF, bond 2 Apr. 1849;
  bdsm: Joseph Self.   [AB]
    John E. BURNS & Martha J. SELFE, 3 Apr. 1849. (SMc)   [B2]
BARNES, Moses H., & Elizabeth GILL, bond 12 Sept. 1838;
  bdsm: Sam Gill.   [AB]
    Moses H. Barnes & Elizabeth Gill, 19 Sept. 1838. (JGW)   [B2]
BARNET, Robert, & Ala Ann HILEY, 10 Oct. 1844. (PCy)   [B2]
BARNS, Coleman, & Julia A. MOCKABEE, bond 16 Apr. 1849;
  bdsm: Joseph Mockabee.   [AB]
    Coleman BARNES & Juli A. MOCKIR, 17 Apr. 1849. (SMc)   [B2]
BARNS, Marian C., & Alvisa BARNS, bond 31 Jan. 1849;
  bdsm: Wm. Barns.   [AB]
    Marian Barns & Alizae Barns, 1 Feb. 1849. (SMc)   [B2]
BARNS, Thomas, & Maranda ?MOORES, bond 30 Oct. 1821;
  bdsm: Hugh Love.   [AB]
    Thomas C. BARNES & Maranda MORROW, 1 Nov. 1821. (JPH)   [TP,RS]
BARNS, Thomas, & Nancy HAZELRIGG, bond 14 Sept. 1842;
  bdsm: Perry S. Steel.   [AB]
[BARNS?] Boones, Wm., & Phebe STICKLER, bond 1 March 1815;
  bdsm: Moses Hawkins.   [AB]
    William BARNS & Febe Stickler, 2 March 1815. (CHp)   [S1,JA]
BASFORD, Isaac, & Rene McCARTY, bond 2 Feb. 1832;
  f/g: John Basford; bdsm: John Norris.   [AB]
BASHAW, James B. & Nancy CROUCH, bond 17 June 1824;
  f/b: Jonathan Crouch; bdsm: Issac Crouch.   [AB]
    James B. Bashaw & Nancy Crouch, 20 June 1824.   [S1]

9

BASHAW, James B., & Rachel PERGREM, bond 2 Nov. 1827;
    f/b: James Pergrem; bdsm: John Pergrem? [AB]
    James Bashaw & Rachel Pergrem, 4 Nov. 1827. (SJk) [B2]
BASHAW, Peter, & Fanny PENDLETON, bond 16 Nov. 1819;
    f/b: Rire [Rice?] Pendleton; bdsm: Wm. Crouch. [AB]
    Peter Bashaw & Fanny Pendleton, 18 Nov. 1819. [S1]
BATY, Daniel, & Sally GILMORE, bond 23 Feb. 1828;
    f/b: Mathew Gilmore; bdsm: Joseph Carsley. [AB]
[BAXTER?] Balter, John W., & Mary KING, bond 24 Oct. 1846;
    bdsm: Aaron Garner. [AB]
    John W. BAXTER & Mary King, 25 Oct. 1846. (JMc) [B2]
BAXTER, Samuel, & Nancy ADAMS, 11 Jan. 1818. [S1]
BAYLEY, Robert, & Meca NEAL, bond 28 Jan. 1832;
    f/b: John Neal; bdsm: Wm. L. Hart. [AB]
    Robert BAGBY & Meed[?] Neal, 31 Jan. 1832. (RTh) [B2]
BEADLE, Samuel, & Rebecca FELAND, bond 1 Jan. 1832;
    bdsm: Geo. Feland. [AB]
    Samuel Beadle & Rebecca FOLAND, 18 Jan. 1833. (EBr) [B2]
[BEAL?] Beeale, David, & Elizabeth ?JAMES or S___, 28 May 1850. (SKc) [B2]
BEAL, John, & Fanny JONES, bond 28 May 1838;
    bdsm: Thomas Jones. [AB]
    John Beal (also BEALE) & Fanny GORE, 27 May 1838. (MGs) [B2]
BEAL, John, & Ann NORIS, 8 Apr. 1843. (EBr) [B2]
BEAN, Phaultey R., & Susannah R. ROGERS, bond 2 Dec. 1830;
    bdsm: David F. Foster. [AB]
    Phantly R. Bean & Susan R. Rogers, 9 Dec. 1830. (JMh) [B2]
BEARD [Baird?], Ratliff, & Sally HARDIN, bond 12 March 1829;
    f/b: Presely Hardin; bdsm: Lewis Hardin. [AB]
    Ratliff Beard & Sally Hardin, 5 March 1829. (PHn) [B2]
BEARD, William, & Polly JONES, 18 Oct. 1835. (PHn) [B2]
BEARD, William, & Margarett McFARLING, 19 Jan. 1844. (PHn) [B2]
BECKETT, Janes F., & Malinda ROSEBERRY, bond 9 Sept. 1822;
    bdsm: Alexander Roseberry. [AB]
    James BECKET & Melinda M. ROSEBURY, 12 Sept. 1822. [S1]
BECKNER, Andrew, & Malinda LEDFORD, bond 28 Feb. 1825;
    bdsm: John Ledford. [AB]
BECKNER, Geo. W., & Debby VINKIRK, bond 1 March 1848;
    bdsm: Henry Vinkirk. [AB]
    W. Beckner & Deby VINCERK, 2 March 1848. (PHn) [B2]
BECKNER, Jacob, & Nancy LANCASTER, bond 11 Jan. 1820;

bdsm: H. Davis; [AB]

Jacob L. BEEKNER & Nancy Lancaster, 23 Jan. 1820. [S1]

BECKNER, John, & Peggy LOWRY, bond 24 Feb. 1830;

f/b & bdsm: Moses Lowry. [AB]

John Beckner & Peggy Lowry, 25 Feb. 1830. (JHH) [B2]

BECKNER, Peter, & Polly LEDFORD, bond 28 May 1831;

bdsm: James Ledford. [AB]

Peter Beckner & Polly LEAFORD, 31 May 1821. [S1]

BECKNER, Samson, & Sarah McFARLAND, 27 March 1851. [S1]

BECKNER, Thos. A., & Emaline N. SMOTHERS, bond 6 March 1844;

bdsm: W. M. Sudduth. [AB]

Thomas A. Beckner & Emaline N. Smothers, 7 March 1844. (JnSm) [B2]

BECKNER, Thos. L., & Malinda CANNON, 19 Jan. 1826. (JtSm) [B2]

[BECKNER?] Buckner, Wm., & Catherine SIX, bond 25 March 1823;

bdsm: John Six. [AB]

William BECKNER & Catharine Six, 27 March 1823. [S1]

BECRAFT, Feilds, & Jane BLEVINS, 14 Apr. 1850. (WRg) [B2]

BECROFT, Benjamin, & Dulcina GORE, bond 7 Oct. 1837;

bdsm: John Gore. [AB]

John BECRAFT & Dulcina Gore, 8 Oct. 1837. (JnSm) [B2]

BECROFT, Wm., & Jane DALE, bond 12 Feb. 1825;

bdsm: Joseph Cordurant. [AB]

William BECRAFT & Jane Dale, 13 Feb. 1825. [S1]

BEDELL, Wm., & Nancy SAILOR, bond 9 Dec. 1816;

bdsm: John Sailor. [AB]

William Bedell & Nancy Sailor, 11 Dec. 1816. [S1]

BELL, Samuel, & Sally FIGHTMASTER, 13 Aug. 1826. (JPk) [B2]

BELL, Wm., & Francis TAYLOR, bond 29 June 1824;

bdsm: Geo. Berry. [AB]

William Bell & Frances TALER, 23 May 1824. [S1]

BELL, Wm., & Polly WALKER, bond 24 July 1833;

bdsm: Wm. Danby. [AB]

BELLIS, Thomas, & Betsy CRAIG, bond 20 Sept. 1819;

bdsm: Peter Craig. [AB]

Thomas Bellis & Betsey Craig, 23 Sept. 1819. [S1]

BERKLY, Edward F., & Sarah Ann Slaughter MAURY, 2 May 1839. (MFM) [B2]

BERRY, Harrison, & Anna HOW, bond 2 Feb. 1839;

bdsm: Peter How. [AB]

Hareson BERY & Anna HON, 7 Feb. 1839. (PHn) [B2]

BERRY, Morgan, & Mabela ACKERMAN, bond 19 Apr. 1842;
    bdsm: John Hornback. [AB]

BESHEAR, James W., & Melinda WILSON, bond 18 Oct. 1831;
    f/b: Joseph Wilson; bdsm: Agella Sampson. [AB]
    James W. BESHEARS & Melinda Wilson, 18 Oct. 1831. (ASh) [B2]

BEST, Thomas, & Betsy WALKER, bond 11 July 1822;
    bdsm: Wm. Frome. [AB]
    Thomas Best & Betsy Walker, 17 July 1822. [S1]

BIGSTAFF, Add L. [Odd S.?], & Fentan ARNOLD, bond 1 Jan. 1834;
    bdsm: Spencer Boyd. [AB]

BLACK, Ephriam, & Liddy FREELAND, bond 30 Dec. 1819;
    bdsm: James ?Frelland. [AB]
    Ephraim Black & Siddy FARLOW, 20 March 1820. [S1]

BLACK, Ezchiah, & Jane McCLURE, bond 3 Sept. 1829;
    bdsm: Robert Steele. [AB]
    Ezekiel Black & Jane McClure, 8 Sept. 1829. (DWh) [B2]

BLACK or Blake, Henry, & Caty GOOLSBERRY, widow, bond 11 Jan. 1822;
    bdsm: Frederick Book. [AB]
    Henry Black & Caty GOODBERRY, 17 Jan. 1822. [S1]

BLACK, John, & Nancy B. CROOKS, bond 16 Dec. 1822;
    bdsm: Arzel Crooks. [AB]
    John Black & Nancy B. Crooks, 19 Dec. 1822. (JPH) [TP,RS]

BLACKBURN, Absolem, & Rebecca KELSO, bond 20 Dec. 1828;
    bdsm: Wm. Kelso. [AB]
    Absolem H. Blackburn & Rebecca KELSOE, 21 Dec. 1828. (JnSm) [B2]

BLACKBURN, Benjamin, & Elizabeth WHITE, bond 21 Aug. 1821;
    bdsm: James White. [AB]

BLACKBURN, William F., & Susan GOODPASTER, 28 March 1850. (SKc) [B2]

BLACKWELL, James, & Agnes CANNON, bond 22 Oct. 1828;
    f/b: Geo. Cannon; bdsm: Nubald Cannon. [AB]
    James Blackwell & Agnes Cannon, 23 Oct. 1828. (JEv) [B2]

BLAKE, John, & Kisei (Kisiah?) HANERS, 27 Nov. 1850. (SKc) [B2]

BLAKE, Thomas, & Ally ROBINSON, bond 15 Aug. 1838;
    bdsm: James Ellison. [AB]
    Thomas Blake & Abby ROBISON, 16 Aug. 1838. (DST) [B2]

BLEVINS, Daniel, & Sarah CHORAY, bond 18 May 1830;
    f/g & bdsm: James Blevins. [AB]

BLEVINS, Eli, & Tilitha STEVENS, bond 3 Apr. 1840;
    bdsm: James Blevins. [AB]
    Eli Blevins & Tabitha STEPHENS, 6 Apr. 1840. (SMc) [B2]

BLEVINS, James, & Nancy YATES, bond 13 Nov. 1840;
    bdsm: Hiram Collins. [AB]
    James Blevins & Nancy Yates, 13 Nov. 1840. (SAR?) [B2]
BLEVINS, James, & Nancy WILLHITE, 15 May 1850. (WRg) [B2]
BLEVINS, William, & Nancy SMITH, 4 Feb. 1841. (SMc) [B2]
BLISS, Charles A., & Mary A. BADGER, 19 Nov. 1844. (SMc) [B2]
BOARDMAN, James R., & Sally HAZELRIGG, bond 29 Dec. 1820;
    bdsm: John Hazelrigg. [AB]
    James B. Bo(a)rdman & Sally HAZLERIGGS, 2 Jan. 1821. [S1]
BOAZ, Austin, & Polly HIGGINS, bond 19 March 1821;
    bdsm: James Young. [AB]
    Austin BOUZ & Polly Higgins, 29 March 1821. [S1]
BOAZ, James, & Elizabeth HIGGINS, bond 9 Feb. 1824;
    f/g & bdsm: Austin Boaz. [AB]
    James Boaz & Elizabeth Higgins, 12 Feb. 1824. [S1]
BOGIE, James N., & Polly HUGHES, bond 27 Sept. 1831;
    bdsm: John S. Hughes. [AB]
BOHANNON, John, & Cathrine R. WRIGHT, bond 21 July 1830;
    bdsm: Flemsted R. Wright. [AB]
    John Bohannon & Katharine R. Wright, 14 July 1830. (JHH) [B2]
BOODE or Birde?, John, & Melah HARDIN, 25 Nov. 1841. (PHn) [B2]
BOON, Joel, & Martha SIVELIAR, bond 27 Aug. 1816;
    bdsm: Thomas Sinclair, J. Boon. [AB]
    Joel Boon & Patsey SINCLAIR, 1816. [S1]
BOON, Richard, & Hannah ADAMS, bond 14 Oct. 1845;
    bdsm: John Adams. [AB]
    Richard Boon & Hannah Adams, 16 Oct. 1845. (WWn) [B2]
BOONE, Joseph, & Cassy KIRK, bond 26 Aug. 1819;
    bdsm: Elijah Lemaster. [AB]
    Joseph BOON & Cassy Kirk, 26 Aug. 1819. [S1]
BOTT, John F., & Mary H. WILSON, bond 29 Sept. 1845;
    f/b: M. R. Wilson; bdsm: Harry Willson. [AB]
    John F. BETT & Ma(r)y H. WILLSON, 1 Oct. 1845. (JRa) [B2]
BOTTS, Archibald, & Peggy WADE, bond 4 Sept. 1816;
    bdsm: James Wade & F. Botts. [AB]
    Archible Botts & Peggy WAID, 8 Sept. 1816. [JA]
    Archible BATTS & Peggy Waid, 28 Dec. 1816. [S1]
BOTTS, Benjamin, & Francis McGOWIN or McGlowdin, 1 Aug. 1839. (SMc) [B2]
BOTTS, Jefferson, & Emily BASHAW, 14 Dec. 1848. (RWM) [B2]

BOTTS, Jefferson, & Nancy S. BOTTS, 15 Nov. 1851. (SMc)   [B2]
BOTTS, Joseph, & Juliann MYERS, bond 26 May 1834;
    f/b: Solomon Myers; bdsm: Robert Botts.   [AB]
    Joseph Botts & Juliah Ann MYRES, 27 May 1834. (HSD)   [B2]
BOTTS, Washington, & Amanda JONES, bond 18 Jan. 1837;
    bdsm: Thos. Jones.   [AB]
    Washing(ton) Botts & Amanda Jones, 19 Jan. 1837. (JGW)   [B2]
BOWRTY[?], Albert, & Polly JACKSON, bond 10 Aug. 1825;
    f/b: Samuel Jackson; bdsm: Wm. Jackson.   [AB]
BOWEN, Harvy, & Elizabeth MICHEL, 25 Sept. 1851. (ISh)   [B2]
BOWEN?, Walker, & Clarrai M. PAYNE, bond 21 March 1829;
    bdsm: Ryon More.   [AB]
    Walker BOWIN & Clarrisa M. Payne, 24 March 1829. (JnSm)   [B2]
BOWEN, Wm., & Caroline STONE, 12 Sept. 18[44?]. (JRg)   [B2]
BOYD, Alexander, & Mary Ann BRUCE, bond 13 Feb. 1845;
    bdsm: James Bruce.   [AB]
BOYD, Drury B., & Lydia L. JONES, bond 21 Apr. 1823;
    f/b: John Jones; bdsm: Hiram Bridges.   [AB]
    Drusy D. Boyd & Lydia Jones, 24 Apr. 1823.   [S1]
BOYD, Gallington, & Elizabeth VICE, bond 28 March 1838;
    bdsm: Aron Vice.   [AB]
BOYD, George, & Mahaly GREGORY, 11 (or 14) Apr. 1827. (AMx)   [B2]
BOYD, Harris, & Hetty BECRAFT, bond 31 March 1830;
    bdsm: Joshua Power.   [AB]
    Harrison Boyd & Hetty Becraft, 31 March 1830. (JHH)   [B2]
BOYD, Harrison, & Lucy YARBER, bond 8 Sept. 1840;
    bdsm: Wm. Yarber.   [AB]
    Harrison Boyd & _____, 8 Sept. 1840. (SJn)   [B2]
BOYD, James G., & Elizabeth G. PERKINS, bond 16 Sept. 1839;
    bdsm: Joseph Walker.   [AB]
    James Boyd & Elizbeth Perkins, 16 Sept. 1839. (JWR)   [B2]
BOYD, John, & Nancy BOYD, 1816.   [S1]
BOYD, John, & Polly HENDRIX, bond 25 Aug. 1825;
    bdsm: John Hendrix.   [AB]
    John Boyd & Polly Hendrix, 1 Aug. 1825.   [S1]
BOYD, Joseph, & Anna KING, bond 23 Jan. 1831;
    f/b: Jesse King; bdsm: Elijah King.   [AB]
    Joseph Boyd & Anna King, 25 Jan. 1821. (JPH)   [TP,RS]
BOYD, Moses, & Jane BRACKEN, bond 27 Nov. 1819;
    m/g: Dorcas Boyd; m/b: Nancy Bracken; bdsm: Theopilis Hendrix;   [AB]

McClure, *Early Marriages in Bath Co., KY*

Moses Boyd & Jane BRAKEN, 28 Nov. 1819.   [S1]

BOYD, Rambard [Rowland], & Susannah PERKINS, bond 13 Feb. 1832;
    bdsm: Elizabeth Perkins.   [AB]

BOYD, Russian, & Malissa TRUMBO, bond 5 Feb. 1849;
    parent & bdsm: M. F. Trumbo.   [AB]

BOYD, Thomas, & Lucy McINTIRE, bond 26 Oct. 1811;
    bdsm: Thos. Boyd, Alexander McIntire.   [AB]
    Thomas Boyd & Lucy McIntire, 31 Oct. 1811. (JPH)   [TP,RS]

BOYD, Thomas, & Catherine ?BALLOW, bond 27 Apr. 1825;
    bdsm: W. T. Sudith.   [AB]

BOYD, W. D., & May LONG, bond 4 Dec. 1849;
    bdsm: F. F. Wade.   [AB]

BOYD, Washington, & Elizabeth BUTLER, bond 15 Feb. 1825;
    bdsm: Nathan Butler.   [AB]
    Washington Boyd & Elizabeth Butler, 28 Feb. 1825.   [S1]

BOYD, Wm., & Joyce COFFERS, bond 9 Jan. 1812;
    f/g: John Boyd; bdsm: Wm. Boyd, Jesse Coffer.   [AB]
    William BOYED & Fonizy or Lonizy COFFER, 9 Jan. 1812.   [JA,S1]

BOYD, Wm. & Sally ROGERS, bond 23 Sept. 1822;
    bdsm: James Rogers.   [AB]
    William Boyd & Sally Rogers, 26 Sept. 1822. (JPH)   [TP,RS]

BOYD, Wm., & Elizabeth DOGGETT, bond 29 Oct. 1822;
    f/b: Thomas Doggett; bdsm: Arthur Doggett.   [AB]
    William Boyd & Elizabeth Doggett, 31 Oct. 1822.   [S1]

BOYD, Wm., & Vilinda CLATON, bond 9? Jan. 1837;
    bdsm: Charles Claton.   [AB]
    William Boyd & Vilinda CLAYTON, Jan. 1837. (TIs)   [B2]

BRACKEN, James, & Fanny VICE, bond 5 Jan. 1811 or 1814;
    bdsm: John Vice.   [AB]
    James BUCKEN & Fanny Vice, 6 Jan. 1819.   [S1]

BRACKEN, James, & Jane SCOTT, 30 March 1851. (JDy)   [B2]

BRACKEN, Thomas, & Nancy VICE, bond 30 Dec. 1824;
    bdsm: Robt. Vice.   [AB]
    Thomas Bracken & Nancy Vice, 20 Oct. 1825.   [S1]

BRACKEN, Walter, & Dorothy HORNBACK, bond 28 Oct. 1812;
    f/b: Abraham Hornback; bdsm: Walter Bracken, Reuben Jones.   [AB]
    Walter Bracken & Dorothy Hornback, 30 Oct. 1812.   [JA,S1]

BRADLEY, Elisha, & Martha HORNBACK, bond 2 Aug. 1824;
    bdsm: Abraham Hornback.   [AB]

15

BRADLEY, James, & Sary SUMMERS, 16 July 1844. (SKc)   [B2]
BRADLEY, Jesse, & Mary FERGUSON, bond 14 Apr. 1832;
   bdsm: Elisha Bradley.   [AB]
BRADLY?, William, & Sarah Ann SOPSHER [Shropshire], 28 July 1850.(SKc) [B2]
BRADSHAW, David, & Rebecca SEARCY or SWICEY, bond 18 Nov. 1815;
   f/b: James ?Frier.   [KM]
   [Rebecca LEONEY?; James LEONEY]   [AB]
   David Bradshaw & Rebecah SEARSCEY, Nov. 1815   [JA]
   Darick BARDSHAW & Rebecah LEANSCY, 15 Nov. 1815.   [S1]
BRADSHAW, David, & Rebecca McCLARIN, bond 18 March 1847;
   bdsm: Samuel Mitchell.   [AB]
BRADSHAW, Harrison, & Radah KINCAID, bond 7 Dec. 1847;
   f/b & bdsm: John Kincaid.   [AB]
   Harrison Bradshaw & Rodah? KINCADE, 9 Dec. 1847. (BHr)   [B2]
BRADSHAW, Harvy, & Minerva HENDRIX, bond 7 Sept. 1836;
   bdsm [f/b]: Theophilus Hendrix.   [AB]
   Harvey Bradshaw & Minerva Hendrix, 8 Sept. 1836. (JVc)   [B2]
BRADSHAW, James, & _____, bond 9 March 1847;
   bdsm: Geo. Rolls.   [AB]
BRADSHAW, Thomas, & Elizabeth JOHNSON, bond 30 Aug. 1814;
   bdsm: Thos. Bradshaw, Robt. Barns.   [AB]
BRADSHAW, Thomas, & Jane CAN [Carr?], 26 Jan. 1826. (JtSm)   [B2]
[BRADSHAW] Brashaw / Brasham, Wm., & Fanny DARNALL, bond 31 July 1833;
   f/b: David Darnell; bdsm: Elliott Dorsett [Darnell].   [AB]
   William BRADSHAW & Fany DARNOLD, 1 Aug. 1833. (SJn)   [B2]
BRAFORD, Anderson, & Elizabeth BRADLEY, bond 21 May 1838;
   bdsm: Elishua Bradley.   [AB]
BRAIN, James, & Nancy GREEN, bond 4 Dec. 1832;
   f/b: Fielding Green; bdsm: Thos. Green.   [AB]
   James M. Brain & Nancy Green, 4 Dec. 1832. (SJk)   [B2]
[BRAMBLE?] Brammell, Elias, & Jane ATHA, bond 23 Aug. 1836;
   bdsm: Henry Brammell.   [AB]
   Ellias BRAMBLE & Jane ATHE, 25 Aug. 1835. (SRg)   [B2]
BRAMBLE, Em, & Nancy MORGAN, bond 26 July 1834;
   f/b: J. Morgan; bdsm: Jacob Craig.   [AB]
BRAMBLE, Nath, & Sally TINCHER, 19 Nov. 1844. (WRg)   [B2]
[BRAMBLE?] Brumble, Wm., & Giny LAW, bond 27 March 1823;
   bdsm: Benj. Law.   [AB]
   William BRAMBLE & Gracy LOW, 29 March 1823.   [S1]
BRAMBLET, Nathaniel, & Lucinda BARBER, bond 1 Nov. 1821;

bdsm: Robert Barber [Barbee?].   [AB]

Nathan BRAMTEL & Lucy BARBEE, 3 Sept. 1821.   [S1]

BRAMMES, Joseph, & Polly McGIN, bond 18 June 1823;

   bdsm: B. F. Johnson.   [AB]

Joseph BRAMMER & Polly McGin, 19 June 1823.   [S1]

BRANCH, James, & Sarah WHALEY, 21 March 1838. (DST)   [B2]

BRANCH, Nelson, & Elizabeth ROBERTSON, bond 24 Jan. 1814;

   bdsm: Nelson Branch, Lawson Robertson.   [AB]

Nelson Branch & Elizabeth Robertson, 27 Jan. 1814.   [JA,S1]

BRANDER, John, & Anna Gray, bond 21 Dec. 1819;

   bdsm: Joseph Gray.   [AB]

John BRANDON & Anna Gray, 23 Dec. 1819.   [S1]

BRANDON, Malon, & Margritte SHIPMAN [Chipman?], bond 29 Feb. 1820;

   f/b: Darper Shipman; bdsm: Perry Chipman.   [AB]

Malon BARNSON & Margarett CHIP, 24 Feb. 1820.   [S1]

BRANER, Isaac, & Martha CHIPMAN, 7 June 1818.   [S1]

BRAVAN, Lewis, & Margaret MORGAN, bond 9 Aug. 1830;

   bdsm: Wm. Morgan.   [AB]

BRECKINRIDGE, John, & Jane PEEBLE, bond 7 Sept. 1820;

   f/b: John Peeble; bdsm: Wm. Peeble.   [AB]

John D. Breckinridge & Jane PEEHLY, 28 Sept. 1820.   [S1]

BRECKINRIDGE, Rody, & Jane ELIS, bond 12 Sept. 1831;

   bdsm: John Elis.   [AB]

Rody Breckenridge & Jane ELES, 15 Sept. 1831. (PHn)   [B2]

BRECKMAN, Tunis, & Sarah FREELAND, bond 26 Nov. 1840;

   bdsm: James Curtright.   [AB]

BRIDGES, Andrew? L., & Hariet N. HUBLE, 8 Apr. 1841. (SJn)   [B2]

BRIGHT, William, & Sibellar ROGERS, bond 19 Feb. 1814;

   consent: Hinson Bright, Stephen Rogers; bdsm: Nathaniel Garrard. [KM]

William Bright & Libellen or Sibellen Rogers, 25 Oct. 1814.   [JA,S1]

[BRIGHT?] Brite, Wm., & Elizabeth CHANDLER, bond 19 Feb. 1816;

   bdsm: Isaac Powell.   [AB]

William BRIGHT & Elizabeth Chandler, 20 Aug. 1816.   [JA,S1]

BRINDLEY, Wm., & Susannah McCLANAHAN [widow?], bond 20 June 1814;

   consent/b: Susannah McClanahan; bdsm: Robt. Barkley, Wm. Brundly. [KM]

BRINEGAR, Ezra, & Maria HARPER, 29 Apr. 1841. (SJn)   [B2]

BRINGAR, Benj., & Malinda SHANKLIN, bond 15 Feb. 1821;

   bdsm: Andrew Shanklin.   [AB]

Benjamin BRINIGAR & Malinda Shanklin, 15 Feb. 1821. (JPH)   [TP,RS]

BRINGLAR, Isaac, & Emily HARPER, bond 30 Oct. 1837;
    bdsm: John Harper.   [AB]
BRISTO, Andrew, & Elizabeth KERRICK, bond 20 June 1828;
    bdsm: James Sudduth.   [AB]
    Andrew Bristo & Eliz. Kerrick, 21 June 1828. (EHw)   [B2]
BROCK, Miles, & Sarah PEARCE, bond 28 Feb. 1842;
    bdsm: Charles Pearce.   [AB]
    Miles Brock & Sarah Pearce, 18 March 1842. (MGs)   [B2]
BROCK, Pleasant, & Nancy McDOWELL, bond 15 Apr. 1830;
    bdsm: Tarlton Brock.   [AB]
    Pleasant Brock & Nancy McDOWEL, 15 Apr. 1831. (RTh)   [B2]
BROMAGEN, Allen, & Angelina JOHNSON, bond 1 Jan. 1840;
    m/g: Martha Bromagen; f/b & bdsm: Levi Johnson.   [AB]
    Allen BROMAGEM & Angeline JOHNSTON, 2 Jan. 1840. (SRg)   [B2]
BROMGANE, Jeremiah, & Martha LINVILLE, 9 Oct. 1817.   [JA]
    Jeremiah BROMAGEN & Martha LINVILL   [S1]
BROOKS, Lenay, & Ellen ROBERTS, 5 Jan. 1817.   [JA]
    Leroy Brooks & Ellen ROBERTSON   [S1]
BROOKS, Wm. A., & Emily RATLIFF, bond 14 June 1842;
    f/b: Caleb Ratliff; bdsm: Sanford Ratliff.   [AB]
    W. A. Brooks & Emily Ratlif, 16 June 1842. (SJn)   [B2]
[BROTHERS?] Brather, James, & Elnira VICE, bond 18 July 1829;
    bdsm: Andrew Trumbo.   [AB]
    Jas. BROTHERS & Elvira Vice, 22 July 1829. (JHH)   [B2]
BROWN, Alvin, & Mary SMOTHERS, bond 28 Feb. 1848;
    bdsm: Joseph Smathers.   [AB]
    Alvin Brown & Mary Smoth(ers?), 2 March 1848. (RFC)   [B2]
BROWN, Coleman, & Inonna GREGORY, bond 8 Dec. 1848;
    bdsm: Nathaniel Gregory.   [AB]
BROWN, Eli, & Emily ?PERGLIN, bond 14 Oct. 1848;
    bdsm: John ?Pergorn.   [AB]
    Eli Brown & Emily PURGRON, 15 Oct. 1848. (RWM)   [B2]
BROWN, George, & Sally HOW, 1 July 1818.   [S1]
BROWN, James, & Nancy PATRICK, bond 11 March 1840;
    bdsm: Wm. Mynheir.   [AB]
BROWN, John, & Frances F. DALE, bond 3 May 1824;
    bdsm: Elias ?Scatt.   [AB]
    John Brown & Frances A. Dale, 3 May 1824.   [S1]
BROWN, John A., & Mary Jane MOFFETT, bond 31 Aug. 1846;

f/b: James Moffett; bdsm: Zephaniah T. Moffett. [AB]

John A. Brown & M. J. MAFFITT, 1 Sept. 1846. (RFC) [B2]

BROWN, Thomas E., & Elizabeth DONALDSON, bond 18 Sept. 1845;
bdsm: Wm. Donaldson. [AB]

Thomas E. Brown & Elizabeth Donaldson, 23 Sept. 1845. (MGs) [B2]

BROWN, Wm., & Polly BROWN, bond 5 Oct. 1816;
bdsm: Alexander Brown. [AB]

William (L.?) Brown & Polly Brown, 8 Oct. 1816. [JA,S1]

BROWN, Wm., & Katharine MYERS, bond 25 Aug. 1820;
bdsm: Sam C. Myers. [AB]

William Brown & Catharine Myers, 28 Aug. 1820. [S1]

BROWN, Wm., & Polly SPARKS, bond 15 July 1828;
bdsm: Alexander Donaldson. [AB]

William Brown & Polly Sparks, July 1828. (AGg) [B2]

BROWN, Wm., & Polly SHARP, bond 30 Apr. 1833;
bdsm: Wm. B. Kirk. [AB]

William Brown & Polly Sharp, 30 Apr. 1833. (SMc) [B2]

BROWN, Wm. W., & Mary Ann DONALDSON, bond 20 March 1846;
bdsm: Alexander Donaldson. [AB]

William W. Brown & Mary Jane Donaldson, 5 March 1846. (MGs) [B2]

BRUCE, James, & Han. [Hannah?] JONES, 21 Jan. 1817. [JA]

BRUCE, Samuel, & Elizabeth CALL, bond 13 Apr. 1846;
f/b: Hamilton Call; bdsm: F. T. Snelling. [AB]

S. Bruce & E. HALL, 14 Apr. 1846. (JHu) [B2]

BRUNTY, Barnabas, & Elizabeth LINEY, bond 12 Jan. 1822;
bdsm: Geo. Liney. [AB]

Barnabas BRUNTA or Bronta & Elizabeth SINNY, 13 Jan. 1822. [S1]

BRYAN, Joseph, & Lydiann MASON, bond 22 Dec. 1825;
f/b: Peter Mason; bdsm: Jesse Tant. [AB]

BRYANT, Daniel, & Elizabeth COSHAW, bond 6 Feb. 1821;
bdsm: John Coshow. [AB]

Daniel Bryant & Elizabeth CASHAN, 8 Feb. 1821. [S1]

BUCKHANNON, Fielding, & Eliz. EDWARDS, bond 27 Oct. 1829;
f/b: Joseph Edwards; bdsm: Samuel Pierce. [AB]

Fielding Buckhannon & Eliza ann Edwards, 18 Oct. 1831. (RTh) [B2]

BUCKNER, Abraham, & Elizabeth HINES, bond 24 March 1823;
bdsm: Geo. Kincaid. [AB]

Abraham Buckner & Elizabeth KINCIAD, 26 March 1823. [S1]

BUFORD, Alexander, & Mary SLAUGHTER, bond 29 Oct. 1832;
bdsm: Wm. Mauphom; [AB]

Alexander Buford & Mary Slaughter, 29 Oct. 1832. (RTh)   [B2]

BUNGARDNER, Jacob, & Nancy LINCOLN, bond 16 Oct. 1812;
    f/b: Daniel Lincoln.   [AB]
    Jacob BUMBGAMER or Bunganer & Nancy LINCH, Oct. 1815. (CHp)   [JA,S1]

BURBRIDGE, Abraham, & Ann UNDERWOOD, bond 1 Aug. 1820;
    bdsm: Robt. Burbridge.   [AB]
    Absalon Burbridge & Anna Underwood, 27 June 1820.   [S1]

BURBRIDGE, John, & Rachel SHROUT, bond 6 March 1821;
    bdsm: John Crockett.   [AB]
    John Burbridge & Rachel Shrout, 8 March 1821.   [S1]

BURBRIDGE, Joseph, & Elizabeth UNDERWOOD, bond 4 June 1822;
    bdsm: John Burbridge.   [AB]
    Joseph Howe Burbridge & Elizabeth Underwood, 6 June 1822. (JPH)   [TP]

BURCH, John, & Patience BARNS, bond 10 Sept. 1822;
    bdsm: Tushatha Barns.   [AB]
    John Burch & Patience BARNES, 11 Sept. 1822.   [S1]

BURFFORD, John, & Polly LOWE, bond 26 March 1838;
    bdsm: Isaac Lowe.   [AB]
    John BRAHFORD & Poly LOW, 21 March 1838. (JSt)   [B2]

BURK, Gilson, & Elizabeth BURKE, 2 Nov. 1826. (JPk)   [B2]

BURK, Wm., & Rebecca McCLAIN, bond 11 Aug. 1825;
    bdsm: John Norris.   [AB]

BURKE, George, & Anna STOOPS, 1813. (LTu)   [KM]
    George BURK & Ann Stoops   [JA]

[BURNES?] Burris, Mathew, & Hannah HINES, bond 10 Apr. 1829;
    bdsm: Adam Burris.   [AB]
    Mathew BURNES & Hanner HINDS, 12 Apr. 1829. (JPk)   [B2]

BURNES, Rice, & Elizabeth HARDIN, bond 31 Jan. 1825;
    bdsm: Presly Hardin.   [AB]

BURNES, Westly, & Nancy F. McILHENNY, 5 Oct. 1829. (DWh)   [B2]

BURNETT, Griffin, & Phebe CANTRILL, bond 28 Dec. 1811;
    f/b: Christopher Cantrell; bdsm: Griffin Burnett, Mark McCollister.   [AB]
    Grifen BAEVENT & Phebe CANTREL, 31 Dec. 1811.   [JA]
    Grifen BENNET & Phebe CANTVEL   [S1]

BURNETT, Thos. H., & Vianns[?] JOHNSON, bond 28 Aug. 1849;
    bdsm: E. J. Wright.   [AB]

[BURNS] Bines?, Adam, & Cinthia GOODPASTURE, bond 31 July 1828;
    bdsm: Jacob Goodpasture.   [AB]
    Adam BURNS & Cyntha Goodpasture, 3 July 1828. (JPk)   [B2]

BURNS, Alfred, & Nancy STEEL, 10 May 1841. (SJn)   [B2]

BURNS, Dennis, & Mary Ann WILLSON, 27 July 1837. (DST)   [B2]

BURNS, Enoch, & Maria STEEL, bond 5 Feb. 1845;
    bdsm: Jacob Steel.   [AB]
    Enock BURNES & Maria O. Steel, 6 Feb. 1845. (RFC)   [B2]

BURNS, Enos, & Elizabeth DUTY, bond 19 Jan. 1821;
    bdsm: Daniel Duty.   [AB]
    Ewin Burns & Elizabeth Duty, 23 Jan. 1821.   [S1]

BURNS, Enos, & Naricissa KINCAID, bond 21 Oct. 1829;
    bdsm: John Kincaid.   [AB]
    Enos BURNES & Narcissa KINCADE, 23 Oct. 1829. (DWh)   [B2]

BURNS, John, & Polly WHITECRAFT, bond 26 June 1811;
    f/b: John Whitecraft; bdsm: John Burns, John Whitecraft.   [AB]
    John Burns & Polly Whitecraft, 27 June 1811. (JPH)   [TP,RS]

BURNS, John, & Nancy RALLS, bond 26 Jan. 1830;
    bdsm: James F. Stone.   [AB]
    John Burns & Nancy Ralls, 28 Jan. 1830. (SJn)   [B2]

BURNS, John, & Eliza SAFFORD, bond 2 Nov. 1847;
    bdsm: John L. Willson.   [AB]
    John Burns & Eliza STAFFORD, 4 Nov. 1847. (RFC)   [B2]

BURNS, Joseph W., & Mary Ann BURNS, bond 9 Nov. 1846;
    bdsm: Enos Burns.   [AB]
    Joseph W. Burns & Ma(r)y Ann Burns, 10 Dec. 1846. (RFC)   [B2]

BURNS, Nicholas, & Sally EVANS, bond 18 Dec. 1811;
    bdsm: Nichols Burns, John Evans.   [AB]
    Nicholas Burns or BURNES & Sarah Evans, 19 Dec. 1811.   [S1,JA]

BURNS, Nicholas, & Susannah CANN, bond 8 May 1820;
    m/b: Jane Cann; bdsm: Nicholas Byrns, James Byrns.   [AB]

BURNS, Rice, & Elizabeth BAIRD, bond 20 Jan. 1837;
    f/b: John Baird; bdsm: Wm. Hazelrigg.   [AB]
    Rice Burns & Elisabeth D. Baird, 26 Jan. 1837. (DST)   [B2]

BURNS, Robert, & Lewie BALLA, bond 7 June 1814;
    f/b: George Balla; bdsm: Robt. Burns, Geo. Balla.   [AB]

BURTON, Josiah, & Lewis or Leuiez JOANS, bond 5 March 1821;
    bdsm: Isaac Cogers.   [AB]
    Josiah Burton & Luisa GOANS, 6 March 1821.   [S1]

BUSBY, Alfred, & Margaret WEBB, bond 10 Oct. 1842;
    f/b: G. M. Webb; bdsm: B. F. Webb.   [AB]
    Alfred Busby or BUSLY? & M. E. Webb, 13 Oct. 1842. (RFC)   [B2]

BUSBY, Isaac, & Lucy ENGLAND, 16 Oct. 1817.   [JA,S1]
[BUSBY?] Bucbay?, James, & Nancy MORGAN, bond 8 Feb. 1827;
   bdsm: Wm. Cartwell.   [AB]
   James BUSBE & Nancy B. Morgan, 11 Feb. 1827. (JEv)   [B2]
[BUSBY] Burby?, Wm., & Jane COLIVER, bond 16 Aug. 1847;
   f/b: Joseph ?Coliver; bdsm: Rice Burns.   [AB]
   William BUSBY & Lydia J. COLLIVER, 19 Aug. 1847. (BHr) [B2]
BUTCHER, George, & Mary SMOOT, bond 14 Aug. 1824;
   bdsm: Daniel Pierce.   [AB]
   George Butcher & Mary Smoot, 19 Aug. 1824.   [S1]
BUTCHER, George, & Debiah [Deborah] BEDELL, 19 March 1835. (SKM) [B2]
BUTCHER, James, & Margaret LYONS, bond 6 Jan. 1829;
   bdsm: Wm. Thomas.   [AB]
BUTCHER, Samuel, & Jane THOMAS, 5 March 1818.   [S1]
BUTCHER, William, & Sall MORGAN, 17 Dec. 1818.   [S1]
BUTCHER, Wm., & Jane NELSON, bond 2 Jan. 1837;
   bdsm: James Nelson.   [AB]
   William BUCHER & Jan Nelson, 1 Jan. 1837. (JEv) [B2]
BUTLER, Alfer [Alpheus], & Rhodah ENGLISH, bond 2 June 1831;
   f/b: John English.   [AB]
BUTLER, Clif(f)ord, & Lucinda BOON, 16 June 1818.   [S1]
BUTLER, David [Davis], & Susan HENDRIX, bond 7 Jan. 1836;
   bdsm: Wesley Arrosmith.   [AB]
BUTLER, George, & Deavna [Diana?] LANDELSS, bond 18 Dec. 1839;
   f/b: Henry Landess; bdsm: William Lee.   [AB]
BUTLER, Ignatius, & Easter Ann SCOT, 23 Aug. 1837. (JVc)   [B2]
BUTLER, Israel, & Deveas [Dorcas] BUTLER, 6 Oct. 1818.   [S1]
BUTLER, Jesse, & Elizabeth TRAYLOR, bond 2 Nov. 1848;
   bdsm: John Butler.   [AB]
BUTLER, John, & Agnes TRAYLER, bond 25 Oct. 1829;
   bdsm: Robert Johnston.   [AB]
BUTLER, Sylvesus, & Margarett Ann FLETCHER, bond 5 Dec. 1838;
   bdsm [f/b]: William Fletcher.   [AB]
   Sylvanus Butler & Margaret Ann Fletcher, 5 Dec. 1838. (JVc) [B2]
BUTLER, Wm., & Polly McLAIN, bond 7 Feb. 1823;
   bdsm: Charles Jones.   [AB]
   William Butler & Polly McLain, 9 Feb. 1823.   [S1]
BYRAM, Alfred, & Sally Ann DAVIS, bond 1 Sept. 1832;
   bdsm: Thomas Davis;   [AB]

Alfred Byram & Sally Ann Davis, 6 Sept. 1832. (MGs)   [B2]

BYRAM, Augustine, & Sally TOULSON, bond 29 Nov. 1816;
   bdsm: Bernit Toulson, A. Byram.   [AB]

Augustus Byram & Sally Toulson, 1 Dec. 1816.   [JA]

Angurtin BYRAN & Sally TANLSON, 28 Dec. 1816.   [S1]

BYRANS, Wesely, & Cynthian TEMPLEMAN, bond 20 Nov. 1829;
   f/b: Ephrum Templeman; bdsm: Wm. Gregory.   [AB]

BYROM, G. W., & Mary TEMPLEMAN, bond 9 Jan. 1836;
   parent/b: E. Templeman; bdsm: Ephraim Templeman.   [AB]

BYROM, Geo. W., & Margaret COYLE, bond 23 Aug. 1838;
   bdsm: Joseph Coyle.   [AB]

George W. BYRAM & Margaret Coyle, 22 Aug. 1838. (JSt)   [B2]

CALDWELL, Alexander, & Hannah B. SAMPLE, 1813. (LTu)   [KM]

CALDWELL, Alexander, & Patsey CUSHAW, 7 Dec. 1826. (Rth)   [B2]

CALDWELL, Burnsides, & _____ GRAY, 15 Feb. 1829.   [S1]

[CALDWELL] Coldwell, Epuraim [Ephraim?], & Patty PENIC, 1816.   [S1]

CALDWELL, Greenberry, & Mary GRAY, bond 10 Feb. 1827;
   bdsm: Isaac Gray.   [AB]

CALL, John, & Tully F. KINGCADE, bond 16 Aug. 1838;
   bdsm: Joseph Kingcade.   [AB]

John Call & Jully A. Kingcade, 23 Aug. 1838. (MGs)   [B2]

CALL, John M., & Essina CLARK, bond 3 Aug. 1846;
   bdsm: Thomas Clark.   [AB]

John M. CAUL & Essene Clark, 6 Aug. 1846. (MGs)   [B2]

CALVERT, Wm., & Sally Lane LYNAM, bond 10 Feb. 1840;
   f/b: Richard Lynam; bdsm: Seth Hunt.   [AB]

CALVERT, Wm., & Eliza Ann ?BARNARD or Barnat, bond 10 May 1847;
   bdsm: Richard Lyram.   [AB]

William Calvert & Eliza BARBABY, 11 May 1847. (BHr)   [B2]

CAMEL?, John, & Amanda BUSLEY, bond 2 Feb. 1830;
   bdsm: John Busley.   [AB]

John Camel & Amanda CUSBY, 7 Jan. 1830. (JGL)   [B2]

CAMPBELL, Andrew, & Polly MARTIN, bond 12 May 1849;
   bdsm: Wm. Romins.   [AB]

CAMPBELL, James, & Mary BAIRD, bond 17 Dec. 1827;
   f/b: George Baird; bdsm: W. D. Ralston.   [AB]

James Campbell & _____ Baird, 20 Dec. 1827. (PHn)   [B2]

CAMPBELL, Joel, & Elizabeth LYNAM, bond 7? Dec. 1837;
   f/g: Alexander Campbell; f/b: Richard Lynam; bdsm: Absolom Lysom.   [AB]

Joel CAMBEL & Elizabeth Lynam, 27 Dec. 1837. (AHu)   [B2]

CAMPBELL, Joshua, & Margaret ARNETT, bond 1 Oct. 1836;
    bdsm: Wm. Workman. [AB]
CAMPBELL, Wm., & Dolly READE, bond 31 Dec. 1842;
    bdsm: Wm. Reade. [AB]
    William Campbell & Dolly Reade, 1 Jan. 1843. (JnSm) [B2]
CAMPBELL, Williamson, & Nancy COSHOW, bond 20 June 1816;
    bdsm: Williamson Campbell, John Coshow. [AB]
    William Campbell & Nancy Coshow, 30 June 1816. [JA]
    W. William Campbell & Nancy Coshow, 12 Sept. 1816. [S1]
CAMPLIN, John H., & Sarah E. TRIPLETT, 14 May 1850. (RFC) [B2]
CAMPLIN, Jonathan L., & Louisa MOORE, bond 11 Feb. 1826;
    bdsm: John Ralls. [AB]
CANNADA, Joseph, & Delila GRIMES, bond 28 Apr. 1821;
    bdsm: Wm. Grims. [AB]
    Joseph Cannada & Delila Grimes, 29 Apr. 1821. [S1]
CANNON, Charles, & Rachell S. PATRICK, bond 10 Sept. 1827;
    bdsm: Herad Patrick. [AB]
    Chas. C. Cannon & Rachel S. Patrick, 11 Sept. 1827. (JEv) [B2]
CANNON, Charles, & Rebecca LOCK, bond 27 Apr. 1842;
    bdsm: James F. Locke. [AB]
CANNON, Clement, & Sally FREEMAN, bond 25 Feb. 1822;
    bdsm: Benj. Lemaster. [AB]
    Clement Cannon & Sally FERSMAN, 11 Nov. 1822. [S1]
CANNON, Henry, & Elizabeth D. CROOKS, bond 7 Jan. 1824;
    bdsm: John Crooks. [AB]
    Henry Cannon & Elizabeth D. Crooks, 8 Nov. 1824. [S1]
CANNON, John C., & Jean ?GARONER, bond 4 Jan. 1829;
    bdsm: John Crooks? [AB]
    J. Cannon & _____ GARDEN, 25 Jan. 1829. [S1]
CANNON, Robert, & Sarah HOUSE, bond 3 Apr. 1827;
    f/b: Wm. House; bdsm: Theophilus Steele. [AB]
    Robt. Cannon & Sarah House, 5 Apr. 1827. (JtSm) [B2]
CANNON, Wm., & Martha Ann WILSON, bond 4 Feb. 1847;
    f/b: Joel Wilson; bdsm: Newton Cannon. [AB]
    William K. Cannon & Marthann WILLSON, 28 Feb. 1847. (PHn) [B2]
CANTRALL, Christopher, & Sally LAFFERTY, bond 20 Jan. 1824;
    bdsm: Richard Lomas. [AB]
    Christopher CANDRELL & Sally Lafferty, 30 Jan. 1824. [S1]
CANTRALL, Wyatt, & Sally ENGLAND, bond 12 Aug. 1812;

f/b: Stephen England; bdsm: Wyatt Cantrall, Stephen England. [AB]

Wyett CANTRELL or CANTWELL & Sally England, 14 Aug. 1811. [JA,S1]

CARPENTER, Absolem, & Emil ?HUNT or Hurt, bond 13 Oct. 1845; bdsm: Hrron[?] Moore. [AB]

CARPENTER, Daniel, & Patsy McNABB, bond 18 May 1812; f/g: Daniel Carpenter, Sr.; f/b: Abner McNabb; bdsm: Daniel Carpenter, Abner McNabb. [AB]

CARPENTER, Henry, & Cintha MOORE, bond 25 Feb. 1820; bdsm: Allen Ficklin. [AB]

CARPENTER, John, & Fanny JONES, bond 31 Aug. 1816; bdsm: Charles Jones, John Carpenter. [AB]

John Carpenter & Fanny Jones, 1 Sept. 1816. [JA,S1]

CARPENTER, Levi, & Susannah MOORE, bond 15 Sept. 1820; bdsm: John Moore. [AB]

Levi Carpenter & Susannah Moore, 17 Sept. 1820. [S1]

CARPENTER, Michael, & Sally JONES, bond 4 Oct. 1822; bdsm: Charles Jones. [AB]

Michael Carpenter & Sally Jones, 5 Oct. 1822. [S1]

CARPENTER, Robert, & Lucinda JONES, 27 Sept. 1843. (SMc) [B2]

CARPENTER, Shelby, & Judy Ann LUTTRELL, bond 4 Apr. 1848; f/g: Squire Carpenter; bdsm: Andrew Suttell. [AB]

[CARR?] Kerr, Samuel, & Nancy BROWN, bond 24 Nov. 1823; bdsm: Atkin Fannin. [AB]

Samuel CARR & Nancy Brown, 24 Nov. 1823. [S1]

CARR, Samuel, & Nancy JACKSON, 26 Dec. 1826. (JPk) [B2]

CARR, Wm., & Jane HAMILTON, bond 4 June 1836; f/b: Samuel Hamilton; bdsm: Samuel C. Hamilton. [AB]

William Carr & Jane Hamilton, 5 Jan. 1836. (SJn) [B2]

CARR, Wm., & Sythania KINARD, bond 14 Feb. 1848; bdsm: Wm. Thompson. [AB]

CARREL, James, & Honor HART, 12 Apr. 1841. (SMc) [B2]

CARRICK, William, & Martha McCLANE, 28 Aug. 1844. (SMc) [B2]

CARRINGTON, James, & Mary WIGGINGTON, bond 17 Jan. 1848; bdsm: James Armitage. [AB]

W. Carrington & M. E. WIGGINTON, 20 Jan. 1848. (AGW) [B2]

CARROLL, Joseph, & Rebecca CLAYTON, bond 17 Aug. 1816; bdsm: Joseph Carroll, Phillip Williams. [AB]

CARROLS, John, & Polly WINCKLEBLACK, bond 24 Nov. 1832; bdsm: John Winckleblack; [AB]

John CARROLL & Polly WINKLEBLACK, 27 Nov. 1832. (JPk) [B2]

CARSON or Carrson, David, & Mossalite GILL, 4 Sept. 1844. (JGW) [B2]

CARSON, James, & Susannah LEDFORD, bond 12 June 1824;
    bdsm: James Ledford. [AB]
    James Carson & Susannah LEAFORD, 12 June 1824. [S1]

CARTER, Andrew, & Nancy RANDOLPH, bond 22 Nov. 1825;
    f/g: Joseph Carter; bdsm: David Carter. [AB]

CARTER, David B., & Virginia McKINNEY, bond 7 Sept. 1825;
    bdsm: Joseph Carter. [AB]

CARTER, Elijah, & Eliza RAGLAND, bond 4 July 1821;
    bdsm: Silas Chastin. [AB]

CARTER, Joseph, & Elizabeth SCOTT, bond, 2 Jan. 1812;
    f/g: Joseph Carter; f/b: Robert Scott; bdsm: Joseph Carter, Thos. Ferrell. [AB]

CARTER, ?Oatka, & Artimila GRIMES, bond 2 June 1825;
    bdsm: Edward Grimes. [AB]

CARTER, Rane, & Magdalene CHASTAIN, bond 6 Sept. 1819;
    bdsm: Silas Chastin. [AB]
    Rane Carter & Magdalen CHASTEEN, 9 Sept. 1819. [S1]

CARTMILL, Charles, & Elizabeth CAR, bond 7 Jan. 1830;
    bdsm: Thos. Cartmill. [AB]
    Charles CARTMEL & Eliza CARR, 27 Jan.1830. (JHH) [B2]

CARTMILL, J. M., & Eliz. DUREAL, bond 5 July 1828;
    bdsm: James Dureal. [AB]

CARTMILL, John, & Rebecca HENDERSON, bond 23 Jan. 1822;
    bdsm: Thos. Welch. [AB]
    John Cartmill & Rebecca HENDRIX, 21 Feb. 1822. [S1]

CARTMILL, John, & Lucinda CLEM, bond 3 Nov. 1849;
    bdsm: Geo. Thomas. [AB]
    John Cartmill & Lucinda CLEMON, 4 Nov. 1849. (JHe) [B2]

CARTMILL, John M., & Mildred TACKETT, bond 22 March 1830;
    f/b: Archibald Tackett; bdsm: Jas. H. Cartmill. [AB]
    John M. CARTMEL & Mildred Tackett, 23 March 1830. (JHH) [B2]

CARTMILL, Thomas, & Asinah ANDER(S)ON, bond 1 Dec. 1836;
    bdsm: James A. Hazelrigg. [AB]

CARTMILL, Wm., & Polly CROCKETT, bond 28 Dec. 1832;
    bdsm: Robert Crockett. [AB]

CARTWRIGHT, David, & Harriet WELCH, bond 6 March 1822;
    f/b: John Welch; bdsm: David Williamson; [AB]
    David CARTRIGHT & Harriet Welch, 7 March 1822. [S1]

CARTWRIGHT, Isham, & Jane BAXTER, bond 15 Jan. 1842;

bdsm: Wm. Baxter. [AB]

CARTWRIGHT, Levi H., & Elizabeth FLETCHER, bond 12 Nov. 1842;
    bdsm: Peter Cartwright. [AB]

CARY, James, & Betsy FLETCHER, bond 11 June 1821;
    bdsm: Benj. Snelling. [AB]
    James CORY & Betsy Fletcher, 14 June 1821. [S1]

CARY, John, & Sally Ann SEXTON, bond 20 July 1830;
    bdsm: John B. Warren. [AB]

CASE, Benjamin S., & Polly QUILLIN, 6 Aug. 1818. [S1]

CASH, Shelly, & Nancy McCORMICK, bond 18 Sept. 1848;
    bdsm: Reuben McCormick. [AB]
    Shelby Cash & Nancy Ann McCormick, 18 Sept. 1848. (RWM) [B2]

CASSITY, Allen, & Mary Ann HOLSEY, bond 28 Oct. 1837;
    f/g: Jesse Cassity; bdsm: G. W. Cassity. [AB]
    Allen Cassity & Mary Ann HALSEY, 29 Oct. 1837. (JGW) [B2]

CASSITY, Alvah, & Elizabeth TRUMBO, bond 10 Feb. 1834;
    bdsm: F. Trumbo, Jr. [AB]

CASSITY, Alvin, & Mary E. CASSITY, bond 27 Sept. 1848;
    bdsm: Mathais Griffin. [AB]

CASSITY, Armstrong, & Ruth TRUMBO, bond 30 Sept. 1828;
    bdsm: John Trumbo. [AB]
    Armstrong Cassity & Ruth Ann Trumbo, 2 Oct. 1828. (PCy) [B2]

CASSITY, David, & Susan JOHNSTON, bond 12 Sept. 1829;
    bdsm: David Johnston. [AB]
    David Cassity & Suszan Johnston, 17 Sept. 1829. (JGW) [B2]

CASSITY, David, & Elizabeth Jane McCORMICK, bond 8 Oct. 1842;
    bdsm: Samuel McCarmick. [AB]

CASSITY, Harvey, & Susan CARRINGTON, bond 7 Nov. 1831;
    bdsm: Timothy Carrington. [AB]

CASSITY, Henry, & Nancy RICHARDS, bond 26 Jan. 1822;
    bdsm: Daniel Peveler. [AB]
    Henry Cassity & Nancy Richards, 28 Jan. 1822. [S1]

CASSITY, Hiram, & Delila PERATT, bond 22 March 1828;
    bdsm: John Hensely. [AB]

CASSITY, Isaac, & Delilah McNAB, bond 19 Oct. 1819;
    bdsm: Isaac Cassity, David Cassity. [AB]
    Isaac Cassity & Delitah McNab, 31 Oct. 1819. [S1]

CASSITY, Jesse, & Elizabeth ELLINGTON, bond 23 May 1812;
    f/b: David Ellington; bdsm: Jesse Cassity, Isaac Ellington. [AB]

CASSITY, John, & Margaret CHARNOWIF, bond 8 Feb. 1813;
  consent from f/b; bdsm: John Cassity, Jacob Cassity.   [KM]
  John Cassity & Margaret RICHARDS   [AB]
CASSITY, Reuben, & Elizabeth BROWN, bond 11 Jan. 1813;
  f/b: James Brown; bdsm: Reuben Cassity, Edmond Wells.   [AB]
  Reubin Cassity & Elizabeth Brown, 12 Jan. 1815.   [S1]
  Reubin Cassity & Elizabeth BROW, 12 Jan. 1813.   [JA]
CASSITY, Stephen, & Peggy BROWN, bond 10 Feb. 1816;
  f/g: Wm. Cassity; bdsm: Geo. Brown.   [AB]
  Stephen Cassity & Peggy Brown, 11 Feb. 1816.   [JA]
  7 Dec. 1816.   [S1]
CASSITY, Stephen, & Sally CROUCH, bond 29 Oct. 1838;
  bdsm: Isaac Crouch.   [AB]
CASSITY, Wm., & Dorothy TRUMBO, bond 7 Feb. 1828;
  bdsm: John Trumbo.   [AB]
  William CASSADY & Doritha Trumbo, 14 Feb. 1828. (PCy)   [B2]
CASSITY, Willix, & Nancy CARTMILL, bond 23 Jan. 1828;
  f/b: Andrew Cartmill; bdsm: Harrison Cartmill.   [AB]
  Willis Cassity & Nancy Cartmill, 24 Jan. 1828. (JCm)   [B2]
CASSITY, Woneduck, & Melinna FICKLIN, bond 14 March 1829;
  bdsm: Charles Ficklin.   [AB]
CAUDILL, John, & Nancy ROBERTS, bond 12 Feb. 1822;
  bdsm: Mare Roberts.   [AB]
  John CORDIAL & Nancy Roberts, 12 Feb. 1822.   [S1]
CAYWOOD, ?Evarner, & Rachel GRIMES, bond 25 Nov. 1833;
  bdsm: Wm. Grimes.   [AB]
  Erasmus Caywood & Rachael Grimes, 26 Nov. 1833. (HEv)   [B2]
CHAMBERS, Wm., & Rebecca GILL, bond 21 March 1814;
  bdsm: Wm. Chambers, Peter R. Gill.   [AB]
  William Chambers & Rebecca Gill, 22 March 1814. (JPH)   [TP,RS]
CHANDLER, Anderson, & Amanda ADAMS, bond 13 Apr. 1849;
  f/b: Wm. Adams; bdsm: Joseph Howard.   [AB]
  Anderson Chandler & Amanda Adams, 13 Apr. 1849. (SMc)   [B2]
CHASTAIN, Levi, & Louisa MARTIN, bond 26 Jan. 1831;
  bdsm: John Davis.   [AB]
  Levi CHASTINE & Louisa Martin, 3 Feb. 1831. (JnSm)   [B2]
CHASTAIN, Silas, & Nancy RAGLAND, bond 14 July 1821;
  bdsm: Elijah Carter.   [AB]
CHILES, Henry, & Eliza WHITE, bond 28 Aug. 1830;
  bdsm: John M. White.   [AB]

CHIPMAN, ?Dresse, & Posey AMOS, bond 10 May 1815;
    bdsm: Archibald Baird.   [AB]
    Draper Chipman & Polly Amos, 10 May 1815.   [JA,S1]
CHRISTIAN, James, & Melinda G. ROSS, bond 16 March 1846;
    bdsm: Phillip Ross.   [AB]
    James Christian & Malinda G. Ross, 18 March 1846. (BHr)   [B2]
CHURCH, Isaiah, & Malinda MITCHELL, bond 15 Dec. 1829;
    f/g: Thos. Church; bdsm: James Crow.   [AB]
    Isaiah Church & Melinda MICHEL, 20 Dec. 1829. (ALy)   [B2]
CHURCH, Isaiah, & Barbary SAP, bond 16 Aug. 1839;
    bdsm: Jacob Sap.   [AB]
    Isaih Church & Barbary Sap, 19 Aug. 1839. (PHn)   [B2]
CHURCH, Thomas, & Berea? JOHNSON, bond 30 Aug. 1831;
    bdsm: Richard Johnson.   [AB]
CLACK or Black, M. L., & Cena MYRES, 2 Sept. 1850. (BBv)   [B2]
CLARK, David, & Elizabeth CRAIG, bond 17 May 1847;
    bdsm: Jacob Craig.   [AB]
CLARK, Hugh, & Livia SPENCER, 18 Apr. 1844. (SKc)   [B2]
CLARK, James, & Comfort INGRAM, bond 1 Feb. 1815;
    bdsm: James Clark, Wm. Sexton.   [AB]
    James Clark & Cumford ENGRAM / Comfort Engname, 2 Feb. 1815.   [S1,JA]
CLARK, James, & Lucinda CLAYTON, bond 23 Aug. 1848;
    parent/g: C. Clark; bdsm: Geo. B. Clayton.   [AB]
    James Clark & Lucretia Clayton, 23 Aug. 1848. (WRg)   [B2]
CLARK, John, & Nancy MABEL, bond 27 July 1815;
    bdsm: John W. Mabel.   [AB]
CLARK, John, & Mary JONES, 14 Nov. 1845. (BBv)   [B2]
CLARK, Robert, & Lucy WILLIAMS, 18 Apr. 1841. (SMc)   [B2]
CLARK, Thompson, & Deboraugh WILSON, bond 22 March 1820;
    bdsm: Nathaniel Wilson.   [AB]
CLARKE, Fieldin, & Abigail SETTER, bond 29 Oct. 1821;
    bdsm: Wm. Ward.   [AB]
    Fieldin Clarke & Abigal SETTE, 30 Oct. 1821.   [S1]
CLARKE, John, & Susannah WILLSON, bond 15 March 1819;
    bdsm: Nathaniel Wilson.   [AB]
    John CLARK & Arsenath WILSON, 18 March 1819.   [S1]
CLARKSON, Wm., & Sarah ALEXANDER, bond 18 June 1832;
    f/b: Thomas Alexander; bdsm: John Bayley.   [AB]
    William M. Clarkson & Sarah Alexander, 19 June 1832. (WBL)   [B2]

CLAY, Samuel, & Amanda PHELPS, bond 17 Nov. 1849;
    bdsm: Wm. Phelps. [AB]
CLAYPOLE / Claypoole, David, & Lucinda VANNATTON, 11 July 1839. (EBr) [B2]
CLAYPOLE, John, & Huldah BIDDELL, bond 3 Apr. 1827;
    bdsm: Henry Reed. [AB]
CLAYTON, Charles, & Dorothy BARNS, bond 7 Dec. 1814;
    f/b: Thos. Barns; bdsm: Chas. Clayton, Wm. Barns. [AB]
    Charles Clayton & Dorothy BARNES, 8 Dec. 1814. (CHp) [JA]
    Charles CLOTON & Dorothy Barns [S1]
CLAYTON, George, & Nancy BAILEY, bond 7 July 1821;
    f/b: Jno. Bailey; bdsm: Enoch McDonnald. [AB]
    George Clayton & Nancy BAILY, 15 July 1821. [S1]
CLAYTON, Jasper, & Malinda BOYD, 28 March 1817. [JA,S1]
CLAYTON, Stephen, & Mebule? GOODPASTER, 30 July 1841. (SMc) [B2]
CLAYTON, Warner, & Louisa BAILEY, bond 6 March 1848;
    bdsm: Charles Bailey. [AB]
CLAYTON, William, & Virginia SMITH, ?bond 5 June 1843. [AB]
    William Clayton & Virginia Smith, 6 June 1843. (JnSm) [B2]
CLEM, Joseph, & Patsy THOMPSON, 26 Oct. 1843. (JFs) [B2]
CLICK, Jon, & Margaret McGLOTHIN, bond 1 Apr. 1836;
    bdsm: John M. McGlothin. [AB]
CLIN, Levi, & Lydia COLLINS, bond 3 March 1849;
    bdsm: S. M. Trumbo. [AB]
CLINE, James, & Margaret JAMES, bond 24 July 1823;
    bdsm: Challis Cooper. [AB]
    James Cline & Margaret James, 24 July 1823. [S1]
CLINE, John, & Elizabeth CLINE, bond 16 Dec. 1848;
    f/b: James Cline; bdsm: John L. Cline. [AB]
    John Cline & El(i)zabeth Ann Cline, 16 Dec. 1846. (BCs) [B2]
CLINE, John G., & Mary Ann CLINE, bond 3 May 1847;
    f/b & bdsm: Samuel Cline. [AB]
CLINE, Landon, & Sally MOORE, bond 12 Jan. 1830;
    bdsm: Robt. Haydon. [AB]
CLINE, Samuel, & Doll CLINE, bond 31 March 1847;
    f/g: James Cline; bdsm: John Cline. [AB]
CLOW, John, & Patsey SHARP, 3 Oct. 1826. (RTy) [B2]
CLOW, Petnam H., & Margaret JACKS, 25 May 1826. (AMx) [B2]
CLUB, Phillip, & Evelery RANDOLPH, bond 8 Oct. 1827;
    bdsm: James Randolph. [AB]
    Phillip Club & Emily Randolph, 9 Oct. 1827. (JnSm) [B2]

COATS, James, & Polly PATTERSON, bond 21 Aug. 1827;
   bdsm: Aaron Gorne [Garner?].   [AB]
[COCHRAN?] Jonnathan, Cochran, & Suzy MYRES or Myers?, bond 3 March 1812;
   m/b: Elizabeth Myres (Myers, Myroe?); bdsm: Joseph Williams.   [AB]
Jonathan COUGHNEN & Susan MOYERS, 6 March 1812.   [S1]
Jonothan COUGHREN & Susan or Sarah Moyers, 16 Apr. 1812.   [JA]
COCHRAN, Jonathan, & Rachall RICE, bond 13 Aug. 1840;
   bdsm: Richard Lynam.   [AB]
COCKRELL, John, & Sarah BARNES, bond 10 June 1822;
   bdsm: Ch. Oakley.   [AB]
John COCKSIT & Sarah Barnes, 11 June 1822.   [S1]
COFER, George, & Elizabeth CUMINGHAM, 27 Aug. 1818.   [S1]
COFER, Haram, & Nancy Jane MARVEL, 28 Nov. 1850. (ISh)   [B2]
COFER, Reuben, & Gincey McCLANAHAN, 24 Feb. 1826.   [S1]
COFFEE, Ambrose, & Margarett NORMAN, bond 17 Dec. 1823;
   bdsm: Thomas Norman.   [AB]
Ambrose Coffee & Margaret Norman, 18 Dec. 1823.   [S1]
COFFER, Anderson, & Margaret ALEXANDER, bond 2 Jan. 1824;
   bdsm: Robert Alexander.   [AB]
Anderson COPHER & Margaret Alexander, 23 Jan. 1824.   [S1]
COFFER, Wm. H., & Phebe SPENCER, bond 4 Aug. 1847;
   bdsm: Lewis Spencer.   [AB]
W. H. Coffer & Phebe Spencer, 5 Aug. 1847. (SKc)   [B2]
COFFERS, Jacob, & Guzilla NESBIT, bond 29 July 1823;
   bdsm: Hugh Nesbitt.   [AB]
Jacob COPHER & Grizella Nesbit, 31 July 1823.   [S1]
COGSWELL, Issac, & Charlotte ROZER or Roger, bond 21 May 1821;
   f/g: Yedariah Cogswell; bdsm: Wm. Martin.   [AB]
Issac Cogswell & Mary Charlott RAZOR, 24 May 1821.   [S1]
COGSWELL, Isaac, & Ann DAVIS, 3 Oct. 1850. (JWW)   [B2]
COGSWELL, James, & Lucinda JOHNSON, bond 21 Sept. 1836;
   bdsm: David Johnson.   [AB]
James Cogswell & Lucinda JOHNSTON, 25 Sept. 1836. (JGW)   [B2]
[COLBERT?] Calvert, James, & Jenetta ?ROZAR or Roger, bond 18 Jan. 1837;
   bdsm: Spencer Boyd.   [AB]
James COLBERT & Jennett RAZOR, 19 Jan. 1837. (TIs)   [B2]
COLBERT, Wesley, & Mahaly MOOR, bond 20 March 1837;
   bdsm: Robt. Haydon.   [AB]
Jesse TABERT & Mahaly MOORE, 28 March 1837. (PCy)   [B2]

COLDAZURE, Phillip, & Polly GORRELL, bond 16 June 1819;
    f/b: John Gorrell; bdsm: Philip Caldmore [Colglazier], John Gorrell. [AB]
    Philip COLGLAIZER & Polly GORREL, 7 June 1819. [S1]
COLE, George, & Rebecca SIX, 25 Sept. 1829. (PHn) [B2]
COLELASURE, Jacob, & Elizabeth GORRELL, bond 18 Feb. 1823;
    f/b: John Gorrell; bdsm: Wm. D. Gorrell. [AB]
    Jacob COLCLAISUER & Elizabeth Gorrell, 19 Feb. 1823. [S1]
COLEMAN, Alexander, & Serilda WARNER, bond 19 Jan. 1846;
    bdsm: Wm. Warner. [AB]
COLEMAN, George, & Francis GOODLOWE, bond 9 Feb. 1824;
    bdsm: Thomas Ficklin. [AB]
    George COALMAN & Frances GOODWIN, 10 Feb. 1824. [S1]
COLLINS, B., & _____, 26 Feb. 1843. (PCy) [B2]
COLLINS, Benjamin, & Martha PEARCE, bond 11 May 1816;
    bdsm: Wm. Harper. [AB]
COLLINS, Bohannon, & Lydia MOXLEY, bond 25 Feb. 1821;
    f/g: Joseph Collins; bdsm: Harlan Moores. [AB]
    Bohannon Collins & Lydia MANLY, 25 Feb. 1831. (JVc) [B2]
COLLINS, Jackson, & Mary Ann COLLINS, bond 12 Jan. 1847;
    f/b: Willis Collins; bdsm: Wm. Balter. [AB]
    Jackson M. Collins & Mary Ann ?BANTA, 19 Jan. 1847. (BCs) [B2]
COLLINS, Willis, & Ellever POWER, bond 24 Nov. 1816;
    bdsm: Jos. H. Phillips. [AB]
    Willis Collins & Elleanor Power, 25 Dec. 1816. [JA,S1]
COLLIVER?, Jesse, & Sarah DOGGETT, bond 1 March 1847;
    m/b: Franky Doggett; bdsm: Wm. Ryan. [AB]
    Jesse B. COLIVER or Colman & Sarah DOGGET, 3 March 1847. (PHn) [B2]
COMBS?, Ephraim, & Sally HINES, bond 18 Dec. 1827;
    bdsm: Wm. Frazer. [AB]
    Ephraim Combs & Sally Hines, 19 Dec. 1827. (JPk) [B2]
[CONGLETON?] Langleton, Columbus, & Margaret SHARP, bond 25 Feb. 1849;
    bdsm: John Caldwell. [AB]
    Collumbus W. CONGLETON & Mact? E. Sharp, 28 Feb. 1849. (RFC) [B2]
CONLEY, Larkin, & Mary BALLA, bond 25 Dec. 1833;
    bdsm: Harry Hawkins. [AB]
    Larken Conley & Mary BALA, 26 Dec. 1833. (SJn) [B2]
C(O)NNER, R. H., & Sullda LEE, bond 30 Apr. 1849;
    bdsm: J. F. Turner, Jr. [AB]
CONNER, Richard, & Mary Jane BERRY, bond 20 Feb. 1849;
    f/b: Joseph Berry; bdsm: John L. Berry. [AB]

CONSTANT, John, & Elizabeth ATCHISON, 1839. (EBr)   [B2]

CONYERS, Isaac, & Nancy STEVENS, bond 29 Nov. 1824;
    bdsm: W. O. Stephen.   [AB]
    Isaac Conyers & Nancy STEPHENS, 2 Dec. 1824.   [S1]

CONYERS, John, & Agnes TAYLOR, bond 27 Sept. 1819;
    bdsm: John Taylor.   [AB]
    John Conyers & Agness Fay COX, 3 Sept. 1819.   [S1]

CONYERS, Thomas, & Nancy KERNS, bond 7 Sept. 1840;
    f/b: Tilmon Kerns; bdsm: Levi Kerns.   [AB]
    Thomas Conyers & _____ KERNES, 13 Sept. 1840. (TDm)   [B2]

COOK, Abraham, & Luncey HAMILTON, bond 8 March 1810[?];
    bdsm: Lincoln Crone.   [AB]
    Abraham Cook & Tursey Hamilton, 8 March 1815. (JPH)   [TP,RS]

COOK, James, & Lucinda MOORE, bond 15 Feb. 1820;
    bdsm: Joseph Nelson.   [AB]
    James Cook & Lucinda MOREHEAD, 17 Feb. 1820.   [S1]

COOK, James, & JulyAnn SNEDDLY, bond 1834;
    bdsm: James Mitchell.   [AB]

COOK, James, & Nancy GORE, bond 27 Jan. 1847;
    bdsm: Ben Botts.   [AB]

COOK, John, & Suphia [Sophia?] NELSON, 9 Apr. 1818.   [S1]

COOK, Joseph, & Nancy THOMAS, bond 4 Sept. 1833;
    bdsm: Cary Traylor.   [AB]
    Joseph Cook & Nancy Thomas, 5 Sept. 1833. (PCy)   [B2]

COOK, Joseph, & Nell DAVIS, bond 14 May 1849;
    bdsm: Allen Davis.   [AB]

COOKE, Robt. F., & Ann Eliz. SHARP, bond 4 May 1839;
    bdsm: Ben F. Webb.   [AB]
    Robert F. COOK or Cooke & Ann Eliza Sharp, 5 May 1839. (MGs)   [B2]

COON, Christopher, & Polly MYERS, bond 29 Nov. 1811;
    f/b: Henry Myers; bdsm: Christopher Coon, James Cook.   [AB]
    Christopher COONS & Polly Myers, 29 Nov. 1811.   [JA,S1]

COONLEY, Harriet[?], & Francis ATKINS, bond 9 Feb. 1833;
    f/b: Thos. Atkins; bdsm: Dudley Atkins.   [AB]

COOPER, Adam, & Margaret SPOON, bond 6 Feb. 1816;
    bdsm: Adam Cooper.   [AB]
    Adam Cooper & Margaret Spoon, 17 March 1816.   [JA,S1]

COOPER, F. H., & Elizabeth McINTOSH, bond 25 Oct. 1839;
    bdsm: Frederick McIntosh.   [AB]

COOPER, Fleetwood, & Elizabeth HOPPER, bond 4 Oct. 1836;
  bdsm: Levi Hopper. [AB]
  Fleetwood Cooper & Elizabeth Hopper, 6 Oct. 1836. (PCy) [B2]
COOPER, John, & Miranna MAGOWAN, bond 13 July 1846;
  bdsm: John D. Magowan. [AB]
  John Cooper & Cynthaana McGOWAN, 23 July 1846. (GBu) [B2]
COOPER, Thomas, & Elizabeth BRADSHAW, bond 18 Apr. 1828;
  bdsm: John Scott. [AB]
COOPER, Wm. K., & Louisa SWITZER, bond 4 March 1829;
  f/b: Abraham Switzer. [AB]
  Wm. K. Cooper & Louisa Switzer, 5 Apr. 1829. (DWh) [B2]
COPHER, Jesse, & Elizabeth PHELP, bond 5 Apr. 1821;
  bdsm: Ezekiel Copher. [AB]
  Jesse Copher & Elizabeth PHILIPS, 4 Apr. 1821. [S1]
COPHER, John, & Polly MYERS, bond 29 Jan. 1849;
  bdsm: Milton Myers. [AB]
CORBIN, Samuel, & Reuben[?] DENTON, bond 7 Aug. 1834;
  bdsm: Reuben Denton. [AB]
CORBIN, Wm., & Maria BROWN, bond 23 March 1845;
  bdsm: Casus Brown. [AB]
CORBIN, Zachariah, & Lucy BAILEY, 18 Jan. 1819;
  bdsm: Wm. Bailey. [AB]
  Zachariah Corbin & Lucy DAILY, 19 Jan. 1819. [S1]
CORBIN or Carlin?, Zachariah, & Nancy DOGGETT, bond 21 Dec. 1824;
  bdsm: Henry Dogget. [AB]
CORY, Abram, & Sarah SPENCER, 7 Sept. 1843. (SKc) [B2]
COSHOW, Thomas, & Sally ARNETT, bond 21 July 1812;
  f/b: Thomas Arnett; bdsm: Vincent Whaley, Thos. Coshow. [AB]
  Thomas Coshow & Sall(e)y Arnett, 23 July 1812. [JA,S1]
COSTIGAN, Wm., & Elizabeth McCARTY, bond 28 Oct. 1811;
  bdsm: Wm. Costigan, Wm. Hughes. [AB]
  William CONSTIGN & Elizabeth McCarty, 7 Nov. 1811. [S1]
COSTIGAN, Wm., & Lydiann DAVIS, bond? 24 Oct. 1839. [AB]
  William Costigan & LydiAnn Davis, 24 Oct. 1839. (JnSm) [B2]
COSTIGAN, Wm., & Haner ?CORRELL or Carrell, bond 22 March 1845;
  bdsm: James Warren. [AB]
  William Costigan & Honor CARROL, 24 March 1845. (SKc) [B2]
COVINGTON, Coleman, & Matilda DUNCAN, bond 6 Apr. 1822;
  bdsm: Henry Duncan; [AB]

Coleman Covington & Matilda Duncan, 12 Apr. 1822. (JPH) [TP,RS]

COWAN, Alex., & Rachel CUNNINGHAM, 8 July 1828. (HMy) [B2]

COWAN, Caleb C., & Margaret LEDFORD, 18 Jan. 1826. (JtSm) [B2]

COX, Alvin, & Mabley WHITTEN, bond 2 Feb. 1829;
    bdsm: J. H. Hendricks. [AB]
    Alvin ?CAR or Can & Mahala WHITTINGTON, 4 Feb. 1829. (JVc) [B2]

COX, David, & Margaret RABURN, bond 16 June 1845;
    f/g: Solomon Cox; f/b: Seldon Raburn; bdsm: James Cox. [AB]
    David Cox & Margaret Ann RABORN, 18 June 1845. (SMc) [B2]

COX, Solomon, & Anne SEXTON, bond 28 Apr. 1814;
    bdsm: Solomon Cox, Jesse Quillin. [KM]
    Solomon Cox & Ann LEXTON or Lenton, 28 Apr. 1814. [JA]
    Solomon COCKS & Ann Sexton [S1]

COYLE, George, & Peggy LINCH, bond 1 Sept. 1812;
    f/b: Daniel Linch; bdsm: Geo. Coyle, Geo. Linch. [AB]

COYLE, George, & Matilda HARAMON, bond 16 July 1842;
    f/g & bdsm: James Coyle. [AB]

COYLE, James B., & Rebecca KINCAID, 31 July 1835. (SKM) [B2]

COYLE, Joseph, & Nancy G(R)EGORY, 9 Jan. 1839. (JSt) [B2]

COYLE, Peter, & Hester RAIMEY, bond 17 June 1842;
    f/g: James W. Coyle; f/b: Able Raimey; bdsm: Thos. Atchison. [AB]

COYLE, Wm., & Polly CATES, bond 1 March 1832;
    bdsm: Joseph Mefris. [AB]

CRACRAFT, Eli, & Polly COSHAW, bond 21 Jan. 1822;
    f/g: Wm. Cracraft; bdsm: John Coshow. [AB]
    Eli Cracraft & Polly COSHOW, 24 Jan. 1822. [S1]

CRACRAFT, Jeremiah, & Nancy DUTY, bond 4 May 1830;
    bdsm: Daniel Duty. [AB]

CRAIG, David, & Matilda DOYLE, bond 2 May 1846;
    f/b & bdsm: John Doyle. [AB]
    David Craig & Matilda Doyle, 3 May 1846. (JMc) [B2]

CRAIG, Jacob, & Nancy YARBROUGH, bond 14 May 1828;
    bdsm: James Wells. [AB]
    Jacob Craig & Nancy YARBOUGH, 4 May 1828. (AGg) [B2]

CRAIG, James, & Katherine DAUGHERTY, bond Aug. 1830;
    bdsm: Samuel Daugherty. [AB]
    James Craig & Katherine Daugherty, 26 Aug. 1830. (DWh) [B2]

CRAIG, Jessee, & Marthy ADAMS, bond 23 Sept. 1839;
    f/b: Richard Adams; bdsm: Eli Prather. [AB]
    Jesse W. Craig & Martha Adams, 24 Sept. 1839. (ASd) [B2]

CRAIG, John, & Nancy COB, bond 26 Sept. 1814;
    bdsm: John Craig, Robert Craig.   [AB]
    John Craig & Nancy Cob or CAB, 27 Sept. 1814. (CHp)   [JA,S1]
CRAIG, John, & Milly HARREMAN, bond 13 March 1845;
    bdsm: Geo. Coyle.   [AB]
    John Craig & Milly HORSEMAN, 13 March 1845. (SKc)   [B2]
CRAIG, John, & Elizabeth CROUCH, bond 3 Sept. 1849;
    bdsm: Isaac Crouch.   [AB]
    John W. Craig & Elizabeth Crouch, 6 Sept. 1849. (RWM) [B2]
CRAIG, Jonathan, & Patsey KINCAID, bond 25 July 1827;
    bdsm: Ben Wells.   [AB]
    Jonathan Craig & Patsey Kincaid, 2 Aug. 1827. (JPk)   [B2]
[CRAIG?] Crag, Joshua, & Rebecky WARREN, 5 March 1839. (JSt) [B2]
CRAIG, Robert P., & Catherine PORTER, bond 16 Jan. 1823;
    bdsm: Thomas Porter.   [AB]
    Robert P. CRAIN & Catharine Porter, 16 Jan. 1824.   [S1]
CRAIG, Samuel, & Rachel KIRK, bond 7 Dec. 1829;
    bdsm: Wm. Kirk.   [AB]
    Saml. A. Craig & Rachael B. Kirk, 10 Dec. 1829. (DWh) [B2]
CRAIG, Samuel, & Fanny CHANDLER, bond 22 Jan. 1833;
    bdsm: John Spencer.   [AB]
    Samuel Craig & Fanny Chandler, 5 Feb. 1833. (TIs)   [B2]
CRAIG, Thomas, & Eliza CHANDLER, bond 15 Jan. 1834;
    bdsm: Ben Sudduth.   [AB]
CRAIG, Wm., & Mary LOGAN, bond 5 July 1821;
    bdsm: Wm. Logan.   [AB]
    William Craig & Mary Logan, 12 July 1821.   [S1]
CRAIN, John F., & Laticha DILLON, bond 28 March 1849;
    bdsm: Geo. F. Trumbo.   [AB]
CRAIN, Robert, & Fanny MULBERRY, bond 23 Dec. 1811;
    f/b: John Mulberry; bdsm: Robt. Crain, John Mulberry.   [AB]
    Robert DRAIN & Fanny Mulberry, 31 Dec. 1811.   [JA,S1]
CRAIN, Samuel, & Sarah JOHNSON, bond 16 Nov. 1836;
    f/g: James Crain; bdsm: James Shields.   [AB]
CRAIN, Wm. L. or T., & Elizabeth HOPKINS, bond 29 Aug. 1834;
    bdsm: F. Hopkins.   [AB]
CRAINE, Wm., & Rebecca MOFFETT, bond? 26 Dec. 1826.   [AB]
    A. M. CRANE & Rebekah MAFFETT, ?Dec. 1826. (JPH: see Appendix) [TP,RS]
CRANE, Samuel, & Jane MOFFETT, bond 23 Nov. 1819;

bdsm: Wm. Moffett. [AB]

CRASE, Adam, & Mary JONES, 15 Apr. 1852. (SMc) [B2]

CRAWFORD, Geo., & Eliza SMITH, bond 19 June 1847;

    bdsm: J. N. Richards. [AB]

    George W. Crawford & El(i)za Smith, 20 June 1847. (WSh) [B2]

CRAWFORD, James M., & Mariah YOUNG, 30 Oct. 1851. (RFC) [B2]

CRAWFORD, Joseph, & Susannah VANLANDINGHAM, bond 29 Dec. 1834;

    bdsm: John _____. [AB]

    Joseph Crawford & Susannah Vanlandingham, 1 Jan. 1824. [S1]

CRAWFORD, Samuel, & Christian CRAWFORD, bond 21 Feb. 1820;

    bdsm: Joseph Crawford. [AB]

    Samuel CRANE & Christana Crawford, 24 Feb. 1820. [S1]

CRAYCRAFT, John, & Nancy FOSTER, bond 4 Sept. 1833;

    bdsm: James Hazelrigg. [AB]

    John Craycraft & Nancy Foster, 5 Sept. 1833. (JPk) [B2]

CRAYCRAFT, Miles, & Elizabeth CRAYCRAFT, bond 19 Apr. 1847;

    bdsm: Thomas Small. [AB]

    Miles Craycraft & E. Craycraft, 22 Apr. 1847. (RFC) [B2]

CRAYCRAFT, Wm., & Keziah RATLIFF, bond 19 Jan. 1832;

    bdsm: James Sudduth. [AB]

    William Craycraft & Kesiah Ratliff, 19 Jan. 1832. (SJn) [B2]

CRAYCRAFT, Wm., & Myran PARKER, bond 8 Feb. 1834;

    bdsm: Henry Pratt. [AB]

CRAYCRAFT, Wm. & Leticha JONES, bond 22 June 1849;

    bdsm: Barford Goodpaster. [AB]

    William Craycraft & Latia Jones, 1 July 1849. (JHe) [B2]

CRAYCRAFT, Zadock, & Anne HENDRIX, bond 10 March 1812;

    f/b: Phillip Hendrix; bdsm: Zadock Craycraft, Philip Hendrix. [AB]

CROCKET, Eligy, & Polly INGRIM, 20 July 1839. (JSt) [B2]

CROCKETT, James, & Mary CARTMILL, bond 27 May 1834;

    bdsm: Thos. Cartmill. [AB]

CROCKETT, John F., & Adaline MEETER or Milter, bond 15 Jan. 1842;

    bdsm: Therman Meeter. [AB]

    John A. CROCKET & Adalelle MATEER, 19 Jan. 1842. (RFC) [B2]

CROCKETT, Redish, & Polly RICE, bond 10 Sept. 1831;

    bdsm: Nelson Rice. [AB]

CROOKS, Alfred N., & Melinda OWINGS, 13 Aug. 1835. (DST) [B2]

CROOKS, John, & Esther CANNON, bond 8 Sept. 1812;

    bdsm: John Crooks, Newble Cannon. [AB]

    John Crooks & Esther Cannon, 1813. (LTu) [KM]

CROOKS, Robt. F., & Mary BRACKENRIDGE, bond 4 Aug. 1846;
    bdsm: Wm. S. Lane. [AB]
CROSLEY, Edward K., & Frances TRIBBLE, 8 June 1842. (JnSm) [B2]
CROSSTWAIT, Aaron, & Roda WILSON, bond 6 June 1845;
    f/b: Joseph Wilson; bdsm: Reuben Wilson. [AB]
    Aaron CROSTHAITE & Rhoda A. Wilson, 12 June 1845. (JWT) [B2]
CROSTHWAIT, Aaron, & Frances PEARSALL, bond 31 Oct. 1849;
    bdsm: Thornton Pearsall. [AB]
    Aaron CROSSTHWAIT & Francis R. PIERSALL, 1 Nov. 1849. (JWW) [B2]
CROUCH, Abraham, & Louisana SANDERS, bond 12 Feb. 1827;
    bdsm: Oliver Sanders. [AB]
    Absolam Crouch & L. SAUNDERS, 15 Feb. 1827. (DWh) [B2]
CROUCH, Cathbert, & Nancy CASSITY, 6 Oct. 1841. (JGW) [B2]
CROUCH, Curtis, & Caroline P. HYMER, 5 Apr. 1843. (JGW) [B2]
CROUCH, Jesse, & Anne CASSITY, bond 12 June 1830;
    f/b: Benj. Serton; bdsm: Jacob Cassity. [AB]
CROUCH, Jesse, & Nancy CASITY, 5 Aug. 1850. (JHe) [B2]
CROUCH, James, & Mary PENDLETON, bond 15 Feb. 1845;
    bdsm: Christopher Galvin. [AB]
CROUCH, Johnathan, & Sarah RICE, 25 July 1850. (BBv) [B2]
CROUCH, Jonathan, & Patsy PENDLETON, bond 24 Jan. 1820;
    f/b: Rice Pendleton; bdsm: Thacker Pendleton. [AB]
    Jonathan Crouch & Patsy Pendleton, 27 Jan. 1820. [S1]
CROUCH, Thomas, & Melvina RICE, 2 Apr. 1843. (WRg) [B2]
CROUCH, Wm., & Polly BESHAW, bond 10 Jan. 1814;
    bdsm: Wm. Crouch, Jesse Pettit. [KM]
    William Crouch & Polly Beshaw or BESHOW, 13 Jan. 1814. [JA,S1]
CROUCH, Wm., & Amanda CARTMILL, bond 19 July 1847;
    bdsm: Thos. Cartmill. [AB]
CROUCHFIELD, ?Zalslar, & Nancy GOODPASTER, bond 20 March 1847;
    bdsm: Noah Goodpaster. [AB]
CROW, F. M., & Susan R. PATRICK, 13 June 1850. (TDL) [B2]
CROWE, Soloman, & Maryan ATCHISON, bond 11 Feb. 1829;
    bdsm: Theo Hendrix. [AB]
    Solomon CROW & Margarett Atchison, 12 Feb. 1829. (ALy) [B2]
CRUMP, Alsen, & Susan or Swaan? KENT, bond 20 Aug. 1828;
    f/g: Richard Crump; bdsm: Lewis Jackson. [AB]
CRUMP, Melvin, & Cassy ANDERSON, 30 Dec. 1834. (JHu) [B2]
CRUMP, Richard, & Nancy McCARTY, bond 11 Aug. 1823;

bdsm: Levi Herndon. [AB]

Richard Crump & Nancy MEAITE, 12 July 1823. [S1]

CRUTCHFIELD, Zapher, & Judith SHARK, bond 23 July 1828;

bdsm: David W. Fletcher. [AB]

Zopher CRUTHFIELD & Judith SHARP, 25 Dec. 1838. (PHn) [B2]

CULL, Hugh, & Louisa DEEN, bond 28 Nov. 1831;

bdsm: Wm. Tincher. [AB]

CUNNING, Uriah, & Elizabeth McLAIN, bond 31 July 1825;

bdsm: Joseph Donahoe. [AB]

Uriah Cunning & Elizabeth McCLAIN, 26 Aug. 1825. [S1]

CUNNINGHAM, John, & Mary HUGHART, bond 1 March 1842;

bdsm: James Hughart. [AB]

John Cunningham & Mary Hughart, 2 March 1842. (RFC) [B2]

CUN(N)INGHAM, John, & Mary E. GUDGELL, 8 Apr. 1852. (GGd) [B2]

CUP?, George, & Amazrida HYMER, bond 7 May 1845;

bdsm: John F. Turner. [AB]

George CUPS & Amarinda Hymer, 8 May 1846. (JGW) [B2]

[CUPS?] Coper, Cornelius, & Betsy YARBROUGH, bond 18 March 1837;

bdsm: Robert Paterson. [AB]

Cornelius CUPS & Betsey YARBER, 19 March 1837. (TIs) [B2]

CUPS, David, & Rebecca MORRIS, bond 15 May 1816;

bdsm: David Morris, D. Cups. [AB]

CURLE, Stephen, & Mary SHARP, bond 19 Dec. 1838;

bdsm: Zopher Crutchfield. [AB]

Stephen CURL & Mary Sharp, 23 Dec. 1838. (PHn) [B2]

[CUTRIGHT] Cartwright, John, & Mary Grill [GORRELL], bond 21 Feb. 1845;

bdsm: Thomas Sorrell [Gorrell]. [AB]

John CUTRIGHT & Mary GORELL, 23 Jan. 1845. (SMc) [B2]

DABNEY or Depuy?, John H., & Eliza ANDERSON, bond 18 Apr. 1821;

bdsm: R. Dapuy. [AB]

John H. DABURY & Eliza Anderson, 19 Apr. 1821. [S1]

DAILY, Samuel , & Sarah DAILY, bond 2 Nov. 1840;

m/b: Elizabeth Daily; bdsm: Edward Barkley. [AB]

DANIEL, Isam, & Mary PERGEM, bond 25 Nov. 1839;

bdsm: James Pergem. [AB]

DANIEL, Jesse R., & Lucy Ann ROBERTSON, bond 13 Aug. 1849;

f/b: Richard Robertson; bdsm: Jno. F. Robertson. [AB]

Jesse Daniel & Lucy ann ROBTERSON, 16 Aug. 1849. (RFC) [B2]

DANIELS, John N., & Rosy HULS, bond 7 March 1812;

f/b: Paul Huls; bdsm: John N. Daniels, Paul Huls; [AB]

John N. (or John) DANNEL & Rosey HULSE, 8 March 1812.   [JA,S1]

DARNAL or Darnell, John, & Priscilla BARBER, 30 March 1843. (SRg)   [B2]

DARNALL, John, & Eliza VICE, bond 16 Nov. 1837;
  bdsm: Wm. Vice.   [AB]

John DARNEL & Eliza VISE, 17 Nov. 1837. (JVc)   [B2]

DARNOLD, Eliott, & Sarah CONYERS, bond 12 Feb. 1833;
  f/b & bdsm: Isaac Conyers.   [AB]

DAUGHERTY, John, & Louisa McGOWAN, bond 18 Apr. 1833;
  bdsm: Lewis Sudduth.   [AB]

John DAUGHORITY & Louisa McGOWEN, 19 Apr. 1833. (JFY)   [B2]

DAUGHERTY, John M., & M. L. COURA [Sarah Barnett?], bond 24 Aug. 1834;
  bdsm: Chas. Shortridge.   [AB]

DAUGHERTY, Joseph, & Polly SHROUT, bond 30 Jan. 1838;
  f/b: Issac Shrout; bdsm: P. Rice.   [AB]

DAVIS, Andrew, & Kesiah MURA, bond 20 June 1821;
  bdsm: David Munn.   [AB]

Andrew Davis & Risiah MUNZ, 21 June 1821.   [S1]

DAVIS, Barker B., & Betsy DAVIS, bond 2 Jan. 1824;
  bdsm: Even ?Evens.   [AB]

Booker Davis, & Betsy Davis, 4 Jan. 1824.   [S1]

DAVIS, Bennet E., & Narcissa M. P. YOUNG, bond 20 March 1836;
  f/b & bdsm: John E. Young.   [AB]

DAVIS, Daniel [David], & Polly LANCASTER, bond 15 Dec. 1815;
  bdsm: Wm. Sudduth.   [AB]

David Davis, & Polly LANKESTER or [sic] Sankestevin, 17 Sept. 1815.   [JA,S1]

DAVIS, David, & Melinda [Malinda] KERNS, 2 Jan. 1827. (RTh)   [B2]

DAVIS, Eli, & Mary DAVIS, 1 March 1818.   [S1]

DAVIS, Ignatious, & Katherine BROMIGAN, bond 22? Apr. 1830;
  bdsm: Robt. Freeland.   [AB]

Ignatius Davis & Catharine BOMIGIM, 30 Apr. 1830. (JHH)   [B2]

DAVIS, Ignatius, & Sally RICE, 20 March 1815.   [JA,S1]

DAVIS, John, & Cely WHITE, 11 June 1814.   [S1]

DAVIS, John, & Milly DARBEY, bond 19 Nov. 1825;
  f/b: James Darbey; bdsm: Abraham Jones.   [AB]

DAVIS, John, & Milly SORRELL, bond 10 May 1847;
  bdsm: Joseph Sorrell.   [AB]

John Davis & Milly Sorrell, 13 May 1847. (SKc)   [B2]

DAVIS, Joseph, & Carie? BAILEY, bond 22 Dec. 1845;
  bdsm: John Bailey.   [AB]

DAVIS, Josephus, & Mary Jane KNOX, bond 24 Aug. 1847;
    f/g: David Davis; bdsm: James Knox. [AB]
    Joseph Davis & Mary Jane Knox, 15 Sept. 1848. (LCb) [B2]
DAVIS, Lodwick, & Icy (or Jey?) HENDRIX, bond 6 March 1823;
    parent/b: Yourath Hendrix (consent 5 March); bdsm: Theophilus Hendrix. [KM]
    Landwick Davis & Joy Hendrix, 6 March 1823. [S1]
DAVIS, Lewis, & Sally SOESBY, 1816. [S1]
DAVIS, Luke, & Elizabeth THOMAS, 6 Aug. 1818. [S1]
DAVIS, Samuel, & Catherine PERVIS, 4 Aug. 1846. (WRg) [B2]
[DAVIS] Daviss, Thomas, & Eveline HOUSE, bond 5 Sept. 1829;
    f/b: David House; bdsm: David Davis. [AB]
DAVIS, W. S., & Lucy Ann LEACH, bond 24 Feb. 1849;
    bdsm: James Leach. [AB]
    W. S. Davis & Lucy A. Leach, 25 Feb. 1849. (JHe) [B2]
DAWSON?, Joseph, & Nancy BOTTS, bond 31 July 1819;
    bdsm: Thomas Botts. [AB]
    Joseph Dawson & Nancy Botts, 3 Aug. 1819. [S1]
DAY, James, & Eliz. COGSWELL, bond 23 Sept. 1829;
    f/b: Jeddiah Cogswell; bdsm: Jacob Day. [AB]
    James Day & Eliz. COGGSWELL (or Betsa Coggwell), 23 Sept. 1829. (SJk) [B2]
DAY, John, & Lydia COGSWELL, bond 16 Oct. 1832;
    f/g: Peter Day; bdsm: James Day. [AB]
    John Day & Lydia Cogswell, 16 Oct. 1832. (JGW) [B2]
DAY, Sanders P., & Ann CATLETT, bond 11 Aug. 1825;
    bdsm: Sennet Young. [AB]
DAY, Truman, & Margaret UNDERWOOD, bond 5 Apr. 1832;
    bdsm: Wm. Underwood. [AB]
DEAKIN, Isaac, & Morgan RUSSELL, bond 16 Jan. 1827;
    bdsm: Robert Russell. [AB]
DEED, John W., & Jane NESBITT, bond 7 Jan. 1846;
    bdsm: John Nesbitt. [AB]
    _____ DEAN & Jane NESBIT, 13 Jan. 1846. [S1]
DEEN, Joseph, & Elizabeth BOYD, bond 1 Nov. 1825;
    f/b: Wm. Boyd; bdsm: Fielding B. Morgan. [AB]
    Joseph Deen & Eliz. Boyd, 4 Nov. 1825. (PHn) [B2]
DELAY, Saul, & Polly UTTERBACK, 1813. (LTu) [KM]
    Sam Delay & Polly Utterback [JA]
DENBY?, Abner, & Nancy EMMONS, bond 3 Nov. 1828;
    bdsm: Joseph Fenwick. [AB]

DENNIS, John, & Sally PERGREM, bond 29 Oct. 1829;
  bdsm: James Pergrem. [AB]
  John Dennis & Sally PURGREM, 29 Oct. 1829. (SJk) [B2]
DENNIS, Samuel, & Castriva INGRAM, 5 Feb. 1850. (JHn) [B2]
DENNIS, Thomas, & Martha MAUPIN, bond 22 Aug. 1849;
  bdsm: Jesse Dennis. [AB]
DENTON, Abram, & Elizabeth BARBER, bond 14 March 1833;
  bdsm: John Denton.
  Abram Denton & Elizabeth ?BARKER, 18 Sept. 1833. (EBr) [B2]
DENTON, Jonathan, & Elizabeth PERKINS, bond 13 June 1836;
  bdsm: Reuben Denton. [AB]
DENTON, Reuben, & Jane PERKINS, bond 18 Oct. 1827;
  bdsm: Ed Perkins. [AB]
  Reuben or Rubin Denton & Jane Perkins, 18 Oct. 1827. (JHu) [B2]
DENTON, Wm., & Catharine BARBER, bond 21 June 1831;
  bdsm: John Barber. [AB]
  William Denton & Katharine Barber, 31 June 1831. (BHu) [B2]
DESKINS, Elijah, & Nancy Ann ?VICE or Vial, bond 6 July 1836;
  bdsm: Greenberry Vice. [AB]
  Elijah Deskins & Nancy Ann Vice, 7 July 1836. (JVc) [B2]
[DEWIT?] Deeoil or Duvil?, Peter, & Elizabeth ADAMS, bond 23 July 1821;
  f/b: Larkin Adams; bdsm: James Giles. [AB]
  Peter DEWIT & Elizabeth Adams, 2 Aug. 1821. [S1]
DEWITT, Henry, & Polly FERGUSON, bond 4 Aug. 1840;
  bdsm: James W. Thomas. [AB]
  Henry Dewitt & Polly Ferguson, 4 Aug. 1839. (JnSm) [B2]
DICKEN, Aaron, & Maria DEAN, bond 4 Feb. 1828;
  bdsm: Clenthus Arnett. [AB]
  Aaron Dicken & Mariah Dean, 7 Feb. 1828. (PHn) [B2]
DICKEN, Jehu, & Nancy FREELAND, bond 9 Sept. 1828;
  bdsm: Robert Freeland. [AB]
  John Dicken & Nancy Freeland, 12 Sept. 1828. (DWh) [B2]
DICKEN, Jesse, & Margaret MAZE, bond 25 Nov. 1842;
  bdsm: John Maze. [AB]
DILSE?, Elijah, & Lydia SMALLWOOD, bond 29 Dec. 1828;
  bdsm: Bean Smallwood. [AB]
  Eligah DELSE & Lydia Smallwood, 29 Dec. 1828. (JPk) [B2]
DIMMITT, Robt., & Anne MORE, bond 21 July 1811;
  bdsm: Robt. Dimmitt, Benj. Snellin. [AB]
DOGGETT, Daniel W., & Eliza MYRES, bond 4 Apr. 1842;

42

bdsm: Zacheriah Corbin. [AB]

Daniel DOGGET & Eliza Myres, 5 Apr. 1842. (SJn) [B2]

DOGGETT, Joel, & Louisa SMOOT, bond 7 July 1833 (no bdsm). [AB]

DOGGETT, Richard, & Margaret VICE, bond 30 Sept. 1839;
bdsm: M. B. Vice. [AB]

Richard Doggett & Margret Vice, 3 Oct. 1839. (JWR) [B2]

DOLEMAN, John, & Maria LACNAW, 9 June 1817. [JA]

John DALEMAN & Maria SAENWON [S1]

DOLL, Thomas, & Elizabeth GEORGE, bond 30? Oct. 1849;
bdsm: Henry George. [AB]

Thomas DALE & Elizabeth George, 1 Nov. 1849. (PHn) [B2]

DONAHOO, John, & Milieson DENBY, 28 Nov. 1825. [S1]

DONALDSON, Alexander, & Sally POWER, bond 15 Dec. 1814;
m/g: Barbary Donaldson; m/b: Elizabeth Power; bdsm: Alex Donaldson, Jeremiah
Power. [KM]

DONALDSON, Fletcher, & Nancy HARPER, bond 3 Feb. 1834;
bdsm: John Harper. [AB]

Fletcher Donaldson & Nancy Harper, 6 Feb. 1834. (SJn) [B2]

DONALDSON, Flet[c]her & Mary HAWKINS, 11 Dec. 1852. (SMc) [B2]

DONALDSON, John, & Polly SWITZER, bond 5 Oct. 1816;
f/b: Abraham Switzer. [AB]

DONAL[D]SON, Patterson, & Margaret BROMAGEN, 14 March 1826. (JtSm) [B2]

DONALDSON, Patterson, & Susannah SINCLAIR, bond 26 March 1833;
bdsm: Wm. Power. [AB]

Patterson Donaldson & Susanah Sinclair, 26 March 1833. (SJn) [B2]

DONALDSON, Wm., & Eliza TACKETT, bond 21 Sept. 1831;
bdsm: F. Donaldson. [AB]

DONALDSON, Wm., & Ann TURNER, bond 2 Apr. 1845;
bdsm: John F. Turner. [AB]

William Donaldson & Ann E. Turner, 3 Apr. 1845. (MGs) [B2]

DONATHAN, Aaron, & Marthy STATEN, bond 1 Oct. 1845;
f/b: Wm. Staten; bdsm: John Grayson. [AB]

Aaron Donathan & Martha STATON, 1 Oct. 1845. (WRg) [B2]

DONATHAN, Elijah, & Sarah GILLS, bond 24 Feb. 1845;
bdsm: Andrew Walton. [AB]

Elijah Donathan & Sarah GILKINSON, 4 Feb. 1845. (WRg) [B2]

DONATHAN, James, & Lila MULLIN, bond 27 July 1848;
bdsm: Elijah Donathan. [AB]

James Donathan & Delila Mullin or MULLINS, 18 July 1848. (JGW) [B2]

DONATHAN, Martin, & Polly SWIN, bond 19 Jan. 1839;
   bdsm: James Mullen.   [AB]

DONITHEN, John, & Nancy BASFORD, 8 Dec. 1818.   [S1]

DONOHUE, Albine, & Elizabeth GOODPASTER, bond 3 Apr. 1846;
   bdsm: James Goodpaster.   [AB]

DONOHUE, Alford, & Martha Ann JONES, bond 18 July 1849;
   bdsm: Josiah Jones.   [AB]
   Alfred DONAHEW & Martha Ann Jones, 18 July 1849. (JHe)   [B2]

DONOHUE, John, & Celice WHITE, bond 10 June 1824;
   bdsm: David McClain.   [AB]

DONOHUE, Joseph, & Rachel McCLAIN, bond 9 Apr. 1824;
   bdsm: John McClain.   [AB]
   Joseph DONAHOO & Rachel McClain, 12 Apr. 1821.   [S1]

DOTSON, James, & Salley CAREY, bond 3 Jan. 1832;
   bdsm: David Morris.   [AB]

DOUGLAS, John, & Margaret MILLER, bond 16 Apr. 1812;
   bdsm: John Douglas.   [AB]
   John Douglas or DONGLAP & Marg(a)ret Miller, 16 Dec. 1812.   [JA,S1]

DOUGLAS, William, & Mary LINTON, bond 22 Jan. 1830;
   bdsm: Rawley Morgan.   [AB]

DOWNEY, James F., & Susanna SNEDIGER, 3 Feb. 1852. (HCN)   [B2]

DOWNEY, John F., & Zilpha COGGSWELL, bond 23 Sept. 1847;
   f/b: John Coggswell; bdsm: Wm. Mynher.   [AB]
   J. A. DOWNY & Zilphia COGSWELL, 23 Sept. 1847. (AGW)   [B2]

DOWNING, James, & Cynthia McCORMICK, bond 9 Feb. 1846;
   bdsm: Samuel McCormick.   [AB]
   James Downing & Cythian McCORMACK, 11 Feb. 1846. (JnSm)   [B2]

DOWNS, Robert, & Polly INGRAM, bond 22 Dec. 1814;
   bdsm: Robt. Down, Thos. Ingram.   [AB]
   Robert Downs & Polly Ingram, 29 Dec. 1814.   [JA,S1]

DOYLE, John, & Malinda BUTLER, bond 24 July 1827;
   bdsm: Robert Freeland.   [AB]
   John Doyle & Malinda Butler, 25 July 1827. (JVc)   [B2]

DUCKWORTH, Absolem, & Harriet MILLER, bond 12 Oct. 1829;
   bdsm: John Duckworth.   [AB]
   Absolem Duckworth & Harriet Miller, 15 Oct. 1829. (SJn)   [B2]

DUCKWORTH, Alvin, & Narcissa WALKER, bond 27 Oct. 1829;
   f/g: John Duckworth; bdsm: James E. Walker.   [AB]
   Alvin Duckworth & Narcissa Walker, 29 Oct. 1829. (DWh)   [B2]

DUCKWORTH, Francis, & Mary SHARP, bond 17 Dec. 1839;

bdsm: Alfred F. Duckworth. [AB]

Francis Duckworth & Mary Sharp, 18 Dec. 1839. (RFC) [B2]

DUCKWORTH, John, & Catharine MOORE, bond 1 Apr. 1839;

bdsm: Alfred F. Duckworth. [AB]

DUGAN, Hugh, & Mary WILLIAMS, bond 17 Dec. 1821. [AB]

Hugh DUGIN & Mary Williams, 20 Dec. 1821. [S1]

DULY, Abner, & Nancy EVANS, 6 Nov. 1828. (WWn) [B2]

DUNAWAY, Joseph, & Minty TRAYLOR, bond 9 Dec. 1822;

parent/b & bdsm: Cary Traylor. [AB]

Joseph DINAWAY & Mirty TRAILOR, Dec. 1822. [S1]

[DUNCAN?] Dancan, Edward, & Minerva GILVIN, 7 March 1850. (RFC) [B2]

DUNCAN, James, & Ann PROCTOR, bond 19 Nov. 1829;

f/b: James B. Proctor; bdsm: Coleman Covington. [AB]

DUNCAN, Wm. B., & Minerva YOUNG, bond 4 July 1838;

bdsm: Senett Young. [AB]

DUNEWAY, Joseph, & Syntha PROCTOR, bond 30 July 1833;

bdsm: Jeremiah Proctor. [AB]

Joseph DONAWAY & Syntha PROCTER, 1 Aug. 1833. (PCy) [B2]

DUNIWAY, John, & Esther KINDER, bond 14 March 1814. [AB]

John DUNAWAY & Est(h)er Kinder, 20 March 1814. [JA,S1]

DUNLAP, David M., & Polly GUDGELL, bond 19 Nov. 1823;

bdsm: Joseph W. Gudgell. [KM]

David Dunlap & Polly Gray [sic], 20 Nov. 1823. [S1]

DUNLAP, John, & Elizabeth GUDGELL, bond 11 Aug. 1814;

f/b: Andrew Gudgell; bdsm: John Dunlap, Allen Gudgell. [AB]

DUNWAY, Ben, & Amanda COOK, bond _____;

f/g: Joseph Dunway; bdsm: Abraham Cook. [AB]

DURHAM, Jacob, & Rachael VANSCHOIACK, bond 18 Nov. 1840;

bdsm: John Durham. [AB]

Jacob Durham & Rachel J. VANSCHOCK, 19 Nov. 1840. (PHn) [B2]

DUROSSETT, Preston, & Lucinda BENSON, bond 26 Sept. 1832;

f/b: James Benson; bdsm: James Benson, Jr. [AB]

Preston DUROSSET & Lucinda Benson, 26 Sept. 1832. (JCH) [B2]

DUSKIN, William, & Nancy GRIMES, 20 Jan. 1817. [S1]

DUTY, John, & Sarah EADEN, bond 20 July 1819;

bdsm: John Eaden. [AB]

John Duty & Sarah PERDIN, 20 July 1819. [S1]

DUTY, John, & Kern H.[Kerenhappuch?] BURNS, bond 14 Sept. 1828;

bdsm: Emerk Burns; [AB]

John Duty & Kerin BURNES, 14 Sept. 1828. (DWh)　　　　[B2]

DUTY, Littleton, & Sally McALISTER, bond 30 March 1821;

　bdsm: C. Whitecraft.　　　　[AB]

　Littleton Duty & Sally L. McATTISTER, 3 Apr. 1821.　　　　[S1]

DUTY, Simpson, & Mary DAILY, 21 Dec. 1844. (ASd)　　　　[B2]

DUTY, Wm., & Jane PERLEY, bond 23 Oct. 1820;

　bdsm: John Duty.　　　　[AB]

　William Duty & Jane PRESLEY, 24 Oct. 1820.　　　　[S1]

DUVALL, Thomas C., & Ann SHUMATE, 2 Apr. 1822.　　　　[S1]

EASTON, Reuben, & Polly MANIN, bond 8 Oct. 1812;

　m/g: Elizabeth Easton; bdsm: Reuben Easten, Tarlton Brock.　　　　[AB]

　Reubin EASTIN or Easton & Polly MANNON, 9 Oct. 1812.　　　　[JA,S1]

EATON, Andrew, & Jane JOHNSON, bond 15 Aug. 1836;

　m/b: Elizabeth Snedaker; bdsm: M. A. Trumbo.　　　　[AB]

EATON, Benj., & Sharlot ALEXANDER, bond 22 Oct. 1832;

　bdsm: Hugh Alexander.　　　　[AB]

EATON, James, & Jenetta WATTS, bond 11 Apr. 1820;

　f/g: Charles Eaton; f/b: Reuben Watts; bdsm: Wm. Buckley.　　　　[AB]

　James Eaton & Genetta WALLS, 13 Apr. 1820.　　　　[S1]

EATON, Jerry, & Christeena ADAMS, bond 17 Feb. 1834;

　bdsm: Wm. Adams.　　　　[AB]

EATON, Wm., & Nancy VICE, bond 19 Nov. 1832;

　bdsm: Aaron Vice.　　　　[AB]

[EDMONSON] Admondson, Ren., & Elizabeth ENGLISH, bond 20 Apr. 1824;

　bdsm: Joseph Rassmore.　　　　[AB]

　Ren EDMONSON & Elizabeth English, 22 Apr. 1824.　　　　[S1]

EDWARD, Owen, & Elizabeth LONSDALE, bond 8 Aug. 1832;

　bdsm: Charles Whington [Whittington?].　　　　[AB]

EDWARDS, James B., & Peggy CHEN, bond 22 July 1820;

　bdsm: Samuel Cahen.　　　　[AB]

ELLINGTON, Abraham, & Delila ALLEY, bond 28 July 1838;

　bdsm: Henry Casity.　　　　[AB]

　Abram Ellington & Delila Alley, 28 July 1838. (JGW)　　　　[B2]

[ELLINGTON?] Alington, Alvin, & Lucy Jane WILSON, bond 5 Dec. 1842;

　f/b: Joseph Wilson; bdsm: Charles Wilson.　　　　[AB]

　Alvin ELLINGTON & Lucy Jane Wilson, 8 Dec. 1842. (JGW)　　　　[B2]

ELLINGTON, Isaac, & Polly CASSITY, bond 23 May 1812.　　　　[KM]

[ELLINGTON?] Allington, Isaac, & Elizabeth HEARTY, bond 5 Feb. 1834;

　bdsm: Joseph Williams.　　　　[AB]

　Isaac ELLINGTON & Elizabeth HASTY, 9 Feb. 1834. (JGW)　　　　[B2]

ELLINGTON, Jacob, & Catherine EVANS, bond 9 Dec. 1822;
    f/b: James Evans; bdsm: Akalis Fannon. [AB]
    Jacob ALLINGTON & Katharine EVINS, 12 Dec. 1822. [S1]
ELLIOTT, Robert, & Elizabeth McINTIRE or McIntine, bond 15 Dec. 1827. [AB]
ELLIOTT, Samuel R., & Minerva OAKLEY, bond 16 Nov. 1835;
    parent/b & bdsm: A. Oakley. [AB]
ELLIOTT, Thomas, & Eliza MORROW, bond 20 Sept. 1833;
    f/b: Robt. Morrow; bdsm: Nicholas Marsh. [AB]
    Thomas Elliott & Elisa J. ?MORVOM, 26 Sept. 183_. (ACs) [B2]
ELLIS, Jonathan, & Mary Jane GRIMSL[E]Y, 29 Oct. 1835. (SJn) [B2]
ELLIS, Owen, & Matilda FIZAR, bond 29 May 1847;
    bdsm: C. Snedegar. [AB]
    Owen Ellis & Matilda FRAZIER, 1 June 1847. (WSh) [B2]
ELLIS, Thomas, & Jane PATRICK, bond 17 Nov. 1814;
    m/b: Elizabeth Patrick; bdsm: Thomas Ellis, Elizah Atchison. [AB]
    Thomas Ellis & Jane Patrick, 18 Nov. 1814. [JA,S1]
EMBRY, Allen, & Emaline RENFRO, bond 25 June 1847;
    bdsm: James Jones. [AB]
EMMONS, Drury J., & Hanah SHEALS, 29 Jan. 1835. (ALy) [B2]
EMMONS, Wm., & Rachael EATON, bond 21 March 1846;
    bdsm: Lewis Story. [AB]
    W. W. Emmons & R. Eaton, 24 March 1846. (JHu) [B2]
ENGLAND, David, & Martha Ann MORELAND, bond 26 Aug. 1846;
    bdsm: Freeland Moreland. [AB]
ENGLISH, Andrew, & Lucy SANDERS, bond 3 March 1832;
    bdsm: Oliver Sanders. [AB]
    Andrew English & Lucy Sanders, 6 March 1832. (MGs) [B2]
ENGLISH, John, & Maratha ENGLISH, bond 24 Jan. 1829;
    f/b: John English; bdsm: David Kincaid. [AB]
ENSOR, George N., & Mary LOWRY, 22 Feb. 1844. (WRg) [B2]
ENSOR, William P., & Nancy RUDDEN, 26 Aug. 1851. (BBv) [B2]
EPERSON, James, & Maryariah SHOAT, bond 9 Dec. 1833;
    bdsm: Austin Shoat. [AB]
    James Eperson & Margarett CHOAT, 11 Dec. 1833. (JPk) [B2]
EPPERSON, Charles, & Susannah PARK, bond 23 Apr. 1827;
    bdsm: Reuben Gillon. [AB]
EPPERSON, James, & Hanah BLEVINS, bond 2 Apr. 1845;
    bdsm: James Blevins. [AB]
    Samuel EPERSON & Hannah Blevins, 2 Apr. 1845. (WRg) [B2]

EPPERSON, Robert, & Mary EPPERSON, bond 9 Oct. 1813;
    f/b: James Epperson; bdsm: Robt. & James Epperson.   [AB]
EPPERSON, Wm., & Hetty FORSYTHE, bond 1 Apr. 1814;
    f/b: Abraham Forsythe; bdsm: Wm. Epperson, Joseph Thompson.   [AB]
    William Epperson & Hetty FORSITHE, 7 Apr. 1814.   [JA,S1]
ERVIN, Isaac, & Ester HAMILTON, bond 4 Sept. 1833;
    bdsm: David Leyett.   [AB]
    Isaac Ervin & Ester Hamilton, 5 Sept. 1833. (RTy)   [B2]
ERWIN, Henry, & Susan McCLELLEN, bond 21 Sept. 1821;
    bdsm: James Sudduth.   [AB]
    Henry Erwin & Susan MECLECLIN, 3 Sept. 1821.   [S1]
ESTILL, Isaac, & Peggy TRUMBO, bond 2 Jan. 1813;
    bdsm: Isaac Estill, Jacob Trumbo.   [AB]
    Isaac ESTELL & Peg(g)y Trumbo, 7 Jan. 1813.   [JA,S1]
ESTILL, Silister, & Eliza THOMPSON, bond 31 Dec. 1832;
    bdsm: Joseph Swetman.   [AB]
ESTILL, William, & Polly WILLIAMS, 24 Dec. 1817.   [S1]
EULETT, Squire, & Sophia HOWARD, bond 29 Feb. 1828;
    bdsm: Eli Howard.   [AB]
    Squire Eulett & Sophia Howard, 30 Feb. 1828. (EHw)   [B2]
EVAN, Evan, & Eliza McNAB, bond 7 June 1830;
    bdsm: James McNab.   [AB]
EVANS, Evan, & Jane KELSOE, 5 Feb. 1826. (JPk)   [B2]
EVANS, Henry, & Rachel BRYAN, bond 21 Feb. 1829;
    bdsm: Frederick White.   [AB]
EVANS, Jesse, & Nancy FICKLIN, bond 31 Dec. 1825;
    bdsm: Charles Ficklin.   [AB]
    Jesse Evans & _____, 3 Jan. 1826.   [S1]
EVANS, John, & Anna BECROFT, bond 2 June 1815;
    f/b: Ben Becroft; bdsm: Wm. Becroft.   [AB]
    John Evans & Ann or Anne BECRAFT, 4 July 1816.   [JA,S1]
EVANS, John, & Elizabeth MYERS, bond 2 Sept. 1839;
    f/b: Joseph Myers; bdsm: Sam Myers.   [AB]
EVANS, Samuel, & Lucy PENDLETON, bond 17 Nov. 1820;
    bdsm: Heacher Pendleton.   [AB]
    Samuel EVAN & Lucy Pendleton, 19 Nov. 1820.   [S1]
EVANS, Thomas, & Margaret THOMPSON, bond 21 Apr. 1820;
    bdsm: Joseph Thompson.   [AB]
EVANS, Thomas, & Elizabeth GREER, bond 11 Nov. 1834;
    bdsm: Thatcher Heate.   [AB]

EVIN, Benjamin, & Elizabeth MARKLAND, 22 Nov. 1822. [S1]

EVINS, Daniel, & Alley PATRICK, bond 8 Nov. 1824;
    bdsm: Herod Patrick. [AB]
    Daniel D. EVANS & Alley Patrick, 11 Nov. 1824. [S1]

EVINS, Thomas, & Anny MARTIN, 9 Apr. 1818. [S1]

EWING, Benjamin, & Betsy MARTIN, bond 26 Nov. 1821;
    f/b: Wm. Martin; bdsm: Enoch Patrick. [AB]

EWING, Joshua, & Elizabeth CONNER, 18 Oct. 1835. (JnSm) [B2]

EWING, Robert, & Margaret BOTTS, bond 19 Sept. 1832;
    bdsm: Jno. Botts. [AB]
    Robert Ewing & Margarett Botts, 20 Sept. 1832. (WHm) [B2]

EWING, William, & Susan FICKLIN, bond 12 Apr. 1822;
    bdsm: John Ficklin. [AB]
    William Ewing & Susan Ficklin, 12 Apr. 1822. [S1]

FANNING, Isaac, & Amanda M. CASSITY, bond 15 Oct. 1849;
    bdsm: Jonathan Cassity. [AB]
    Isaac FANNIN & Amanda M. Cassity, 18 Oct. 1849. (PCy) [B2]

FANNING, John, & Polly MYERS, bond 4 July 1823;
    bdsm: Jonathan Crouch. [AB]
    John Fanning & Polly Myers, 8 July 1823. [S1]

FANNING, Josiah, & Susanna McCLURE, bond 25 July 1820;
    bdsm: Jonathan Crouch. [AB]
    Iasiah Fanning & Susan McCLINATHAN, 27 July 1820. [S1]

[FANNON?] Farmer, Achellas or Akalis, & Mary MILLER, bond 9 Feb. 1814;
    f/b: Matthew Miller; bdsm: Wm. Miller. [KM]
    also, compare: Wm. MILLER [sic?] & Mary Miller, bond 9 Feb. 1814;
    f/b: Wm. Miller; bdsm: Achillas Fannon, Wm. Miller. [AB]
    Achellas Farmer or FANNON & Mary Miller, 1 Sept. 1814. [JA,S1]

[FARIS?] Fans, J. A., & E. M. BOYD, bond 26 July 1845;
    bdsm: D. B. Boyd. [AB]
    J. A. FARIS & Elizabeth M. Boyd, 18 Aug. 1845. (SJn) [B2]

FARRIS, G. C., & Nancy BOYD, bond 15 May 1848;
    f/g: Michael Farris; bdsm: D. B. Boyd. [AB]
    George C. FARIS & Nancy J. Boyd, 16 May 1848. (SJn) [B2]

FAULTY, Henry, & Sally NESBITT, bond 7 Aug. 1828;
    bdsm: John Nesbitt. [AB]
    Henry FOUTY & Sally NESBIT, 7 Aug. 1828. (JVc) [B2]

FAY, John, & Roda LOWE, bond 26 Jan. 1822;
    bdsm: Samuel Lowe. [AB]

FENWICK, Wm., & July Ann GILL, bond 22 Jan. 1831;
    bdsm: Peter R. Gill. [AB]
    William Fenwick & Julyann Gill, 27 Jan. 1831. (SJn) [B2]
FENWICK, Wm., & Margaret COOPER, bond 23 June 1839;
    bdsm: G. Kincaid. [AB]
    William Fenwick & Margaret Cooper, 23 June 1839. (EBr) [B2]
FENWYCK, Wm., & Elizabeth PORTER, bond? 27 Feb. 1844. [AB]
    William FENWYICK & Elizabeth Porter, 27 Feb. 1844. (JnSm) [B2]
FERRILL, James, & Sarah MAPPIN, bond 19 July 1814;
    bdsm: James Ferrell, John Mappin. [AB]
    James FERREL or FERNEL & Sally Mappin, 21 July 1814. [JA,S1]
FICKLIN, Alexander, & Eliza RICKITTS, bond 19 Jan. 1839;
    f/b: Reuben Ricketts; bdsm: James Young. [AB]
    Alexander Ficklin & Eliza M. RICKETTS, 20 Jan. 1839. (SMc) [B2]
FICKLIN, James A., & Mary A. DAWSON, bond 21 Apr. 1849;
    bdsm: John Burbridge. [AB]
FICKLIN, Jarret P., & Menia? SCOTT, bond 25 Apr. 1849;
    bdsm: Harry Scott. [AB]
    Jarrett P. Ficklin & Maria S__tt, 26 Apr. 1849. (SMc) [B2]
FICKLIN, John, & Polly ANDERSON, bond 5 Jan. 1819;
    bdsm: W. M. Anderson. [AB]
    John Ficklin & Polly Anderson, 7 Jan. 1819. [S1]
FICKLIN, John, & Julieth GOODLOW, bond? 11 July 1826. [AB]
FICKLIN, Thomas, & Mary M. DOODLAR, bond 25 Oct. 1819;
    bdsm: Geo. Coleman. [AB]
    Thomas Ficklin & Mary GOODBE, 27 Oct. 1819. [S1]
FIELD, Thomas, & Polly ATCHINSON, bond 3 Sept. 1822;
    bdsm: Samuel Willson. [AB]
    Thomas FIELDS & Polly ATERCTICHEN, 11 Nov. 1822. [S1]
FIELDERS, Franklin, & Matilda SORRELL, bond 6 Jan. 1842;
    bdsm: Wm. Sorrell. [AB]
    Franklin FILARS & Mallellda SORELL, 13 Jan. 1842. (JGW) [B2]
FILSON, Stephen, & Narcissa FILSON, bond 6 Jan. 1829;
    bdsm: John D. ?Magan. [AB]
    Stephen Filson & Narcissa FELSAN, 6 Feb. 1829. (TCp) [B2]
FISCHER, James, & Emily TAPP, bond 28 Nov. 1849;
    parent/b: N. Tapp; bdsm: Jesse Dennis. [AB]
FISHER, John, & Nancy MOUNTS, bond 18 Nov. 1815;
    bdsm: Andrew Mounts; [AB]

John Fisher & Nancy MOVINSTON or MONINTSON, 20 Nov. 1815.   [JA,S1]

FISHER, Samuel, & Mary DENNIS, bond 2 March 1848;

   f/b: Jesse Dennis; bdsm: Thomas Dennis.   [AB]

   Samuel Fisher & Mary Dennis, 23? March 1848. (JFs)   [B2]

FLEMING, James, & Nancy CANNON, bond 5 Feb. 1836;

   bdsm: Wm. Hardin.   [AB]

   James Fleming & Nancy CANON, 1 Feb. 1836. (PHn)   [B2]

FLEMING, Joshua J., & Nancy TACKET, 16 May 1839. (MGs)   [B2]

FLEMING, William H., & Mary Ann PEARCE, 5 Oct. 1837. (MGs)   [B2]

FLETCHER, David, & Miranda BUSBY, bond 3 Jan. 1849;

   bdsm: Jas. Small.   [AB]

   David W. Fletcher & Marandy Busby, 4 Jan. 1849. (RFC)   [B2]

FLETCHER, Jacob, & Nancy CLARK, bond 7 Feb. 1845;

   bdsm: Ed Wells.   [AB]

   Jacob Fletcher & Nancy Clark, 7 Feb. 1845. (SKc)   [B2]

FLETCHER, John, & Rebecca VICE, bond 23 Sept. 1828;

   bdsm: David Young.   [AB]

   John F. Fletcher & Roberta Vice, 24 Sept. 1828. (JVc)   [B2]

FLETCHER, John, & Margaret McILHENY, bond 21 July 1832;

   f/b: John McIlhenny; bdsm: Thomas Arnett.   [AB]

   John F. Fletcher & Margret McILHENNEY, 22 July 1832. (RTh)   [B2]

FLETCHER, Thomas, & Daniel[?] ANDERSON, bond? 1814.   [AB]

FLETCHER, Thomas, & Margaretta G. BANTLETT, 13 Aug. 1818.   [S1]

   Col. Thomas Fletcher & Margaret G. BARTLETT, 13 Aug. 1818. (JPH)   [RS]

FLETCHER, Verdiman, & Elizabeth ROGERS, bond 6 Apr. 1819;

   f/b: Fletcher Rogers; bdsm: Verdiman Fletcher, John Rogers.   [AB]

   Derdman Fletcher & Elizabeth Rogers, 8 Apr. 1819.   [S1]

FLETCHER, William, & Lydia BROMAGEN, bond 19 Jan. 1820;

   bdsm: Wm. Fletcher, Thos. Bromagen.   [AB]

   William Fletcher & Siddy BROMIGAN, 21 March 1820.   [S1]

FLORA, Daniel, & Kirziah PHELPS, bond 28 Dec. 1811;

   bdsm: Daniel Flora, Wm. Oakley.   [AB]

FODY?, John, & Sally McCLAIN, 21 Feb. 1850. (WRg)   [B2]

FOLAND, Hugh, & Martha AUSTIN, 13 June 1851. (BBv)   [B2]

FORGAY, Hugh, & Margaret ROGERS, 22 March 1837. (SRg)   [B2]

FORGISON, John, & Sarah KANADAY, bond 4 Sept. 1813;

   bdsm: John Fergerson.   [KM]

   John FORGESON or Forgerson & Sarah Kanaday, 5 Sept. 1813.   [JA,S1]

FORRAM, Henry, & Matilda LANCASTER, bond 23 Jan. 1822;

   f/g: Jeremiah Forran; bdsm: John Utterback;   [AB]

Henry FARAN & Matilda Lancaster, 24 Jan. 1822. [S1]

FORTUNE, Thomas, & Mary SAILOR, bond 1 Feb. 1815;
    f/b: Frederick Sailor; bdsm: T. Fortune, Wm. Sailer. [AB]
    Thomas Fortune & Mary Sailor, 2 Feb. 1815. [JA,S1]

FOSTER, David, & Mrs. Susannah ROGERS, 19 Jan. 1817. [JA]
    David T. FORTER & Mrs. Susanna Rogers [S1]

FOSTER, Eli S., & Franky FLETCHER, bond 16 Aug. 1837;
    f/b: Jacob Fletcher; bdsm: Charles Shotridge. [AB]

FOSTER, James, & Ann COSTIGAN, bond 5 Jan. 1838;
    bdsm: James Warren. [AB]

FOSTER, John, & Hester Ann ?LYRAM [Lynam?], bond 12 May 1842;
    bdsm: Richard Lyram. [AB]

FOSTER, Jonathan, & Mary HOPKINS, bond 19 May 1815;
    bdsm: Lot Foster. [AB]
    Jonathan Foster & Mary Hopkins, 11 May 1815. [JA,S1]

FOWLER, Robert, & Nancy OAKLEY, bond 7 Sept. 1813;
    f/b: Christopher Oakley; bdsm: Robt. Fowler, John P. Oakley. [AB]

FOWLER, Thomas, & Cinthia GILL, bond 10 Nov. 1829;
    bdsm: Thomas Fowler. [AB]

FRAKMON, Levi, & America PERRY, bond 25 March 1845;
    bdsm: Juison Perry. [AB]
    Levi FRAKMAN & America Perry, 25 March 1845. (SMc) [B2]

FRANCIS, Andrew, & Leah ANDERSON, bond 17 Sept. 1832;
    bdsm: Wm. Anderson. [AB]

FRAZIER, Alexander, & Betsy GIBSON, bond 12 May 1827;
    bdsm: Juan[?] Taylor. [AB]

FRAZIER, Alexander, & Matilda SNEDEGAR, bond 9 July 1827;
    bdsm: John Clark. [AB]

FRAZIER, Dr., & Ibby Jane COOK, bond 28 May 1842;
    bdsm: Abram Cook. [AB]

FRAZIER, John, & Geo. Ann COOK, bond 30 Dec. 1847;
    bdsm: Dr. Frazier. [AB]
    John FRASIER & George Ann Cook, 29 Dec. 1847. (SKc) [B2]

FRAZIER, Wm., & Susannah THOMAS, bond 13 Nov. 1830;
    f/g: John Frazier; f/b: Isaac Thomas; bdsm: Cawood Traylor. [AB]

FREELAND, John, & Elizabeth OAKLEY, bond 3 July 1830;
    bdsm: Edward Wells. [AB]

FREELAND, Jonas, & Jemima JACKSON, bond 4 Oct. 1827;
    bdsm: Reuben Denton; [AB]

Jonas Freeland & Josemia Jackson, 18 Oct. 1827. (JHu) [B2]

FREELAND, Robert, & Hannah FLEMING, bond 15 Oct. 1821;
    bdsm: John Whitecroft. [AB]

    Robert Freeland & Hannah FLENNIN, 18 Oct. 1821. [S1]

FREELAND, Stephen, & Sarah DICKEN, bond 23 March 1829;
    bdsm: Jesse Dicken. [AB]

    Stephen Freeland & Sarah Dicken, 25 March 1829. (DWh) [B2]

FREEMAN, Edgar S., & Eliza Ann SMITH, 23 March 1843. (AKe) [B2]

FREEMAN, Thomas, & Sally CARBIN, bond 23 July 1827;
    bdsm: Holeman Rice, Jr. [AB]

    Thomas Freeman & Sally CORBING, 23 July 1827. (ALy) [B2]

FREEMAN, Wm. L., & Susan Y. RALLS, bond 26 Oct. 1836;
    bdsm: James F. Stone. [AB]

    William L. Freeman & Susan R. Ralls, 27 Oct. 1836. (JnSm) [B2]

FRIEND, Jonas, & Sarah BUTLER, bond 22 Jan. 1812;
    bdsm: Jonas Friend, Paul Naylor. [AB]

    Jonas or Jones Friend & Sarah Butler, 23 Feb. 1812. [JA,S1]

FUGATE, James, & Sarah McGINNIS, bond 27 Nov. 1813;
    bdsm: James Fugate, James McGinnis. [AB]

    James Fugate & Sarah McGinnis, 1813. (LTu) [KM]

[FUGATE] Frigate, James, & Malinda HAWKINS, bond 24 Sept. 1847;
    bdsm: David Hawkins. [AB]

FUGATE, Reuben, & Katharine SMALLWOOD, bond 28 Feb. 1816;
    bdsm: Beave Smallwood. [AB]

    Rubin FUGATT & Caty Smallwood, 1816. [S1]

FULKERSON, Ben, & Mary EWING, bond 28 July 1825;
    bdsm: Putman Ewing. [AB]

    Benj. F. FALKERSON & Mary Ewing, 29 July 1827. (IGL) [B2]

FUNSTON, James C., & Nancy WARREN, bond 9 Apr. 1838;
    bdsm: John B. Warren. [AB]

FURGUSON, David, & Eliza FITHERGILL, bond 19 Oct. 1822;
    bdsm: Thomas Linton. [AB]

    David FURGERSON & Eliza FEATHERSAIL, 19 Oct. 1822. [S1]

GAINES, Joseph, & Eliza METEAR, bond 17 Feb. 1829;
    bdsm: John Galloway. [AB]

    Joseph Gaines & Eliza METEER, 19 Feb. 1829. (DWh) [B2]

GALLOWAY, John, & Kenin HOPKINS, bond 24 Apr. 1833;
    bdsm: Thos. Richard. [AB]

GALVIN?, Christopher C., & Cintha CROUCH, bond 15 Feb. 1845;
    f/b: Isaac Crouch; bdsm: James Crouch. [AB]

GALVIN, John, & Elizabeth CROUTCH, 20 March 1817.   [S1]

GALVIN, William, & Elizabeth PEARSALL or Pearceall, 20 June 1844. (JGW)   [B2]

GARDNER, John, & Nancy ADKINS, bond 5 Nov. 1831;
   bdsm: Thomas Adkins.   [AB]
   John Gardner & Nancy Adkins, 9 Nov. 1831. (RTh)   [B2]

GARDNER, Samuel, & Tuthila Jane KINDALL, 12 Feb. 1850. (JHn)   [B2]

GARNER, Aaron B., & Matilda BUTLER, bond 4 May 1829;
   bdsm: John Doyle.   [AB]

GARNER, Anderson, & Elizabeth BROWN, bond 5 Oct. 1842;
   bdsm: Alfred Van.   [AB]
   Anderson Garner & Elizabeth Brown, 5 Oct. 1843. (WRg)   [B2]

GARNER, Andrew B., & Nancy LYON, bond 13 Apr. 1819;
   bdsm: Noah Lyon.   [AB]
   Andrew B. Garner & Nancy LYONS, 15 Apr. 1819.   [S1]

GARNER, Isaac B., & Margaret WARNER, bond 28 Oct. 1837;
   bdsm: F. Knox.   [AB]

GARRETT, Wm., & Elizabeth Jane TRUMBO, bond 18 Aug. 1848;
   bdsm: S. M. Trumbo.   [AB]

GATES, Geo., & Sally CHIPMAN, bond 1 Jan. 1816;
   bdsm: Paris Chipman.   [AB]
   George Gates & Sally Chipman, 2 Jan. 1816.   [JA,S1]

GATEWOOD, Robt. H., & Mary Ann STONER, bond 1836;
   bdsm: G. W. Stoner.   [AB]
   Robert H. Gatewood & Mary Ann Stoner, 12 Apr. 1836. (JnSm)   [B2]

GEORGE, Henry, & Ann SHARP, bond 31 Oct. 1829;
   f/g: Bailey George; bdsm: Moore Sharp.   [AB]
   Henry George & Ann Sharp, 5 Nov. 1829. (PHn)   [B2]

GEORGE, William, & Sally JANSON, bond 16 Nov. 1833;
   bdsm: John Traylor.   [AB]
   William George & Sally JOHNSON, 17 Nov. 1833. (PCy)   [B2]

GILASPIE, Alexander, & Maria SCOTT, bond 2 Jan. 1842;
   bdsm: Eliza Scott.   [AB]
   Alexander GALLASPIE & Maria SCOT, 20 Jan. 1842. (PHn)   [B2]

GILASPIE, Calvin, & Lucinda HEDGES, bond 17 Nov. 1842;
   f/b: James Hedges; bdsm: John H. Hedges.   [AB]

GILASPIE, Garnet, & Mary Jane HEDG(E)S, bond 5 Nov. 1832;
   bdsm: James Hedgs.   [AB]

GILBERT, Barnett, & Elizab(e)th HASTY, bond 29 Jan. 1824;
   bdsm: Wm. Hasty;   [AB]

Barnett Gilbert & Nancy Hasty, 30 Jan. 1824. [S1]

GILBERT, Stephen, & Nancy JACKSON, bond 28 Oct. 1828;
  bdsm: Wm. Griffin. [AB]

  Stephen Gilbert & Nancy Jackson, 1? Nov. 1828. (AGg) [B2]

GILBERT, Stephen, & Hetty BADGESON, 25 Aug. 1851. (SKc) [B2]

GILKERSON, James, & Sarah WALTON, bond 28 Oct. 1836;
  f/b: Wm. Walton; bdsm: Andrew Walton. [AB]

  James Gilkerson & Sarah Walton, Dec. 1836. (TIs) [B2]

GILL, Jonathan, & Sytha INGRAM, bond 16 Sept. 1837;
  bdsm: Abraham Ingram. [AB]

  Jonathan Gill & Sytha Ingram, 17 Sept. 1837. (JGW) [B2]

GILL, Samuel, & Elizabeth REED, bond 1 Nov. 1849;
  f/b: William Reed; bdsm: W. M. Sudduth. [AB]

  Salm C. Gill, Esq., & Elisabeth Reed, 1 Nov. 1849. (RFC) [B2]

GILL, Shilock, & Sarah A. ANDERSON, bond 2 Oct. 1849;
  bdsm: Wm. Anderson. [AB]

  Shiloh Gill & Sarah A. Anderson, 2 Oct. 1849. (JWc) [B2]

GILLASPIE, John H., & Rutha Ann ALLISON, bond 9 June 1845;
  bdsm: James Allison. [AB]

  John H. GILLSPIE & Ruth Ann ALISON, 11 June 1845. (RFC) [B2]

GILLISPIE, Clark L., & Eliza Ann McCORMIE, bond 19 Sept. 1837;
  bdsm: Wm. McCormick. [AB]

  Charles L. GILLASPY & Eliza ann McCORMICK, 19 Sept. 1837. (DST) [B2]

GILMORE, William, & Jane GILLASPIE, 28 June 1841. (RMx) [B2]

GILVIN, Harrison, & Lucinda MITCHELL, bond 30 May 1839;
  bdsm: Joseph Gilvin. [AB]

  Harrison GELVIN & Lucinda MITCHEL, 31 May 1839. (RTh) [B2]

GINN, James, & Lucy Wyatt GINN, bond 29 March 1825;
  bdsm: Eady Beck. [AB]

GINN, John, & Abigail BOACHEN, 6 Jan. 1820. [S1]

GINN, Thomas, & Susanna KIGGINS, bond 5 Apr. 1824;
  bdsm: John Munns. [AB]

  Thomas Ginn & Susannah FRIGGINS, 8 Apr. 1824. [S1]

GINTER, Conrad, & Elizabeth McGLOTHLIN, bond 4 March 1834;
  bdsm: Cobbert Manley. [AB]

GINTER, Jacob, & Patsy McGLOCKLIN, bond 12 Sept. 1833;
  bdsm: James Ragland. [AB]

  Jacob Ginter & Patsy McGLOCKTIN, 12 Sept. 1833. (JPk) [B2]

GINTER, John, & Polly OAKLEY, 2 Apr. 1826. (JPk) [B2]

GLOVER, Cread F., & Maria A. W. CHOTE, bond 24 June 1814;

bdsm: Cread F. Glover, Augustus Choat.   [AB]

   Creed Glover & A. W. CHOAT, 28 June 1814.   [JA]

   Creed T. Glover & H. W. Choat   [S1]

GLOVER, Creed, & Nancy HINES, bond 26 May 1842;

bdsm: C. B. Boyd.   [AB]

GLOVER, E. G., & Elizabeth J. TIPTON, bond 26 Apr. 1846;

bdsm: Joshua Tipton.   [AB]

   B. G. Glover & Elizabeth J. Tipton, 30 Apr. 1846. (TRk)   [B2]

GLOVER, Robert, & Elizabeth EPPERSON, bond 6 Sept. 1836;

f/b & bdsm: Peter Epperson.   [AB]

GLOVER, Walker, & Fanny MOORE, bond 9 Aug. 1830;

bdsm: Robert Moore.   [AB]

[GODDARD?] Gadd, Edwin Frederick, & Elenor Miner SIMS, bond 10 Apr. 1836;

f/b: Joe Sims; bdsm: Hutchis Wickliffe.   [AB]

   Edwin F. GODDARD & Eleanor M. LINS, 11 Apr. 1836. (DST)   [B2]

GOIN, Wm., & Susan RATLIFF, bond 18 Oct. 1829;

f/b: Caleb Ratliff; bdsm: Lorenzo Phillip.   [AB]

GOOCH, Thomas S., & Rachel TRUMBO, bond 15 Nov. 1832;

bdsm: John Trumbo.   [AB]

   Thomas S. Gooch & Rachael Trumbo, 4 Nov. 1833. (EBr)   [B2]

GOODEN?, Samuel, & Susan WELLS, bond 2 Aug. 1838;

bdsm: Joseph Wills or Wells.   [AB]

GOODING, Lewis, & Mary WARREN, bond 20 Nov. 1840;

bdsm: John B. Warren.   [AB]

GOODMAN, Absalem, & Nancy YOUNG, bond? 25 Feb. 1826.   [AB]

GOODPASTER, Abraham, & Rhoda GOODPASTER, bond 12 Oct. 1825;

bdsm: Hardin Goodpaster.   [AB]

   Abraham Goodpaster & Rhoda GOODPASTURE, 12 Oct. 1825.   [S1]

GOODPASTER, Carlisle, & Emily BOTTS, 16 Apr. 1839. (SMc)   [B2]

GOODPASTER, David, & Rebecca PEN, bond 17 Nov. 1821;

bdsm: Samuel Pen.   [AB]

GOODPASTER, Hardin, & Polly GOODPASTER, 12 Feb. 1818.   [S1]

GOODPASTER, Jackson, & Cythia CARPENTER, 19 Sept. 1844. (SMc)   [B2]

GOODPASTER, James, & Eliza BOON, bond 16 Sept. 1845;

bdsm: Samuel Goodpaster.   [AB]

GOODPASTER, John, & Patricia TURNER, bond 16 March 1811;

bdsm: John Goodpaster, Joseph Goodpaster.   [AB]

GOODPASTER, John, & Betsy PERATT, 17 Aug. 1826. (JPk)   [B2]

GOODPASTER, Michael, & Margaret CARPENTER, bond 19? Apr. 1813;

f/g: Cornelius Goodpaster; bdsm: Michael Goodpaster, John Hazel.   [AB]

GOODPASTER, Perry, & Magdaline JONES, bond 22 Nov. 1846;

   m/b: Elizabeth Jones; bdsm: Martin Jones.   [AB]

GOODPASTER, Robert, & Mary GOODPASTER, bond 25 Oct. 1849;

   bdsm: James Becroft.   [AB]

   Robert Goodpaster & Mary Goodpaster, 20 Oct. 1849. (JHe)   [B2]

GOODPASTER, Shelby, & Nancy SMITH, 6 March 1850. (EJo)   [B2]

GOODPASTER, Wm., & Sally BOTTS, bond 2 Feb. 1825;

   bdsm: Thomas Botts.   [AB]

GOODPASTURE, Anderson, & Henryetta PAYNE, bond 2 June 1840;

   f/b & bdsm: John Payne.   [AB]

   Anderson GOODPASTER & Henretta Payne or Payen, 13 June 1840. (SMc) [B2]

GOODPASTURE, Barefoot, & Margaret CANNADY, bond 8 Sept. 1819;

   bdsm: Cornelius Goodpaster.   [AB]

   Barfood GOODPASTER & Margarett KENNEDAY, 13 Sept. 1819.   [S1]

GOODPASTURE, Geo. W., & Elizabeth PERRAT, bond 16 Oct. 1833;

   bdsm: James Peratt.   [AB]

   George W. Goodpasture & Elizabeth PERATT, 18 Oct. 1833. (JPk)   [B2]

GOODPASTURE, John, & Lucinda PAYNE, bond 29 Aug. 1838;

   bdsm: John Payne.   [AB]

   John GOODPASTER & Lucinda Payne, 29 Aug. 1838. (SMc)   [B2]

GOODPASTURE, Seaton or Beaton, & Betsy BELL, bond 29 March 1837;

   bdsm: B. F. Sudduth.   [AB]

   Seaton GOODPASTER & Betsy BEAL, 29 March 1837. (JnSm)   [B2]

GOODWIN, Aaron, & Nancy F. HENDRIX, bond 1 Dec. 1838;

   bdsm [f/b]: Peter Hendrix.   [AB]

   Aaron Goodwin & Nancy F. Hendrix, 6 Dec. 1838. (JnSm)   [B2]

GOODWIN, Bradford, & Almira DAVIS, bond 29 Apr. 1830;

   bdsm: Jonah Freeland.   [AB]

   Bradford GOODIN & Alvira Davis, 2 May 1830. (JEv)   [B2]

GOODWIN, Levi, & Gounee? CROUCH, bond 1 Dec. 1815;

   bdsm: David Crouch, L. Goodman.   [AB]

   Levi GOODAN & Cauner Crouch / Garner GROUVH, 3 Dec. 1815.   [S1,JA]

[GORREL?] Sorrel, James, & Rebecca HITEN, bond 13 May 1816;

   bdsm: Henry Rice.   [AB]

   James GORNEL & Rebecca or Rebekah HYTEN, 13 May 1816.   [JA,S1]

[GORREL] Gowd, John, & Ann CROW, 26 Feb. 1818.   [S1]

[GORREL] Gorvel, Thomas, & Sarah BUTCHER, 13 March 1817.   [S1]

   Thos. Garvel & Sarah Butcher.   [JA]

GORREL, William, & Minerva HOUSE, 6 March 1827. (JBn)   [B2]

[GOSSETT?] Glassett?, Isaac, & Caroline ATKINSON, bond 31 Aug. 1847;

   bdsm: John Atkinson.   [AB]

   Isaac GOSSETT or Gassett & Caraline Atkinson, 2 Sept. 1847. (MGs)   [B2]

GOSSETT, Jacob, & Joann Francis RATLIFF, bond 31 Aug. 1846;

   f/b: Caleb Ratliff; bdsm: Rich I. Ratliff.   [AB]

   Jacob D. Gossett & Joann Francis Ratliff, 2 Sept. 1846. (SJn)   [B2]

GOSSETT, Martin ?C., & Mary Ann ATCHISON, 22 Aug. 1844. (SJn)   [B2]

GRAHAM, Adam, & Elizabeth WARREN, bond 25 Oct. 1811;

   bdsm: Adam H. Graham, John Warren.   [AB]

GRAHAM, Samuel, & Susanna ?BRENIN or Brwin[?], bond 29 Oct. 1827;

   bdsm: W. M. Sudduth.   [AB]

   Samuel GRAYHAM & Susanna IRVIN, 29 Oct. 1827. (JEv)   [B2]

GRAVES, Ben W., & Julian OWINGS, bond 25 March 1827;

   f/b: Elihu Owings; bdsm: Samuel Owings.   [AB]

   Benjamin H. Graves & Julian Owings, 22 March 1827. (JnSm)   [B2]

GRAVES, Thomas, & Nancy GALLOWAY, bond 19 Dec. 1820;

   f/b & bdsm: Robert Galloway.   [AB]

   Thomas Graves & Nancy GALLAWAY, 28 Dec. 1820. (JPH)   [TP,RS]

GRAY, Andrew, & Margaret COOPER, bond 5 Feb. 1816;

   bdsm: Adam Cooper.   [AB]

   Andrew Gray & Margaret(t) Cooper, 8 Feb. 1816.   [JA,S1]

GRAY, David, & Elizabeth ?MORIS, 1813. (LTu)   [KM]

   David Gray & Elizabeth MORRIS   [JA,S1]

GRAY, James H., & Emily E. HOPKINS, 15 March 1837.   [S1]

GRAY, William, & Margaret CAMPLETT, 1813. (LTu)   [KM]

   William Gray & Margaret(t) CAMPBELL, 1813.   [JA,S1]

GRAY, William, & Betsey FRANKLIN, 1813. (LTu)   [KM]

GRAY, William, & Frances GORRELL, 11 Dec. 1851. (WDA)   [B2]

GRAYHAM, Adam U., & Elizabeth WARREN, 31 Oct. 1811.   [JA]

   U. Adam Grayham & Elizabeth WAVEN   [S1]

GRAYSON, J. J., & Susannah McCLAIN, bond 27 Aug. 1842;

   bdsm: David Warner.   [AB]

   J. J. Grayson & Susannah McClain, 5 Aug. 1842. (WRg)   [B2]

GRAYSON, John, & Daisy HOPKINS, bond 5 March 1816;

   bdsm: Patrick Eringan.   [AB]

   John GRASON & Dainey Hopkins, 1816.   [S1]

GRAYSON or Gayson, John, & Polly SMITH, 18 July 1841. (PCy)   [B2]

GRA(Y)SON, Joshua, & Polly ?CONAH, bond 24 June 1823;

   bdsm: John Grason;   [AB]

Joshua GRAYSON & Polly CARAH, June 1823. [S1]
GRAYSON, Robert, & Elizabeth BLAIR, bond 23 July 1814;
    bdsm: Robt. Grayson, Wm. Caldwell. [AB]
GREEN, Fieldin, & Milly PURVIS, bond 12 Sept. 1822;
    bdsm: Geo. Purvis. [AB]
    Fieldin Green & Milly Purvis, 15 Sept. 1822. [S1]
GREEN, Fielding, & Elizabeth MOORE, bond 21 May 1845;
    bdsm: Wm. Moore. [AB]
    Fielding Green & Elizabeth Moore, 22 May 1845. (BBv) [B2]
GREEN, Gooseberry, & Yenna MITCHELL, bond 22 Aug. 1811;
    f/b: Alexander Mitchell; bdsm: Gooseberry Green, James Mitchell. [AB]
    Goulsber Green & Jenna MICHEL, 7 Sept. 1811. [JA]
    Goldsberry Green & Jeana Michel [S1]
GREEN, Richard, & Artemicea LYNAM, 3 Oct. 1850. (JDy) [B2]
GREEN, Simpson, & Elizabeth BAILY, 1 Jan. 1845. (SMc) [B2]
GREEN, Thomas, & Armida? R. JONES, 3 March 1841. (MGs) [B2]
GREGG, James, & Polly GREEN, bond 28 Aug. 1833;
    f/g: John Gregg; bdsm: Goldsberry Green. [AB]
GREGORY, Hugh, & Margaret ROGERS, bond 22 March 1837;
    bdsm: Alfred Rogers. [AB]
GREGORY, James, & Jane HYLERT or [?]Hgbert, bond 23 Apr. 1824;
    bdsm: Lewis Templeman. [AB]
    James Gregory & Jane HEGGARD, 23 Apr. 1824. [S1]
GREGORY, John, & Jane CUNNINGHAM, bond 17 March 1842;
    bdsm: John Cunningham. [AB]
    John Gregory & Jane Cunningham, 17 March 1842. (RFC) [B2]
GREGORY, Nathan, & Mahala TEMPLEMAN, bond 25 Jan. 1842;
    f/b: Ephriam Templeman; bdsm: Jesse Templeman. [AB]
GREGORY, William, & Ann CARR, 13 Aug. 1835. (SJn) [B2]
GRIFFIN, Andrew, & Lucinda ?SHAIN, bond 17 June 1822;
    bdsm: Thos. Bellows. [AB]
    Andrew Griffin & Lucinda GOV, 19 June 1822. [S1]
GRIFFIN, George, & Phebe MORRIS, 28 Feb. 1850. (WRg) [B2]
GRIFFIN, Joan[?], & Sarah McKINNEY, bond 15 May 1849;
    bdsm: James Maze. [AB]
GRIFFIN, John, & Sally McKINNEY, bond 23 June 1849;
    bdsm: Thomas Maze. [AB]
    John Griffin & Sally McKinney, 24 June 1849. (WRg) [B2]
GRIFFIN, Matthew, & Susan CASSITY, bond 30 Jan. 1834;

bdsm: Andrew Griffin. [AB]

GRIFFIN, Matthias, & Phebe SHOALTZ, widow, bond 11 Sept. 1812;
    bdsm: Matthias Griffin, Edward Parsons. [AB]
    Mathias GRIFFING & Phebe SHOOTS, 11 May 1813. [JA,S1]

GRIFFIN, William, & Ann JACKSON, 1 Dec. 1817. [JA]
    William GRIFFEN & Ann Jackson [S1]

GRIMES, Randle, & Elizabeth SPENCER, 13 Aug. 1835. (JVc) [B2]

GRIMES, Stephen, & Peomelia BOMAN, bond 17 July 1812;
    bdsm: Stephen Grimes, Thos. Alexander. [AB]
    Stephen Grimes & Parmelia Boman or BOWAN, 23 July 1812. [JA,S1]

GRIMES, Wm., & Ann D. JONES, bond 23 July 1831;
    f/b: Amos Jones; bdsm: Wm. Arosmith. [AB]

GRIMES, Wm. B., & Peggy ALEXANDER, bond 23 Sept. 1822;
    bdsm: Hugh Alexander. [AB]
    William B. Grimes & Peggy Alexander, 26 Sept. 1822. [S1]

[GRIMSLEY] Grimsby, Gabriel, & Malinda BOYD, bond 12 Dec. 1849;
    f/b: George Boyd; bdsm: John Barber. [AB]
    Gabrel GRIMSLY & Malinda Boyd, 13 Dec. 1849. (EJo) [B2]

GRIMSLEY, John, & Susan America JONES, 24 Aug. 1837. (MGs) [B2]

GRIMSLEY, Nimrod, & Frances MORELAND, bond 15 Aug. 1836;
    bdsm: Samuel Morelan. [AB]
    Nimrod Grimsley & Frances Moreland, 15 Aug. 1836. (SJn) [B2]

GROOVE, James, & Eliza MOCKBEE, bond 14 May 1828;
    bdsm: Stephen Mockbee. [AB]
    James M. GROOMS & Eliza McOCBEE, 15 May 1828. (JPk) [B2]

GROOVE?, Wm., & Alinina HOUSE, bond 3 March 1827;
    f/b: David House; bdsm: John Clark. [AB]

GROSE, Wm., & Sarah ATCHISON, bond 9 Jan. 1849;
    bdsm: James Atchison. [AB]

GROVE, James H., & Emily HOPKINS, bond 13 March 1837;
    bdsm: Wm. Hopkins. [AB]
    James H. GRAVES & Emily E. Hopkins, 15 March 1837. (DST) [B2]

GROVER, Wm. E., & Lucia HEFFLIN, bond 28 Sept. 1825;
    bdsm: Reuben Underwood. [AB]

GROVES or Graves?, Willy, & Menerva OWINGS, bond 14 Feb. 1832;
    f/b: Elihu Owings; bdsm: Sam Owings. [AB]
    Willis Groves & Manerva ?OOUNGS, 16 Feb. 1832. (DWh) [B2]

GUDGELL, Joseph, & Minerva Ann BUSBY, bond 25 Jan. 1848;
    bdsm: Jackson Busby. [AB]

GUDGELL, Thomas F., & Mary M. POWER, bond 8 Feb. 1837;

bdsm: Geo. Power. [AB]

GUERANT, Henry E., & Marcy H. OWINGS, 8 July 1835. (DST) [B2]

GUYER, Jacob, & Louisa MOORE, bond 1 Oct. 1829;

    bdsm: Silas Moore. [AB]

    Jacob GEIGER & Louisa MORE, 1 Oct. 1829. (JVc) [B2]

HACKETT, Daniel, & Madlin HICKS, 5 May 1817. [S1]

HAGANS, Francis, & Jane COFFER, 2 Jan. 1823. [S1]

HALE, Matthew, & Mahala LEDFORD, bond 29 March 1821;

    bdsm: James Ledford. [AB]

    Mathew Hale & Mahaley LYONS, 5 Apr. 1821. [S1]

HALE, Thomas, & Mrs. Malinda WALKER, 14 March 1843. (RFC) [B2]

HALL, Archibald P., & Jamima SONNEY [Sorency], 19 Nov. 1818. [S1]

HALL, Barton, & Melinda Ann RYON, bond 11 Oct. 1837;

    bdsm: Moses Ryan. [AB]

    Barton W. Hall & Melinda Ann RYAN, 12 Oct. 1837. (JnSm) [B2]

HALL, Benjamin H., & Susan ATKINSON, bond 26 Aug. 1840;

    f/b & bdsm: John Atkinson. [AB]

    Benjamin H. Hall & Susan Atkinson, 27 Aug. 1840. (MGs) [B2]

HALL, Elijah B., & Sally GRAHAM, bond 2 March 1816;

    bdsm: James McIcbury [McIlhenny?]; Elijah B. Hall. [AB]

    Elijah B. Hall & Sally Graham, 4 March 1816. [JA]

    18 Dec. 1816 [S1]

HALL, Mahlan, & Nancy TRUETT, bond 26 July 1823;

    bdsm: Riley Steel. [AB]

HALL, Robert, & Betty WILLIAMS, bond 19 Feb. 1821;

    bdsm: James Williams. [AB]

    Robert Hall & Betsy Williams 22 Feb. 1821. [S1]

HALL, William, & Mary TRAYLOR, bond 9 Feb. 1846;

    bdsm: Thomas Sorrell. [AB]

    Matison Hall & Mary Traylor, 10 Feb. 1846. (SKc) [B2]

HAM?, Preston, & Elizabeth BERRY, bond 22 Dec. 1848;

    bdsm: Jesse Berry. [AB]

    Preston Ham & Elizabeth ?Berry, 28 Dec. 1848. (JnSm) [B2]

HAMER, Hanner, Homes?, Joseph, & Julyan RAIBORN, 27 Apr. 1838. (SMc) [B2]

HAMILTON, Abner, & Elizabeth ELLIOTT, bond 1 Jan. 1812;

    f/b: James Elliott; bdsm: Abner Hamilton, James Elliott. [AB]

    Abner Hamilton & Elizabeth Elliott, 2 Jan. 1812. (JPH) [RS]

HAMILTON, Alexander, & Mary CARTMILL, bond 21 March 1848;

    bdsm: John Cartmill. [AB]

HAMILTON, Allen, & Elizabeth SHULTZ, bond 1 Jan. 1834;
  bdsm: John Parker.   [AB]
HAMILTON, Andrew, & Elizabeth RANDOLPH, bond 9 Oct. 1823;
  bdsm: Reuben Young.   [AB]
  Andrew Hamilton & Elizabeth BARDOLPH, 11 Oct. 1823. (AMx)   [B2]
HAMILTON, Daniel D., & Hannah EATON, bond 19 Feb. 1820;
  bdsm: Wm. E. Graves or Groves.   [AB]
  David D. HAWDTON & Hannah Eaton, 20 Feb. 1820.   [S1]
HAMILTON, Eli J., & Nancy J. M. GILLMORE, 8 Jan. 1850. (JHe)   [B2]
HAMILTON, George, & Ellen ASHLEY or Ashbey?, bond 20 Oct. 1845;
  f/b: M. I. Ashley or Ashbey; bdsm: John Sanford.   [AB]
  George Hamilton & Ellin J. ASHLY or Ashby, 22 Oct. 1845. (RFC)   [B2]
HAMILTON, James, & Drucilla JACKSON, bond 29 Jan. 1849;
  bdsm: John Jackson.   [AB]
  James Hamilton & Drucilla Jackson, 30 Jan. 1849. (JHe)   [B2]
HAMILTON, Mathew F., & Betsey CRAYCRAFT, bond 17 Aug. 1821;
  bdsm: Peter R. Gill.   [AB]
  Mathew A. Hamilton & Betsy CRACRAFT, 17 Aug. 1821.   [S1]
HAMILTON, Thomas B., & Frances RENDALL, 23 Oct. 1850. (JHe)   [B2]
HAMM, John, & Polly JONES, 25 Apr. 1821.   [S1]
HAMPTON, Geo. M., & Jane McCORMICK, bond 8 June 1837;
  bdsm: Wm. McCormick.   [AB]
  George M. Hampton & Jane McCormick, 15 June 1837. (DST)   [B2]
HANNA, John, & Heziah [Keziah?] ASBURY, bond 31 Aug. 1830;
  bdsm: John Tincher.   [AB]
HARDIN, Edgar, & Caroline ROGERS, bond 5 May 1846;
  bdsm: William Rogers.   [AB]
  Edgar Hardin & Caroline Rogers, 7 May 1846. (TRk)   [B2]
HARDIN, James, & Huldah VICE, bond 10 Nov. 1846;
  bdsm: Lawrence Vice.   [AB]
HARDIN, Jno. B., & Lydia CASSITY, 4 June 1843. (DDn)   [B2]
HARDIN, Joseph S., & Melinda McCULLA, bond 7 Oct. 1830;
  bdsm: Reuben Hughes.   [AB]
HARDIN, Lewis, & Polly McHENRY, bond 12 Nov. 1828;
  bdsm: J. P. ?Hugin.   [AB]
  Lewis Hardin & Polly N. McILHENNY, 13 Nov. 1828. (DWh)   [B2]
HARDIN, Presley, & Sarah E. TAYLOR, bond 25 Feb. 1842;
  f/g: Lewis Hardin; bdsm: Charles Taylor.   [AB]
  Presly Hardin & Sarah E. Taylor, 24 Feb. 1842. (RFC)   [B2]
HARDIN, Wesely, & Philladelphia BAIRD, bond 19 March 1829;

f/b: H. Baird; bdsm: Ratliff Baird. [AB]

    Wesley Hardin & Philadelphia BEARD, 22 March 1829. (JEv) [B2]

HARDIN, William, & Patsy FLEMING, bond 5 Sept. 1833;

    bdsm: Wm. Fleming. [AB]

    William Hardin & Poly Fleming, 10 Sept. 1833. (PHn) [B2]

HARMAN, Philip, & Nancy JACKSON, bond 9 March 1825;

    f/b: Samuel Jackson; bdsm: Joseph Jackson. [AB]

    Philip HARRISON & Nancy Jackson, 10 March 1825. [S1]

HARMON, Daniel, & Unica INGRAM, bond 16 Dec. 1845;

    bdsm: James Scuddith [Sudduth?]. [AB]

    Daniel Harmon & Nica INGRUM, 7 Dec. 1845. (OSx) [B2]

[HARMON?] Hennan, Jannard, & Mary An SHROUT, bond 30 Nov. 1816;

    bdsm: John Litter. [AB]

    Jarrord HARMON & Mary Shrout, 1 Dec. 1816. [JA]

    Jarrard HARRON & Mary Shrout, 21 Oct. 1816. [S1]

HARNEY, Adam W., & Mary Ann LANE, bond 8 July 1839;

    f/b: Robert Lane; bdsm: Robt. G. Lane. [AB]

    Adams William Harney & Mary Ann Lane, 9 July 1839. (MGs) [B2]

HARPER, Alfred, & Hannah CARE, bond 13 Sept. 1837;

    f/g: James Harper; bdsm: John D. Magowan. [AB]

HARPER, Daniel, & Sally GUDGELL, bond 14 Sept. 1846;

    bdsm: Thomas Gudgell. [AB]

HARPER, George, & Elizabeth ROBERSON, bond 31 Jan. 1842;

    f/b: Richard Robertson; bdsm: Wm. Roberson. [AB]

    George Harper & Elizabeth Roberson, 2 Feb. 1842 (MGs);

    also: George Harper & Elizabeth ROBINSON, 20 Feb. 1842. (MGs) [B2]

HARPER, Reuben, & Prudence STEEL, 28 Aug. 1851. (SRg?) [B2]

HARRIS, James, & Sally Lyde WHITECRAFT, bond 8 May 1846;

    bdsm: John Whitecraft. [AB]

    James Harris & Sally ?Late Whitecraft, 12 May 1846. (TRk) [B2]

HARRISON, Alfred, & Sally VICE, bond 7 Aug. 1824;

    f/b: Joseph Vice; bdsm: Greenberry Vice. [AB]

    Alfred Harrison & Sally Vice, 8 Aug. 1824. [S1]

HARRISON, Bartley, & Elizabeth BUSBY, bond 12 Jan. 1824;

    bdsm: James Busby. [AB]

    Bartley Harrison & Elizabeth BUSBEY, 15 Jan. 1824. [S1]

HARRISON, Jacob, & Comfort IGO, bond 4 Sept. 1849;

    bdsm: N. Igo. [AB]

    Jacob ?HARMON & Comfort IGOW, 5 Sept. 1849. (OSx) [B2]

HARRISON, James, & Jemima BROWN, bond 26 Nov. 1812;
    m/g: Mary Hawkins; bdsm: James Harrison. [AB]
    James Harrison & Jemima Brown, 26 Nov. 1812. [JA,S1]

HARRISON, John C., & Polly EPPERSON, bond 9 Jan. 1824;
    bdsm: Peter Epperson. [AB]

HARROW, Thomas C., & Margaret McDAVID, 16 Sept. 1826. (AMx) [B2]

HART, Benjamin, & Elizabeth Jane WARREN, 12 Apr. 1841. (SMc) [B2]

HART [or Hunt?], David, & Nancy SPENCE, 5 Dec. 1817. [S1]

HART, David, & Elizabeth PARKS, bond 30 July 1831;
    bdsm: James Johnson. [AB]

HART, David, & Mary CLARK, bond 24 Jan. 1845;
    bdsm: John Clark. [AB]
    David Hart & Marty Clark, 24 Jan. 1845. (SKc) [B2]

HART, F. M., & Mary BOGIE, bond 10 Feb. 1849;
    bdsm: John Hughes. [AB]

HART, Henry, & Milly Jane STREET, bond 13 Apr. 1849;
    bdsm: Thos. Spencer. [AB]
    Hay? Hart, & Jane ?St___, 19 Apr. 1849. (SKc) [B2]

HART, John, & Catherine WILHITE, 26 ___ 1839. (SMc) [B2]

HART, John, & Alvira WRIGHT, bond 13 Apr. 1846;
    bdsm: F. R. Wright. [AB]
    John Hart & Alvira Wright, 16 Apr. 1846. (SKc) [B2]

HART, John P., & Louisa Ann BRADSHAW, bond 4 June 1833;
    bdsm: David Bradshaw. [AB]
    John P. Hart & Loisa an Bradshaw, 7 June 1838. (JWR) [B2]

HART, Michael, & Susan FERGUSON, bond 3 May 1849;
    bdsm: R. T. Howard. [AB]
    Michael Hart & Susan J. FURGASON, 3 May 1849. (RFC) [B2]

HART, Samuel, & Nancy COSTIGAN, bond 29 Jan. 1836;
    bdsm: James Sudduth. [AB]

HART, Thomas D., & Margarett C. HONAKER, bond 20 Dec. 1848;
    f/b: Martin Honaker; bdsm: P. J. Honaker. [AB]
    Thomas D. Hart & Margarett E. HANAKER, 20 Dec. 1849. (SMc) [B2]

HART, William, & Sally STATON, 18 March 1850. (WRg) [B2]

HARTY, James, & Polly ?MINNEAR, bond 20 Nov. 1820;
    bdsm: Joseph Williams. [AB]

HARTY, John, & Mariah FICKLIN, bond 7 Jan. 1829;
    bdsm: M. Harty. [AB]

HASTY, Moreduck, & Meranda HICKLIN [Ficklin?], 17 ___ 1829. (JGW) [B2]

HATTAN, Martillis, & Sarah Ann JACKSON, bond 22 March 1842;

f/b: Thos. Jackson; bdsm: Allen Jackson. [AB]

Martillus HATTON & Sarah Ann Jackson, 27 March 1842. (JFs) [B2]

HATTON, Benjamin, & Elizabeth THOMPSON, bond 6 Feb. 1840;
bdsm: Wm. I. Tapp. [AB]

Bemjamin HATTEN & Elizabeth TOMPSON, 6 Feb. ____. (WSd) [B2]

HAVERMALE?, James, & Elizabeth CARRINGTON, bond 31 July 1839;
bdsm: Timothy Carrington. [AB]

James HOOVERMALE & Elizabeth Carrington, 31 July 1839. (JGW) [B2]

HAWKEN or Hawkins, John, & Eliza A. HART, 26 Dec. 1847. (LCb) [B2]

HAWKINS, Alpheus, & Nancy DAVIS, 17 Sept. 1850. (GMr) [B2]

HAWKINS, David, & Abegail BUTLER, bond 8 Feb. 1830;
parent/g: David Hawkins; f/b: Nathan Butler; bdsm: Alphens Butler. [AB]

HAWKINS, Felix, & Eliza McFARLAND, 8 Oct. 1850. (TDL) [B2]

HAWKINS, Gregory, & Sally CANNON, bond 3 Jan. 1815;
bdsm: Noble Cannon, G. Hawkins. [AB]

HAWKINS, James, & Eliza BOYD, bond 27 Dec. 1828;
bdsm: Rolling Boyd. [AB]

James Hawkins & Elizabeth Boyd, 8 Feb. 1829. (PHn) [B2]

HAWKINS, John, & Jane ROGERS, bond 31 Oct. 1815;
bdsm: J. Hawkins, James Rogers. [AB]

John Hawkins & Jane ROGEN, 21 Nov. 1815. [JA]

2 Nov. 1815 [S1]

HAWKINS, John M., & Polly RALSTON, bond 12 Feb. 1821;
bdsm: John Ralston. [AB]

HAWKINS, Thomas, & Polly DEAN, bond 6 Apr. 1824;
bdsm: Nancy Dean. [AB]

Thomas Hawkins & Polly DEANE, 6 Apr. 1824. [S1]

HAWKINS, Walker, & Elizabeth ADAMS, bond 21 July 1849;
bdsm: Mathews Jones? [AB]

HAWKINS, Walter R., & Angelina SNEDEGAR, bond 4 March 1840;
f/b: Robert Snedegar; bdsm: Wm. Snedegar. [AB]

HAZELRIGG, D. H., & Amelica ROBERTS, bond 30 Dec. 1846;
f/g: J. H. Hazelrigg; bdsm: Ramison Kendall. [AB]

?J. O. H. Hazelrigg & America?? Roberts, 7 Jan. 1847. (PHn) [B2]

HAZELRIGG, David, & Catharine HUGHES, bond 17 Nov. 1828;
f/b: John Hughes; bdsm: Sam Duckworth. [AB]

HAZELRIGG, Eli, & Ruth BYRAM, bond 15 March 1845;
bdsm: W. M. Sudduth. [AB]

HAZELRIGG, Harry, & Margaret STONE, bond 23 Sept. 1830;

bdsm: Charles Stone. [AB]

  Harvy G. HAZLERIGG & Margaret Stone, 23 Sept. 1830. (JMh) [B2]

HAZELRIGG, James F., & Polly CRAYCRAFT, bond 20 Feb. 1821;

  bdsm: Wm. M. Sudduth. [AB]

HAZELRIGG, Robert, & Susan BURNS, bond 25 Jan. 1847;

  bdsm: Rice Burns. [AB]

  R. H. Hazelrigg & S. R. Burns, 28 Jan. 1847. (RFC) [B2]

HAZELRIGG, Wm., & Angeline BAIRD, bond 1 May 1827;

  bdsm: Samuel Baird. [AB]

  Wm. ?W. Hazlerigg & Ann Gelina Baird, May 1827. (JtSm) [B2]

HEAD, Oliver C., & Nancy ARROWSMITH, bond 22 May 1829;

  bdsm: Abner Arrowsmith. [AB]

HEART, John G., & Eliz. MORELAND, 8 Oct. 1826. (RTh) [B2]

HEART, Samuel, & Elizabeth WILLS, bond 25 Dec. 1819;

  bdsm: Samuel Heart, David Heart. [AB]

  Samuel Heart & Elizabeth Wills, 27 Dec. 1819. [S1]

HEDGES, Benj. F., & Elizabeth BAIRD, bond 15 June 1840;

  bdsm: Joseph Chipman. [AB]

  Benjamin F. Hedges & Elizabeth BERDE, 18 June 1840. (TWn) [B2]

HEDGES, James, & Susan STONE, bond 4 Dec. 1848;

  f/g: Robert Hedges; parent/b: Gary Stone; bdsm: Johnson Stone. [AB]

  James HEDGER & Susan Stone, 7 Dec. 1848. (SJn) [B2]

HEDGES, John, & Sarah SMITH(ERS?), bond 17 Jan. 1848;

  bdsm: Joseph Smithers. [AB]

  John H. Hedges & Sarah ?SMOTHERS, 18 Jan. 1848. (JnSm) [B2]

HEDGES or Hedger?, Joseph F., & Nancy Jane BROWN, bond 4 Jan. 1847;

  bdsm: John F. Brown. [AB]

  J. F. Hedges & Nancy J. BROWNE, 7 Jan. 1847. (RFC) [B2]

HEDGES, Richard, & Jane EMMETT, bond 24 Apr. 1827;

  bdsm: Alexander Emmett. [AB]

  Richard Hedges & Jane Emmett, 29 Apr. 1827. (JGW) [B2]

HEDRICK, James, & Abrget ROE or Raw?, bond 11 June 1849;

  bdsm: Solem Roe. [AB]

  James Hedrick & Abiga(i)l Roe, 14 June 1849. (BBv) [B2]

HEDRICK, John, & Eliza FLETCHER, bond 24 Sept. 1838;

  bdsm: Jacob Fletcher. [AB]

HEDRICK, Michael, & Margaret DOUGHERTY, bond 4 May 1832;

  bdsm: John Dougherty. [AB]

HEDRICK, Wm., & Elizabeth DOUGHERTY, bond 7 Sept. 1831;

bdsm: John Dougherty.   [AB]

HENDERSON, Elders, & Letty FANNING, bond 8 Oct. 1821;
   f/b: John Fanning; bdsm: Geo. Colman.   [AB]

HENDRIX, Grant [Garret], & Nancy NAYLOR, bond 7 Jan. 1848;
   f/b: Ignatius Naylor; bdsm: Wm. Naylor.   [AB]

HENDRIX, John, & Sarah DAVIS, bond 12 March 1849;
   bdsm [f/b]: David Davis.   [AB]
   John Hendrix & Sarah C.(or H.?) Davis, 15 March 1849. (EJo) [B2]

HENDRIX, Levi, & Rebecca HART, bond 23 Sept. 1824;
   bdsm [f/g]: Peter Hendrix.   [AB]
   Levi Hendrix & Rebecca Hart, 26 Sept. 1824.   [S1]

HENDRIX, Peter, & Katharine LANCASTER, bond 7 Aug. 1820;
   bdsm: Thos. Raine.   [AB]
   Thomas RAIN & Catharine LOUCASTER, 13 Aug. 1820.   [S1]

HENDRIX, Sanford, & Ferin [Kerenhappuch] HENDRIX, bond 10 Dec. 1832;
   f/b: Peter Hendrix; bdsm: Thomas McFerran.   [AB]

HENDRIX, Squire, & Elizabeth MAPPINE, bond 29 Dec. 1821;
   bdsm [f/g]: Peter Hendrix.   [AB]
[HENDRIX?] Hendmin, Squire, & Polly MAPIN, 11 Nov. 1822.   [S1]

HENLY, John, & Susan SHARPE, bond 11 Apr. 1836;
   bdsm: Moses Sharpe.   [AB]
   John HANLEY & Susan SHARP, 12 Apr. 1836. (DST)   [B2]

HENRY, James, & Drusilla McINTIRE, bond 7 July 1845;
   bdsm [f/b?]: Peter Hendrix.   [AB]
   James Henry & Drucilla McIntire, 14 July 1845. (RFC)   [B2]

HENRY, Simphan, & Margaret SORRELL, bond 16 March 1842;
   bdsm: James Sorrell.   [AB]
   Simpson Henry & Margret SORRELLS, 17 March 1842. (PCy)   [B2]

HENSLEY, John, & Ludia McCULLAH, bond 1 Jan. 1823;
   bdsm: Reuben Hugh.   [AB]
   John HENSLY & Lydia McCullah, 2 Jan. 1823.   [S1]

[HEWETT?] Henis(s)tt?, Josephus, & Luscilla PAYNE, bond 27 Apr. 1831;
   bdsm: John Payne.   [AB]
   Josephus HEWETT & Lusilla H. Payne, 5 May 1831. (JnSm)   [B2]

HICKS or Hicky?, Jesse, & Polly McDOYLE, 8 June 1826. (PCy)   [B2]

HICKS, Saul, & Elizabeth McDOUDALE, bond 1 Jan. 1827;
   bdsm: Solomon McKinnan.   [AB]
   Samuel Hicks & Elizabeth McDOWDLE, 10 Apr. 1827. (PCy)   [B2]

HIGGINS, Thomas, & Margaret BLAKE, bond 10 Sept. 1839;
   bdsm: Geo. Blake;   [AB]

Thomas HEGGINS & Margaret Blake, 12 Sept. 1839. (MGs)   [B2]
HILEY?, Bird, & Judy SEXTON, bond 28 Aug. 1834;
  bdsm: Ben Sexton.   [AB]
HILEY, George W., & Elizabeth SHROUT, 22 Nov. 1843. (JMc)   [B2]
HILL, Thomas, & Jane HALL, bond 22 March 1827;
  bdsm: James Donaldson.   [AB]
HILTON, Wm., & Nancy ARRASMITH, 6 Jan. 1851. (SRg)   [B2]
HIMER, James P., & Amanda MARTIN, 8 Oct. 1835. (JGW)   [B2]
HIMER or Hymer, Jas. P., & Elizabeth CASSITY, 5 Sept. 1844. (JGW) [B2]
HINES, James, & Lucinda WALKER, bond 18 Aug. 1831;
  bdsm: Wm. Dandy.   [AB]
HINES, James, & Geo. Ann HARPER, bond 15 Dec. 1849;
  bdsm: Wm. Frame.   [AB]
  James Hines & Georgeann Harper, 15 Nov. 1849. (JHe) [B2]
HINES, Robert, & Malisa L. TAYLOR, bond 14 Sept. 1846;
  bdsm: Benoni Taylor.   [AB]
  Robert Hines & Malisa L. Taylor, 17 Sept. 1846. (JMc?) [B2]
HODGE, Samuel, & Dolly ATCHISON, bond 14 Nov. 1831;
  bdsm: Wm. Atchison.   [AB]
HOGAN, Michael, & Margaret HOPKINS, bond 2 Sept. 1831;
  bdsm: Geo. Harper.   [AB]
HOGERMAN, John, & Elizabeth SHROPSHIRE, bond 16 Jan. 1827;
  f/b: James Shropshire; bdsm: Geo. Lansdown.   [AB]
  John Hogerman & Eliz. Shropshire, 11 Jan. 1827. (JGW) [B2]
HOGIN, John, & Anne ?McCLEMAHEN, bond 31 July 1822;
  bdsm: Alexander Emmet.   [AB]
  John HAGGAN & Anna McCLANIHAN, 15 Aug. 1822.   [S1]
HOLLAND, Benjamin, & Grizzella PRIEST, bond 6 Oct. 1840;
  bdsm: Agustin Sanford.   [AB]
  Benjamin Holland & _____, 6 Oct. 1840. (SJn)   [B2]
HOLLIDAY, Hiram, & Agnes LEMON, bond 10 Nov. 1812;
  f/g: Charles Holliday; f/b: Jacob Lemon; bdsm: Hiram Holliday, Wm. Martin. [AB]
  Hiram HOLLIDAYS & Agnes Lemon, 11 Sept. 1812;   [JA]
  Hiram Holliday & Agness Lemon, 12 Nov. 1812.   [S1]
HOLMES, John, & Lura CALDWELL, bond 25 June 1821 (or 51?);
  f/b: Walter Caldwell; bdsm: James Caldwell.   [AB]
  John HELLMUS & Laru COLDWELL, 28 June 1821.   [S1]
HON, Andrew, & Prudence HON, 28 June 1839. (PHn)   [B2]
HONAKER, John, & Eliza HART, bond 24 Dec. 1847;

bdsm: John Hart.	[AB]
HONAKER, Martin, & Nancy ENGLAND, bond 27 Apr. 1822;	
f/b: Jesse England; bdsm: Salem Roe.	[AB]
Martin Honaker & Nancy England, 2 May 1822.	[S1]
HONAKER, Wm., & Elizabeth HARRIMAN, bond 28 Apr. 1828;	
bdsm: Jon? Whaley.	[AB]
William Honaker & Elizabeth HORSMAN, 30 Apr. 1828. (JEv)	[B2]
HONAKER, Wm., & Mary Ann COYLE, bond 20 Nov. 1845;	
bdsm: Geo. Coyle.	[AB]
William HONECKER & Mary ann COIL, 20 Nov. 1845. (SKc)	[B2]
HONICKER, Francis M., & Louisa Ann KINCADE, 9 Oct. 1851. (SKc)	[B2]
HOPE, Wm., & Ann C. FRY, bond 13 Jan. 1820;	
bdsm: Francis Manny.	[AB]
William Hope & Ann C. Fry, 20 July 1820.	[S1]
HOPEWELL, Isaac, & Charlotte MAGOWAN, bond 4 Apr. 1849;	
bdsm: James Summers.	[AB]
Isaac D. Hopewell & Charlott MAGOWEN, 7 Apr. 1849. (EJo)	[B2]
HOPEWELL, W. M., & Francis MESSERICK, bond 13 Dec. 1849;	
bdsm: B. D. Nixon.	[AB]
William H. Hopewell & Frances H. MESSICK, 13 Dec. 1849. (EJo)	[B2]
HOPKINS, Francis, & Cele MULBERRY, bond 27 Feb. 1815;	
bdsm: John Mulberry.	[AB]
Francis Hopkins & Celia Mulberry, 28 Feb. 1815.	[S1]
28 Feb. 1813	[JA]
HOPKINS, Franke, & Frances ROE, bond 13 Nov. 1837;	
bdsm: James Roe.	[AB]
Frank Hopkins & Frances Roe, 15 Nov. 1837. (JnSm)	[B2]
HOPKINS, Henry, & Catherine CLAYTON, 26 Oct. 1817.	[JA,S1]
HOPKINS, Jacob, & L. BAILEY, bond 19 Nov. 1840;	
f/g & bdsm: Francis Hopkins; f/b: David Bailey.	[AB]
HOPKINS, Joslin, & Betsy BOYD, 13 March 1817.	[JA]
Joshia Hopkins & Besty Boyd	[S1]
HOPKINS, Joslin J. J., & Jane JONES, 17 Nov. 1851. (SJn)	[B2]
HOPKINS, Peter, & Mary MULBERRY, 24 Apr. 1817.	[JA,S1]
HOPKINS, William, & Betsy BRINTON, bond 9 Sept. 1815;	
bdsm: Wm. Hopkins, Thos. Fletcher.	[AB]
William Hopkins & Betsey BRINSON, 9 Sept. 1815.	[JA,S1]
HOPPER, William, & Katherine HOPPER, 3 Jan. 1834. (JHu)	[B2]
HORN, James, & Mary YOCOM, bond 20 Feb. 1830;	
f/b: John Yocom; bdsm: Fielden Buchanan.	[AB]

HORN, John, & Polly JONES, bond 22 Jan. 1821;
  f/b: Thomas Jones; bdsm: Joseph Jones. [AB]
[HORNBACK?] Hamback, Abraham, & Elizabeth BRACKEN, 20 Sept. 1817. [S1]
HORNBACK, Abraham, & Ruth DARNELL, bond 5 Apr. 1823;
  bdsm: David Darnell. [AB]
  Abraham Hornback & Ruth DARNEL, 5 Apr. 1823. [S1]
HORNBACK, Abram, & Anna ARROSMITH, bond 13 Dec. 1847;
  bdsm: Ignatius Naylor. [AB]
HORNBACK, David, & Margarette BROMAGER, bond 16 June 1845;
  bdsm: Allen Bromager. [AB]
HORNBACK, Elliott, & Minerva J. BARBER, bond 12 Nov. 1849;
  parent/g: F. Hornback; f/b & bdsm: Landon Barber. [AB]
HORNBACK, Isaac, & Elizabeth MOCBEE, bond 5 Jan. 1819;
  bdsm: Wm. Marker. [AB]
  Isaac Hornback & Elizabeth MACKBEE, 6 Jan. 1820. [S1]
HORNBACK, Ishamel, & Sylvia CLAYTON, bond 1831;
  bdsm: Jacob Hornback. [AB]
HORNBACK, James, & Eliza LEE, 16 May 1844. (JnSm) [B2]
HORNBACK, Jefro, & Elizabeth BRACKEN, bond 9 Dec. 1823;
  f/b: James Bracken; bdsm: Robert Bracken. [AB]
HORNBACK, Milton, & Margaret JOHNSON, 6 March 1851. (LGH) [B2]
HORNBACK, Samuel C., & Margaret JOHNSON, bond 2 Sept. 1830;
  m/b: Elizabeth Cooper; bdsm: Jacob Hornback. [AB]
HORNBACK, Simon, & Margaret CONYERS, bond 24 Jan. 1825;
  bdsm: John Conyers. [AB]
  Simon Hornback & Margaret Conyers, 25 Jan. 1825. [S1]
HORNBACK, Zephariah, & Susan LEAVY, bond 14 Sept. 1839;
  bdsm: John Hornback. [AB]
[HORSEMAN] Harreman, Fielder, & Sally MARKLAND, bond 9 Aug. 1834;
  bdsm: Johnson Whaley. [AB]
  Fieldin HORSEMAN & Sally Markland, 21 Aug. 1834. (SJn) [B2]
HORSEMAN, John, & Nancy CARTMELL, bond 27 Aug. 1838;
  bdsm: Thomas Cartmill. [AB]
HORSEMAN, Joseph, & Armon TRAYLOR, bond 21 Nov. 1849;
  bdsm: John Traylor. [AB]
HORTON or Harten?, Hiram, & Susan PAYNE, bond 14 July 1832;
  bdsm: Robert Baler. [AB]
  Hiram Horton & Susan Payne, 19 July 1832. (RTh) [B2]
HOUSE, Alvin, & Malinda MAHANY, bond 21 Sept. 1829;

    bdsm: Larkin Turner.   [AB]

    Alvin House & Malinda MALEOND, 22 Sept. 1829. (JCm)   [B2]

HOUSE, Richard, & Nancy HENSLEY, bond 13 Apr. 1815;

    bdsm: James Birson.   [AB]

    Richard House & Nancy HENSLY, 13 Apr. 1815.   [JA,S1]

HOUSE, Wm., & Margaret HIGGINS, bond 10 Feb. 1823;

    bdsm: Asher Boaz.   [AB]

HOUSE, Worthy, & Elizabeth McCLAIN, bond 17 Apr. 1832;

    bdsm: John McClain.   [AB]

HOUSTON, Mathew, & Agness McCLURE, bond 6 Oct. 1815;

    m/b: Jane McClure; consent/b & bdsm: Thomas McClure.   [KM]

    Mathew Houston & Agnes McClure, 12 Oct. 1815.   [JA]

    Mathew Housten & Agness McCline [sic]   [S1]

HOWARD, David, & Peggy FORT, bond 4 March 1816;

    f/b: Peter Fort.   [AB]

    David Howard & Peggy FONT, 7 March 1815.   [JA,S1]

HOWARD, Frederick, & Janey GRANT, 8 May 1817.   [JA]

    Frederick Howard & Jailey Grant   [S1]

HOWARD, Guidian, & Elizabeth HUNT, bond 27 Dec. 1814;

    bdsm: Guidon Howard, Hiram Hunt.   [KM]

HOWARD, James O., & Rebecca MUNS, bond 10 June 1846;

    bdsm: Wm. ?Mulholn.   [AB]

    James O. Howard & Rebecca Muns, 11 June 1846. (TRk)   [B2]

HOWARD, Joseph, & Mary Jane CHANDLER, bond 2 Aug. 1836;

    m/g: Nancy Howard; parent/b: Lanny Craye?; bdsm: Bohannon Collins.   [AB]

    Joseph Howard & Mary Jane Chandler, 2? Aug. 1836. (JVc)   [B2]

HOWARD, Joseph, & Nancy WARD, bond 21 July 1849;

    bdsm: David Traylor.   [AB]

HOWARD, Richard, & July DUTY, bond 30 May 1849;

    bdsm: John Duty.   [AB]

HOWE, Wm. I., & Sarah Jane WHALEY, bond 3 Nov. 1847;

    bdsm: Charles Whaley.   [AB]

    Wm. ?H. Howe & Sarah J. WHALY, 9 Nov. 1847. (RFC)   [B2]

HUFFMAN, Thornton, & Sophiah NOE, bond 25 Aug. 1825;

    bdsm: James Williams.   [AB]

HUGGART, James, & Nancy OWINGS, bond 4 May 1815;

    bdsm: Eli Owings.   [AB]

HUGHART, Ben, & Mary Jane COX, bond 24 Feb. 1848;

    f/b: John Cox; bdsm: W. M. Sudduth.   [AB]

HUGHES, Alexander, & Nancy SHUAR, bond 30 May 1815;

bdsm: Thos. Ingram, F. Hughes.   [AB]

HUGHES, Harrison, & Mary PRATHER, bond 13 Dec. 1832;
  parent/g: Liverzy Hughes; bdsm: James Hughes.   [AB]
  Harrison HUGZ & Mary Prather, 16 Dec. 1832. (ASh)   [B2]

HUGHES, James, & Elizabeth PRATHER, bond 6 July 1831;
  f/b: J. Prather; bdsm: Jeremiah Prather.   [AB]

HUGHES, John, & Elizabeth BOYD, bond 2 Jan. 1823;
  f/g: James Hughes; bdsm: Geo. Boyd.   [AB]
  John Hughes & Elizabeth Boyd, 2 Jan. 1823.   [S1]

HUGH(E)S, Reuben, & Elizabeth McCULLY, bond 27 Aug. 1813;
  bdsm: Reubin Huges, Jas. McCully.   [AB]
  Rheubin HUGHES & Elizabeth McULLEY, 1813. (LTu)   [KM]

HULS?, Foreman, & Susan LIGGETT, bond 30 Jan. 1833;
  bdsm: Asa Pettit.   [AB]
  Freeman Huls & Susan LEGGET, 30 Jan. 1833. (JCH)   [B2]

HUMPHREYS, Alexander, & Nancy WHITECRAFT, bond 22 Sept. 1827;
  bdsm: Charles McAlister.   [AB]

HUMPHRIES, Thomas, & Sally FOSTER, bond 4 May 1822;
  bdsm: Henry Saunders.   [AB]
  Thomas HUMPHERY & Sally Foster, 25 May 1822.   [S1]

HUNT, David, & Letty SPENCER, bond 24 (or 4?) Aug. 1821;
  bdsm: Wm. Spencer.   [AB]
  David HART & Lelly SPENCE, 31 Aug. 1821.   [S1]

HUNT, Deaton, & Martha Ann TINCHER, 28 Nov. 1843. (SKc)   [B2]

HUNT, Isaac, & Margaret YATES, bond 16 Apr. 1836;
  bdsm: J. A. Cassity.   [AB]
  Isaac Hunt & Margaret Yates, 24 July 1836. (JGW)   [B2]

HUNT, John, & Saley HUNT, bond 8 May 1829;
  f/b: Abraham Hunt; bdsm: Lewis Hunt.   [AB]

HUNT, John, & Jane CAMPBELL, bond 27 July 1839;
  f/g: Jeremiah Hunt; bdsm: Melvin Crump.   [AB]

HUNT, Joseph D., & Rebecca R. WILLIAMS, 7 Dec. 1826. (JGW)   [B2]

HUNT, Joshua P., & Elen or Elenora? DENTON, bond 22 Aug. 1828;
  f/b: Reuben Denton; bdsm: John Hunt.   [AB]
  Joshua P. Hunt & Elinor Denton, 25 Aug. 1828. (JHu)   [B2]

HUNT, Lewis, & Fanny ANDERSON, bond 21 June 1834;
  bdsm: Richard Anderson.   [AB]

HUNT, Lewis, & Amanda DAILEY, bond 11 Jan. 1847;
  f/g: Jeremiah Hunt; f/b: Ralph Dailey; bdsm: Richard Hunt.   [AB]

HUNT, Reuben, & Eliz. CRUMP, bond 20 or 30 Sept. 1829;
    m/b: Maryan Crump; bdsm: Isaac Jackson.   [AB]
HUNT, Wm. S., & Katherine G. WILLIAMS, bond 30 March 1832;
    f/b: Joseph G. Williams; bdsm: Alexander Swim.   [AB]
    Wm. S. Hunt & Katharine G. Williams, 25 Apr. 1832. (JGW)   [B2]
HURT, Berry, & Elizabeth L. BERRY, bond 18 May 1846;
    f/b: Joseph Berry; bdsm: William Allen.   [AB]
    B. Hurt or HUNT & Elizabeth ?Berry, 18 May 1846. (GGd)   [B2]
HUTCHISON, Isaac, & Lucinda MORGAN, bond 22 Feb. 1848;
    f/b: James Morgan; bdsm: John Clark.   [AB]
    Isaac N. HUTCHERSON & Lucinda Morgan, 24 Feb. 1848. (DBk)   [B2]
[HYDEN?] Keyton, Otho, & Elizabeth ALEXANDER, bond 20 Sept. 1828;
    bdsm: Hirman Alexander.   [AB]
    Otha HYDEN & Elizabeth Alexander, 28 Sept. 1828. (WCS)   [B2]
HYNEMAN, David, & Martha LONSDALE, 2 Jan. 1817.   [JA]
    David Hyneman & Martha Lousdale [sic], 10 Feb. 1817.   [S1]
IGO, Nathaniel, & Phebe An INGRAM, 19 July 1844. (DDn)   [B2]
ILES, Wm., & Jane GEORGE, bond 1 Feb. 1827;
    bdsm: Wm. George.   [AB]
    William Iles & Jane George, 1 Feb. 1827. (JBn)   [B2]
INGRAHAM, Isaac, & Elizabeth LYONS, 24 June 1844. (SKc)   [B2]
INGRAM, Abraham, & Eliza JACKSON, bond 12 May 1824;
    f/g: Thomas Ingram; bdsm: John Neal.   [AB]
    Abraham Ingram & Eliza Jackson, 12 May 1824.   [S1]
INGRAM, Abraham, & Polly JONES, 27 Apr. 1844. (JFs)   [B2]
INGRAM, Hiram, & Julian STATON, bond 2 Apr. 1830;
    f/b: Samuel Staton; bdsm: Samuel C. Gill.   [AB]
    Hiram INGRAHAM & Julian Staton, 8 Apr. 1830. (SJk)   [B2]
INGRAM, Isaac, & Polly LOSSON, bond 31 Oct. 1814;
    f/b: Travis Losson; bdsm: Isaac Ingram, Jesse Quillin.   [AB]
    Isaac Ingram & Polly LAWSON, 3 Nov. 1814.   [JA,S1]
INGRAM, James, & Margaret JACKSON, bond 4 Aug. 1828;
    bdsm: Geo. Welch.   [AB]
    James INGHAM & Margret Jackson, 4 Aug. 1828. (JPk)   [B2]
INGRAM, James, & Marerny CARTMILL, bond 19 Dec. 1831;
    bdsm: Thos. Cartmill.   [AB]
INGRAM, Thomas, & Elizabeth McCLAIN, bond 4 June 1840;
    f/b & bdsm: James McClain.   [AB]
INGRAM, Thomas, & Franky SMITH, bond 25 Feb. 1846;

bdsm: L. M. Nesbitt. [AB]

    Thomas Ingram or Inggorum & Fanny Smith, 3 March 1846. (WSd) [B2]

INGRAM, William, & Mary Jane CASIDY, 9 Oct. 1851. (SRg?) [B2]

ISHMORE, Isaac, & Elizabeth BEARD, bond 6 Aug. 1849;
    bdsm: Jacob Goff or Loff. [AB]

JACKS, Wm., & Sarah Ann MOORE, bond 16 Oct. 1848;
    bdsm: Henry Moore. [AB]

JACKSON, Alfred, & Nancy EPPERSON, bond 6 Jan. 1829;
    bdsm: Robert Epperson. [AB]

    Alfred Jackson & Nancy Epperson, 9 Jan. 1829. (JPk) [B2]

JACKSON, Allen, & Malinda FROME, bond 27 Aug. 1842;
    f/b: Wm. Frome or Frame?; bdsm: Wm. Hings. [AB]

JACKSON, Andrew, & Margaret BOAT, bond 22 Nov. 1821;
    bdsm: Caleb Evin. [AB]

JACKSON, Elias, & Elizabeth SWETNAM, bond 14 Sept. 1837;
    f/b: Wm. Swetnam; bdsm: Sareney Thompson. [AB]

JACKSON, Elias, & Fanny TACKET, bond 9 Dec. 1840;
    bdsm: Abram Hornback. [AB]

    Elias Johnson [sic] & Fanny TACKETT, 10 Dec. 1840. (SJn) [B2]

JACKSON, Elitha, & Alma HARMAN, bond 3 Sept. 1828;
    f/b: George Harman. [AB]

    Elitha or Elisha? Jackson & Anna Harman, 11 Sept. 1828. (SJk) [B2]

JACKSON, Garrett, & Rachel BARNES, bond 18 Nov. 1830;
    bdsm: Thomas Barnes. [AB]

JACKSON, George, & Michael MORRIS, 28 Sept. 1843. (SKc) [B2]

[JACKSON?] Henry, Jackson, & Ruth FRELAND, bond 26 Feb. 1812;
    bdsm: William Lansdale, Thos. Fletcher, CBC [Clerk, Bath Co.]. [AB]

    Henry JACKSON & Ruthy FREELAND, 29 Feb. 1812. [JA]

    27 Feb. 1812 [S1]

JACKSON, James, & Polly McCLANSEY, bond 7 March 1827;
    bdsm: Aaron Angland. [AB]

    James JOHNSON & Polly McILHENNY, 8 March 1827. [S1]

JACKSON, John, & Marcby[?] GRAYSON, 4 Apr. 1836. (JPk) [B2]

JACKSON, Josiah, & Martha MYERS, bond 2 May 1822;
    bdsm: John Myers. [AB]

JACKSON, Josiah, & Nancy FANNING, bond 25 Oct. 1825;
    bdsm: Elenor Henderson. [AB]

    Josiah Jackson & Nancy Fanning, 3 Nov. 1825. [S1]

JACKSON, Leanda, & Eliza GRIFFIN, bond 22 Sept. 1847;
    bdsm: Allen Jackson. [AB]

JACKSON, Russell, & Margaret BECROFT, bond 12 Aug. 1822;
  bdsm: Levi Fortune.   [AB]
JACKSON, Samuel, & Sarah THOMAS, bond 25 Jan. 1814;
  bdsm: Samuel Thomas, Larkin Thomas.   [AB]
  Samuel Jackson & Sarah Thomas, 27 June 1814.   [JA]
  27 Jan. 1814   [S1]
JACKSON, Thomas, & Nancy OAKLY, 30 Oct. 1817.   [S1]
JACKSON, Thomas, & Nancy BARBER, bond 2 Dec. 1832;
  bdsm: Thos. Barber.   [AB]
JACKSON, Thomas, & Martha Ann WILLIAMSON, bond 12 Aug. 1846;
  f/b: David Williamson; bdsm: Thomas Jackson.   [AB]
  Thomas Jackson & Martha Ann Williamson, 12 Aug. 1846. (SKc)   [B2]
JACKSON, Wm., & Elizabeth HARMON, bond 24 March 1821;
  f/g: Samuel Jackson; f/b: John Harmon; bdsm: Josiah Jackson.   [AB]
  William Jackson & Elizabeth HAMON, 29 Mar. 1821.   [S1]
JAMES, John, & Margarett ?BOW or Bon, bond 20 Aug. 1819;
  bdsm: Henry Chiles.   [AB]
  John JONES & Margarett BALL, 24 Aug. 1819.   [S1]
JAMES, Sylvester, & Mary TOMLINSON, bond 18 Dec. 1847;
  bdsm: John Richards.   [AB]
  Sylvester L. James & Mary L. Tomlinson, 14 Dec. 1847. (JnSm)   [B2]
JAMESON, James, & Elizabeth PALMER, bond 28 July 1840;
  bdsm: Daniel Palmer.   [AB]
  James JIMERSON & Elizabeth PARMER, 28 July 1840. (SJn)   [B2]
JAMISON, John T., & Elizabeth S. CRAIGG, 12 July 1843. (RFC)   [B2]
JAMISON, Robert, & Elizabeth CLAYTON, bond 2 Sept. 1839;
  f/b: Joseph Clayton; bdsm: Wm. D. Abbott.   [AB]
JOHNSON, Arnold, & Elizabeth WRIGHT, bond 23 May 1838;
  bdsm: Flem Wright.   [AB]
JOHNSON, Barney, & _____, bond 30 Sept. 1816;
  bdsm: John Trumbo.   [AB]
  Barney or Barry Johnson & Betty TRUMBO, 15 Oct. 1816.   [JA,S1]
JOHNSON, Benj., & Susanna BRETON, 9 Oct. 1844. (WBT)   [B2]
JOHNSON, Dan M. F., & Polly STEPHENSON, bond 11 March 1833;
  bdsm: Hugh Mays.   [AB]
JOHNSON, David, & Hatty WARNER, 25 Dec. 1817.   [S1]
JOHNSON, George, & Mary ROGERS, bond 23 Feb. 1847;
  bdsm: Allen Burgear.   [AB]
JOHNSON, Isack, & Sarah ?A. BIVEN, 20 March 1851. (BBv)   [B2]

JOHNSON, Jacob, & Malinda WILLIAMS, bond 19 Feb. 1821;
    bdsm: James Williams. [AB]
    Jacob Johnson & Malinda Williams, 22 Feb. 1821. [S1]
JOHNSON, Jacob, & Jane BRACKEN, bond 6 Aug. 1823;
    bdsm: Theophilus Bracken. [AB]
    Jacob JOHNSTON & Jane Bracken, 10 Aug. 1823. [S1]
JOHNSON, James, & Polly McILHENNY, 8 March 1827. (SJo) [B2]
JOHNSON, James, & Polly EPPERSON, bond 11 March 1829;
    bdsm: Alfred Jackson. [AB]
    James Johnson & Polly Epperson, 11 Feb. 1829. [S1]
JOHNSON, James, & Eliza WILLSON, bond 14 July 1845;
    bdsm: David Wilson. [AB]
JOHNSON, Jefferson, & Racheal SORRELL, bond 10 Aug. 1842;
    bdsm: Issac Johnson. [AB]
    Jefferson Johnson & Racheal SORREL or Sorell, 11 Aug. 1842. (JGW) [B2]
JOHNSON, John, & Polly SMITH, bond 31 May 1819;
    bdsm: John Johnson, Joseph Smith. [AB]
    John Johnson & Polly Smith, 3 June 1819. [S1]
JOHNSON, John, & Abigail McINTIRE, bond 22 March 1823;
    bdsm: Samuel Jones. [AB]
    John JOHNSTON & Abigail McIntire, 23 March 1823. [S1]
JOHNSON, John, & Phebe HUNT, bond 28 Feb. 1827;
    bdsm: Samuel Kerr. [AB]
    John Johnson & Phebe Hunt, 1 March 1827. (SJo) [B2]
JOHNSON, Jonathan, & Nelly YARBROUGH, 8 Feb. 1844. (WRg) [B2]
JOHNSON, Pleasent, & Margaret PARKS, bond 5 March 1845;
    bdsm: James Coyle. [AB]
    Pleasant Johnson & Margaret Parks, 6 March 1845. (SKc) [B2]
JOHNSON, Robert, & Lemensey CHURCH, bond 4 Apr. 1831;
    f/b: Thomas Church; bdsm: Isiah Church. [AB]
    Robert Johnson & Louisa Church, 5 Apr. 1831. (ALy) [B2]
JOHNSON, Simpson, & Elizabeth SORRELL, bond 12 Feb. 1842;
    f/g: Arman Johnson; bdsm: Walter West. [AB]
JOHNSON, Thos., & Nancy JOHNSON, bond 19 Feb. 1829;
    bdsm: Robert Johnson. [AB]
    Thomas Johnson & Nancy Johnson, 19 Feb. 1829. (JHH) [B2]
JOHNSON, Thomas, & Melinda ?ALLINDEN, bond 13 Nov. 1849;
    bdsm: Silas Atchison. [AB]
    Thomas Johnson & Malinda ?ALENDEN, 14 Nov. 1849. (PCy) [B2]
JOHNSON, Thomas M., & Juliett NEALEY, bond 4 Aug. 1823;

bdsm: John Ralston. [AB]

Thomas JOHNSTON & Jude NEABY, 4 Aug. 1823. [S1]

JOHNSTON, James, & Jane YOUNG, bond 25 May 1830;
f/b: Edwin Young; bdsm: Robt. T. Hart. [AB]

JOHNSTON, James, & Rebecca YOUNG, bond 29 May 1846;
bdsm: Archibald Paxton. [AB]

JOHNSTON, Jonathan, & Hannah EPPERSON, bond 2 July 1830;
f/b & bdsm: Robert Epperson. [AB]

JOHNSTON, Thomas, & Delany DEEN, bond 1 Oct. 1836;
bdsm: Thos. Hawkins. [AB]

Thomas JOHNSON & Deborah Deen, 6 Oct. 1836. (PHn) [B2]

JOHNSTON, Wm., & Cynthia WILLIAMS, bond 1 Sept. 1823;
bdsm: James Williams. [AB]

JOLLY, John, & Polly BERDEN, 1813. (LTu) [KM]

JONES, Ambrose, & Deborah WILSON, bond 2 Aug. 1830;
f/b: Washington Wilson; bdsm: Franklin Jones. [AB]

Ambrose Jones & _____, 4 Aug. 1830. (SJn) [B2]

JONES, Benjamin, & Polly JONES, bond 13 Apr. 1816;
f/g: John Jones; bdsm: Thomas Jones. [AB]

Benjamin Jones, Jr., & Polly Jones, 16 Apr. 1816. [JA,S1]

JONES, Benjamin, & Hannah SNELLING, bond 1 Oct. 1819;
bdsm: Benj. Jones, Benj. Snelling. [AB]

Benjamin Jones & Hannah SNILLING, 14 Oct. 1819. [S1]

JONES, Caldwell, & Betty RAYAN, bond 10 Sept. 1816;
bdsm: John Rogers. [AB]

Cadwalder Jones & Betsey ROGERS, 12 Sept. 1816. [JA]

Cadwaldern Jones & Betsy ROGAN, 18 Apr. 1816. [S1]

JONES, Charles, & Jane KEITHLEY, bond 29 Nov. 1825;
bdsm: John Keithley. [AB]

Charles Jones & Jane Keithley, 30 Nov. 1825. (PHn) [B2]

JONES, Charles, & Rebecca ROBBINS, bond 30 March 1836;
bdsm: James Robbins. [AB]

JONES, Chas. T., & Renulia BRIDGES, bond 29 Dec. 1827;
f/b: Hiram Bridges; bdsm: D. B. Boyd. [AB]

Closs? T. Jones & Permelia Bridges, 3 Jan. 1828. (JnSm) [B2]

JONES, Daniel R., & Mary L. GROVES or Graves?, bond 23 Oct. 1849;
bdsm: Willis Groves. [AB]

Daniel R. Jones & Mary L. Groves, 24 Oct. 1849. (RFC) [B2]

JONES, David L., & Margaret JONES, 2 May 1844. (SJn) [B2]

JONES, Eliza [Braxton?], & Susan KERNS, bond 22 Aug. 1848;
    f/g: Jones Jones; bdsm: Wm. Jones. [AB]
JONES, Franklin, & Sarah WILSON, bond 30 June 1828;
    f/b: Uriah Wilson; bdsm: Frances Jones. [AB]
    F. Jones & S. Wilson, 2 July 1828. (SJn) [B2]
JONES, Geo. W., & Elizabeth GARNER, bond 15 Dec. 1849;
    bdsm: Andrew Garner. [AB]
JONES, Henry C., & Nancy PEARCEALL, bond 15 Dec. 1840;
    bdsm: Thomas Hicks. [AB]
    Henry C. Jones & Nancy PIERCEALL, 17 Dec. 1840. (TJW) [B2]
JONES, James, & Permela McDANIEL, bond 27 Feb. 1813;
    bdsm: James Jones, Wm. Jones. [AB]
    James Jones & Permellea McDaniel, 28 Feb. 1813. [S1]
JONES, James, & Lydia B. RALLS, bond 3 Aug. 1813;
    f/b: Nathaniel W. Ralls; bdsm: James Jones, Coleman Ratliff. [AB]
    James Jones & Lydia B. RAWLS, 2 Sept. 1813. (JPH) [TP,RS]
JONES, James, & Dicey GREGORY, bond 28 Dec. 1816;
    bdsm: Elizah Gregory. [AB]
    James Jones & Dicey Gregory, 28 Dec. 1816. [JA,S1]
JONES, James or Jones, & Betsy BUTLER, bond 14 Dec. 1819;
    bdsm: John Armstrong. [AB]
    James Jones & Betty Butler, 19 Dec. 1819. [S1]
JONES, James, & Elizabeth CURRY, bond 17 Apr. 1820;
    bdsm: Wm. Fleming. [AB]
    James Jones & Elizabeth CAIRG, 7 Apr. 1820. [S1]
JONES, James, & Elizabeth STEPEN, bond 23 July 1821;
    bdsm: Wm. Stepena. [AB]
    James Jones & Elizabeth JONES, 26 July 1821. [S1]
JONES, James or Jones, & Deborah TRUMBO, bond 2 May 1831;
    f/b: John Trumbo; bdsm: Andrew Trumbo. [AB]
JONES, James, & Lydea Ann JONES, 19 May 1844. (MGs) [B2]
JONES, John, & Susan AUSBURN, bond 12 Jan. 1813;
    bdsm: John Jones, Wm. Ausburn. [AB]
    John Jones & Susan Ausburn, 12 Jan. 1813. [JA,S1]
JONES, John, & Betsy THOMPSON, bond 27 Dec. 1820;
    bdsm: Charles Whitington. [AB]
    John Jones & Betsy Thompson, 28 Dec. 1820. [S1]
JONES, John, & Mary Ann HORNBACK, bond 12 Feb. 1839;
    f/g: James Jones; bdsm: Abram Hornback. [AB]
JONES, John, & Martha ATKINS, bond 26 Oct. 1846;

bdsm: Eber Atkins.	[AB]

JONES, John, & Caty Ann VANUELLS, bond 7 Oct. 1848;

   bdsm: Daniel Vanuells. [AB]

   John Jones & Caty Ann VANULE or Varule?, 9 Oct. 1848. (RFC) [B2]

JONES, Jno. E. F., & Elizabeth CRAIG, bond 8 Aug. 1833;

   bdsm: Samuel Hart. [AB]

   John E. F. Jones & Elizabeth Craig, 9 Aug. 1833. (JPk) [B2]

JONES, Jonathan, & Sarah Jane (or Jane) GOSSETT, 30 Nov. 1843. (SJn) [B2]

JONES, Joseph, & Milly YARBROUGH, bond 12 Feb. 1816;

   f/b: John Yarbrough; bdsm: Robert Ford. [AB]

   Joseph Jones or JONE & Milly Yarbrough, 15 Feb. 1816. (CHp) [S1,JA]

JONES, Joseph, & Rebecca CROOKS, bond 11 Dec. 1820;

   f/b: William Crooks; bdsm: Francis Jones. [AB]

   Joseph Jones & Rebecca Crooks, 14 Dec. 1820. [S1]

JONES, Joseph, & Emily BOYD, bond 23 Feb. 1832;

   bdsm: Spencer Boyd. [AB]

   Joseph Jones & Emily Boyd, 27 Feb. 1832. (EBr) [B2]

JONES, Joshua, & Elizabeth JONES, bond 3 Nov. 1830;

   bdsm: James Sudduth. [AB]

JONES, Josiah, & Sally DONAHUE, bond 9 March 1822;

   bdsm: Matthew Donahue. [AB]

   Josiah Jones & Sally DUNIHOO, 10 Apr. 1822. [S1]

JONES, Northcutt, & Lucy ENGLAND, bond 23 Oct. 1838;

   bdsm: John Moreland. [AB]

   Northcut Jones & Lucy England, 23 Oct. 1838. (GWM) [B2]

JONES, Oliver, & Mary CLAYTON, bond 13 Jan. 1823;

   f/g: John Jones; bdsm: Samuel Line. [AB]

   Oliver Jones & Mary Clayton, 16 Jan. 1823. [S1]

JONES, Patrick D., & _____ MORGAN, 5 Oct. 1826. (JtSm) [B2]

JONES, Riley, & Latisa GOODPASTER, 23 Oct. 1844. (SMc) [B2]

JONES, Samuel, & Marian RALLS, bond 6 Apr. 1814;

   f/g: Francis Jones; f/b: Nathaniel W. Ralls; bdsm: Samuel & Francis Jones. [KM]

   Samuel Jones & Mary Ann Ralls or ROLLS, 7 Apr. 1814. [S1,JA]

JONES, Samuel, & Nancy BAILEY, bond 11 Feb. 1828;

   bdsm: Wm. Bailey. [AB]

   Samuel Jones & Nancy Bailey, 12 Feb. 1828. (JCm) [B2]

JONES, Spencer, & Han(n)ah E. BAILY, 27 Sept. 1851. (SJn) [B2]

JONES, Thomas, & Patsy TOLLY, bond 11 June 1821;

   bdsm: Clabourn Tolly. [AB]

Thomas Jones & Patsy SALLY, 14 June 1821. [S1]

JONES, Thomas, & Eliza RATLIFF, bond 1 Jan. 1827;
f/b: Coleman Ratliff; bdsm: Henry Ratliff. [AB]
Thomas Jones & Eliza Ratliff, 4 Jan. 1827. (RTh) [B2]

JONES, Thomas, & Mary BYRAM, 22 Oct. 1835. (SJn) [B2]

JONES, Thos. I., & Elizabeth F. BOYD, bond 12 Apr. 1830;
f/b: Spencer Boyd; bdsm: Benj. T. Jones. [AB]
Thomas T. Jones & Elizabeth T. Boyd, 15 Apr. 1830. (SJn) [B2]

JONES, Thos. J., & Elizabeth SNELLING, 17 July 1851. (MGs) [B2]

JONES, Thompson, & Lucy TACKET, bond 26 Sept. 1836;
f/b & bdsm: Baylis Tacket. [AB]
Tompson Jones & Lucy Tacket, 29 Sept. 1836. (SJn) [B2]

JONES, Thompson, & Julia HUGHARD, 13 Apr. 1843. (SJn) [B2]

JONES, Thompson, & Catharine LOY, bond 27 Dec. 1845;
f/b: Geo. C. Loy; bdsm: Andrew Loy. [AB]

JONES, William, & Elizabeth CHASTIN, bond 30 Oct. 1824;
bdsm: Ramey Chastin. [AB]
William Jones & Elizabeth CHASTAIN, 30 Oct. 1824. [S1]

JONES, Wm., & Nancy Ann KERNS, bond 31 Aug. 1846;
bdsm: James Sudduth. [AB]

KANNADY, Wm., & Nancy CLEM, bond 29 May 1821;
bdsm: John Crooks. [AB]
William KINNADA & Nancy Clem, 3 May 1821. [S1]

KARICK, John, & Evelina KARICK, 29 Feb. 1844. (SKc) [B2]

KARRICK, Washington, & Amanda McCARTY, 28 June 1852. (WRg) [B2]

KEATON, Wm., & Elizabeth RAMEY, bond 22 Aug. 1823;
bdsm: Acho Ramey. [AB]
William KETON & Elizabeth RAMY, 22 Aug. 1823. [S1]

KEITH, Gabriel, & Lucy RANDOLPH, bond 18 Jan. 1829;
bdsm: James Randolph. [AB]
Gabriel Keith & Lucy Randolph, 20 Jan. 1829. (IGL) [B2]

KELLY, Thomas, & Cordelia MORROW, bond 17 Dec. 1824;
f/b: Robert Morrow; bdsm: John L. Brent. [AB]
Thomas Owings Kelly & Cordelia Morrow, 17 Dec. 1824. [S1]

KELSO, Robert, & Jalcy? UNDERWOOD, bond 3 March 1816;
f/b: John Underwood; bdsm: Robt. Kelso, Joseph Kelso. [AB]
Robert Kelso & Gala Underwood, 4 Apr. 1816. (JPH) [TP,RS]

KELSOE, Wm., & Susan WYMOUTH, bond 24 Oct. 1827;
bdsm: Fielding Cassity. [AB]

KENNEDY, Cyrus, & Mariah EVANS, bond 18 Jan. 1830;

bdsm: Francis Evans. [AB]

    Cyrus KENADY & Mariah Evans, 20 Jan. 1830. (JHu) [B2]

KENNY, Archibald, & Susan RITE [Wright], bond 28 Nov. 1839;

    f/b: Ben Wright; bdsm: James Kenny. [AB]

KENNY, James, & Nancy BRUCE, bond 23 March 1847;

    bdsm: H. M. Butcher. [AB]

    James KINNEY & Nancy BOON, 24 May 1847. (BCs) [B2]

KERICK, Thos., & Martha PENDLETON, bond 8 Feb. 1836;

    bdsm: Thacker Pendleton. [AB]

    Thomas Kerick & Martha Pendleton, 21 Jan. 1836. (SJk) [B2]

KERICK, Thomas, & Genela McCLAIN, 14 Nov. 1843. (JMc) [B2]

KERICK, Walter K., & Clarissa PENDLETON, bond 36 [26?] Jan. 1836;

    f/g & bdsm: Hugh Kerick. [AB]

    Walter Kerick & Clarissa Pendleton, 3 Jan. 1836. (SJk) [B2]

KERNS, John, & Martha BLAIR, bond 18 Oct. 1839;

    bdsm: Noah Patrick. [AB]

KERNS, Jonathan, & Franky VICE, bond 13 Feb. 1845;

    bdsm: Wm. Vice. [AB]

KERNS, Levi, & Martha CONYERS, bond 9 Apr. 1838;

    bdsm: Isaac Conyers. [AB]

    Levi Kerns & Martha Conyers, 10 Apr. 1838. (JWR) [B2]

KERNS, Wm., & Sally BROWN, bond 29 Feb. 1829;

    bdsm: Norman Taylor. [AB]

KERNS, Wm. & Nancy DARNELL, bond 18 Feb. 1834;

    f/g: Tilmon Keirns; f/b: David Darnell; bdsm: Abraham Hornback. [AB]

    William KERNES & Nancy DARNAL, 18 Feb. 1834. (SJn) [B2]

KERREY, Elisha, & May NEAL, bond 19 June 1820;

    bdsm: John Neal. [AB]

    Elisha KENSEY & Mary Neal, 22 June 1820. [S1]

KERRICK, James J., & Nancy CASE, bond 4 Dec. 1845;

    bdsm: B. S. Right (Wright). [AB]

    James T. Kerrick & Nancy Case, 11 Dec. 1845. (BBv) [B2]

KERSEY, James, & Nancy NEAL, bond 25 Oct. 1830;

    bdsm: Henry Neal. [AB]

    James KEREY & Nancy Neal, 28 Oct. 1830. (JEv) [B2]

KIBBLE, William, & Sarah VICE, 26 Aug. 1818. [S1]

KIDWELL, Wm., & Hester ARMITAGE, bond 25 June 1823;

    f/b: Wm. Armitage; bdsm: Wm. Armitage ?Linn. [AB]

    William Kidwell & Hester ARNITAGE, 25 June 1823. [S1]

KIGGINS, Thomas, & Elizabeth LINZLIN, bond 18 March 1815;
    bdsm: James Busby, T. Kiggins.   [AB]
KILE, George, & Peggy LYNCH, 11 Sept. 1812.   [JA,S1]
KILLION, Edwin, & Rachel RAMEY, bond 11 May 1830;
    f/b: Archabell Ramey; bdsm: John Allfrey.   [AB]
    Edward H. Killion & Rachel Ramey, 13 May 1830. (SJk)   [B2]
KINCADE, Asa, & Marg(a)ret HOUSE, 23 Sept. 1852. (LGH)   [B2]
KINCADE, John, & Emma HAWKINS or Hawkings, 24 Jan. 1851. (TDL)   [B2]
KINCAID, Andrew, & Malinda MOPPIN, bond 10 Jan. 1831;
    bdsm: Wm. Moppin.   [AB]
    Andrew E. Kincaid & Malinda MAPPIN, 13 Jan. 1831. (JHu)   [B2]
KINCAID, George, & Polly HEATON, bond 15 Sept. 1812;
    guardian/b: Wm. Caldwell; bdsm: Geo. Kincaid, Wm. Caldwell.   [AB]
KINCAID, James, & Polly SANDERS, bond 5 May 1816;
    f/b: Robert Sanders; bdsm: Robert Sanders, J. Kincaid.   [AB]
    James CINNAIC & Polly Sanders, 1816.   [S1]
KINCAID, James or Jones, & Elizabeth CASSITY, bond 27 Apr. 1833;
    bdsm: Jacob Cassity.   [AB]
    James Kincaid & Elizabeth Cassity, 28 Apr. 1833. (WWh)   [B2]
KINCAID, James, & Mary Ann HAWKINS, bond 22 Jan. 1838;
    bdsm: John Hawkins.   [AB]
    James Harvy KINDLE & Mary Ann HOIKINSON, 25 Jan. 1838. (PHn)   [B2]
KINCAID, Joseph, & Nancy ROGERS, bond 9 Sept. 1822;
    bdsm: Samuel Rogers.   [AB]
    Joseph Kincaid & Nancy Rogers, 12 Sept. 1822. (JPH)   [TP,RS]
KINCAID, Joseph, & Emily CASSITY, bond 23 July 1834;
    bdsm: Jacob Cassity.   [AB]
    Joseph KINCADE or Kincaid & Emily CASITY, 24 July 1834. (WWh)   [B2]
KINCAID, Joseph, & Minerva J. BRADSHAW, bond 10 Feb. 1846;
    bdsm: Jas. F. Bradshaw.   [AB]
    Joseph Kincaid & Minerva J. Bradshaw, 12 Feb. 1846. (TRk)   [B2]
KINCAID, Samuel, & Lucy SMITH, 13 Sept. 1826. (JPk)   [B2]
KINCAID, Wm., & Polly SMALL, bond 7 Jan. 1810;
    bdsm: Geo. Small.   [AB]
    Willaim KINKEAD & Polly Small, 10 Jan. 1815.   [JA,S1]
KINCAID, Wm., & Lematha GOODPASTURE, bond 5 Nov. 1828;
    bdsm: J. P. Goodpasture.   [AB]
KINCAID, Wm., & Barbary ?NEAT, bond 14 Jan. 1829;
    bdsm: James Caldwell;   [AB]

William Kincaid & Bailasy WEST, 14 Jan. 1829. (DWh) [B2]

KINCAID, William, & Jane FLETCHER, bond 6 Feb. 1832;
bdsm: Jacob Fletcher. [AB]

KINCAID, William C., & Berrilla N. HILL, 16 Nov. 1837. (MGs) [B2]

[KINCAID?] Cincaid, William T., & Betey MACE, 1813. (LTu) [KM]

KINDER, Bonebo or Bourbon?, & Jane ARMSTRONG, bond 23 June 1819;
bdsm: John Dunaway. [AB]

Barnbas J. KUDER & Jane Armstrong, 27 June 1819. [S1]

KINDLE, Jackson, & Elizabeth JACKSON, bond 20 Nov 1837;
f/g: Banford Kindle; bdsm: Thomas Jackson. [AB]

Jackson Kindle & Elizabeth Jackson, 20 Nov. 1837. (JnSm) [B2]

KING, Elijah, & Eliza CROOKS, 28 March 1826. (JtSm) [B2]

KING, Wm., & Ann MINNEAR, 24 Dec. 1826. (JGW) [B2]

KINKAID, John T., & Julian TAYLOR, bond 7 Jan. 1840;
bdsm: Wesley Taylor. [AB]

KIPHART, Henry, & Polly THOMPSON, 5 May 1816. [JA]

Henry KEPHART & Polly Thompson [S1]

KIRK, Hugh, & Mary JONES, 17 Aug. 1817. [S1]

KIRK, John, & Sally FARIS, bond 1 Feb. 1812;
bdsm: James E. Walker. [AB]

John Kirk & Sally FERIS, 4 Feb. 1812. (JPH) [TP,RS]

KIRK, Thomas, & Carsanna LEMASTER, bond 28 July 1812;
f/b: Richard Lemaster; bdsm: Thos. Kirk, Richd. Lemaster. [AB]

Thomas Kirk & _____ LEMASTERS, 28 July 1812. (JPH) [TP]

KNOX, Ben, & Jane KINCAID, bond 25 Dec. 1845;
bdsm: James Coyle. [AB]

Benjamin F. Knox & Jane KINCADE, 25 Dec. 1845. (SKc) [B2]

KNOX, Benjamin F., & Rebecca TACKETT, bond 24 Oct. 1837;
bdsm: Geo. Knox. [AB]

KNOX, Charles, & Mary TRAYLOR, bond 29 Sept. 1847;
bdsm: John Traylor. [AB]

Charles Knox & Ma(r)y Traylor, 30 Sept. 1847. (SKc) [B2]

KNOX, James, & Sally ATKINS, bond 1 March 1829;
bdsm: John Rice. [AB]

KNOX, James, & Sally STEPHENS, 11 Nov. 1829. (SJn) [B2]

KNOX, Joseph S., & Elisabeth STAMPER, 14 Sept. 1852. (LGH) [B2]

LACEY, James, & Nancy WILSON, bond 29 Aug. 1844. [AB]

James H. LACY & Nancy WILLSON, 1 Sept. 1844. (JnSm) [B2]

LAIN?, Isaac, & Cyntha FERGUSON, bond 15 March 1820;
bdsm: John Smith; [AB]

Isaac LOW & Cynthia FUGUSON, 16 March 1820.   [S1]

LANCASTER, Achiles, & Susan VANLANDINGHAM, bond 20 Sept. 1823;

    bdsm: Francis Hopkins.   [KM]

    Achilles LAMEASTER & Susan VANLAND, 20 Sept. 1823.   [S1]

LANCASTER, Samuel L., & Harriet DAVIS, 12 Feb. 1840;

    bdsm: Thomas Davis.   [AB]

    Samuel SAND [sic] & Harriet Davis, 30[?] Feb. 1840. (TDm)   [B2]

LANDER, Wm., & Lydia HOWARD, bond 10 May 1831;

    f/b: Eli Howard; bdsm: Jno. McLane.   [AB]

LANDERS, Felix, & Sarah OCKERMAN, bond 4 Dec. 1811;

    f/b: Daniel? Ockerman; bdsm: Felix Landers, Daniel Ockerman.   [AB]

LANDERS, Oliver, & Maria BURNS, bond 4 June 1831;

    bdsm: W. M. Sudduth.   [AB]

LANDESS or Landers?, Henry, & Kata MOLERE, bond 2 Apr. 1811;

    bdsm: Henry Landers, Joseph Molere.   [AB]

LANE or Love, C. G., & Emily SWINEY, bond 29 Jan. 1849;

    f/b: Miles Swiney; bdsm: D. Lockridge.   [AB]

LANE, Hugh, & Louina GRAHAM, bond 23 Jan. 1824;

    f/b: James Graham; bdsm: Albert Harrison.   [AB]

    Hugh Lane & Louisa P. Graham, 28 Jan. 1824. (JPH)   [TP,RS]

LANE, Hugh, & Melinda WALKER, bond 30 Jan. 1837;

    bdsm: Wm. Sudduth.   [AB]

    Hugh Lane & Malinda Walker, 2 Feb. 1837. (MGs)   [B2]

LANE, Hugh, & Sally MONTJOY, bond 7 Aug. 1843.   [AB]

    Hugh Lane & Sally Montjoy, 10 Aug. 1843. (JnSm)   [B2]

LANE or Love, Wm., & Dolly WADE, bond 21 July 1822;

    bdsm: James Wade.   [AB]

    William Lane & Polly Wade, 23 June 1822.   [S1]

LANE, Wm. A., & Elizabeth LANE, bond 19 Aug. 1846;

    bdsm: W. N. Lane.   [AB]

    William A. Lane & Elizabeth Lane or LAW, 19 Aug. 1846. (JnSm)   [B2]

LANE or Love, Wm. S., & Eleanor SUDDUTH, bond 9 Sept. 1834;

    bdsm: Lewis Sudduth.   [AB]

LANSDALE, Jacob, & Martha WARNER, 11 March 1851. (JHe)   [B2]

LANSDALE, James, & Hetty WARNER, bond 1 Nov. 1814;

    f/b: Jacob Warner; bdsm: James Lansdale, Hetty Warner.   [AB]

    James LONSDALE & Hetty Warren / Netty Warner[sic], 6 Nov. 1814. (CHp) [JA,S1]

LANSDOWN, George, & [Mrs.] Mary MENIFEE, bond 23 Oct. 1819;

    bdsm: Wm. Suddith;   [AB]

George Lawsdown [sic] & Mary Menifee, 24 Oct. 1819. [S1]

LANSDOWN, George, & Nancy ALLEN, bond 28 Oct. 1849;
f/b: John Allen; bdsm: David Trumbo. [AB]

George Lansdown & Nancy Allen, 30 Oct. 1849. (DBk) [B2]

LATHRAM, Anthony, & Atevura? HORNBACK, bond 4 Feb. 1845;
bdsm: Isaac Hornback. [AB]

LATHRAM, David, & Eliza Jane JONES, bond 6 Nov. 1849;
f/b & bdsm: Ambrose Jones. [AB]

LATHRAM, George, & Elizabeth DARNALL, bond 30 Nov. 1822;
bdsm: David Darnale. [AB]

George LATHNANS & Elizabeth DARNAL, 5 Dec. 1823. [S1]

LAW, John, & Sarah MINNEAR, bond 4 Aug. 1846;
bdsm: David Minnear. [AB]

John Law & Sarah MYNHEIR, 6 Aug. 1846. (JGW) [B2]

[LAW?] Lane or Love?, John, & Mary NICHOLAS, bond 27 Dec. 1846;
bdsm: Francis Sinclair. [AB]

John LAW & Mary Nicholas, 27 Dec. 1846. (SKc) [B2]

LAW, Wm., & Elizabeth SMITH, bond 17 Feb. 1814;
bdsm: Wm. Law, Michael Smith. [AB]

William LOW or Law & Betsey Smith, 17 Feb. 1813. [JA,S1]

LAWRENCE, Wm., & Delila WALLS, bond 28 Sept. 1824;
bdsm: Zachariah Walls. [AB]

William Lawrence & Delila Walls, 28 Sept. 1824. [S1]

LAWSON, Edmond, & Cassanan? JOHNSON, bond 20 Nov 1849;
bdsm: Isaac Johnson. [AB]

Edward Lawson & Cassandria Johnson, 22 Nov. 1849. (JWW) [B2]

LAWSON, Joseph, & Mary Jane JOHNSON, bond 19 Oct. 1849;
f/b & bdsm: Isaac Johnson. [AB]

Joseph R. Lawson & Ma(r)y Jane Johnson, 30 Oct. 1849. (JWW) [B2]

LAYTON, John, & Anna JACK, bond 23 Jan. 1822;
bdsm: Wm. White. [AB]

John TAYLOR & Anna Jack, 27 Jan. 1822. [S1]

LEACH, Wm., & Judith CHASTAIN or Cheatam?, bond 9 Apr. 1816;
f/b: Silas Chastain; bdsm: John Leach, Wm. Leach. [AB]

William Leach & Judith CHATAIN, 11 Apr. 1816 [JA,S1]

also: Wm. Leach & Judeth Chatain, 11 Oct. 1816. [JA]

LEDFORD, Nathaniel, & Betsey TAYLOR, bond 14 March 1825 (or 35?);
bdsm: B. Taylor. [AB]

Nathaniel Ledford & Betsey Taylor, 31 March 1825. [S1]

LEDFORD, Wm. & Mary ARNETT, bond 27 Feb. 1811;

f/b: Thos Arnett; bdsm: Wm. Ledford, Richard Stamper. [AB]

LEDFORD, William S. P., & Philladelphia SMITHERS, bond 5 Oct. 1833;
bdsm: Joseph Smithers or Smothers. [AB]
William G. P. Ledford & Philadelphia SMOTHERS, 10 Oct. 1833. (PHn) [B2]

LEE, Henry, & Eda FLETCHER, bond 13 Feb. 1839;
bdsm: Y. Smith. [AB]

LEE, James A. J., & Mariah M. SMITH, bond 5 March 1840;
f/b: John Smith; bdsm: B. A. Webb. [AB]
James S. P. Lee & Maria M. Smith, 8 March 1839. (JnSm) [B2]

LEE, John?, & Maria MOCKABEE, bond 24 Nov. 1847;
bdsm: Wm. McClain. [AB]

LEE, Joseph, & Abigal MOPPIN of Fleming Co., Ky., bond 5 Apr. 1814;
m/g: Susanah Lee; m/b: Jane Moppin; bdsm: Joseph Lee, Wm. Lee. [AB]

LEE, Wm. G., & Eliza McGOWN, bond 27 June 1821;
bdsm: James Sudduth. [AB]
William G. Lee & Eliza McGRAVEN, 27 June 1821. [S1]

LEFORGE, Lewis, & Hestar LEDFORD, 19 Dec. 1850. (TDL) [B2]

LEGAH?, David, & Mary ROBERTSON, bond 13 Apr. 1837;
bdsm: Sam Rogers. [AB]
David LEGOT & Mary ROBBERSON, 13 Apr. 1837. (MGs) [B2]

LEMASTER, Michael, & Richard[?] LEMASTER, bond 6 July 1816;
f/g: Richard Lemaster; bdsm: R. Lemaster, M. Lemaster. [AB]

LEMASTER, Richard, & Polly SMITH, bond 7 Apr. 1815;
bdsm: Richard Ross, R. Lemaster. [AB]
Richard LAMASTERS & Polly Smith, 9 Apr. 1815. [JA]
Richard LAMASTER & Polly Smith, 8 Sept. 1815. [S1]

LEVANEY, Edward, & Elizabeth A. CALDWELL, bond 21 June 1819;
bdsm: Ephriam Caldwell. [AB]

LEVERSON, Michael, & Ellen KING, bond 6 Oct. 1821;
f/b: John King; bdsm: James Forsythe. [AB]
Michael LAMEMAN & Eleanor King, 7 Oct. 1821. [S1]

LEWIS, John, & Betsey ELLIOTT, bond 15 Feb. 1817;
bdsm: (not legible). [AB]
John Lewis & Betsey Elliott, 23 Feb. 1817. [S1]

LEWIS, Thomas, & Elizabeth ?MINNEAR, bond 24 Sept. 1823;
f/b: John Minnear or Minner; bdsm: Wm. Sailor. [AB]
Thomas Lewis & Elizabeth MINEAR, 28 Sept. 1823. [S1]

LEWIS, Thos., & Elizabeth COGSWELL, 14 Feb. 1843. (JGW) [B2]

LIKES, Thomas, & Charity LATHROM, bond 24 Oct. 1849;

bdsm: Anthony Lathram. [AB]

LIKES, Wm., & Ailsy JONES, bond 29 Feb. 1816;
    bdsm: John Jones, Wm. Likes. [AB]

LINCH, Sylvester, & Nancy GARNER, bond 4 Feb. 1824;
    bdsm: Jane B. Garner. [AB]
    Sylvester LYNCH & Mary B. GAINES, 4 Feb. 1824. [S1]

LINE, Samuel, & Mary Ann Levina JONES, bond 7 Dec. 1824;
    f/g: Samuel Line; f/b: John Jones; bdsm: Samuel Line, Oliver Jones. [AB]
    Samuel LYONS & Maryann Larina Jones, 9 Dec. 1824. [S1]

LINEY, Wm., & Margaret CROCKETT, bond 2 Sept. 1834;
    bdsm: Maryann Crockett. [AB]

LINK, James, & Katharine ?MINNEAR, bond 16 Nov. 1832;
    f/b: Jonathan Minnear; bdsm: Wm. Walton. [AB]
    James ?LINPS & Katherine Minnear, 19 Nov. 1832. (SJk) [B2]

LINK, Peter, & Nancy BROWN, bond 24 Feb. 1821;
    bdsm: Caleb Brown. [AB]

[LINK?] Luke, Gaul, & Polly ?MINNEAR, bond 15 Aug. 1828;
    f/b: Jonathan Minnear; bdsm: Thos. Fitzgood. [AB]
    Simon LINK & Polly MANIER, 17 Aug. 1828. (JGW) [B2]

LINVILLE, James, & Polly HONAKER, 19 June 1817. [JA]
    James LINVILL & Polly Honaker [S1]

LINVILLE, John, & Elizabeth DONALDSON, bond 4 Oct. 1815;
    consent/b: James Donaldson; bdsm: J. Donaldson, John Linvill. [AB]

LINVILLE, Josiah, & Polly SNELLING, bond 15 Sept. 1812;
    f/g: Elisha Linville; f/b: Wm. P. Snelling;
    bdsm: Josiah Linville, Wm. P. Snelling. [AB]

LOCKRIDGE, James or Jones, & Rachel JONES, bond 14 May 1814;
    bdsm: Jones Lockridge, Benj. Jones. [AB]
    James Lockridge & Rachel Jones, 17 May 1814. (JPH) [TP,RS]

LOCKRIDGE, John, & Adalia PEEBLES, bond 1 Aug. 1827;
    bdsm: James S. Noe. [AB]
    John Lockridge & Alecia PEPLES, 2 Aug. 1827. (PHn) [B2]

LOCKRIDGE, Joseph (or Elijah) H., & Patsy CASSITY, bond 23 Apr. 1823;
    bdsm: Alexander Cassity. [AB]
    Joseph H. Lockridge, & Patsy Cassity, 1 May 1823. [S1]

LOGIN, Edward W., & Queen TABER, 20 Dec. 1839. (PCy) [B2]

LOLY or Toly?, George, & Polly SMITH, 31 Jan. 1826. (RGd) [B2]

LONG, Alexander, & Matilda OWINGS, bond 26 Oct. 1830;
    bdsm: Elihu Owings. [AB]

LONG, Henry, & Betsey WARFIELD, bond 3 Oct. 1812;

f/b: Calib Warfield; bdsm: Henry Long, John Long; mar. 20 Oct.   [KM]

 Henry Long & Betsey Warfield, 12 Oct. 1812.   [JA]

 Henry Long & Betsey WANFIELD, 20 Oct. 1812.   [S1]

LONG or Lary?, Henry, & Matilda COOK, 5 Feb. 1835. (MGs)   [B2]

LONG, John C., & Elizann WADE, bond 4 June 1834;

 bdsm: Samuel Wade.   [AB]

LOOKNDY?, John H., & Margaret EDWARDS, 6 Oct. 1843. (SJn)   [B2]

LOVE, Lewis, & Mary CHOAT, bond 24 Dec. 1814;

 f/b: Augustine Choate; bdsm: Lewis Lane, Wm. Sexton.   [KM]

 Lewis LANE & Polly SHOAT or Chout, 25 Dec. 1814.   [JA]

 Lewis LONE & Polly SMOOT   [S1]

LOVE, Mark, & Elizabeth PRATOR, bond 26 Sept. 1819;

 bdsm: Palmer Rice.   [AB]

 Mark LOU & Elizabeth PRTOR[?], 26 Sept. 1819.   [S1]

LOVE or Lane, Thos., & Sally WILSON, bond 5 March 1828;

 bdsm: Joseph Wilson.   [AB]

[LOWERY?] Lamerz, John, & Patsy ROBINSON, bond 29 Dec. 1833;

 bdsm: Wm. Barry.   [AB]

 John LOWERY & Patsy ROBERSON, 3 Dec. 1833. (TIs)   [B2]

LOWERY, Moses, & Elizabeth THOMAS, 18 June 1851. (BBv)   [B2]

LOWREY?, Kary, & Mary Ann SEXTON, bond 8 Jan. 1834;

 bdsm: Bry Sexton.   [AB]

LUMBLESON?, John, & Sarah LADDERS, bond 15 Jan. 1823;

 bdsm: Henry Ladders.   [AB]

 John TUMBLESON & Sarah SODERS, 16 Jan. 1823.   [S1]

LYKIN, William, & Lucy LAIN, 1816.   [S1]

 William LYKINS & Rebekah COFFEE, 18 Jan. 1816. (JPH)   [TP,RS]

LYMAN, Andrew, & Jane RICE, bond 2 March 1836;

 f/b & bdsm: Holman Rice.   [AB]

LYMAN, J., & Debera ?GARRET, 8 July 1846. (JHu)   [B2]

LYMAN, Richard, & Sarah HUNT, bond 13 Feb. 1812;

 f/b: Ab Hunt.   [AB]

 Richard LYNAM & Sarah Hunt, 16 Feb. 1812.   [JA,S1]

LYNAM, Absolum, & Nancy EATON, bond 25 Oct. 1837;

 f/b: Jeremiah Eaton; bdsm: Jery Eaton.   [AB]

 Absalom Lynam & Nancy Eaton, 26 Oct. 1837. (TLy)   [B2]

LYNAM, Charles, & Winny GREEN, bond 12 Jan. 1816;

 f/b: Z. Green; bdsm: Thomas Fletcher.   [AB]

 Charles Lynam or LYMAN & Winn(e)y Green, 14 Jan. 1816.   [JA,S1]

LYNAM, John, & Lucinda ATHA, 16 March 1843. (SRg)   [B2]

[LYNAM?] Lyram, John, & Elizabeth DAVIS, bond 22 Dec. 1845;
    bdsm: Jonathan Davis.   [AB]

LYNAM, Lee, & Elizabeth DUNCAN, bond 13 Nov. 1815;
    bdsm: Wm. Duncan.   [AB]

    Lee LYMAN & Elizabeth DUNKIN, 16 Nov. 1815.   [JA,S1]

LYNAM, Lee, & Mary A. WILSON, 14 Apr. 1850. (JDy)   [B2]

LYNAM, Wm., & Jane REED, bond 19 Jan. 1821;
    bdsm: David England.   [AB]

    William H. Lynam & Jane RICE, 26 Jan. 1821.   [S1]

LYNAM, William H., & Levina RICE, 8 Nov. 1835. (SJn)   [B2]

LYONS, John, & Sally READ, bond 15 Dec. 1827;
    bdsm: Hyram Barnes.   [AB]

    John Lyons & Sally Read, 18 Dec. 1827. (PCy) [B2]

LYONS, John, & Martha Ann JONES, bond 11 March 1833;
    bdsm: Thos. Jones (or James?).   [AB]

    John Lyons & Martha Ann Jones, 11 March 1833. (SMc) [B2]

LYONS, John, & Sarah EMSIGM[?], 9 Feb. 1843. (WRg)   [B2]

LYONS, Robert, & Scytha Ann SEXTON, bond 21 Aug. 1846;
    bdsm: Dye Teal.   [AB]

    Robert Lyons & Syntha Ann Sexton, 24 Aug. 1846. (WRg) [B2]

MABERRY, Joseph, & Hannah McCILVAIN, 2 July 1819.   [S1]

MACE, Job, & Cata MOLES, 1813. (LTu)   [KM]

    Jacob Mace & Caty MOLER   [JA,S1]

MACE, Jobe, & Esther MOLER, bond 20 Jan. 1814;
    f/b: Joseph Moler; bdsm: John Mace, Joseph Moler. [AB]

MACKEY, Wm., & Dilly ?LANE, bond 13 Jan. 1829;
    bdsm: Wm. Lane.   [AB]

    William MACKY & Dilly Lane, 13 Jan. 1829. (ATd) [B2]

MADISON, James, & Salley WARNER, bond 26 Nov. 1831;
    bdsm: F. Oakley.   [AB]

MAHAN?, Samuel, & Margarett McCARNISH, bond 15 June 1824;
    bdsm: Adam McCornish.   [AB]

    Samuel MAGHHAN & Margaret McCAMISH, 18 June 1824. [S1]

MAHANY or Mahony?, Wm., & Polly FOONS or Koons, bond 6 Dec. 1814;
    f/g: John Mahony; bdsm: Wm. Mahony, John Foons. [AB]

MAHONEY, Henry, & Polly Ann STEELE, bond 30 Apr. 1838;
    bdsm: Wm. Storm.   [AB]

    Henry H. Mahoney & Polly Ann STEEL, 30 Apr. 1838. (SMc) [B2]

MAN, Solomon, & Lucinda McCLANNAHAN, bond 26 Jan. 183_;
    bdsm: James McClanahan. [AB]
    Solomon MAIN & Lucinda McCLANIHAN, 31 Jan. 1822. [S1]
MANIER, D. S., & Cassey BROWN, 27 June 1847. (AGW) [B2]
MANIER, Jonathan, & Jane MANIER, bond 11 June 1849;
    f/b: John Manier; bdsm: Wm. Walton (or Walter?). [AB]
    Jonathan MINNER & Martha MINNER, 14 June 1849. (OSx) [B2]
MANLEY or Maynley, Andrew, & Sarah WARREN, 2 May 1839. (JSt) [B2]
MANLEY, David, & Robertta CLAYTON, bond 27 Oct. 1846;
    bdsm: James Manley. [AB]
MANLEY, Peter, & Julia Ann REED, bond 1 Jan. 1847;
    bdsm: David Manley. [AB]
    Peter Manley & Julia A. Reed, 1 Jan. 1847. (SKc) [B2]
MANLEY, Samuel, & Anne RICHART, bond 8 Apr. 1811;
    f/b: James Richart; bdsm: Samuel Manley, Dunkin Richart. [AB]
    Samuel Manley & Anna Richart, 9 Apr. 1811. (JPH) [TP,RS]
MANLEY, Wm., & Nancy DAVIS, bond 28 Apr. 1815;
    bdsm: John Cherry; mar. 28 Apr. [KM]
    Willam MANLY & Nancy Davis, 28 Apr. 1813. [JA,S1]
MANLEY, Wm., & Lydy Ann S. MITCHEL, bond 18 Feb. 1840;
    bdsm: David Bailey. [AB]
MANLY, Harvy, & Polly CLAYTON, bond 25 June 1836;
    bdsm: Jonas Warner. [AB]
MANLY, Isick, & Sarah CHILDRES, bond 4 Apr. 1814;
    bdsm: Isaac Manly, Nicholas Burns; mar. 7 Nov. [KM]
    Isick Manly & Sarah CHILDERS, 30 Apr. 1814. [JA]
    Isick MANLEY & Sarah CHILDNES, 7 Nov. 1814. [S1]
MANNIN, Henry, & Nancy ADAMS, bond 29 Aug. 1812;
    f/g: Meredith Mannin; f/b: James Adams; bdsm: Henry Mann, James Adams. [AB]
    Henry MANNON or MAMMON & Nancy Adams, 30 Aug. 1812. [JA,S1]
MANNIN, John, & Phebe CHILDERS, bond 18 May 1811;
    bdsm: John Mannin, Claburn Burnitt. [AB]
MANNIN, John, & Susannah SHEWBERT, bond 30 Sept. 1812;
    bdsm: John Mannin, Wilton Brook. [AB]
    John MANNON & Susannah SHEUBERT, 4 Oct. 1812. [JA]
    John MAMMON & Susannah SHENBERT [S1]
MANNIN, Tarlton, & Hester Ann HIAT, bond 4 May 1826;
    bdsm: Thos. I. Young. [AB]
MANNON, Meredith, & Rachel FUGATE, bond 14 Feb. 1825;
    bdsm: Reuben Fugate. [AB]

MAPPIN or Moppin, James, & Alizanna JOHNSON or Johnston, bond 9 Apr. 1823;
   bdsm: Jessy Atchison. [AB]
   James MASSIN & Alizana Johnson, 16 Apr. 1823. [S1]
MAPPIN, Thomas, & Louisa F. BARBER, 12 Sept. 1850. (SKc) [B2]
MAPPIN or Moppin, Wm., & Cintha ALEXANDER, bond 7 Dec. 1839;
   bdsm: Thomas Alexander. [AB]
   William Mappin or Mappine & Cynthia Alexander, 10 Dec. 1839. (TWC) [B2]
MARKLAND, Jonathan, & Elizabeth PRATOR, bond 27 Feb. 1833;
   bdsm: Wm. Harnaker. [AB]
   Johnathan Markland & Elizabeth PRATER, 18 Feb. 1833. (SJn) [B2]
MARKLAND, Jonathan, & Mary CRAIG, bond 24 Oct. 1839;
   bdsm: Joshua Craig. [AB]
MARKLAND, Nathaniel, & Hannah HORSEMAN, bond 9 Dec. 1846;
   bdsm: George Coyle. [AB]
MARPLE, John, & Sarah WILSON, bond 3 Apr. 1845;
   parent/b: S. F. Wilson; bdsm: H. F. Wilson. [AB]
   John Marple & Sarah Wilson, 3 Apr. 1845. (SJn) [B2]
MARRS, John, & Mae BRIDGES, bond 16 July 1825;
   bdsm: Hiram Bridges. [AB]
MARTIN, David, & Polly RAYLAND, bond 2 Dec. 1829;
   bdsm: Raney Ragland. [AB]
   David Martin & Polly RAGLAND, 2 Dec. 1829. (JnSm) [B2]
MARTIN, James, & Tily Ann McFETUS, bond 26 Apr. 1831;
   bdsm: James Moreland. [AB]
   James Martin & Tely (or Fely?) ann McFETERS, 2 Apr. 1831. (JVc) [B2]
MARTIN, Robert, & Lucy ROUTT, bond, no date [1820s];
   f/b: George Routt; bdsm: Herod Patrick. [AB]
[MAXEY?] Masey, John C., & Lydia B. GROVER, bond 21 March 1842;
   bdsm: James Whaley. [AB]
   John C. MAXY & Ly[d]ia B. CRAVER, 23 March 1842. (SJn) [B2]
MASON, Geo. C., & Sally HARPER, bond 8 Feb. 1831;
   bdsm: John Harper. [AB]
   George C. WASSON & Sally Harper, 10 Feb. 1831. (SJn) [B2]
MASON, John C., & Ann E. OWING, bond 6 Apr. 1847;
   bdsm: John W. Richards. [AB]
   John C. Mason & Ann E. OWINGS, 6 Apr. 1847. (WSh) [B2]
[MASTERSON] Mastenan?, Hathway, & Nancy Ann HAWKINS, bond 26 Feb. 1845;
   bdsm: Thomas Hawkins. [AB]
   Hathaway MASTERSON & Nancy Ann Hawkins, 4 March 1845. (PHn) [B2]

MATHEWS, Thomas A., & Eliza A. FLETCHER, 28 March 1843. (RFC) [B2]
MATTHEW, Franklin, & Elizabeth COSTIGAN, bond 24 Aug. 1846;
   m/b: Sarah Costigan; bdsm: James Warren. [AB]
   Franklin MATHEWS & Elizabeth Costigan, 5 Aug. 1846. (BCs) [B2]
MATTHEW, Wm., & Eunice TRUMBO, bond 24 Oct. 1827;
   bdsm: Geo. Trumbo. [AB]
   William MATTHEWS & Eunice Trumbo, 24 Oct. 1827. (JVc) [B2]
MATTHEWS, Anthony, & Polly HUNT, bond 22 Apr. 1822;
   f/b: Reuben Hunt; bdsm: Meredith Hasty. [AB]
   Anthony Matthews & Polly Hunt, 21 Sept. 1822. [S1]
MATTHEWS, William, & Lucinda SNELLING, bond 2 Sept. 1815;
   f/b: Benjamin Snelling; bdsm: Wm. Matthews, Spencer Boyd. [AB]
MAUPIN, Simon, & Mary Ann MARKWELL, bond 11 March 1846;
   f/b: Abel Markwell; bdsm: N. E. Bradley. [AB]
   Simon Maupin & Mary Jane Markwell, 19 March 1846. (DBk) [B2]
MAUPIN, Thomas, & Peggy McCLINE, 1 March 1818. [S1]
MAYS, Andr(e)w, & Harriett BARBER, 13 March 1850. (SKc) [B2]
MAYS, John, & Mattea BRISTO, 12 Feb. 1818. [S1]
MAZE, James, & Mary Ann HART, bond 26 Feb. 1845;
   bdsm: Wm. Rogers. [AB]
   James Maze or MAYS & Mary Ann Hart, 26 Feb. 1845. (WRg) [B2]
MAZE, Thomas, & Jane JACKSON, bond 22 May 1847;
   bdsm: Geo. Jackson. [AB]
   Thomas Maze & Jane Jackson, 23 May 1847. (WRg) [B2]
McALLISTER, Charles, & Katharine LANCASTER, bond 14 Jan. 1829;
   bdsm: Charles McAllister. [AB]
   Charles H. McCALISTER & Katharine Lancaster, 15 Jan. 1829. (WCS) [B2]
McARTINE, Van, & Grace GOODIN, bond 9 Nov. 1829;
   bdsm: W. Richards. [AB]
McBEE, Joseph, & Louina CORBIN, bond 29 May 1824;
   bdsm: Zachariah Corbin. [AB]
   Joseph McBee & Lavina Corbin, 30 May 1824. [S1]
McBEE, Wm., & Ann SCOTT, bond 28 Nov. 1822;
   bdsm: John Scott. [AB]
   William McBee & Ann Scott, 29 Nov. 1822. [S1]
McCARTY, Augustine, & July an FIELDIN, 1 Jan. 1852. (WRg) [B2]
McCARTY, Andrew Jackson, & Frankie McCLANE, bond 7 July 1836;
   bdsm: James McClane. [AB]
   Andrew J. McCarty & Franky McCLAIN, 7 July 1836. (SJk) [B2]
McCARTY, Ezekiel, & Margaret PEVELER or Peebles, bond 28 Dec. 1814;

m/b: Sibby Peveler; bdsm: Ezekiel McCarty, Reuben Underwood. [KM]

Ezekiel MANLY & Marget PERILER, 29 Dec. 1814. [S1]

Ezekiel McAUTY & Marget PEVLER [JA]

McCARTY, James, & Maud KARRICK, bond 22 Apr. 1829;
bdsm: Hugh Karrick. [AB]

McCARTY, James, & America FIELDER, bond 6 Sept. 1838;
f/b: Wm. Fielder; bdsm: John Norris. [AB]

McCARTY, Robert, & Polly CLONILL, bond 2 Apr. 1833;
bdsm: Eli Clovill. [AB]

Robert McNULTY & Polly CLAVILL, 4 Apr. 1833. (PHn) [B2]

McCARTY, William, & Mary Ann SORREL, bond 11 July 1833;
bdsm: Joshua Sorrel. [AB]

William McARTA & Mary Ann SORRELL, 12 ____ 1833. (TIs) [B2]

McCAUL, Wm. H, & Ann WILLIAMS, bond 19 Jan. 1820;
f/b: John Williams. [AB]

William H. McCARD & Ann Williams, 25 Jan. 1820. [S1]

McCLAIN, Alexander, & Elizabeth BARNES, 10 March 1833. (SMc) [B2]

McCLAIN, Augustin, & Janella McCLAIN, bond 13 Apr. 1840;
f/b: John McClain; bdsm: David Norris. [AB]

McCLAIN, Cornelius, & Salley DAVIS, bond 7 Feb. 1833;
f/b: Jesse Davis; bdsm: B. Goodpasture. [AB]

Cornelus McClain & Sally Davis, 7 Feb. 1833. (ALy) [B2]

McCLAIN, Garrett, & Elizabeth SORRELL, bond 27 June 1832;
bdsm: Jean Sorrell. [AB]

Garrot McClain & Elizabeth SORREL, 28 June 1832. (WFg) [B2]

[McCLAIN?] McClane, George, & Caty ROBERTS, bond 28 May 1811;
f/b: John Roberts; bdsm: Geo. McClain, John Robert. [AB]

George McCLAIN & Caty Roberts, 30 May 1811. [JA,S1]

(In Nicholas Co., KY; license from Bath) [JA]

McCLAIN, George, & Elizabeth RICHARDSON, bond 24 March 1834;
bdsm: John Norris. [AB]

George McClain & Elizabeth RICHARDS, 30 March 1834. [S1]

McCLAIN, George, & Martha SPENCER, bond 10 Aug. 1846;
bdsm: John B. Warren. [AB]

McCLAIN, Howard, & Mary EDEN, bond 17 March 1845;
bdsm: Jeremiah Eden. [AB]

McCLAIN, James, & Caty ROBINSON, bond 14 Feb. 1825;
bdsm: Hugh Karrick. [AB]

James McClain & Caty Robinson, 22 Feb. 1825. [S1]

McCLAIN, James, & Malvina NORRIS, bond 5 Feb. 1842;
 bdsm: John Norris. [AB]
McCLAIN, James, & Nancy KARRICK, bond 17 Apr. 1845;
 bdsm: John Karrick. [AB]
 James McClain & Nancy KERRICK, 18 May 1845. (BBv) [B2]
McCLAIN, James, & Nancy SHROPSHIRE, bond 12 July 1847;
 bdsm: Wm. Shropshire. [AB]
McCLAIN, John, & Patsey JONES, bond 19 Jan. 1813;
 f/b: Charles Jones; bdsm: John McClain, Charles Jones. [AB]
 John McClain & Patsey Jones, 21 Jan. 1813. [JA,S1]
McCLAIN, John, & Phebe McCARTY, bond 12 Feb. 1814;
 f/b & bdsm: Augustin McCarty; mar. 13 Feb. [KM]
 John McClain & Phebe McCarty, 15 Feb. 1814. [JA]
 13 Feb. 1813 [S1]
McCLA(I)N, John, & Nancy MITCHELL, bond 29 Apr. 1825;
 bdsm: Samuel Mitchell. [AB]
McCLAIN, John, & Mayamy RICHISON, bond 1 Oct. 1834;
 bdsm: Joshua Sorrell. [AB]
 John McClain & Naomy Richison, 2 Oct. 1834. (SMc) [B2]
McCLAIN, John M., & Hannah McCARTY, bond 12 Apr. 1847;
 bdsm: John McClain. [AB]
 John McLAIN & Hannah McCarty, 14 Apr. 1847. (BBv) [B2]
McCLAIN, Joseph, & Isabella KELSO, bond 30 Sept. 1840;
 f/b: Walker Kelso; bdsm: Robt. O. Chapman. [AB]
McCLAIN, Josiah, & Melinda NICHOLS, bond 1 Jan. 1836;
 bdsm: Wm. Ward. [AB]
 Josiah McClain & Matinda[?] Nichols, 3 Jan. 1836. (GSz) [B2]
McCLAIN, Solomon, & Nancy SMITH, bond 2 Oct. 1819;
 bdsm: John McClain. [AB]
 Solomon McClain & Paucy Smith, 3 Oct. 1819. [S1]
McCLAIN, William, & Malinda OAKLEY, 30 Nov. 1817. [S1]
McCLANAHAN, Wm., & Rebecca MITCHELL, bond 2 Jan. 1828;
 bdsm: Sam Mitchell. [AB]
 William McClanahan & Rebecca MITCHAL, 2 Jan. 1828. (SJk) [B2]
McCLANE, John, & Lucy BOYD, 14 March 1844. (SKc) [B2]
McCLAUGHLIN, John, & Mary STATON, bond 29 July 1828;
 bdsm: James Staton. [AB]
 John McGLAUTHLIN & Mary Staton, 4 Aug. 1828. (EHw) [B2]
McCLELAND, Alexander, & Elizabeth BARNES, bond 9 March 1833;
 bdsm: Charles Clayton. [AB]

McCLURE, Landon, & Elizabeth CALDWELL, bond 12 Jan. 1846;
    bdsm: John A. Crocket.   [AB]

McCLURE, Martin [Matthew], & Larnia [Terissa] GUDGELL, bond 16 Sept. 1845;
    bdsm [f/b]: Allen Gudgell.   [AB]

[McCLURE] Mclure, Peter, & Emily Ann METEER, 9 Jan. 1845. (RFC)   [B2]

McCLURE, Samuel, & Jane HENDRICKS, bond 20 Oct. 1814;
    f/b: Peter Hendricks; bdsm: Samuel McClure, Peter Hendri[c]ks.   [KM]
    Samuel McClure & Jane Hendricks, 20 Feb. 1814.   [JA]
    Samuel McClune [sic] & Jane Hendricks, 25 Oct. 1814.   [S1]

McCLURE, Samuel, & Elizabeth POWER, bond 27 Feb. 1839;
    bdsm: James Mitchell.   [AB]

McCLURE, Thomas, & Virlinda McILHENNY, bond 5 Jan. 1815;
    bdsm: John Duckworth; bride "heretofore married."   [KM]
    Thomas McClure & Villinda McIlhenny, 5 Jan. 1815.   [JA]
    Thomas McClune [sic] & Villinda Molhenny, 5 June 1815.   [S1]

McCLURE, Wm., & Martha SPRATT, bond 22 Jan. 1848;
    bdsm: Solmon Spratt.   [AB]

McCOLLOUGH, Peter, & Levina MERIS, bond 10 Nov. 1811;
    bdsm: Jas. Johnson.   [AB]
    Peter McCollough & Levina MENIS or Meris, 17 July 1811. [JA,S1]

McCORMICK, Joseph, & Louisana ALLEN, bond 17 Sept. 1834;
    f/b: George Allen; bdsm: Reuben McCormick.   [AB]
    Joseph M. McCORMAC & Louisa Allen, 18 Sept. 1834. (SMc) [B2]

McCORMICK, Wm., & Emily PURGAM, bond 25 Aug. 1847;
    bdsm: Daniel Allen.   [AB]
    William McCormick & Emily ?PURGRON, 26 Aug. 1847. (RWM) [B2]

McCOSLIN or McCaslin, James, & Angeline WRIGHT, 23 July 1846. (SKc) [B2]

McCUE, John, & Nancy KENDLE, bond 12 Nov. 1836;
    f/b & bdsm: Sandford Kendle.   [AB]

McCULLON, Jonathan, & Elizabeth STATON, bond 19 Oct. 1815;
    bdsm: Reuben Staton.   [AB]

McCULLOUGH, John, & Salley STATEN, bond 11 June 1813;
    f/b: Thomas Staton; bdsm: John McCullough, Reuben Staton. [KM]
    John McCULLER & Sally STATEN, 17 June 1813.   [JA,S1]

McCULLY, Samuel, & Elizabeth BASHFORD, bond 21 Sept. 1840;
    f/b: John Bashford; bdsm: Elijah Bailey.   [AB]
    Samuel McCULLEY & Elizabeth BASFORD, 22 Sept. 1840. (PCy) [B2]

McDANAL, Jeremiah, & Elizabeth FAWSIT, 23 July 1818.   [S1]

McDANIEL, John, & Matilda CAWOOD, bond 10 Jan. 1822;

bdsm: Thomas Caywood. [AB]

   John McDaniel & Matilda CAYWOOD, 27 Jan. 1822. [S1]

McDANIEL, Wm., & Angeline McCLANE, 8 Jan. 1852. (ISh) [B2]

McDONALD, Daniel, & Elizabeth POWER, 24 Oct. 1817. [JA]

   Daniel McDANIEL & Elizabeth Power [S1]

McDONALD, Henry, & Anna HOPKINS, bond 23 Apr. 1819;

   bdsm: Francis Hopkins. [AB]

   Henry McDonald & Ann Hopkins, 29 Apr. 1819 [S1]

McDONALD, James, & Polly TRAYLOR, bond 11 March 1833;

   bdsm: Thos. Iles. [AB]

   James McDONNOLD & Polly Traylor, March 1833. (TIs) [B2]

McDONALD, John, & Elizabeth INS, bond 8 Oct. 1822;

   bdsm: Wm. Sudduth. [AB]

   John E. McDonald & Elizabeth ILES, 8 Oct. 1822. [S1]

McFARLAN, Fleix [Felix?], & Nancy ?GILTKENS, bond 28 Feb. 1849;

   bdsm: Wm. Baird. [AB]

McFARLAND, Robert, & Elizabeth MARTIN, bond 16 Jan. 1823;

   bdsm: John Nesbitt. [AB]

   Robert McFARLING & Elizabeth NEASBET, 23 Jan. 1823. [S1]

[McFERRAN] Phennin, Thomas, & Lucinda HENDRIX, bond 1 March 1831;

   bdsm [f/b]: Peter Hendrix. [AB]

   Thomas McPhercen / McPhurson & Lucinda Hendrix, 3 March 1831. (MGs) [B2]

McGAHY, John C., & Polly BOYD, bond 31 Jan. 1822;

   m/b: Dorcus Boyd; bdsm: Wm. Boyd. [AB]

   John McGaln & Dolly Boyd [sic], 3 Feb. 1822. [S1]

McGINNIS, Francis, & Jane COFER, bond 31 Dec. 1822;

   f/b: Reuben Cofer; bdsm: Wm. McGinnis. [AB]

McGINNIS, Wm., & Jane BROWN, bond 25 Oct. 1819;

   bdsm: Reuben Cassity. [AB]

   William McGRIMES & Jane Brown, 29 Oct. 1819. [S1]

McILVAIN, Wm., & Elizabeth MOCKBEE, bond 1 Sept. 1824;

   bdsm: Stephen Mockbee. [AB]

   William McIlvain & Elizabeth Mockbee, 1 Sept. 1824. [S1]

McINTIRE, D. W., & Elizabeth SNEDEGAR, 30 July 1851. (BBv) [B2]

McINTIRE, James, & Rachel OACLY, bond 2 Dec. 1822;

   bdsm: Prior Oacly. [AB]

   James McINTOSH & Rachel ARSEBY, 4 Dec. 1822. [S1]

McINTOSH, Frederick, & Rebecca HELPHINSTINE, bond 20 March 1820;

   f/b & bdsm: John Helphinstine. [AB]

   Frederick McINTUSH & Rebekah McCLIHRUSINA[?], 24 March 1820. [S1]

McINTOSH, More, & Polly EVAN, bond 30 Aug. 1822;
    f/b: James Even; bdsm: Joshua Price.   [AB]
McKEE, James, & Polly McQUIDDY, bond 21 Sept. 1813;
    bdsm: Jas. McKee, Archibald Mitchell.   [AB]
    James McKee & Polly McQUADY, 1813. (LTu)   [KM]
[McKEE] Kee, John, & Caroline SWINEY, bond 12 Sept. 1848;
    f/b: Miles Swiney; bdsm: F. M. Webster.   [AB]
    John McKEE & Caroline M. SWINNY, 13 Sept. 1848. (EAD)   [B2]
McKEE, Robert, & Julia Ann SHARP or Sharpe, 13 Nov. 1850. (LGH)   [B2]
McKINNEY, Andrew, & Eliza RICE, 26 Jan. 1850. (SKc)   [B2]
McKINNEY, Charles, & Elizabeth JACKSON, bond 13 Sept. 1813;
    bdsm: Chas. McKinney, Geo. G. Jackson.   [AB]
McKINNIN, Solomon, & Ganter BROMER or Bramer, bond 19 Feb. 1825;
    bdsm: Robert Bromer.   [AB]
[McKINNY, Joseph?] Carter, Joseph, & Virginia CARTER, bond 27 July 1819;
    bdsm: Joseph Carter.   [AB]
    Joseph McKINNY & Virginia Carter, 29 July 1819.   [S1]
McLANE, Charles, & Caufoot [Comfort?] SEXTON, bond 24 May 1820;
    bdsm: John Sexton.   [AB]
    Charles McCANE & Counfort Sexton, 26 May 1820.   [S1]
McLANE, John, & Micha JACKSON, bond 10 Jan. 1849;
    bdsm: Wm. Spencer.   [AB]
    John McLAINE & Michal Jackson, 11 Jan. 1849. (WRg)   [B2]
McLAUGHLIN, James, & Luann TRAYLOR, 13 Apr. 1851. (WRg)   [B2]
[McLAUGHLIN?] Laughlin, Wm., & Eleanor PLEVIS, bond 28 July 1820;
    bdsm: Thos. Pervis.   [AB]
    William McLOCKLAN & Ellendor PERVIS, 30 July 1820.   [S1]
McMANNIS, Wm. P., & Sarah ATCHISON, bond 19 Feb. 1824;
    bdsm: Jesse Atchison.   [AB]
McNAB, Abner, & Esther CASSITY, bond 1 Aug. 1814;
    f/b: Stephen Cassity; bdsm: Abner McNab, Stephen Cassity.   [AB]
    Abner McNab & Hester Cassity, 7 Aug. 1814.   [JA,S1]
McNAB, Andrews, & Judith CROUCH, bond 9 Sept. 1839;
    f/b: Wm. Crouch; bdsm: Cuthbert Crouch.   [AB]
McNAB, Hicklin, & Rebecca McDONALD, bond 16 Dec. 1820;
    bdsm: John McNab.   [AB]
    Thiklin McNab & Rebecca McDonald, 28 Dec. 1821.   [S1]
McNAB, John C., & Jane CLUBB, bond 15 Aug. 1825;
    f/g: John McNab; bdsm: Francis Hopkins.   [AB]

John C. McNabb & Jane Clubb, 16 Aug. 1825. (JPH)   [TP,RS]
[McNARY] Nany?, Samuel, & Elizabeth C. WALKER, bond 29 Oct. 1833;
   bdsm: Joseph Walker.   [AB]
   Samuel McNARY & Elizabeth Walker, 31 Oct. 1833. (SGW)   [B2]
McNEILL, Alexander, & Minerva ILES, 30 Jan. 1844. (SAR)   [B2]
McPHERSON, Jesse, & Nancy CANNON, bond 27 Dec. 1824;
   bdsm: Stephen McPherson.   [AB]
   Jessee McPherson & Nancy Cannon, 6 Aug. 1825.   [S1]
McPHERSON, Stephen, & Nancy McNABB, bond 7 Jan. 1812;
   f/b: S. McNabb; bdsm: Stephen McNabb, Andrew McNabb. [AB]
McVEY, James, & Susan SHROUT, bond 29 July 1815;
   bdsm: John Sett.   [AB]
   James McVey & Susan (Sarah?) SROUTT or Srautt, 29 July 1815. [JA,S1]
MEEKS, Wm., & Lucinda PORTER, bond 13 Aug. 1840;
   f/b & bdsm: Thomas Porter.   [AB]
MENIFEE, Alven, & Jane Nelley RICHARDS, bond 2 Apr. 1828;
   f/b: Robert Richard; bdsm: Robert Richards, Geo. Landon [Lansdown?]. [AB]
MERRIDITH, Thomas, & Eliza ANDERSON, bond 16 July 1849;
   bdsm: Sanford Anderson.   [AB]
METEER, James, & Elizabeth HILL, 16 July 1835. (MGs)   [B2]
MILLER, Alfred, & Adelin FREELAND, bond 11 Feb. 1845;
   bdsm: Robt. Freeland.   [AB]
   Alfred L. Miller & Adaline PREELAND, 13 Feb. 1845. (RFC) [B2]
MILLER, Broaddham, & Rebecca KEATH, bond 16 Jan. 1823;
   f/b: Couth Keath; bdsm: James Miller.   [AB]
   Bratchshaw Miller & Rebecca HEATH, 26 Jan. 1823.   [S1]
MILLER, George, & Elizabeth SWINEY, bond 10 March 1829;
   bdsm: Joshua Barnes.   [AB]
   George Miller & Elizabeth SWINNEY, 12 March 1829. (DWh) [B2]
MILLER, George E., & Henrietta BARNES, 20 Jan. 1852. (SPL)   [B2]
MILLER, James, & Seby HANKS, bond 23 Feb. 1816;
   bdsm: David Bradshaw, J. Miller.   [AB]
   James Miller & Siby Hanks, 23 Feb. 1816.   [S1]
   James MILLY & Sebey Hanks   [JA]
MILLER, John, & Missmi LEE, bond 5 June 1849;
   bdsm: C. Whitington.   [AB]
   John Miller & Missouri Lee or SEE, 5 June 1849. (EJo) [B2]
MILLER, Robert A., & Julia Ann GARRETT, bond 8 March 1847;
   bdsm: Flemming Garret.   [AB]

MILLER, Thomas, & Polly WELCH, 22 March 1814;
    m/b: Martha Welch; bdsm: Thos. Miller, Jos. Lancaster. [AB]
    Thomas Miller & Polly Welch, 22 March 1814. [JA,S1]
MILLER, Wm., & Cassandrew ROSS, bond 28 Sept. 1813;
    bdsm: Wm. Miller, Archibald Kincaid. [AB]
    William Miller & Casandra Ross, 30 Sept. 1813. (JPH) [TP,RS]
MILLER, Wm., & Rachel BUTLER, bond 26 Dec. 1820;
    f/b & bdsm: Nathan Butler. [AB]
    William Miller & Rachael Butler, 28 Dec. 1821. [S1]
MILROY, James, & Betsy PENIX, bond 13 July 1811;
    f/b: John Penix; bdsm: James Milroy, Thos. Triplett. [AB]
MINEAR, Solomon, & Almira LITRO, 5 Nov. 1826. (JGW) [B2]
MINEAR, Wm., & Lidia HIMER, bond 9 June 1834. [AB]
MINNEAR, John, & Jerusha McCARTY, bond 23 July 1811;
    bdsm: John Mannear, John McCarty. [AB]
    John MINNER & Jerusha McCarty, 15 Apr. 1811. [JA,S1]
MIRCKLY, Diego Wall, & Polly Ann PICKLEHEJIMER, bond 21 Jan. 1839;
    bdsm: Travis Daniel. [AB]
    Diego ?Watt MERKLY & Polly Ann PICKLEHIMER, 21 Jan. 1839. (MFM) [B2]
MITCHEL, James, & Anah GREEN, bond 15 Oct. 1811;
    f/g: Alex Mitchell; bdsm: James Mitchell. [AB]
    James MITCHELL & Lara Green, 17 Sept. 1811. [S1]
    James MICHEL & Ona Green [JA]
MITCHEL, John F., & Ann E. STEEL, 22 Oct. 1850. (SJn) [B2]
MITCHEL, Samuel, & Nancy FLOROUGH, bond 18 Apr. 1811;
    bdsm: Samuel Mitchell, Benj. Heaton. [AB]
    Samuel MITCHELL & Nancy FLORAH, 19 Apr. 1811. [JA,S1]
MITCHEL, Wesley, & Lavina McKEE, bond 14 Apr. 1846;
    bdsm: James Mitchel. [AB]
    W. MITCHELL & L. MOLL, 14 Apr. 1846. [B2]
MITCHELL, Henry, & Elizabeth McCLAIN, bond 21 Jan. 1847;
    f/b: Solman McClain; bdsm: Thos. Gudgell. [AB]
[MITCHELL?] Michel, Hiram, & Lorency[?] BALEY, 5 Nov. 1826. (ALy) [B2]
MITCHELL, Hiram, & Elizabeth FLETCHER, bond 3 Jan. 1846;
    m/g: Jane Mitchell; f/b: Feilding Fletcher; bdsm: James Jackson. [AB]
    H. Mitchell & E. Fletcher, 3 Jan. 1846. (SHo) [B2]
MITCHELL, James, & Rosannah LADDERS, bond 16 Dec. 1822;
    bdsm: Henry Ladders. [AB]
    James Mitchell & Rosanna SODERS, 17 Dec. 1822. [S1]
MITCHELL, James, & Nancy STONE, bond 30 July 1839;

bdsm: Robt. Stone. [AB]
MITCHELL, James, & Mary STEVENSON, bond 13 Apr. 1846;
   bdsm: Wesley Mitchel. [AB]
   Jos. Mitchell & M. ?STUNSON, 14 Apr. 1846. (SHo) [B2]
MITCHELL, ?Loue, & Eliza BAIRD, bond 3 Aug. 1846;
   bdsm: Hardon Baird. [AB]
   Samuel MITCHAL & Elizabeth ?BORD, 6 Aug. 1846. (SHo) [B2]
MITCHELL, Orville, & Mahala MYERS, bond 12 Aug. 1822;
   f/g: Matthew Mitchell; bdsm: Henry Myers. [AB]
   Oville Mitchell & Mahaly MIVES, 15 Aug. 1822. [S1]
MITCHELL, Samuel, & Rebecca GUDGELL, bond 15 Nov. 1824;
   bdsm: Joseph Gudgell. [AB]
   Samuel W. Mitchell & Rebeccah Gudgell, 16 Nov. 1824. [S1]
MITCHELL, Samuel, & Delilo HAVERMILL, bond 5 Nov. 1833;
   bdsm: James McClain. [AB]
   Samuel MICHEL & Dilila HOVERMILL, 6 Nov. 1833. (MGs) [B2]
[MITCHELL] Mitchial, Samuel, & Elizabeth RUNNELS, 24 March 1844. (SKc) [B2]
MITCHELL, Samuel, & Sally RUMMELLE, bond 19 May 1845;
   bdsm: James McClain. [AB]
   Samuel MITCHEL & Susanna RUNNELS, 20 May 1845. (WRg) [B2]
MITCHELL, Thomas, & Drusilla McCORD, bond 21 May 1825;
   bdsm: Samuel Mitchell. [AB]
MITCHELL, W., & L. WELLS?, 14 Apr. 1846. (SHo) [B2]
MITCHELL, Warren G., & Mary A. COOK, 21 Dec. 1843. (SMc) [B2]
MITCHELL, Wm., & Mary Ann CLINES, bond 16 Feb. 1848;
   bdsm: Thomas Sap. [AB]
   Wm. Mitchell & Ma(r)y ann ?CLINE, 22 Feb. 1848. (SHo) [B2]
[MITCHELL?] Michel, William, & Colgate STEEL, 26 Aug. 1851. (SRg?) [B2]
MITT, Cyrus, & Patsy BURBRIDGE, 22 Sept. 1818. [S1]
MOFFITT, James, & Nancy RATLIFF, bond 10 Apr. 1811;
   bdsm: Jas. Moffitt, Cal(e)b Ratliff. [AB]
   James MOFFETT & Nancy Ratliff, 11 Apr. 1811. [JA,S1]
MOFFITT, Willis, & Caroline STONE, bond 3 Jan. 1825;
   bdsm: Robert Stone. [AB]
MOLES, John, & Anna OCKERMAN, bond 6 Nov. 1816;
   bdsm: Daniel Ockerman. [AB]
   John MALER & Ann Ockerman, 7 Nov. 1816. [JA]
   John Moles & Anna Ockerman [S1]
MONTGOMERY, James, & Julia MANIER, bond 10 Apr. 1827;

f/b: John Manier; bdsm: John Minnear. [AB]

James Montgomery & Julia MINEAR, 17 Apr. 1827. (JGW) [B2]

MOOR, Benjamin, & Jane ALEXANDER, bond 23 Dec. 1822;

f/b: Hugh Alexander; bdsm: Wm. Alexander. [AB]

Benjamin MOORE & Jane Alexander, 24 Jan. 1823. [S1]

MOOR, James, & Mary C. DEAN, bond 17 Dec. 1811;

bdsm: James Moor, Daniel Dean. [AB]

James Moor & Mary C. Dean, 19 Dec. 1811. (JPH) [TP,RS]

MOOR, James, & Sarah Ann CRAVER, bond 5 May 1832;

bdsm: Geo. Craver. [AB]

James Moor & Sarahann Craver, 6 May 1832. (SJn) [B2]

MOOR, James K., & Louisana BOYD, bond 22 Jan. 1837;

f/b: Spencer Boyd; bdsm: D. B. Boyd. [AB]

MOOR, Jonathan, & Susanna SMITH, bond 14 June 1819;

bdsm: Michael Smith. [AB]

Jonathan MOORE & Suzanna Smith, 17 June 1819. [S1]

MOOR, Milton B., & Margarett DUTY, 17 Oct. 1844. (ODB) [B2]

MOOR, Thomas, & Sally MILLER, bond 27 Aug. 1816;

bdsm: Henry Moore. [AB]

Thos. (S.?) MOORE & Sally Miller, 29 Aug. 1816. [JA,S1]

MOORE or Moor, Harlan, & Mary Ann STONE, bond 29 Apr. 1834;

bdsm: Charles Stone. [AB]

Harland MOOR & Mary Ann Stone, 1 May 1834. (SJn) [B2]

MOORE, Hiram, & Polly McLAUGHTIN, bond 26 Jan. 1832;

bdsm: Sinnett Young, Jr. [AB]

MOORE, James, & Mary CRONER, bond 11 Nov. 1839;

bdsm: James Sudduth. [AB]

MOORE, James W., & Mary Virginia LANE, bond 21 Nov. 1846;

bdsm: W. M. Sudduth. [AB]

MOORE, John, & Emily BUTLER, bond 4 Dec. 1816;

f/b & bdsm: Wm. Butler. [AB]

John Moore & Emily Butler, 26 Dec. 1816. [S1]

MOORE, John, & Mary HOPKINS, bond 12 Feb. 1849;

bdsm: Wm. Moore. [AB]

MOORE, John F., & Mahala HUNT, bond 5 Feb. 1839;

f/b: Henry Hunt; bdsm: Thos. Spencer. [AB]

John F. Moore & Mahala HART, 10 Feb. 1839. (SMc) [B2]

MOORE, Lloyd, & Margaritte STEEL, bond 27 Feb. 1846;

bdsm: Jacob Steel. [AB]

MOORE, Presley, & Rhody ENGLISH, bond 10 Dec. 1822;

bdsm: John Duckworth. [AB]

 Presley Moore or MORE & Rhoda English, 12 Dec. 1822. [S1]

MOORE, Reuben P., & Polly COFER, bond 2 May 1820;

 bdsm: Wm. Martin. [AB]

 Rubin P. Moore & Polly COFFER, 4 May 1820. [S1]

MOORE, Silas, & Pauline COLLINS, bond 8 March 1830;

 f/g: Harlan or Harlon Moore; f/b: Josiah Collins; bdsm: Jeremiah Bromigan. [AB]

 Silas Moore & Pailina Collins, 9 March 1830. (SJn) [B2]

MOORE, Solomon, & Peggy SMITH, bond 4 Sept. 1820;

 bdsm: Michael Smith. [AB]

 Solomon Moore & Peggy Smith, 7 Sept. 1820. [S1]

MOORE, Thomas, & Lorenzo MOORE, bond 19 Jan. 1819;

 bdsm: Jacob Moore. [AB]

 Thomas MOOR & Louiwzo MOOR, 21 Jan. 1819. [S1]

MOORE, Thomas, & Sarah HINKLE, bond 14 Jan. 1848;

 bdsm: Manly Hardin. [AB]

 Thomas MOOR or Moore & Sary Hinkle, 16 Jan. 1848. (PHn) [B2]

MOORE, Valna, & Matilda SMITH, bond 30 Aug. 1839;

 f/g: Elisha Moore; bdsm: Solmon Blevin. [AB]

 Vonly Moore & Matilda Smith, 26 May 1839. (WSd) [B2]

MOORE, William, & Polly SMITH, 30 Dec. 1818. [S1]

MOORE, Wm. ?B., & Eliza Jane DOWNS, bond 29 May 1845;

 bdsm: Wm. Downs. [AB]

 William G. Moore & Eliza Jane Downs, 1 June 1845. (JSt) [B2]

MOORES, Rollings, & Elizabeth Martha DOGGETT, 14 Jan. 1851. (SJn) [B2]

MORE, George, & Elizabeth COLLINS, bond 15 March 1824;

 f/b: Josiah Collins; bdsm: Will Collins. [AB]

 George MOORE & Elizabeth Collins, 17 March 1824. [S1]

MORE, Noah, & Dorothy E. CRONOR, bond 17 Dec. 1842;

 bdsm: John Maly. [AB]

MORE, Reuben, & Emily THOMPSON, bond 1 Oct. 1822;

 bdsm: Solomon Steel. [AB]

 Reuben MOORE & Emily Thompson, 3 Oct. 1822. [S1]

MORELAND, Amos D., & Sarah ATHY, bond 12 Jan. 1839;

 bdsm: James Martin. [AB]

 Amos D. Moreland & Sarah Athy, 12 Jan. 1839. (JVc) [B2]

MORELAND, Fidder, & Nancy GRAHAM, 6 Aug. 1825. [S1]

MORELAND, John, & Malvina ENGLAND, bond 20 Apr. 1832;

 bdsm: David England. [AB]

John Moreland & Melvina England, 23 Apr. 1832. (SJn) [B2]

MORELAND, Samuel, & Martha CLAYTON, bond 9 March 1832;
bdsm: Charles Bartley. [AB]

Samuel Moreland & Patsy CLATON, 10 March 1833. (SJn) [B2]

MORELAND or Moorliand, Zenes, & Matilda ATHE, 28 Apr. 1839. (SRg) [B2]

MORGAN, Ambrose D., & Eliza BROWN, bond 22 Feb. 1836;
bdsm: Richard D. Brown. [AB]

MORGAN, James, & Elizabeth STEWART, bond 21 Jan. 1842;
bdsm: James Emmons. [AB]

James Morgan & Elizabeth Stewart, 22 Jan. 1842. (TMy) [B2]

MORGAN, Samuel, & Sarah CLAYTON, bond 10 Feb. 1830;
f/g: J. Morgan; f/b: Wm. B. Clayton; bdsm: Wm. Bailey. [AB]

Samuel Morgan & Sarah Clayton, 12 Feb. 1830. (JHH) [B2]

MORGAN, William, & Sarah HANNAHS, 12 Oct. 1844. (WRg) [B2]

MORGAN, Zachariaz, & Pevlina? HAZELRIGG, bond 23 March 1821;
f/b: Eli Hazelrigg; bdsm: James G. Hazelrigg. [AB]

Zachariah Morgan & Perlina Hazlerigg, 25 March 1821. [S1]

MORRIS, Joseph, & Susy MORRIS, bond 29 Nov. 1811;
bdsm: Joseph Morris, Geo. Kincaid. [AB]

MORRIS, Wm., & Mary SWITZER, bond 2 May 1846;
f/g & bdsm: Daniel Morris. [AB]

William Morris & Mary SWISHER, 10 Apr. 1846. (SKc) [B2]

MORRIS, Wm. D., & Clarinda BROWN, bond 8 Sept. 1812;
f/b: Mathew Brown. [AB]

Wm. D. Morris & Clarinda Brown, 9 Sept. 1812. [JA]

William Morris & Clanindia Brown [S1]

MOSS, William H. ?T., & Mary SNELLING, 17 July 1851. (SJn) [B2]

MOTT?, Almarian, & Charlotte GREGORY, bond 27 Jan. 1842;
bdsm: John Gregory. [AB]

MULLEN, James, & Elizabeth DONATHAN, bond 15 June 1836;
bdsm: Thos. Donathan. [AB]

James MULLIN & Elizabeth Donathan, 19 June 1836. (SJk) [B2]

MUNAHOLN, Wm., & Sarah HOWARD, bond 26 Dec. 1838;
bdsm: Joseph Howard. [AB]

William S. MUNHOLN & Sarah Howard, 26 Dec. 1838. (DST) [B2]

MUNHOLLEN or Menallen?, Wm. L., & Sarah CRIEGHTEN, bond 20 Oct. 1846;
bdsm: James Howard. [AB]

Wm. S. MULHOLIN & Sarah CRAYCRAFT, 21 Oct. 1846. (RFC) [B2]

MUNNS, Wm., & Jane DAVIS, bond 30 July 1823;
bdsm: Jesse Davis. [AB]

William MORIS & Jane Davis, 30 July 1823.   [S1]
MURFREY, Morrow, & Louisa SAILOR, 15 Nov. 1839. (SJk)   [B2]
[MURPHY?] Humphrey, Peter, & Caroline BECKNER, bond 8 Oct. 1849;
   f/b & bdsm: Peter Beckner.   [AB]
   Peter MURPHY & Caroline Beckner, 11 Oct. 1849. (TDL)   [B2]
MUSICK, Josiah, & Sally PRATER, bond 3 March 1819;
   bdsm: Josiah Musick, Wm. Prater.   [AB]
   Josiah Musick & Sally Prater, 4 March 1819.   [S1]
MYERS, Anderson, & Alcy PATRICK, bond 26 Sept. 1837;
   bdsm: Sam Myers.   [AB]
MYERS, Christopher, & Elizabeth ALFREY (Alphery?), bond 18 Apr. 1814;
   f/b: John Alfrey; bdsm: Christopher Myers, Henry Myers.   [KM]
   Chrisopher MYNES or Myres & Elizabeth Alfrey, 21 Apr. 1814.   [JA]
   Christopher Myers & Elizabeth Alfrey, 21 Apr. 1813.   [S1]
MYERS, George, & Peggy KERR, bond 20 Aug. 1832;
   f/b: Samuel Kerr; bdsm: John Kerr.   [AB]
MYERS, Hiram, & Debila [Delila] NAILOR, bond 12 March 1827;
   bdsm: Wm. Vice.   [AB]
   Hiram Myers & Delila BUTLER, 12 March 1827.   [B2]
MYERS, James, & Elizabeth ELLINGTON, 10 Nov. 1844. (JSt)   [B2]
MYERS, Jamison, & Margaret PATRICK, bond 25 Jan. 1837;
   f/g: Christopher Myers; bdsm: Fielding Alfrey.   [AB]
   Jamerson MYRES & Margaret PATTERICK, 26 Jan. 1837. (JGW)   [B2]
MYERS, John, & Emily NICKOLS, bond 15 Feb. 1842;
   bdsm: James R. Moxley.   [AB]
   John MYRES & Emily NICHOLAS, 21 March 1842. (BCs)   [B2]
MYERS, Jonathan, & Margaret SUDDUTH, bond 20 Dec. 1837;
   bdsm: Wm. Sudduth.   [AB]
   Jonathan Myers & Margaret Sudduth, 21 Dec. 1837. (PHn)   [B2]
MYERS, Joseph, & Rachel ALFREY, bond 2 Oct. 1816;
   bdsm: Thos. Williams.   [AB]
   Joseph MYNES or Myres & Rachel Alfrey, 21 Oct. 1816.   [JA]
   Joseph MYNER & Rachel Alfrey   [S1]
MYERS, Joseph, & Elizibeth HOVERMILL, 24 Oct. 1844. (RFC)   [B2]
MYERS or Mesers, Marcus, & Susan F. BURNS, 14 Feb. 1850. (RFC)   [B2]
MYERS, Philip, & Elizabeth RICHARD, bond 13 Oct. 1823;
   bdsm: Wm. Turley.   [AB]
   Philip MYAS & Elizabeth RICHARDS, 18 Oct. 1823.   [S1]
MYERS, Samuel, & Sarah Ann JOHNSTON, 20 Dec. 1837. (SJk)   [B2]

MYERS, Samuel C., & Polly BROWN, bond 8 Dec. 1821;
    bdsm: Wm. Brown. [AB]
    Samuel Myers & Polly Brown, 9 Dec. 1821. [S1]
MYHIER, David, & Copy BROWN, bond 26 June 1847;
    bdsm: Wm. Walton. [AB]
MYNER, Jacob, & Lucy CORBIN, 19 Oct. 1817. [JA,S1]
MYRES, Lewis, & Nancy Ann RALLS or Rolls, bond 1 Sept. 1842;
    bdsm: George W. Ralls or Rolls. [AB]
    Lewis Myres & Nancy ann ROLLS, 4 Aug. 1842. (SJn) [B2]
NASH, Thomas B., & Elizabeth MAURY, bond 20 Aug. 1840;
    bdsm: Matthew Maury. [AB]
NASSELL, Andrew, & Nancy CRAYCRAFT, bond 5 Feb. 1815;
    bdsm: Wm. Craycraft. [AB]
NAYLOR, George T., & Molly Ann JONES, bond 28 Oct. 1830;
    m/b: Susen Jones; bdsm: Alpheus Butler. [AB]
    George T. Naylor & Mollyann Jones, 28 Oct. 1830. (ALy) [B2]
NA[Y]LOR, Ignatus, & Mary ARROSMITH, bond 1 Jan. 1834;
    bdsm: Wm. Arrosmith. [AB]
NAYLOR, Paul, & Polley BARBER, 27 Oct. 1836. (EBr) [B2]
NEAL, George, & Rebecca SIX, bond 24 Sept. 1828;
    bdsm: Phiber Six. [AB]
NEAL, Wm., & Elizabeth PETTIT, bond 21 Sept. 1846;
    bdsm: Ewell Sylcox. [AB]
    William Neal & Elizabeth PETIT, 22 Sept. 1846. (WRg) [B2]
NELSON, James, & Nancy Ann PEARCE, bond 25 Dec. 1827;
    bdsm: Charles Pearce. [AB]
    James Nelson & Nancy ann PERCE, 20 Dec. 1837. (PHn) [B2]
NELSON, James, & Elvira I. HAWKINS, bond 6 Feb. 1840. [AB]
NELSON, John, & Nancey George GOODLOE, bond 11 March 1829;
    bdsm: Thos. McIntosh. [AB]
NESBET, Deean, & Jane NESBET, 13 Jan. 1846. (PHn) [B2]
NESBET, Hugh, & Mouier[?] McOLISTER, 19 May 1818. [S1]
NESTAR, Andrew, & Anna NARBRY, bond 6 July 1829;
    bdsm: Eliser Bradley. [AB]
NEWLAND, Wm. B., & Autimesa ?LEVENCY [Sorency], bond 25 Apr. 1823;
    f/b: David ?Lovevey; bdsm: John Lovency. [AB]
    William B. Newland & Artimisia Lorvency [sic], 1 May 1823. [S1]
NEWMAN, David, & Louissiana GRAY, bond 3 March 1829;
    bdsm: Isaac Grey. [AB]

David Newman & Louisa ana Gray, 3 March 1829. (DWh)   [B2]

NEWTON, Andrew, & Jane BASHAW, 3 Apr. 1826. (AMx)   [B2]

NICHERSON, Wm., & Addaline NOAH [Noe?], bond 25 March 1839 (29?);
    f/b: George Noah; bdsm: David Cowan.   [AB]

    William VIOSON? & Adelinah Noah, 26 March 1829. (PHn)   [B2]

NICHOLAS or Nickell, George, & Febe SORRELL, Sept. 1849.   [AB]

[NICHOLL?] Nichare?, James M., & Hannah BURCH, bond 5 Apr. 1825;
    bdsm: David Burch.   [AB]

    James H. NICHOLL & Hanah Burch, 14 Apr. 1825.   [S1]

NIELSON, Jesse, & Cintha COPHER, bond 18 Apr. 1827;
    bdsm: Reuben Copher.   [AB]

NOLAND, Richard, & Milinda HARPER, bond 12 Aug. 1833;
    bdsm: John Harper.   [AB]

    Richard NOLOND & Melinda Harper, 1833. (MGs)   [B2]

NORMAN, Thomas, & Sarah DAVIS, bond 2 Jan. 1823;
    bdsm: Ignatius Davis.   [AB]

    Thomas Norman & Sarah Davis, 5 Jan. 1823.   [S1]

NORRIS, David, & Mariah SPENCER, bond 9 June 1820;
    bdsm: John Norris.   [AB]

    David Norris & Mevier Spencer, 11 June 1820.   [S1]

NORRIS, David, & Rachel McCLAIN, bond 24 Feb. 1829;
    bdsm: James McClain.   [AB]

NOR(R)IS, James, & Sal(l)y Jane ROBISON, 10 July 1851. (BBv)   [B2]

NORRIS, John, & Anne GOODPASTURE, bond 8 May 1821;
    bdsm: Neale Goodpasture.   [AB]

    William Norris & Ann GOODPASTER, 8 May 1821.   [S1]

NORRIS, John, & Patsy RICHARDS, bond 12 Jan. 1823;
    bdsm: David Norris.   [AB]

    John Norris & Patsy Richards, 12 Jan. 1823.   [S1]

NORRIS, John, & Hannah McCARTY, bond 30 Dec. 1829;
    bdsm: James Sudduth.   [AB]

    John Norris & Hannah McCarty or McCARTA, 3 Dec. 1829. (SJk)   [B2]

NORRIS, John W., & Ann M. PAYNE, bond 29 Feb. 1836;
    bdsm: Walker Brown.   [AB]

NORRIS, Richard, & Nancy KARRICK, bond 3 Jan. 1829;
    bdsm: Hugh Karrick.   [AB]

    Ric'd. Norris & Nancy Karrick, 11 Jan. 1829. (CBw)   [B2]

NORTH, Layfeyette, & Katherine ROBERSON, 6 Feb. 1851. (BBv)   [B2]

NORTH, Myson, & Julia WHALEY, bond 2 June 1842;
    bdsm: Wm. Sudduth;   [AB]

Myrun North & Julia Whaley, 2 June 1842. (RFC) [B2]

NORTON or Narton?, James, & Hetty McCULLOUGH, bond 22 March 1823;
  bdsm: Reuben Hughes. [AB]

OAKLEY, Anderson, & Maria OAKLEY, bond 28 Nov. 1833;
  f/b: E. Oakley; bdsm: Austin Oakley. [AB]
  Anderson Oakley & Mariah Oakley, 28 Nov. 1833. (JPk) [B2]

OAKLEY, Austin, & Eliza BOTTS, bond 12 Dec. 1831;
  bdsm: Ben Botts. [AB]

OAKLEY, Christopher, & Elizabeth GINTER, bond 20 June 1825;
  bdsm: Thos. Noselly. [AB]
  Christopher Oakley & Elizabeth Ginter, 27 June 1825. [S1]

OAKLEY, Edward, & Sarah BURCH, bond 4 July 1829;
  bdsm: John Burch. [AB]

OAKLEY, Gee, & Polly GOODPASTER, bond 1 Aug. 1827;
  bdsm: Joseph Goodpaster. [AB]
  George Oakley & Polly GOODPASTURE, 2 Aug. 1827. (JPk) [B2]

O(A)KLEY, James B., & Alis Ann CRAYCRAFT, 29 Aug. 1850. (JHe) [B2]

OAKLEY, Pleasant E., & Mary CRAYCRAFT, bond 27 March 1848;
  f/b: John Craycraft; bdsm: Andrew Suttell. [AB]

OAKLEY, Wm., & Elizabeth CASSITY, bond 19 Aug. 1826;
  bdsm: Madeson Cassity. [AB]

OALDHAM, Thompson B., & Nancy B. PHELPS, bond 11 Feb. 1843;
  bdsm: James Sudduth. [AB]
  Thomas B. OLDHAM & Nancy B. Phelps, 23 Feb. 1843. (JnSm) [B2]

OIRE, Tallent, & Nancy THOMPSON, 22 June 1833. (JPk) [B2]

ORNESBY, W. M., & Margaret A. TRUMBO, 4 July 1844. (DBk) [B2]

ORNSBY?, J. Henry, & Meromes? LOCKE, 22 Apr. 1852. (LGH) [B2]

OTIS, John, & Elizabeth SORRELL, bond 25 Jan. 1845;
  bdsm: Joseph Sorell. [AB]

OTIS, Jonathan, & Hannah FIGHMASTER or Highmaster, bond 5 Apr. 1820;
  bdsm: Frederick Fighmaster. [AB]
  Jonathan Otis & Hannah FIGHTMASTER, 6 Apr. 1820. [S1]

OTIS, Jonathan, & Jane TOMPSON, bond 26 Nov. 1832;
  bdsm: Austin Choat. [AB]
  Jonathan Otis & Jane THOMPSON, 26 Nov. 1832. (JPk) [B2]

OTIS, Wm., & Nancy WRIGHT, bond 9 March 1846;
  bdsm: F. R. Wright. [AB]
  William Otis & Nancy Wright, 13 March 1846. (SKc) [B2]

OWEN, James, & Carolinah? JONES, bond 6 Oct. 1845;

bdsm: Abraham Jones. [AB]

OWINGS, John, & Hetty PLATT, bond 1 Feb. 1814;

m/b: Ann Platt; bdsm: John Owings, Robert Fowler. [AB]

John Owings & Hetty or Hatty PLAT, 6 Feb. 1814. [JA,S1]

OWINGS, Reason G., & Mary KELSOE, 26 Nov. 1835. (DST) [B2]

OWINGS, Samuel, & Lucy COLEMAN, bond 8 Sept. 1827;

bdsm: Ben Graves. [AB]

Samuel Owings & Lucy Coleman, 11 Sept. 1827. (JnSm) [B2]

OWINGS, Thomas, & Mary BYRAM, bond 15 March 1816;

bdsm: Richard Owings. [AB]

Thomas C. Owings & Mary BRYAN, 17 March 1816. [JA]

C. Thomas OWINS & Mary BUGAM [S1]

OWSLEY, Edward, & Frances TRIBLE, bond 8 June 1842;

bdsm: Michel Staver or Stover. [AB]

Edward K. Owsley & Frances TRIBBLE, 8 June 1842. [S1]

PADGETT, Nicholas, & Cordelia M. ROSS, bond 27 Feb. 1840;

f/b: James Ross; bdsm: Samuel Ross. [AB]

Nicholas Padgett & Cordelia M. Ross, 30 July 1840. (PCy) [B2]

PAGET, Washington, & Harriet CALVERT, bond 10 Feb. 1834;

bdsm: Robb Paget. [AB]

Washing(ton) Paget & Harrit COLBERT, 18 Feb. 1834. (PCy) [B2]

PAINTER, Solomon, & Polly ADAMS, bond 20 Sept. 1814;

f/g: James Painter; bdsm: Henry Mannus. [AB]

Solomon Painter & Polly Adams, 22 Sept. 1814. [JA,S1]

PANTHER, William, & Rebeckah STAMPER, 26 March 1835. (PHn) [B2]

PARISH, Daniel, & Elizabeth LEACH, 16 July 1833. (JVc) [B2]

PARISH, David, & Elizabeth LOCKE, bond 15 July 1833;

f/b: Richard Locke; bdsm: Wm. Locke. [AB]

David Parish & Elizabeth LOCH, 16 July 1833. (JVc) [B2]

PARISH, Obie, & Sarah FRANKLIN, bond 21 Sept. 1812;

f/b: George Franklin; bdsm: Obie Parish, Geo. Knox. [AB]

Obe PARRIS & Sarah Franklin, 24 Sept. 1812. [JA,S1]

PARK, David, & Elizabeth CRAIG, 18 May 1847. (SKc) [B2]

PARKER, Joel, & Rhoday MAXEY, bond 14 March 1814;

m/g: Ethel Parker; bdsm: Joel Parker, Wm. Storm. [KM]

Joel Parker & Rhoday Maxey, 30 March 1814. [JA]

Joel Parker & Rhoday MANEY, 31 March 1814. [S1]

[PARKER?] Porter, John, & Julian ANDERSON, bond 3 Oct. 1827;

bdsm: Wm. Anderson. [AB]

John PARKER & Julian J. Anderson, 4 Oct. 1827. (JnSm) [B2]

PARKER, John, & Catharine SHULTZ, bond 19 Dec. 1832;
    bdsm: John Shultz. [AB]
    John Parker & Catharine Shultz, 21 Dec. 1832. (JPk) [B2]
PARKER, William, & Patsey LEMASTER, bond 8 Feb. 1820;
    bdsm: Joel Parker. [AB]
PARKS, George, & Abigail KINCAID, bond 6 Aug. 1821;
    bdsm: John Keithly. [AB]
    George Parks & Abigail Kincaid, 7 Aug. 1821. [S1]
PARKS, John, & Izabel FENWICK, bond 8 July 1825;
    bdsm: Thomas Barker. [AB]
PARNELL, Robert, & Leah MURPHY, 8 June 1815. [S1]
PARSONS, James, & Sally STATON, 11 March 1850. (WRg) [B2]
PARSONS, John, & Elizabeth CRAIG, bond 20 Aug. 1849;
    bdsm: James Parsons. [AB]
    John W. Parsons & Elizabeth Craig, 22 Aug. 1849. (RWM) [B2]
PARSONS, Nathan, & Nancy CRAIG, bond 30 March 1815;
    f/b: David Craig; bdsm: Nathan Parsons, David Craig. [AB]
PARSONS, Osburn, & Katharine DAY, bond 7 Aug. 1821;
    bdsm: Jeremiah Eaton. [AB]
    Asturn PARSON & Katharine Day, 12 Aug. 1821. [S1]
PARSONS, Thomas W., & Emily NELSON, 12 Oct. 1851. (BBv) [B2]
PARVER?, Joseph, & Rachel OWINGS, bond 2 Oct. 1838;
    bdsm: Jesse Crouch. [AB]
PATERSON, Robert, & Polly YARBROUGH, bond 15 March 1837;
    bdsm: B. F. Sudduth. [AB]
    R. PATTERSON & Saly Yarbrough, 16 March 1837. (TIs) [B2]
PATRICK, Enoch, & Polly MARTIN, bond 1 Oct. 1821;
    f/b: Wm. Martin; bdsm: Jeremiah Patrick. [AB]
    Enock Patrick & Polly Martin, 3 Oct. 1821. [S1]
PATRICK, Gabriel, & Kiziah WILLIAMS, 18 Sept. 1826. (WMt) [B2]
PATRICK, Herod, & Minerva LANCASTER, bond 4 Jan. 1836;
    bdsm: Thos. L. Lancaster. [AB]
    Herod Patrick & Menerva LANDCASTER, 5 Jan. 1836. (DST) [B2]
PATRICK, Noah, & Polly BAIRD, bond 1 March 1831;
    bdsm: Samuel Baird. [AB]
    Noah Patrick & Polly BEARD, 3 March 1827. (PHn) [B2]
PATTEN, Robert, & Nancy BYRAM, bond 6 Feb. 1832;
    m/b: Ruth Byram; bdsm: Thomas Bynam. [AB]
    Robert PATTON & Nancy Byram, 9 Feb. 1832. (SYG) [B2]

PATTON, Alexander D., & Jane MARSHAL, 26 Nov. 1851. (GGd)   [B2]
PAXTON, Archer, & Eliza YOUNG, bond 25 Aug. 1834;
  bdsm: Edwin Young.   [AB]
  Archer S. Paxton & Eliza Ann Young, 2 Sept. 1834. (JnSm)   [B2]
PAXTON, Wm., & Mary SHROPSHIRE, bond 17 Apr. 1832;
  bdsm: James Shropshire.   [AB]
  William Paxton & Mary SHROPSHER, 18 Apr. 1833. (JPk)   [B2]
PAYNE, Amos, & Malinda BUSBY, bond 24 Sept. 1834;
  bdsm: Isaac Busby.   [AB]
PAYNE, Edwin D., & Maria E. RYON, 27 Jan. 1846. (JnSm)   [B2]
PAYTON, Jacob, & Caty JOHNSON, bond 7 Aug. 1823;
  f/g: Wm. Payton; bdsm: Samuel Kerr.   [AB]
  Jacob PEYTON & Caty Johnson, 8 Aug. 1823.   [S1]
PEARCE, John, & Mary SAPP, bond 12 June 1848;
  bdsm: James Jackson.   [AB]
  John PIERCE & Ma(r)y SAP, 13 June 1849. (SHo)   [B2]
PENDLETON, Rice, & Eliza JONES, bond 24 Jan. 1848;
  f/g: W. Pendleton; bdsm: James Crouch.   [AB]
PERATT, Henry, & Malinda HAMILTON, bond 10 Feb. 1828;
  f/b: Wm. Hamilton; bdsm: Saul Hamilton.   [AB]
PERATT, James, & Sally SHULTZ, bond 26 March 1814;
  f/g: Valentine Peratt; m/b: Elizabeth Shultz; bdsm: James Peratt, John Shultz. [AB]
  James PERUTT & _____ Shultz, March 1814.   [JA]
  James PRATT & _____ SHUTLY, 1814.   [S1]
[PERATT?] Pirat, John, & Anna MAXEY, bond 8 Oct. 1814;
  guardian/b: Martin Chastain, Silas Chastain, Asa Maxey; bdsm: John Peratt, Asa
  Maxey, Joel Parker.   [KM]
  John PINATT & Anne MASEY (Maxey?), 9 Oct. 1814.   [JA]
  John PRATT & Anna MANEY.   [S1]
PERATT, John, & Deborah GOODPASTER, bond 27 June 1839;
  bdsm: John Goodpaster.   [AB]
  John Peratt or PEERATT & Deborah Goodpaster, 27 June 1839. (SMc)   [B2]
PERGRAM, John, & Minerva CROUCH, bond 17 Apr. 1828;
  f/b: John Crouch; bdsm: Isaac Crouch.   [AB]
  John Pergram & Minerva Crouch, 24 Apr. 1828. (PCy)   [B2]
PERGRAM, Robert, & Nancy WARNER, bond 27 Oct. 1848;
  bdsm: Jefferson Botts.   [AB]
  Robert C. PURGROM & Nancy Warner, 29 Oct. 1848. (RWM)   [B2]
PERKINS, Elijah, & Celia DENTON, bond 11 Aug. 1828;
  bdsm: Isa Hunt.   [AB]

PERKINS, Isaac, & Elizabeth MOORE, bond 26 Feb. 1814;
   f/b: Samuel Moore; bdsm: Isaac Perkins. [AB]
   Isaac Perkins & Elizabeth Moore, 1813. (LTu) [KM]
PERRY, Absolom, & Elizabeth SNELLING, bond 7 Jan. 1824;
   f/b: Ben Snelling; bdsm: Lewis Perry. [AB]
   Absalom Perry & Elizabeth Snelling, 8 Jan. 1824. [S1]
PERRY, Benjamin, & Polly SNELLING, bond 3 March 1834;
   bdsm: Ben Snelling. [AB]
PERRY, Ben F., & Eliza BARNS, bond 29 Oct. 1849;
   bdsm: Juison Perry. [AB]
PERRY, Elijah, & Cholloth[?] TRUMBO, bond 26 Jan. 1846;
   bdsm: John L. Trumbo. [AB]
PERRY, J____, & Sally POWER, bond 17 March 1824;
   bdsm: Carnelius Vanarsdal. [AB]
   Juason Perry & Sally Power, 19 March 1824. [S1]
PERRY, John W., & Margarette KINCAID, bond 30 Aug. 1847;
   bdsm: Ben Perry. [AB]
   John W. Perry & Margarett KINCADE, 30 Aug. 1847. (BHr) [B2]
PERRY, Lewis, & Elizabeth TRUMBO, bond 10 Feb. 1834;
   f/b & bdsm: John Trumbo. [AB]
   Lewis Perry & Elizabeth Trumbo, 12 Feb. 1834. (JVc) [B2]
PERRY, Lucis, & Ellinor HOGGINS, bond 21 Aug. 1821;
   parent/b: C. Y. Higgins; bdsm: John Allen. [AB]
   Lewis Perry & Ellinder KIGGINS, 22 Aug. 1821. [S1]
PERSALL, Zachariah, & Margaret GOODLOW, bond 31 Dec. 1832;
   bdsm: Geo. Colman. [AB]
PERVIS, Allen, & P.? Ann PERVIS, 23 Jan. 1843. (WRg) [B2]
PERVIS, Asa, & Nancy HEILY, 29 Feb. 1843. (WRg) [B2]
PERVIS, John, & Ann GELASBY, 18 Sept. 1817. [S1]
   John PARRIS & Ann GALASBY [JA]
PERVIS, Thomas, & Polly WARREN, bond 1 July 1815;
   bdsm: John Warren. [AB]
   Thomas Pervis & Polly WARNER, 18 Oct. 1815. [S1]
   Thomas PERRIS & Polly Warren, 2 July 1813. [JA]
PETERS, Marcus, & Miranda YOUNG, bond 9 May 1838;
   f/b: Thomas Young; bdsm: T. P. Young. [AB]
PETTIT, Hiram, & Rebecca FELAND, bond 9 Sept. 1846;
   bdsm: Geo. Feland. [AB]
   Hiram TILLET & Rebeca FOLAND, 10 Sept. 1846. (JMc) [B2]

PETTITT, Samuel, & Nancy SHARP, bond 29 Dec. 1828;
    bdsm: Geo. Sadler. [AB]
    Samuel PETTIT & Nancy Sharp, 30 Dec. 1829. (WCS) [B2]
[PEVELER] Plueler?, Daniel, & Elizabeth SAILOR, bond 20 Sept. 1819
    bdsm: John Saylor (Taylor?). [AB]
    Daniel PEVELER & Elizabeth SAILER, 23 Sept. 1819. [S1]
PEVLER, David, & Sally McCART, bond 15 Dec. 1821;
    bdsm: John McCart. [AB]
    David Pevler & Sally McCart, 16 Dec. 1821. [S1]
PEVILER, David, & Ruth CASSITY, bond 26 Jan. 1822;
    bdsm: Henry Cassity. [AB]
    Daniel PEVLER & Ruth Cassity, 27 Jan. 1822. [S1]
PEYTON, Daniel, & Frances CARTMILL, bond 7 Nov. 1849;
    bdsm: W. Cartmill. [AB]
    Daniel PAYTON & Francis A. Cartmill, 14 Nov. 1849. (JHe) [B2]
PHILIPS, Andrew, & Jane NESBIT, bond 26 Sept. 1821;
    f/g: Nimwood Philips; bdsm: Andrew Nesbit. [AB]
    Andrew Philips & Jane NEASBET, 2 Oct. 1821. [S1]
PHILLIPS, George, & Matthew BOON, 7 March 1817. [S1]
PHILLIPS, Wm., & Polly ARMSTRONG, bond 16 Oct. 1839;
    bdsm: Wm. Iles. [AB]
PHILPS, Curtis G., & Nancy LORENCY [Sorency?], bond 1 Nov. 1834;
    bdsm: Silas Lorency. [AB]
PHILPS, Wm., & L. F. SANDERSON, bond 11 Nov. 1847;
    bdsm: F. W. Allen. [AB]
    William PHELPS & L. A. SANDERS, 11 Nov. 1847. (JnSm) [B2]
PICKLEHIMER, Jesse, & Eliza GILL, bond 14 March 1831;
    bdsm: Samuel Gill. [AB]
    Jesse P. HIMER & Eliza Gill, 16 March 1831. (JGW) [B2]
PIERCE, David T., & Elizabeth GREGORY, 10 Aug. 1826. (AMx) [B2]
PIERCE, Peter, & Philadelphia LEDFORD, bond 2 March 1829;
    f/b: James Ledford; bdsm: John Nesbit. [AB]
    Peter Pierce & Philadelphia Ledford, 5 March 1829. (JHu) [B2]
PIERSALL, Samuel, & Mary YOUNG, bond 2 Jan. 1849;
    bdsm: Reuben Young. [AB]
    Samuel PEARSAULL & Mary Young, 4 Jan. 1849. (JGW)
    also: Saml. Pearsall & _____, 4 Jan. 1849. (AGW) [B2]
PLUMMER, Mason, & Ann NICKLSON, bond 17 Jan. 18__;
    bdsm: John Whitleroph. [AB]
    Mason CLUMMEN & Ann NICOSON, 19 Jan. 1832. (PHn) [B2]

POINTER, William, & Cassandra LYLEY, 7 Apr. 1839. (RTh)   [B2]

POOR, James, & Celice DOWNING, 4 Aug. 1817.   [S1]

POOR, John, & Martha COYLE, bond 9 Jan. 1839;
  bdsm: Joseph Coyle.   [AB]
  John Poor & Matha Coyle, 10 Jan. 1839. (JSt)   [B2]

POOR, Moses, & Cidney DOWNING, bond 15 June 1819;
  bdsm: Moses Poor, Wm. Poor.   [AB]
  Moses Poor & Cidney DOWNEY, 15 June 1819.   [S1]

POOR, Samuel, & Rachel STAUSBERRY, 22 Sept. 1817.   [S1]

POOR, Wm., & Elinor POWER, bond 15 Apr. 1815;
  f/b: James Power; bdsm: Wm. Poor, Alexander Boon.   [AB]
  William Poor & Elener POOR, 16 Apr. 1814.   [JA,S1]

POOR, W., & Nancy BURNS, 9 June 1836. (SJn)   [B2]

POTTS, Henry, & Izza HAZELRIGG, bond 30 Apr. 1815;
  bdsm: Joshua Hazelrigg, H. Potts.   [AB]

POUFRET, Lemual, & Melissa C. GUNN, 18 Feb. 1851. (LGH)   [B2]

POWEL, Ashford, & Maria Elizabeth VISE, 2 Feb. 1851. (LGH)   [B2]

POWEL, John, & Rebecca MAPPIN, 25 Jan. 1827. (JEv)   [B2]

POWELL, Ashford, & Sally EVANS, bond 8 Oct. 1828;
  bdsm: Stoker Emmons.   [AB]
  Asford POWEL & Sally EMMONS, 9 Oct. 1828. (CBw)   [B2]

POWELL, Jeremiah, & Amanda NOE, bond 21 Nov. 1831;
  f/b: Geo. Noe; bdsm: Joseph Noe.   [AB]
  Jeremiah POWEL & Amanda Noe, 24 Nov. 1831. (JMh)   [B2]

POWELL, John, & Betsey PATRICK, bond 16 March 1833;
  bdsm: John Kerrey.   [AB]
  John Powell & Betsy Patrick, 19 March 1833. (TEv)   [B2]

POWELL, Joseph, & Nancy ARGO, bond 10 March 1832;
  bdsm: Turnell Argo.   [AB]

POWELL, Nathan, & Nancy BURNS, bond 12 March 1822;
  bdsm: Enoch Burns.   [AB]
  Nathan Powell & Nancy BYRNS, 14 March 1822. (JPH)   [TP,RS]

POWELL, Nathan, & Sally METER, bond 29 Oct. 1829;
  bdsm: Charles Whaley.   [AB]
  Nathan Powell & Sally METEER, 29 Oct. 1829. (DWh)   [B2]

POWELL, Robert, & Sealy MURPHY, 8 Jan. 1815.   [JA]

POWELL, William, & Nancy BURNS, bond 6 June 1836;
  bdsm: Dennis Burns.   [AB]

POWER, Bryan, & Sarah VARNARSDALL, bond 4 Feb. 1819;

bdsm: James Donaldson. [AB]

Bryant Power & Sarah VANNAVSALL, Feb. 1819. [S1]

POWER, Edmund, & Patsey THOMPSON, bond 4 Feb. 1828;

f/b: Win Thompson; bdsm: Joseph Sweatman. [AB]

POWER, George, & Nancy WILLIAMS, bond 5 Feb. 1820 (or 50?);

bdsm: Wm. Williamson or Willenson. [AB]

George POWERS & Nancy WILEACKSON, 10 Feb. 1820. [S1]

POWER, James, & Betsy McPHERSON, bond 19 Feb. 1820;

bdsm: Jesse McPherson. [AB]

James POWERS & Betsy McPLURSON, 24 Feb. 1820. [S1]

POWER, Jeremiah, & Leah McCARTY, bond 11 Sept. 1823;

bdsm: Wm. Coatigan. [AB]

POWER, John, & Louisa WILLSON, bond 11 Apr. 1838;

f/b: Uriah Willson; bdsm: John McDonald. [AB]

POWER, Joshua, & Catharine WILSON, bond 31 July 1833;

f/b: Uriah Wilson; bdsm: James Sudduth. [AB]

Joshua S. Power & Catharine Wilson, 1 Aug. 1833. [S1]

POWER, Robert, & Linly MURPHY, bond 5 July 1815;

parent/b: Zepha Murphy; bdsm: James McCoy. [AB]

POWER, Thomas, & Cynthia anna WELLS, 4 Jan. 1845. (WRg) [B2]

POWER, Wm., & Hullerry CARR, bond 5 May 1832;

bdsm: Jacob Craig. [AB]

POWER, Woodson B., & Eliza GALDEN, 4 Sept. 1841. (SJn) [B2]

[PRATER?] Porter, Isaac C., & Margarett BAIRD, bond 15 Feb. 1845;

f/g: Archibald Porter; f/b: Sam Baird; bdsm: John Freeman. [AB]

Isaac C. PRATER & Margarett Baird, 20 Feb. 1845. (WWn) [B2]

PRATER, James, & Polly WILLSON, bond 28 Apr. 1831;

bdsm: John Jacks. [AB]

James PRATHER & Polly WILSON, 28 Apr. 1829. (PHn) [B2]

PRATHER, Allen D., & Maranda HAWKINS, 21 Feb. 1843. (PHn) [B2]

PRATHER, Andrew, & Paulina DRESKIN, bond 11 Sept. 1848;

bdsm: Isaac Dreskin. [AB]

PRATHER, Eli, & Jane BEAL, bond 7 May 1840;

f/b: John Beal; bdsm: U. S. McIntire. [AB]

Eli Prather & Jane BEAN, 10 May 1840. (TDm) [B2]

PRATHER, James, & Polly WHITE, bond 12 Nov. 1821;

bdsm: Henry Prather. [AB]

PRATHER, Wm., & Esther CRANDLE, bond 16 Dec. 1816;

f/b: J. Crandle; bdsm: Bean Smallwood. [AB]

William PRATTS & Easter CRANDEL, 1816. [S1]

PRATTS, Johnathan, & Sally WILSON, 1813. (LTu) [KM]

PRESELY, John, & Providence WARFIELD, bond 25 Sept. 1820;
    bdsm: Wm. Griffin. [AB]

PRICE, Henry, & Polly HARMON, bond 7 Oct. 1823;
    bdsm: Geo. Razor. [AB]
    Henry Price & Polly Harmon, Oct. 1823. [S1]

PRINCE, David, & Lucy JOHNSON, bond 12 Aug. 1832;
    bdsm: John Prince. [AB]
    David Prince & Biney or Piney? Johnson, 14 Aug. 1833. (JPk) [B2]

PRINCE, Levi, & Grizzy FUGATE, bond 21 May 1822;
    f/b: Reuben Fugate; bdsm: David W. Fletcher. [AB]
    Levi Prince & Enezezy[?] Fugate, 23 May 1822. [S1]

PRINCE, Mason, & Asamith KYGINS, 3 July 1822. [S1]

PRINGLE, Robert, & Martha Ann CHEATHAM, bond 10 Feb. 1840;
    bdsm: Wm. M. Ragland. [AB]
    Robert Pringle & Martha Ann Cheatham, 11 Feb. 1839. (JnSm) [B2]

PROCTOR, Jeremiah, & Mary STANDCRIFF, bond 13 Dec. 1828;
    bdsm: Jas. Standcriff. [AB]

PROCTOR, Moses, & Eliza DUNCAN, 30 Aug. 1827. (RTy) [B2]

PUBLES, W. B., & Margaret CRAIG, bond 14 July 1823;
    bdsm: Andrew Gudgell. [AB]
    William B. Publes & Margaret Craig, 13 July 1823. [S1]

PURGRAM, Enoch, & Peggy ann MONTJOY, 3 Apr. 1844. (SMc) [B2]

PURGRAM or Purgarum, James, & Ann CROUCH, 31 Aug. 1843. (SMc) [B2]

PURVIS, Frank, & Margaret SORREL, 1 March 1852. (WRg) [B2]

PURVIS, Matthew, & Rebecca GLASPA, bond 30 May 1831;
    bdsm: Wm. Moore. [AB]

PURVIS, Samuel, & Cynthiana PURVIS, bond 3 Aug. 1846;
    bdsm: Thomas Purvis. [AB]

PURVIS, Thomas, & Cynthia THOMAS, bond 3 Apr. 1823;
    bdsm: John Cooper. [AB]
    Thomas Purvis & Cynthia Thomas, 8 Apr. 1823. [S1]

PURVISS, George, & Nancy MOORE, 12 May 1841. (PCy) [B2]

QUILLIN, William, & Sarah CREE, 6 March 1817. [S1]

RABNER, Franklin, & Malvina JACKSON, bond 15 July 1849;
    bdsm: Tudor Ratland. [AB]
    Franklin RABERN or Rabarn & Malinda Jackson, 17 June 1849. (JHe) [B2]

RAE, Hugh, & Susan BROWN, bond 21 Feb. 1831;
    bdsm: Richard Brown. [AB]

RAGAN, Richard, & Lucy HUGHES, 26 Jan. 1826. (JPk) [B2]

RAGLAND, James, & Lucinda MOCKBEE, bond 5 Nov. 1828;
   f/b: Stephen Mockbee; bdsm: Alfred Menfee. [AB]
   James Ragland & Luicindia McABEE, 6 Nov. 1828. (JPk) [B2]

RAIMEY, Jeremiah, & Unice MANLY, bond 2 Oct. 1845;
   f/b: J. R. Manly; bdsm: James R. Manly. [AB]
   Jeremiah RAMEY & Unice MANLEY, 2 Oct. 1845. (TRk) [B2]

RALLS, George, & Martha THOMPSON, bond 28 Sept. 1812;
   f/g: Nathan Ralls; f/b: John Hawkins; bdsm: George Ralls, James Hawkins. [AB]

RALLS, Nathaniel, & Eliza Jane BURNS, bond 18 Feb. 1831;
   bdsm: Samuel Stone. [AB]
   Nathaniel P. ROLES & Eliza Jane BURNES, 23 Feb. 1831. (DWh) [B2]

RALLS, Valentine Stone, & Catherine FREELAND, bond 26 Nov. 1845;
   bdsm: Robt. Freeland. [AB]
   Valentine S. Ralls & Catharine FREELING, 27 Nov. 1845. (__) [B2]

RALPH, Ben, & Lucy STEPHENS, bond 9 Aug. 1842;
   bdsm: James F. Jones. [AB]

RALSTON, Boyd, & Eliza SPARKS, bond 9 Aug. 1847;
   bdsm: John Bainbridge. [AB]

RAMEY, Able, & Sally PHILPS, bond 5 Dec. 1821;
   bdsm: Henry Cofer. [AB]
   Abb Ramey & Sally Philps, 5 Dec. 1821. [S1]

RAMEY, James, & Mary D. HENRY, bond 17 Jan. 1840;
   f/b: Lane D. Henry; bdsm: John S. Pierce. [AB]
   James S. RANEY & Mary D. RANEY, 17 Jan. 1840. (RFC) [B2]

RAMSEY, John, & Catherine DO [ditto?], 28 Sept. 1826. (RGd) [B2]

RAMSEY, William W., & Martha Ann BARNES, 21 Nov. 1843. (JAn) [B2]

RANDALL, Harvy, & Sally MAPPIN, bond 24 June 1824;
   bdsm: Henry Reed. [AB]

RANDOLPH, Albert, & Eliz. SWARTZER, bond 30 Sept. 1829;
   f/b: Abraham Swartzer; bdsm: P. F. Young. [AB]
   Albert Randolph & Eliza SWITZER, 1 Oct. 1829. (JnSm) [B2]

RANKIN, Joseph K., & Rebecca KINCAID, bond 7 March 1825;
   bdsm: John Kincaid. [AB]

RASER, Jackson, & Epsey or Essey? TRAYLOR, 25 Dec. 1834. (PCy) [B2]

RATLIFF, Caleb, & Nancy STONE, bond 7 Aug. 1819;
   bdsm: Geo. ?Laudrdom [Lansdown?]. [AB]
   Caleb Ratliff & Nancy Stone, 19 Aug. 1819. [S1]

RATLIFF, Caleb, & Elizabeth WHALEY, bond 28 Jan. 1842;

bdsm: James Whaley. [AB]

Caleb Ratliff & Elizabeth WHELEY, 1 Feb. 1842. (SJn) [B2]

RATLIFF, Caleb, & Elizabeth BAIRD, bond 28 June 1847;

bdsm: Ratliff Baird. [AB]

Caleb Ratliff & Elizabeth Ellen Baird, 2 July 1847. (MGs) [B2]

[RATLIFF] Ratcliff, Coalman, & Margaret ROBINSON, bond 28 March 1815;

bdsm: Lawson Robinson. [AB]

Coleman or W. Colman RATLIFF & Peggy ROBERSON, 30 March 1815. [JA,S1]

RATLIFF, Colman, & Susan McGILL, bond 14 Apr. 1834;

bdsm: Harlan Moor. [AB]

Coleman Ratliff & Susan M. GILL, 24 Apr. 1834. (SJn) [B2]

RATLIFF, Harrison, & Jully Ann FREEMAN, bond 24 March 1834;

f/b: Wm. Freeman; bdsm: B. F. Sudduth. [AB]

Henry H. Ratliff & Julyann Freeman, 27 March 1834. (WWh) [B2]

RATLIFF, Richard, & Martha HICKMAN, bond 29 Aug. 1846;

bdsm: Wm. Hickman. [AB]

RAWLINGS, Henry, & Caroline HAZELRIGG, bond 25 June 1849;

bdsm: D. D. Duty. [AB]

Henry S. Rawlings & Carroline W. Hazelrigg, 27 June 1849. (RFC) [B2]

RAY, John, & Sarah ?DIXCON or Discon, bond 22 July 1824;

bdsm: Henry Discon. [AB]

John Ray & Sarah DIXEN, 23 July 1824. [S1]

RAY, Wm., & Martha HAWKINS, bond 29 Apr. 1815;

bdsm: John Hawkins. [AB]

RAYSON, Samu(e)l, & Sally McDANEL, 16 June 1839. (PCy) [B2]

RAZER or Rozar?, Wm. B. H., & Mary CAREY, bond 3 Sept. 1838;

bdsm: Isaac Cogswell. [AB]

N. B. H. RAZOR & Mary CARY, 4 Sept. 1838. (JGW) [B2]

RAZOR or Rozar?, Wm., & Permelia BARNES, bond 3 Nov. 1837;

bdsm: Wm. Burns. [AB]

REED, Ben, & Malvina NICHOLAS, bond 7 Apr. 1819 (49?);

bdsm: Allen Chandler. [AB]

Benjamin REEDE & Malvina Nicholas, 7 Apr. 1849. (SKc) [B2]

REED, David, & Lucy ?LANE, bond 12 July 1825;

f/b: Sam Lane; bdsm: Aursted White. [AB]

David Reed & Lucy LOVE, 12 July 1820. [S1]

REED, Garnett B., & Nancy WORKMAN, bond 14 Apr. 1825;

bdsm: Geo. Workman. [AB]

Garnett B. Reed & Nancy B. Workman, 24 Apr. 1824. [S1]

REED, Geo. W., & Elizabeth HOSSTETTER, bond 11 Aug. 1842;

bdsm: Solmon Hostetler. [AB]

George W. REEDE & Elizabeth HOSTELLER, 18 Aug. 1842. (PHn) [B2]

REED, Henry, & Elizabeth BIDELL, bond 14 Jan. 1823;

bdsm: Samuel Bedell. [AB]

Henry Reed & Elizabeth BEDELL, 14 Jan. 1823. [S1]

REED, Henry, & Jane DENTON, bond 17 Oct. 1831;

bdsm: Wm. Denton. [AB]

Henry Reed & Jane Denton, 18 Oct. 1831. (BHu) [B2]

REED, Isaac, & Polly MANIS, bond 1828;

bdsm: J. P. Manis. [AB]

REED, John, & Elizabeth McBEE, bond 8 Feb. 1819. [AB]

REED, Jonathan, & Nancy DONATHAN, bond 3 March 1827;

bdsm: Thomas Donathan. [AB]

Jonathan Reed & Nancy DONITHAN, 1 March 1827. (SJo) [B2]

REED, Jonathan, & Serrilda WOOD, bond 6 Sept. 1847;

bdsm: John Waganer. [AB]

Jona(t)han Reed & Ganlda HOOD, 8 Sept. 1847. (AGW) [B2]

REED, Joseph, & Marilla Jane BRADSHAW, bond 10 Jan. 1846;

bdsm: Thomas Bradshaw. [AB]

Joseph Reed & M. J. Bradshaw, 11 Jan. (or June?) 1846. (RFC) [B2]

REED, Josiah, & Juirley COLDWELL [Caldwell?], 9 Oct. 1818. [S1]

REED, Stephen, & Mary A. BRYANT, 18 Nov. 1850. (SKc) [B2]

REEVES, Elijah, & Sarah HILEY, bond 2 Aug. 1836;

bdsm: Wm. Hiley. [AB]

Elijah Reeves & Sarah Hiley, 3 Aug. 1836. [S1]

REEVES, Elijah, & Lucinda FRAZIER, bond 9 Feb. 1847;

bdsm: Dr Frazier. [AB]

Elijah REAVES & Lucinda Frazier, 9 Feb. 1847. (SKc) [B2]

REEVES, Lewis, & Betsy PURVIS, bond 29 Sept. 1831;

bdsm: Thomas Purvis. [AB]

REFFET, Dusset, & Catharine BLEVINS, bond 24 May 1839;

bdsm: James Blevins. [AB]

Deret Reffet or REPPET? & Katharine BLEVENS, 26 May 1839. (WSd) [B2]

REGINS or Rigins, Simpson, & Lucy O. ARNOLD, 15 Apr. 1851. (LGH) [B2]

REPHANT, Henry, & Polly THOMPSON, bond 3 May 1816;

f/b: Wm. Thompson; bdsm: Wm. Thompson, H. Rephant. [AB]

RETHERFORD, James, & Polly CROW, 19 March 1835. (JVc) [B2]

REYNOLDS, Jesse, & Mary BROUCH, bond 13 March 1811;

bdsm: Jesse Reynolds, John Delay. [AB]

RHUE, Isiah, & Melissa BRUNGER, bond 20 Sept. 1842;
    f/g: Abraham Rhue; bdsm: Sam Brunger. [AB]
RIADON, Samuel, & Angelina RABURN, bond 30 Sept. 1845;
    bdsm: Joseph Warner. [AB]
RICE, Alfred G., & Malinda RICHARD, bond 26 May 1829;
    bdsm: William Richard. [AB]
    Alfred G. Rice & Malinda RICHARDS, 28 May 1829. (SJn) [B2]
RICE, Charles, & Rachel LYNAM, 23 Jan. 1826. (JVc) [B2]
RICE, Corban, & Elizabeth CALVERT, bond 27 Jan. 1840;
    bdsm: Jesse Calvert. [AB]
    Corban Rice & Elizabeth COLBERT, 29 Feb. 1840. (ALy) [B2]
RICE, F. B., & Eliza SHUMATE, bond 12 Nov. 1829;
    bdsm: Wm. Bailey. [AB]
RICE, Henry, & Anne DARNELL, bond 28 May 1814;
    bdsm: Henry Rice, Asa Kaywood; mar. 30 May. [KM]
    Henry Rice & Ann or Anne Darnell, 30 May 1814. [JA,S1]
RICE, Holman, & Margaret CORBIN, bond 27 June 1814;
    bdsm: Holman Rice, Zachariah Corbin; mar. 30 June. [KM]
    Holdman or Hodlman Rice & Margaret Corbin, 30 June 1814. [S1,JA]
RICE, Holman, & Polly FATHERGILL, bond 20 June 1816;
    f/b: Thomas Fathergill; bdsm: John Murr, H. Rice. [AB]
RICE, James, & Margarett BRADLEY, bond 1 Jan. 1846;
    m/b: Martha Bradley; bdsm: Alexander Bradley. [AB]
    James Rice & Margret Bradley, 1 Jan. 1846. (SKc) [B2]
RICE, Jefferson, & Nancy RICHARD, bond 6 Apr. 1829;
    bdsm: Elza Richard. [AB]
    Jefferson Rice & Nancy RICHARDS, 3 Apr. 1829. (SJn) [B2]
RICE or Ries?, John, & Juliann BURNES, bond 31 Dec. 1828;
    bdsm: Enoch Burnes. [AB]
    John Rice & Julian BYRNES, 1 Jan. 1829. (DWh) [B2]
RICE, John, & Polly STEPLEN or Stephen?, bond 2 Feb. 1829;
    bdsm: Wm. Steples or Steplen. [AB]
RICE, John E., & Margaret BRISTOW, bond 18 Jan. 1840;
    bdsm: Joseph Wilson. [AB]
    John E. Rice & Margaret BRISTOE, 19 Jan. 1840. (SJk) [B2]
RICE, John Holeman, & Margaret Ann RICHARDS, bond 29 June 1839;
    bdsm: James Richards. [AB]
    John Holeman Rice & Margaret Richards, 22 June 1839. (ALy) [B2]
RICE, M. C., & C. T. ROE, 26 Oct. 1843. (SMc) [B2]
RICE, Ma(r)cus B., & Elizabeth ROBERSON, 28 Feb. 1844. (WRg) [B2]

119

RICE, Nelson, & Martha CARTMELL, bond 24 Apr. 1813;

    m/b: Mary Cartmell; bdsm: Nelson Rice, David M. Cartmell; mar. 24 Apr.   [KM]

    Nelson Rice & Martha CARTMEAL, 25 Apr. 1813.   [JA,S1]

RICE, Nelson, & Frances A. RICHARDS, bond 23 March 1836;

    bdsm: Jefferson Rice.   [AB]

    Nelson T. Rice & Francis A. Richards, 29 May 1836. (JnSm)   [B2]

RICE, Samuel, & Robertta BAILEY, bond 12 Oct. 1846;

    bdsm: Robert Bailey.   [AB]

RICE, Washington, & Mahaly REEVES, bond 25 May 1847;

    bdsm: Isable Reeves.   [AB]

    Washington W. Rice & Mahala RIEVES, 27 May 1847. (SKc)   [B2]

RICE, Wm., & Perlina RAINE, bond 19 Oct. 1822;

    bdsm: Wm. Raine.   [AB]

    William C. Rice & Paulina W. RONE, 20 Oct. 1822.   [S1]

RICE, Wm., & Sarah LYNAM, bond 1 Jan. 1827;

    bdsm: Wm. Smallwood.   [AB]

    William Rice & Sally Lynam, 2 Jan. 1827. (JEv)   [B2]

RICE, Wm., & Mary BRADLEY, bond 17 March 1845;

    bdsm: Martha Bradley.   [AB]

    William Rice & Mary BRADLY, 24 March 1845. (SKc)   [B2]

RICE, Wm., & Sally Ann BAILEY, bond 22 Sept. 1846;

    f/g: Wm. ?Rice (or Royse); bdsm: Robert Bailey.   [AB]

RICE, Wm. F., & Mary E. VANARSDELE, 2 Oct. 1851. (TDL)   [B2]

RICHARDLY, James, & Pollina COLLINS, bond 30 Jan. 1837;

    f/b: Willis Collins; bdsm: Bohanan Collins.   [AB]

RICHARDS, James, & Barbara BURNES, bond 20 Sept. 1830;

    bdsm: Thomas I. Young.   [AB]

    James Richards & Barbara BURNER, 22 Sept. 1830. (JHH)   [B2]

RICHARDS, James H., & Eliza SHROUTT, bond 27 Feb. 1838;

    bdsm: Isaac Shrout.   [AB]

    James H. Richards & Eliza SHROUT, 28 Feb. 1838. (JnSm)   [B2]

RICHARDS, James I., & Mary MOORE, bond 27 Jan. 1840;

    bdsm: William Moore.   [AB]

    James J. Richards & Mary Moore, 28 Jan. 1840. (EBr)   [B2]

RICHARDS, John, & Margaret ROBBINS, bond 26 Dec. 1825;

    f/b: James Robbins; bdsm: Samuel Webster.   [AB]

    John Richards & Margarett ROBINS, 3 Jan. 1826.   [S1]

RICHARDS, John L., & Elizabeth MOOR, bond 5 Jan. 1837;

    bdsm: James Stoneclift or Stoneleft.   [AB]

Longley Richards & Elizabeth MOORE, Jan. 1837. (TIs) [B2]

RICHARDS, Josiah, & _____ SNEDAGER, 22 March 1844. (SMc) [B2]

RICHARDS, Washington, & Elenor GOODWIN, bond 26 Feb. 1825;
bdsm: Solomon Taylor. [AB]

Washington Richards & Eliner GOODING, 4 March 1825. [S1]

RICHARDSON, James, & Mary (Polly) BARNES, bond 13 Apr. 1812;
f/b: William Barnes; bdsm: James Richardson, Josiah Richardson. [AB]

James RICHARDS & Polly BARNS, 11 June 1812. [JA]

James Richards & Polly Barns, 14 Apr. 1812 [S1]

RICHARDSON, Joshua, & Lucretia STATON, 10 Nov. 1845. (BBv) [B2]

RICHARDSON, Lewis, & Jane TAP, bond 26 Dec. 1828;
bdsm: Elizabeth Tapp. [AB]

RICHARDSON, Natha P., & Nancy INGRAM, bond 26 Feb. 1830;
bdsm: Robt. Downes. [AB]

RICHART, Duncan, & Patsy SHARP, bond 26 Aug. 1813;
f/g: Duncan D. Richart; f/b & bdsm: Richard Sharp. [AB]

Duncan O. Richart & Patsey Sharp, 31 Aug. 1813. (JPH) [RS]

RIDDLE, Harrison, & Lydia BOYD, bond 24 Jan. 1848;
bdsm: Gabriel Grimsly. [AB]

RIDDLE, John, & Mary Adaline MEYERS, bond 24 Dec. 1824;
bdsm: Henry Meyers. [AB]

RIDDLE, Robert, & Lucinda BRADSHAW, bond 15 Aug. 1834;
bdsm: David Bradshaw. [AB]

Robert RIDLE & Lucind Bradshaw, 15 Aug. 1834. (JVc) [B2]

RIDDLE, Stephen C., & Sally Ann KERNS, bond 10 Sept. 1838;
f/b: Filmore [Tilman] Kerns; bdsm: Robert Riddle. [AB]

Stephen C. D. RIDLE & Sally an KERENS, 11 Sept. 1838. (JWR) [B2]

RIGES?, John, & Martha Ann TOMLINSON, bond 30 Jan. 1838;
bdsm: James Tomlinson. [AB]

RINGO, Jackson, & Sary INGRAM, bond 3 Jan. 1837; [AB]

Jackson Ringo & Sally GARGRAHAM[?], 5 Jan. 1837. (WSd) [B2]

RINGO, James D., & Emily PLEAK or Pleakslaver, 19 Dec. 1850. (SRg) [B2]

RINGO or Ringor?, Richard, & Nancy JONES, bond 17 Sept. 1819;
bdsm: John Jones. [AB]

Richard Ringo & Nancy Jones, 19 Sept. 1819. [S1]

RINGO, Richard, & Elizabeth B. STONE, bond 29 Jan. 1840;
bdsm: Thomas I. Jones. [AB]

Richard Ringo & Elizabeth B. SONE, 3 Jan. 1840. (MGs) [B2]

RINGO, Wm. H., & Harriet B. MOFFETT, bond 25 Nov. 1839;

bdsm: James B. Moffett. [AB]

   William H. Ringo & Harriet B. MOFFITT, 27 Nov. 1839. (RFC) [B2]

ROACH, John, & Elizabeth MORGAN, bond 18 Sept. 1815;

bdsm: John Morgan. [AB]

ROACH, Henry, & Mariah THATCHER, bond 10 March 1820;

bdsm: Hoden Thatcher. [AB]

   Henry Roach & Maira THATHER, 12 March 1820. [S1]

ROAK, Samuel, & Mary CARTWELL [Cartmill?], bond 31 July 1824;

bdsm: Zebulen Cartmill. [AB]

ROBBINS, Andrew, & Hester CUP, bond 10 Nov. 1840;

bdsm: John Richards. [AB]

   Andrew ROBINS & Hester CUPS, 19 Nov. 1840. (WBL) [B2]

ROBBINS, John, & Elizabeth KENAILL, bond 27 Apr. 1812;

bdsm: John Robbins, Henry Baird. [AB]

ROBERSON, Benjamin, & Petty McCLAIN, bond 15 Apr. 1834;

bdsm: Jones Roberson. [AB]

ROBERSON, Green L., & Trenella GRIGORY, 2 Apr. 1844. (SMc) [B2]

ROBERSON, Harrison, & Mary DOLAND, bond 15 Jan. 1834;

bdsm: John Roberson. [AB]

ROBERTS or Robertson?, Francis, Jr., & Peggy BAKER, bond 8 June 1815;

f/b: Rezin Baker; bdsm: Edwin Baker. [AB]

   Francis Roberts, Jr., & Peggy Baker, 8 June 1815. [JA,S1]

ROBERTS, Henley, & Susan DARNELL, bond 19 March 1824;

bdsm: W. M. Sudduth. [AB]

   Menley Roberts & Susan McDONEL, 23 March 1824. [S1]

ROBERTSON, John, & Mary HAZELRIGG, bond 14 March 1828 (or 38?);

f/b: Eli Hazelrigg; bdsm: John F. Hazelrigg. [AB]

   John M. Robertson & Mary HAZILRIGG, 15 March 1838. (GWM) [B2]

ROBINS, John, & Eliza Ann RANDOLPH, bond 30 Sept. 1830;

bdsm: James Randolph. [AB]

ROBINSON, James, & Pressilla McCLAIN, bond 19 July 1828;

bdsm: James McClain. [AB]

   James Robinson & Prissilla McClain, 24 Aug. 1828. (SJk) [B2]

ROBINSON, Samuel, & Jane RICHART or Richey, bond 11 Nov. 1811;

bdsm: Samuel Robinson, Duncan Richart. [AB]

   Samuel Robinson & Jane RICHEY, 19 Nov. 1811. (JPH) [TP,RS]

ROBINSON, Sylvester, & Martha RIADON, bond 6 Sept. 1845;

bdsm: Geo. Riadon. [AB]

   Sylvester ROBERSON & Sarah RHIDON or Rhedon, 10 Nov. 1845. (BBv) [B2]

ROBINSON, Wm., & Sally ROBINSON, bond 4 Aug. 1834;

bdsm: B. F. Sudduth. [AB]

ROBINSON, William, & Mary W. GLOVER, bond 30 Apr. 1842;
    bdsm: Creed Glover. [AB]
    William Robinson & Mary W. Glover, 4 May 1842. (JnSm) [B2]

ROBISON, Jonathan, & Sally BRISTOW, bond 24 June 1823;
    bdsm: John Bristow. [AB]
    Jonathan Robison & Sally Bristow, June 1823. [S1]

ROE, Daniel, & Lucy JAMISON, bond 26 Feb. 1821;
    bdsm [f/b]: Wm. Jamison. [AB]
    Daniel Roe & Lucy Jamison, 27 Feb. 1821. [S1]

ROE, M. I., & Lucinda CASSITY, bond 3 Nov. 1845;
    bdsm: Rubel Noland. [AB]

ROE, M. J., & Francis CASSITY, 25 Oct. 1843. (SMc) [B2]

ROE, Salem, & Eliza B. RICHARTS, 21 Sept. 1826. (AMx) [B2]

ROE, Salem or Solem, & Hester HUNT, bond 23 Aug. 1847;
    bdsm: Wilson Hunt. [AB]

[ROE?] Ros, Samuel, & Elizabeth McCOY, 14 May 1835. (PHn) [B2]

ROE, Samuel, & Louisa TEMPLEMAN, bond 14 Sept. 1846;
    bdsm: Skidmore Field. [AB]
    J. ROE & S. Templ(e)man, 17 Sept. 1846. (SVL) [B2]

ROE, Wm. B., & Amanda I. HEDRICK, bond 9 Nov. 1846;
    bdsm: J. C. Hedrick. [AB]

ROGAN?, Dempsey, & Lucretia McINTIRE, bond 9 Dec. 1825;
    bdsm: John McIntire. [AB]

ROGERS, Harry, & Elizabeth GIPSON, bond 10 Nov. 1827;
    f/g & bdsm: Wm. Rogers. [AB]

ROGERS, Jacob, & Anna CARTER, bond 5 July 1815;
    bdsm: Joseph Carter. [AB]

ROGERS, James, & Chithy ?OFFICERA or Officula, bond 4 Oct. 1832;
    f/g: Wm. Rogers; bdsm: Alford Rogers. [AB]

ROGERS, James, & Mary SPENCER, bond 2 Sept. 1836;
    bdsm: B. F. Sudduth. [AB]
    James Rogers & Mary Spencer, 28 Sept. 1836. (SRg) [B2]

ROGERS, John, & Sally BROMAGEN, 29 Oct. 1826. (JtSm) [B2]

ROGERS, John, & Eliza Ann SMOOTT, bond 18 July 1832;
    bdsm: Swafford Anderson. [AB]

ROGERS, John, & Zerilda CORY, 8 March 1850. (WRg) [B2]

ROGERS, Madison, & Hestty SMITH, bond 17 May 1833;
    f/b: Wm. Smith; bdsm: Samuel Kingcade. [AB]

Matison Rogers & Hetty Smith, 16 July 1833. (TIs) [B2]
ROGERS, McIlheney, & Elizabeth WILLSON, 20 Aug. 1835. (SRg) [B2]
ROGERS, S., & Mary Jane POWERS, bond 7 Nov. 1849;
  bdsm: Sam Jones. [AB]
ROGERS, Samuel, & Rebecca LANE or Love?, bond 27 March 1829;
  bdsm: Thomas Lancaster. [AB]
  Samuel Rogers & Rebecca LANCASTER, 31 March 1829. (WCS) [B2]
ROGERS, Samuel, & Sally McDANIEL, bond 15 June 1839;
  bdsm: W. Razor. [AB]
ROGERS, Samuel, & Malinda GREGORY, bond 11 Jan. 1849;
  bdsm: J. Sudduth. [AB]
ROGERS, Silas, & Artimecia BUTLERS [Butler], 21 Sept. 1843. (SRg) [B2]
ROGERS, Thomas, & Peggy ASHLEY, bond 5 May 1821;
  bdsm: Peter Ashley. [AB]
  Thomas Rogers & Peggy Ashley, 13 May 1821. [S1]
ROGERS, Thomas, & Mary Ann WILLIAMS, bond 16 Apr. 1848;
  f/b: Aaron Williams; bdsm: John Sheant. [AB]
  Thomas Rogers & Ma(r)y Ann Williams, 14 Apr. 1848. (WRg) [B2]
ROLLSTEN, Robert, & Susan NOAH, bond 8 March 1833 (38?);
  bdsm: Isaac Nichlas. [AB]
  Robert ROLSTON & Susan NOE, 10 March 1838. (TWn) [B2]
ROMINS, ?Jones & Sarah WELCH, 14 March 1844. (SMc) [B2]
RORSE, William T., & Elizabeth F. CARNES, 22 Feb. 1844. (SMc) [B2]
ROSE, Bowen, & Comfort INGRAM, bond 8 May 1838;
  bdsm: Thomas Ingram. [AB]
  Kowel Rose & Comfort INGRUM, 8 May 1839. (WSd) [B2]
ROSS, Jacob, & Elizabeth DENTON, bond 26 Sept. 1815;
  bdsm: Wm. Denton. [AB]
  Isaac or Jacob Ross & Elizabeth Denton, 28 Sept. 1815. [JA,S1]
ROSS, John N., & Nancy KINIMON, bond 7 Aug. 1839;
  bdsm: Wm. Denton. [AB]
ROSS, Richard, & Catherine McCLESE, bond 29 Aug. 1814;
  bdsm: Richard Ross, Jeremiah Jackson. [KM]
  Richard Ross & Catherine McClese, 29 Aug. 1814. [JA,S1]
ROSS, Washington, & Harriet TRUMBO, bond 4 Jan. 1836;
  f/b & bdsm: Jacob Trumbo. [AB]
  Washington Ross & Harriett Trumbo, 4 Jan. 1836. (GSz) [B2]
ROTHWELL, Solomon, & Hannah DENNIS, 3 Nov. 1848. (RWM) [B2]
ROUTT, Bailey, & Elizabeth ATCHISON, bond 9 Sept. 1822;
  f/g: Geo. Routt; bdsm: Wm. Boyd; [AB]

Bailey Routt & Elizabeth Atchison, 12 Sept. 1822.   [S1]

ROUTT, Wm. F., & Minanda? [Maranda] HENDRIX, bond 25 Jan. 1837;

     bdsm [f/b]: Theophilus Hendrix.   [AB]

     William Routt & Meranda Hendrix, 26 Jan. 1837. (JVc)   [B2]

RUBY, Wm., & Cassy GILL, bond 17 Aug. 1849;

     bdsm: J. F. Moore.   [AB]

     William RIBBY & Cassand(r)a Gill, 19 Aug. 1849. (AGW)   [B2]

RUDDER, David, & Narcissa BOYD, bond 30 June 1838;

     bdsm: David Bailey.   [AB]

     Davis Rudder & Narissa Boyd, 30 June 1838. (JSt)   [B2]

RUDDER, Edward, & Susan CONNEL, bond 6 Nov. 1824;

     bdsm: Wm. Gregory.   [AB]

RUDDER, John, & Lucinda CARTMELL, bond 7 Jan. 1815;

     f/b: Andrew Cartwell; bdsm: Jacob Lawrence.   [AB]

     John Rudder & Lucinda Cartmell, 7 Jan. 1815.   [S1]

     John RUDER & Lucinda CARTMEAL   [JA]

RUDDER, John M., & Elizabeth KENNEDY, bond 5 Nov. 1823;

     bdsm: John Bailey.   [AB]

     John H. Rudder, & Elizabeth KENADY, 6 Nov. 1823.   [S1]

RUDDER, Thomas, & Nancy LATHRAM, bond 5 Apr. 1848;

     f/g: Ed Rudder; f/b & bdsm: George Lathram.   [AB]

RUDDER, Wm. B., & Sally CARTSILL, bond 3 July 1829;

     bdsm: Rudd Cartsill.   [AB]

RUNNELS, Thomas, & George Ann WARNER, 15 Dec. 1843. (SKc)   [B2]

RUSEL, Andrew, & Nancy CRACRAFT, 8 Feb. 1816.   [JA]

     Andrew RUSSELL & Nancy CARCRAFT   [S1]

RUSSELL, Robert, & Lucinda MENNOW, bond 27 Apr. 1825;

     bdsm: John Mannon.   [AB]

     Robert Russell & Lucinda MANSON, 7 Apr. 1825.   [S1]

RYAN, Elijah, & Catherine HORNBACK, bond 2 Feb. 1829;

     bdsm: John Bedell.   [AB]

RYON, John, & Charlotte WEBSTER, bond 20 May 1815;

     bdsm: Sam Budle.   [AB]

SADLER, Geo. W., & Paulina GILMORE, bond 19 Dec. 1838;

     bdsm: Tarlton Meannor.   [AB]

     George W. SADDLER & Paulina Gilmore, 20 Dec. 1838. (SMc)   [B2]

SAFELY, Andrew, & Elizabeth CROOKS, bond 5 Aug. 1838;

     bdsm: Thos. Wigle.   [AB]

     Andrew Jackson Safely & Elizebeth CROOK, 4 (14?) Aug. 1838. (JnSm)   [B2]

SAILOR, George Wm., & Louisa BATTAILE, bond 25 Feb. 1842;
   f/b & bdsm: Wm. Battaile. [AB]
   Geo. W. TAILOR & Louisa M. ?BATTAILLE, 2 March 1842. (RFC) [B2]
SAILOR, Samuel, & Lucinda JOHNSON, bond 4 Dec. 1822;
   bdsm: Isaac Johnson. [AB]
   Samuel Sailor & Lucinda JONSTON, 6 Dec. 1822. [S1]
SAILOR, Jonathan, & Lucinda ELLIOTT, bond 19 Dec. 1821;
   f/b: James Elliott; bdsm: David Perller. [AB]
   Jonathan SAITER & Lucinda ELIOTT, 20 Dec. 1821. [S1]
SANDERS, Henry, & Patsy RALS(T)ON, bond 20 Jan. 1816;
   bdsm: John Ralston. [AB]
   Henry SAUNDERS & Patsey (I.?) ROLSTON or Rotston, 23 Jan. 1816. [JA,S1]
SANDERS or Saunders, Squire, & Martha D. WILLIAMS, 21 Apr. 1839. (ASd) [B2]
SANDERS, Wm. W., & Lucinda TAP, bond 17 Apr. 1834;
   bdsm: Nelson Tap. [AB]
   W. W. SAUNDERS & Lucinda Tap, 17 March 1834. (SMc) [B2]
SANFORD, John, & Margaret FLETCHER, bond 23 Dec. 1846;
   bdsm: John Sanford. [AB]
   John Sanford or Sandford & M. J. Fletcher, 29 Dec. 1846. (RFC) [B2]
SAP, Jonathan, & Dester[?] HUNT, bond 30 May 1832;
   f/b: Jeremiah Hunt; bdsm: Lewis Jackson. [AB]
SAPP or Tapp?, Isaac, & Nancy HUNT, bond 21 June 1827;
   bdsm: Daniel Sapp. [AB]
SAPP, Joseph, & Elizabeth WILLIAMS, bond 12 Nov. 1832;
   bdsm: Joseph Williams. [AB]
   Joseph SAP & Elizabeth Williams, 5 Feb. 1833. (TIs) [B2]
SAPP(E)R, Daniel, & Susannah PRATER, bond 10 Dec. 1825;
   bdsm: Daniel Sapper. [AB]
SARGENT, Elijah, & Malinda NEXTER, bond 12 March 1842;
   bdsm: Joseph Cash. [AB]
   Elijah ?SARGINT & Malinda NESTER, 20 March 1842. (PCy) [B2]
SARGENT, William, & Eliza Jane REED, 4 Feb. 1819. [S1]
S(A)TTERFIELD, William, & Polly W. BRADSHAW, 5 Feb. 1835. (JCC) [B2]
SCHALE, Jesse, & Charity ELEGE, 1 Sept. 1819. [S1]
SCINICS?, Samuel, & Elizabeth WILLIAMS, bond 10 Apr. 1820. [AB]
   Samuel SEIRS & Elizabeth Williams, 10 Apr. 1820. [S1]
SCOT, Samuel, & Perline OCKERMAN, 26 March 1835. (PHn) [B2]
SCOTT, Alexander, & Ellen ROE, bond 8 Oct. 1838;
   bdsm: Francis Hopkins. [AB]
   Alexander Scott & Ellen Roe, 11 Oct. 1838. (JnSm) [B2]

SCOTT, David R., & Swan BARNABY, bond 3 Oct. 1825;
    bdsm: Wm. Barnaby. [AB]
SCOTT, Elias, & Betsey BROWN, bond 10 Apr. 1816;
    bdsm: Walter Caldwell, Elias Scott. [AB]
    Elias Scott & Betsey Brown, 1816. [S1]
SCOTT, Elisha, & Nancy RENER, bond 27 July 1822;
    f/g: Edward Scott; bdsm: Samuel Patrick. [AB]
SCOTT, Geo. W., & Elizabeth CUTRIGHT, bond 20 Sept. 1847;
    f/b & bdsm: Wm. Baxter. [AB]
    George W. Scott & Elizabeth COURTRIGHT, 21 Sept. 1847. (GBu) [S1]
SCOTT, James, & Verva STEMORT [Stewart?], bond 8 Sept. 1845;
    bdsm: Peter Ackerman. [AB]
    James SCOOL & Serena STURT, 11 Sept. 1845. (PHn) [B2]
SCOTT, James, & Ana Eliza GARRET, 5 Sept. 1851. (SMc) [B2]
SCOTT, Joseph, & Sally A. PERKINS, bond 9 Aug. 1837;
    bdsm: Thos. Perkins. [AB]
SCOTT, Ransdall G., & Sarah Jane RICHARD, bond 26 Apr. 1842;
    f/b: J. H. Richard; bdsm: Jefferson Scott. [AB]
SCROGGS, Ebenezer, & Rachel OWINGS, bond 4 Nov. 1826. [AB]
SEAL, Dye, & Malvina SEXTON, bond 27 Feb. 1845;
    bdsm: Robert Clark. [AB]
    Dye TEAL & Malvine Sexton, 27 Feb. 1845. (SKc) [B2]
SECREST, George, & Sophia SAUNDERS, bond 21 Dec. 1820;
    f/b & bdsm: Oliver Saunders. [AB]
    George Secrest & Sophia SANDERS, 14 Dec. 1820. [S1]
SET, John, & Elizabeth ?SROUT, bond 21 Apr. 1811;
    bdsm: Jno. Johnson. [AB]
    John Set & Elizabeth Srout, 21 Apr. 1811. [JA,S1]
    also, compare: John LETT & Elizabeth TROUTT, bond 20 Apr. 1811;
    bdsm: John Lett, Casper Troutt. [AB]
[SETTER?] Gitter, Samuel P., & Sally TINCHER, bond Apr. 1828;
    f/b: Wm. Tincher; bdsm: Francis Tincher. [AB]
    Samuel P. SETTER & Sally SINCHER, 29 Apr. 1828. (JPk) [B2]
SEXTON, Ben, & Delila LAWENCY, bond 12 Apr. 1845;
    bdsm: Wm. Rodgers. [AB]
    Benjamin ?Sexton & Delila LOWRY, 13 Apr. 1845. (WRg) [B2]
SEXTON, Benjamin, & Elizabeth WAITT, 27 March 1833. (OSx) [B2]
[SEXTON?] Senton, James, & Polly STATEN, bond 11 Jan. 1822;
    f/b: Ruban Staten; bdsm: Benj. Calk. [AB]

SEXTON, James Henry, & Nancy NORRIS, bond 21 Sept. 1842;
    bdsm: David Norris.   [AB]
SHANKLIN, Benjamin, & Peggy FURGERSON, 1813. (LTu)   [KM]
SHANKLIN, John, & Elizabeth KIGGINS, bond 3 March 1824;
    bdsm: John Munn.   [AB]
    John Shanklin & Elizabeth HIGGINS, 4 March 1824.   [S1]
SHANKLIN, John, & Christiana ADAMS, bond 21 July 1846;
    f/b: John Adams; bdsm: James Adams.   [AB]
    John H. SHANKLAND & Christe Ann Adams, 24 July 1846. (JDS)   [B2]
SHANKLIN, Joseph, & Amelia JONES, 23 March 1826.   [B2]
SHANKLINS, J. W., & Mariah STAMPER, bond 31 July 1848;
    bdsm: James Lock.   [AB]
[SHANNON?] Shoson, William, & Martha RICE, bond 15 Sept. 1842;
    f/b: Eli Rice; bdsm: W. W. ?Rernley.   [AB]
    William SHANNON & Martha J. RICE, 20 Oct. 1842. (JGW)   [B2]
SHARP, Jesse, & Polly NORRIS, bond 14 July 1829;
    bdsm: John Norris.   [AB]
SHARP, John W., & Mary CRAYCRAFT, bond 22 Nov. 1847;
    bdsm: Thomas Craycraft.   [AB]
    John Sharp & Ma(r)y CRACRAFT, 25 Nov. 1847. (RFC)   [B2]
SHARP, Dr. Joseph, & Katharine RATLIFF, 20 Sept. 1826. (RTy)   [B2]
SHARP, Samuel, & Julia KINCAID, bond 16 July 1840;
    f/b & bdsm: Archibald Kincaid.   [AB]
    Samuel Sharp & Jude KINDALE, 17 July 1841. (SMc)   [B2]
SHARP, Thomas, & Louinda ROBERTSON, bond 4 Aug. 1823;
    bdsm: Richard Robertson.   [AB]
    Thomas Sharp & Lauvinda Robertson, 14 Aug. 1824.   [S1]
SHARP, Wm., & Polly MITCHELL, bond 20 July 1831;
    bdsm: Samuel Mitchell.   [AB]
SHARP, Wm. S., & Mary HORD or Herd, bond 12 March 1845;
    bdsm: Joshua Barns.   [AB]
    William S. Sharp & Mary Hord, 12 March 1845. (ODB)   [B2]
SHEAKLES, Ira, & Pauline BARNETT, bond 28 Jan. 1828;
    bdsm: Abner Rafferty.   [AB]
    Ira SHECKLES & Paulina Barnett, 28 Jan. 1829. (TCp)   [B2]
SHIELDS, Wm., & Geo. Ann COGSWELL, bond 21 Jan. 1846;
    f/b: Isaac Cogswell; bdsm: Geo. Casey.   [AB]
    William Shields & George ann Cogswell, 22 Jan. 1846. (JGW)   [B2]
SHIRLEY, Fortunatus, & Elizabeth S. BROTHERS, 23 Dec. 1851. (RFC)   [B2]
SHOALTZ, Christian, & Philey RICHARDS, bond 13 Dec. 1811;

bdsm: Christian Shoatz, R. Richards. [AB]
   Christian SHUTTS or SHOOTS & Phebe Richards, 15 Dec. 1811. [JA,S1]
SHOAT, Samuel, & Polly GRAYSON, 21 June 1819. [S1]
SHOULTZ, Berry, & Nancy COOPER, bond 31 May 1840;
  bdsm: Leander Cooper. [AB]
SHOULTZ, Jones, & Sally GOODPASTURE, bond 16 Jan. 1834;
  bdsm: Austin Oakley. [AB]
   James SHOOTTS & Sally GOODPASTER, 16 Jan. 1834. (SMc) [B2]
SHOUSE, Hamilton, & Sarah SMALLWOOD, bond 16 Sept. 1833;
  bdsm: Ben Smallwood. [AB]
SHROPSHIRE, Gillmore, & Gegueller[?] SHROUT, bond 10 Feb. 1848;
  f/b: Noah Shrout; bdsm: David Cups. [AB]
   Gilman? SOPSHER & Genela? Shrout, 10 Feb. 1848. (SKc) [B2]
SHROPSHIRE, Wm., & Elizabeth ATCHISON, bond 31 Aug. 1833;
  bdsm: Silas Atchison. [AB]
SHROPSIER, James, & Elizabeth TEEL, bond 19 Feb. 1833;
  bdsm: Joshua Ewing. [AB]
   James SHROPSHIER & Elizabeth Teel, 19 Feb. 1833. (WWh) [B2]
SHROUT, Abram, & Sally B. GARNER, bond 6 Jan. 1812;
  f/b: Jacob Garner; bdsm: Abram Shrout, Jacob Garner. [AB]
SHROUT, David, & Cinthiana WRIGHT, bond 22 Apr. 1842;
  f/g: John Shrout; f/b: F. B. Wright; bdsm: Arnold Johnson. [AB]
   David SROUT & Catharine Wright, 3 May 1842. (JGW) [B2]
SHROUT, Henry, & Eladia ARROSMITH, bond 22 Feb. 1847;
  bdsm: Elijah Clark. [AB]
   Henry Shrout & Eleda? Araminta CLARK, 25 Feb. 1847. (SKc) [B2]
SHROUT, Isaac, & Betsey RICHARDS, 23 Feb. 1817. [S1]
[SHROUT] Srout, John, & Polly SMITH, bond 8 July 1822;
  bdsm: David Ullery. [AB]
   John SHROUT & Polly Smith, 8 June 1822. [S1]
SHROUT, John, & Polly YARBROUGH, bond May 1828;
  f/g: Jehu (or John?) Shrout; bdsm: Thos.? Yarbrough. [AB]
   John SHULTZ & Polly YARBOUGH, 22 May 1828. (AGg) [B2]
SHROUT, Noah, & Nancy McCLAIN, bond 1 Sept. 1827;
  bdsm: John Shrout. [AB]
SHROUT, Shelton, & Hester Ann EDWARDS, bond 13 June 1848;
  bdsm: Owen Edwards. [AB]
[SHROUT] Srout, Samuel, & Hester FITZGERALD, bond 22 Dec. 1824;
  bdsm: John B. Warren; [AB]

Samuel SHROUT & Hester FITZGUALD, 24 Dec. 1824. [S1]

SHROUT, William, & Elizabeth MOORE, 16 June 1844. (JMc) [B2]

SHROUT, William, & Rebecca MYERS, bond 24 Oct. 1846;
    f/b: Joseph Myers; bdsm: John Shrout. [AB]
    William SROUT / Shrout & Rebecca MYRES, 25 Oct. 1846. (JGW or AGW) [B2]

SHRYACK, Wm., & Elizabeth REED, bond 3 Feb. 1819;
    bdsm: Austin Choat. [AB]

SHULES, Henry, & Winnified UTTERBACK, 1813. (LTu) [KM]
    Henry SHUTTS & Winnefred Utterback [JA]

SHUMATE, William, & Milly UNDERWOOD, bond 21 Dec. 1820;
    f/g: Bailey Shumate; f/b & bdsm: Reuben Underwood. [AB]
    William Shumate & Milley Underwood, 21 Dec. 1820. [S1]

SILCOCK, Ewel, & Betsey BEAN, bond 19 Jan. 1820
    bdsm: Edward Hammond. [AB]
    Ewel Silcock & Betsy McBEAN, 2 Jan. 1820. [S1]

SIMON or Smart?, James, & Elizabeth HUGHES, bond 25 Jan. 1825;
    bdsm: John Hughs. [AB]

SIMPSON, Thos. A., & Frances J. SIMPSON, 7 Jan. 1851. (RFC) [B2]

SINSTER, Jeremiah, & Levina CARR, 13 June 1817. [S1]

SIX, G. W., & Elvira J. NELSON, bond 16 July 1846;
    bdsm: Jas. F. Hawkins. [AB]

SIX, John, & Elizabeth BANTA or Burns?, bond 12 March 1812;
    bdsm: John Six, John Williams. [AB]
    John Six or SISA & Elizabeth BURNS, 15 March 1812. [JA,S1]

SIX, John, & Jane McVEY, bond 26 March 1815;
    bdsm: Manining Vice, J. Six. [AB]
    John Six or SISA & Jean McVey, 26 March 1815. [JA,S1]

SIX, John, & Julian CANN [or Carr?], bond 25 Jan. 1836;
    bdsm: Thos. Bradshaw. [AB]

[SLAVENS?] Havens, James, & Polly DAVIS, bond 16 May 1829;
    bdsm: George Owings. [AB]
    James SLAVENS & Polly Davis, 16 May 1829. (JnSm) [B2]

SMALL, Jesse, & Levina GEORGE, bond 17 July 1837;
    bdsm: Bailey George. [AB]
    Jesse Small & Leuce George, 13 July 1837. (RTy) [B2]

SMALL, Moses, & Harriet GEORGE, bond 2 Sept. 1840;
    bdsm: Jesse Small. [AB]

SMALL, Philip, & Eliza GEORGE, 9 July 1835. (MGs) [B2]

SMALL, Philip F., & Martha CLOW, 14 Nov. 1850. (SLH) [B2]

SMALL, Thomas, & Polly Ann SHARP, bond 24 March 1847;
    m/b: Elizabeth Sharp; bdsm: Thomas Craycraft. [AB]
    Thos. Small & Polly Ann Sharp, 25 March 1847. (RFC) [B2]
SMALL, Wm., & Matilda LINCH, 30 Nov. 1843. (RFC) [B2]
SMALLWOOD, David, & Polly MUNS, bond 13 (or 18?) Feb. 1816;
    f/b: Wm. Muns; bdsm: Reuben Fugate. [AB]
    David Smallwood & Polly MOORE, 1816. [S1]
SMALLWOOD, James or Jones, & Elizabeth CELELASURE, bond 4 Sept. 1820;
    bdsm: David Cellelasure. [AB]
    James SMALWOOD & Elizabeth COLGLAZLER, 7 Sept. 1820. [S1]
SMILEY, Robert, & Polly BLACKBURN, bond 18 March 1816;
    bdsm: Joseph Hopkins. [AB]
    Robert SMILY or Swiley & Polly Blackburn, 21 March 1816. [JA,S1]
SMITH, C., & Eliza BURNS or Burnes, bond 21 Nov. 1842;
    bdsm: John F. Turner. [AB]
    Creed Smith & Elizabeth BARNES, 22 Nov. 1842. (JnSm) [B2]
SMITH, Jesse, & Amy or An(n)y COLLINS, 11 Nov. 1851. (JDh) [B2]
SMITH, Joab, & Nancy JOHNSON, bond 1 Feb. 1812;
    f/b: Thomas Johnson; bdsm: Joab Smith, John Johnson. [AB]
SMITH, Jones, & Nancy STATON, 21 Feb. 1826. (JGW) [B2]
SMITH, Mark A., & Sarah YARBROUGH, bond 18 Oct. 1837;
    bdsm: Thomas Yarbrough. [AB]
SMITH, Thomas B., & Martha A. LIGHTFOOT, bond 29 Jan. 1840;
    parent/b: C. Lightfoot; bdsm: Wm. M. Ragland. [AB]
    Thomas B. Smith & Martha A. Lightfoot, 6 Feb. 1840. [S1]
SMITH, Thomas B., & Frances A. M. LIGHTFOOT, 6 Nov. 1840. (TDm)
    also: Thomas B. Smith & Francis W. Lightfoot, 5 Nov. 1850. (EJo) [B2]
SMITH, Washington, & Elizabeth A. SPENCER, 3 Feb. 1851. (LGH) [B2]
SMITH, William, & Sarah BRACKEN, 29 July 1817. [S1]
SMITH, William, & Sharlott GOODLOW, bond 29 Dec. 1830;
    bdsm: Geo. Coleman. [AB]
    William Smith & Charlott Goodlow, 30 Dec. 1830. (JnSm) [B2]
SMITH, William, & Kizzy ARROWSMITH, 4 Aug. 1839. (SJk) [B2]
SMITH, William, & Margar(e)t McFARLAND, 27 March 1851. (LGH) [B2]
SMITH, Wm. R., & Lydia TRUMBO, bond 29 July 1829;
    bdsm: Jacob Trumbo. [AB]
SMOOT, Geo. W., & Rebecca HINES, bond 10 Oct. 1831;
    bdsm: John Hines. [AB]
SMOOT, John, & Eliza BANCE, bond 6 Nov. 1839;
    bdsm: James Bruce; [AB]

John J. Smoot & Eliza J. RICE, 7 Nov. 1839. (SRg)   [B2]
SMOOT or Smott?, Stephen, & Lena JACKSON, bond 17 June 1831;
   bdsm: Jacob Stelle [Steele?].   [AB]
[SMOOT?] Smott, Stephen, & Katharine HYMER, bond 19 Apr. 1847;
   bdsm: C. B. Hymer.   [AB]
   Stephen SMOOT & Katherine P. Hymer, 19 Oct. 1847. (AGW)   [B2]
SMOOT or Smart, W. N(icholas), & Martha A. ROGERS, bond 17 Feb. 1849;
   f/b: Sackett? Rogers; bdsm: J. Boyd.   [AB]
SNAP, George, & Arminea WATKINS, 18 Nov. 1851. (JLk)   [B2]
SNAP, Henry, & Nancy McKINNIS, bond 9 Jan. 1836;
   bdsm: Milton McGinnis.   [AB]
SNEDAKER, James, & Sarah BUTHER [Butcher?], 30 Jan. 1851. (SKc)   [B2]
SNEDEGAR, Christopher, & Kiziah CONYERS, bond 3 Jan. 1825;
   bdsm: Enoch Conyers.   [AB]
   Christopher Snedegar & Kisiah Conyers, 5 Jan. 1825.   [S1]
SNEDEGAR, Mose, & Elizabeth JOHNSON, bond 26 July 1831;
   bdsm: Elish Darnell.   [AB]
SNEDEGAR, William, & Sally TRUMBO, bond 11 Dec. 1820;
   f/b & bdsm: John Trumbo.   [AB]
   William SUEDGER & Sally TURMBO, 14 Dec. 1820.   [S1]
SNEDIEGAR, Isaac, & Elizabeth ARROSMITH, bond 22 Aug. 1849;
   bdsm: A. Hornback.   [AB]
SNEDIGAR, Moses, & Ann Matilda HORSEMAN, 19 Nov. 1851. (SMc)   [B2]
SNEDIGER, Isaac, & Peggy TRUMBO, bond 11 March 1822;
   bdsm: Isaac Trumbo.   [AB]
   Isaac SNEDAGAR & Margaret Trumbo, 15 March 1822.   [S1]
SNELLING, Benjamin, & Rachel FETHERGILL, bond 19 July 1822;
   bdsm: Thornton Snelling.   [AB]
   Benjamin Snelling & Rachel FATHERGILL, 19 July 1822.   [S1]
SNELLING, Benjamin, & Polly DOGGETT, bond 20 Aug. 1838;
   bdsm: Richard Doggett.   [AB]
   Benjamin Snelling & Polly DAGGET, 23 Aug. 1838. (JnSm)   [B2]
SNELLING, Franklin, & Martha CLINE, 10 Jan. 1851. (JDy)   [B2]
SNELLING, Jilson P., & Minerva ATCHISON, bond 29 Jan. 1833;
   bdsm: Wm. Atchison.   [AB]
SNELLING, Toliver, & Elizabeth NEWLAND, 7 March 1844. (SMc)   [B2]
SOMERVILLE, Sterling, & Elizabeth CAMPLIN, bond 4 Oct. 1848;
   bdsm: James Rainey.   [AB]
SORREL, Augustine, & Margaret ?BOGERS, bond 9 Apr. 1849;

bdsm: Wm. Rogers. [AB]

   Augustine SORRELL & Margaret ROGERS, 9 Apr. 1849. (WRg) [B2]

SORREL, Joseph, & Seny HALL, bond 2 Oct. 1816;

bdsm: Thomas Williams. [AB]

SORREL, Lorenzo, & Elizabeth MORE, 16 Oct. 1851. (SKc) [B2]

SORRELL, Alfred, & Sarah F. FIELDER, bond 14 March 1848;

bdsm: Wm. Fielder. [AB]

   Alford Sorrell & Sarah A. FIELDEN, 14 March 1848. (WRg) [B2]

SORRELL, Elijah, & Mary TACK, bond 20 March 1848;

bdsm: Nicholas Traylor. [AB]

[SORRELL?] Collins, Elisha, & Eliza McCULLA, bond 2 Jan. 1840;

bdsm: Joshua Sorrell. [AB]

   Elisha SORREL & Eliza McCulla, 9 Jan. 1840. (SJk) [B2]

SORRELL, Geo., & Elizabeth SORRELL, bond 16 Nov. 1846;

f/g: Wm. Sorrell; f/b: Joseph Sorrell; bdsm: Elisha Sorrell. [AB]

   George W. Sorrell & Elizabeth Sorrell, 17 Nov. 1846. (SKc) [B2]

SORRELL, James, Jr., & Dicey or Diesy FRYERS, bond 15 Oct. 1834;

f/g & bdsm: James Sorrell, Sr. [AB]

   James Sorrell & Disey FRASURE, 16 Oct. 1834. (PCy) [B2]

SORRELL, John, & Peggy TRAILER, bond 19 March 1822;

bdsm: Joel Trailor. [AB]

   John Sorrell & Peggy TRAYLOR, 7 June 1822. [S1]

SORRELL, John, & Margaret STATON, bond 12 June 1824;

bdsm: James Sorrell. [AB]

   John Sorrell & Margaret Staton, 15 June 1824. [S1]

SORRELL, John, & Martha STEARMAN, bond 18 Nov. 1830;

bdsm: Robt. Stearman. [AB]

SORRELL, John, & [Mrs.] Katharine ARROWSMITH, bond 3 Apr. 1845;

bdsm: David Hawkins. [AB]

   John SORREL & Catharine Arrowsmith, 3 Apr. 1845. (TRk) [B2]

SORRELL, John, & Nelly _____, 2 Feb. 1852. (WRg) [B2]

SORRELL, John H., & Polly Anna JOHNSON, bond 10 Sept. 1846;

f/b & bdsm: Jefferson Johnson; [AB]

John H. Sorrell & Polly R. Johnson, 11 Sept. 1846. (BBv) [B2]

SORRELL, Joseph, & Phebe McCARTE, bond 17 March 1824;

f/b: Thomas McCarte; bdsm: Reuben Staten. [AB]

   Joseph Sorrell & Phebe McCarte, 17 March 1824; also, 18 March. [S1]

SORRELL, Joshua, & Edimia McCLAIN, bond 8 Jan. 1834;

bdsm: John Sorrell. [AB]

   Joshua SORREL & Edany McLAIN, 8 Jan. 1834. (TIs) [B2]

[SORRELL?] Sarrell, Thomas, & Gillian THOMAS, bond 6 Feb. 1838;
  f/b: Isaac Thomas; bdsm: James Sorrell. [AB]
SORRELL, Wm., & Catherine McCARTY, bond 31 May 1823;
  bdsm: Reuben Stayton [Staton?]. [AB]
  William Sorrell & Catharine McCARTEE, 6 June 1823. [S1]
SORRELL, William, & Amanda STATON, 16 Apr. 1850. (WRg) [B2]
SORRELL, Wm. R., & Betsey McCOLOUGH, bond 15 May 1845;
  bdsm: Wm. Staten. [AB]
  Ri SORREL & Betsy McCOLLOUGH, 16 May 1845. (BBv) [B2]
SORRELLE, James, & Mary An SORRELL, bond 22 June 1848;
  bdsm: Elisha Sorrell. [AB]
  James SORRELL & Mary A. BAILY, 23 June 1849. (WRg) [B2]
SOUTH, Benjamin, & Polly MOORE, bond 8 Dec. 1823;
  bdsm: Wm. Moore. [AB]
  Benjamin South & Polly Moore, 18 Dec. 1823. [S1]
SOWARD, William, & Betsy SMITH, bond 17 Feb. 1813. [AB]
SPARKS, George, & Hannah GILLASPIE, bond 1 May 1848;
  bdsm: Francis Gillaspie. [AB]
  George Sparks & Hannah Gillaspi(e), 2 May 1848. (ASh) [B2]
SPENCE, Jonathan, & Betsey McCLAIN, 28 Dec. 1826. (JPk) [B2]
SPENCE, More, & Eliza BEDFORD, bond 15 Jan. 1831;
  bdsm: Henry Hart. [AB]
SPENCE, Wm. D., & Jane DUTY, bond 7 May 1849;
  bdsm: More Spencer. [AB]
  William SPENCER & Jane Duty, 3 Apr. 1849. (WMV) [B2]
SPENCER, Aaron, & Mary INGRAM, bond 31 Dec. 1823;
  bdsm: Wm. Ward. [AB]
SPENCER, David, & Kate PERVIS, bond 5 Apr. 1848;
  f/b & bdsm: Thomas Pervis. [AB]
  David SPENCE & Hetty Pervis, 5 March 1848. (SKc) [B2]
SPENCER, George, & Rutha Ann CARROLL, bond 23 Feb. 1842;
  m/b: Rachel Carroll; bdsm: James Carrol. [AB]
SPENCER, John, & Phebe TURNER, bond 23 Aug. 1814;
  bdsm: John Spencer, John Traylor. [AB]
  John Spencer & Phebe Turner, 25 Aug. 1814. (CHp) [JA,S1]
SPENCER, John, & Sally JOHNSON, bond 28 Sept. 1847;
  bdsm: Levi Johnson. [AB]
  John SPENSER or Spencer & Sally Johnson, 28 Sept. 1847. (SKc) [B2]
SPENCER, John, & Cyntha NELSON, 27 Nov. 1851. (BBv) [B2]

SPENCER, Lewis or Louis, & Frames[?] SORRELL, bond 2 Apr. 1812;
  f/b: Elisha Sorrell; bdsm: Elisha Sorrell, Louis Spencer. [AB]
  Lewis Spencer & Frances SORREL, 5 Apr. 1812. [JA,S1]
SPENCER, Moses, & Jane DAVIS, bond 22 March 1848;
  bdsm: Aaron Spencer. [AB]
  Moses SPENCE & Jane PERVIS, 22 March 1848. (SKc) [B2]
SPENCER, Samuel, & Lucy YARBROUGH, 27 July 1840. (SMc) [B2]
SPENCER, Thos., & Margaret HART, bond 22 Oct. 1836;
  bdsm: B. F. Sudduth. [AB]
SPENCER, Wm., & Eleanor GILLIS, bond 11 June 1821;
  bdsm: Wm. Pervis. [AB]
SPENCER, Wm., & Melinda BUSBY, bond 1 Jan. 1833;
  bdsm: John Busby. [AB]
  William Spencer & Malinda Busby, 3 Jan. 1833. (JFY) [B2]
SPENCER, Wm., & Catharine WILLIAMSON, bond 14 Oct. 1848;
  bdsm: Jonathan Spencer. [AB]
  William SPENCE & Catharine Williamson, 15 Oct. 1848. (SKc) [B2]
SPRATT, Andrew, & Mary Ann DUTY, bond 9 March 1840;
  bdsm: John Duty. [AB]
  Andrew Spratt & Maryann Duty, 13? March 1840. (TDm) [B2]
SPRATT, John, & Ann CRAIG, bond 28 July 1845;
  bdsm: James Berry. [AB]
SPURLOCK, John, & Milly PERVIS, bond 11 March 1825;
  bdsm: John Pervis. [AB]
STAMPER, Richard, & Margaret ETCHISON [Atchison?], bond 28 March 1838;
  f/g: Washington Stamper; bdsm: Charles Jones. [AB]
  Richard Stamper & Marget ETCHESON, 21 March 1838. (JSt) [B2]
STAMPER, Richard, & Mary Ann MYERS, bond 13 July 1848;
  bdsm: Thos. Shelton. [AB]
STAMPER, Samuel, & Mariah P. LOCK, bond 29 Aug. 1836;
  f/b: Richard Lock; bdsm: Wm. Lock. [AB]
  Samuel A. Stamper & Maria Lock, 1 Sept. 1836. (WWn) [B2]
STAMPER, Thos. F., & Nancy ROSTON [Ralston?], bond 24 March 1828;
  bdsm: John Roston. [AB]
STANCLIFFE, James, & Susannah MOORE, bond 28 July 1831;
  bdsm: Jeremiah Proctor. [AB]
STANFIELD, James, & Martha MORGAN, bond 28 Oct. 1845;
  bdsm: Henry Morgan. [AB]
STANFIELD, John, & Nancy REED, bond 2 Aug. 1836;
  bdsm: Wm. Reed; [AB]

John Stanfield & Nancy READ, 4 Aug. 1836. (JnSm) [B2]
STANFIELD, Pleasant, & Sarah MORGAN, bond 22 Sept. 1848;
    bdsm: Thos. Manfield. [AB]
    Pleasant Stanfield or Stand Field & Sarah Morgan, 24 Sept. 1848. (SKc) [B2]
STATEN, Ruben, & Susan HALL, widow, bond 13 Aug. 1813;
    bdsm: Reuben Staten, John Purvis. [KM]
    Ruben Staten or STATON & Susan Hall, 14 Aug. 1813. [JA,S1]
STATEN, William, & Sally McCLAIN, bond 31 July 1845;
    f/g: John Staten; bdsm: Mason Spence. [AB]
    William STATON & Sarah McClain, 31 July 1845. (OSx) [B2]
STATON, D. P., & Patsey FIELDER, bond 16 Aug. 1842;
    bdsm: James McCarty. [AB]
    O. P. Staton & Patsy Fielder, 18 Aug. 1842. (WRg) [B2]
STATON, James, & Salley McCARTEY, bond 8 Apr. 1828;
    bdsm: Wm. Staton. [AB]
    James Staton & Sally McCARTEE, 10 Apr. 1828. (EHw) [B2]
STATON, James, & Sally THOMAS, bond 20 Sept. 1829;
    f/b: Isaac Thomas; bdsm: John Sorrel. [AB]
    James Staton & Sally Thomas, 22 Sept. 1829. (EHw) [B2]
STATON, John, & Polley TRALER, bond 31 Dec. 1833;
    bdsm: John Sorrell. [AB]
    James Staton & Polly TRAYLOR, 1 Jan. 1834. (TIs) [B2]
STATON, Samuel, & Druslia SADLER, bond 19 Nov. 1825;
    bdsm: Matthew Pettit. [AB]
STATON, Samuel, & Polly McCULLOUGH, bond 15 July 1830;
    bdsm: John McLaughlin. [AB]
STATON, Samuel, & Lucretia THOMPSON, 4 May 1843. (WRg) [B2]
STATON, Solomon, & Melinda McCLAIN, bond 15 Feb. 1821;
    bdsm: Wm. Staton. [AB]
    Solomon Staton & Malinda McCARTHA, 16 Feb. 1821. [S1]
[STATON] Statan, Wm., & Nancy SEXTON, bond 27 Jan. 1821;
    bdsm: Timothy Terrell. [AB]
    William STATON & Nancy Sexton, 28 Jan. 1821. [S1]
STATON, Wm., & Nancy WILSON, bond 17 Nov. 1846;
    bdsm: Wm. Staton, Sr. [AB]
    William Staton & Nancy WILLSON, 20 Nov. 1846. (BBv) [B2]
STAYTON, James, & Emily FRAZIER, bond 24 Jan. 1838;
    f/b: John Frazier; bdsm: Wm. Frazier. [AB]
STEAL, Elijah, & Emily TOWNSEND, bond 29 Dec. 1828;

f/b & bdsm: Wm. Townsend.   [AB]

STEEL, Elijah, & Rachel HOLT, bond 12 Dec. 1822;

    bdsm: Mahala Holt.   [AB]

    Elijah Steel & Rachel HALL, 13 Dec. 1822.   [S1]

STEEL, Geo. K., & Louisa MITCHELL, bond 27 Jan. 1848;

    bdsm: James Mitchell.   [AB]

STEELE, Fielding B., & Nancy MINNEAR, bond 18 Nov. 1839;

    f/b: Jonathan Minnear; bdsm: Thos. Minnear.   [AB]

    Fielding B. Steele & Nancy MENEAR, 21 Nov. 1839. (JGW)   [B2]

STEELE, John, & Ann BUTLER, bond 20 Jan. 1819;

    f/b: John Butler; bdsm: John Steel, Samuel Steele.   [AB]

    John STEEL & Ann Butler, 21 Jan. 1819.   [S1]

STEELE, John B., & Mary Ann McCLAIN, bond 8 Sept. 1845;

    bdsm: James McClain.   [AB]

STEELE, Larkin, & Casandrid? OWINGS, bond 6 July 1828;

    bdsm: John Jones.   [AB]

STEELE, Robert, & Polly CASSITY, bond 12 Apr. 1830;

    bdsm: Jacob Cassity.   [AB]

STEELE, Solomon, & Martha MOOR, bond 13 Nov. 1813;

    f/b: Robert Moor; bdsm: John Laymon; mar. 12 Nov.   [KM]

    Solomon STEEL & Martha Moor, 14 Nov. 1813.   [JA]

    14 Nov. 1814   [S1]

STEELE, Thomas, & Elizabeth MITCHELL, bond 19 Oct. 1829;

    bdsm: Charles Whaley.   [AB]

STEPHENS, Alvin, & Mildred HUGHES, bond 17 Dec. 1836;

    bdsm: John S. Hughes.   [AB]

    Alvin Stephens & Mildred Hughes, 20 Dec. 1836. (JnSm)   [B2]

STEPHENS, Benjamin, & Nancy BRADSHAW, 27 Dec. 1826. (JHu)   [B2]

STEPHENS, Fairfax W., & Susan BROWN, bond 13 Jan. 1836;

    bdsm: John W. Tydings.   [AB]

STEPHENS, James F., & Milly Jane DOWNS, bond 28 June 1847;

    bdsm: Wm. Downs.   [AB]

STEPHENS, Jerome, & Elender HENRY, bond 25 Oct. 1847;

    bdsm: Jacob Henry.   [AB]

    Jerome Stephens & Elender? Henry, 2 Nov. 1847. (RFC)   [B2]

STEPHENS, John, & Cytha HUGHES, bond 11 Dec. 1815.   [AB]

STEPHENS, Joseph, & Mary CANNINGS, bond 29 Sept. 1847;

    bdsm: Robt. Caldwell.   [AB]

    Joseph Stephens & May COMINGS, 5 Oct. 1847.   [S2]

STEPHENS, Thomas, & Catharine GRAY, bond 3 March 1846;
    bdsm: Elisha Gray. [AB]
[STEPHENS] Stephen, Wm., & Nancy BOYD, bond 18 Aug. 1831;
    bdsm: Wm. Boyd. [AB]
STEPHENSON, William, & Anna WILLIAMS, 1813. (LTu) [KM]
STEVENSON, John, & Eliza COLEMAN, bond 11 May 1848;
    parent/b: F. O. Coleman; bdsm: James Sudduth. [AB]
    John T. STEPHENSON & El(i)za B. Coleman, 16 May 1848. (JnSm) [B2]
STEWART, Alexander, & Nancy TIPTON, bond 14 Nov. 1836;
    bdsm: Mitchel Tipton. [AB]
    Alexander Stewart & Nancy Tipton, 7 Nov. 1836. (RTh) [B2]
STEWART, Isaac, & Emily STEPHENS, bond 28 May 1842;
    f/b: Wm. Staphens; bdsm: John Stephens. [AB]
STEWART, James, & Sarah TIPTON, bond 3 Aug. 1837;
    f/g: Mitchell Stewart; bdsm: Mayor D. Tipton. [AB]
    James Stewart & Sarah Tipton, 3 Aug. 1837. (RTh) [B2]
STEWART, Wm., & Lydia GINTER, bond 30 Aug. 1825;
    bdsm: Thomas Mosely. [AB]
    William STUART & Lydia Ginter, 21 Aug. 1825. [S1]
ST(E)WART, William, & Milly STEPHENS, 17 Jan. 1851. (JDy) [B2]
STILLWELL, Obadiah, & Delila BUTLER, bond 15 Apr. 1815;
    m/b: Delila Butler; bdsm: John Stillwell. [KM]
STITH, Anderson, & Susannah RALLS, bond 27 Sept. 1834;
    f/g: James Stith; bdsm: Geo. W. Ralls. [AB]
    Anderson Stith & Lucinda ROLLS, 2 Oct. 1834. (MGs) [B2]
STITH, Preston, & Lydia RALLS, bond 7 May 1842;
    f/b: George Ralls; bdsm: Valentine Ralls. [AB]
    Preston Stith & Lydeabeck ROLLS, 10 June 1842. (SJn) [B2]
STOART, William, & Elizabeth EMMONS, bond 2 Jan. 1834;
    bdsm: Ashford Powell. [AB]
    William STOARD & Elizabeth Emmons, 2 Jan. 1834. (ALy) [B2]
STOCKTON, Edward, & Polly JOUETT, bond 18 July 1815;
    f/b: John Jouett; bdsm: Sam Willson. [AB]
STOCKTON, Ira, & Ruth FUGETT, bond 2 March 1831;
    bdsm: Andrew Nester. [AB]
    Ira Stockton & Ruth FUGATE, 3 March 1831. (JGW) [B2]
STOCKTON, Robert, & Maria MORRIS or Morros?, bond 11 Nov. 1816;
    bdsm: James McIlhaney. [AB]
STONE, Charles, & Matilda STONE, bond 10 Oct. 1812;
    bdsm: Valentine Stone, Charles Stone. [AB]

STONE, Dudley, & Polly BURNETT, bond 8 Feb. 1816;
 bdsm: Wm. Burnett, D. Stone.   [AB]
 Dudley Stone & Polly BURNET, 1816.   [S1]
STONE, James, & Margaret MARKHAM, bond 29 Sept. 1829;
 bdsm: Wm. Markham.   [AB]
 James F. Stone & Margarett Markham, 1 Oct. 1829. (SJn)   [B2]
STONE, John, & Sophia GRAHAM, bond 18 Apr. 1821;
 f/b: James M. Graham; bdsm: Henry Chiles.   [AB]
STONE, John, & Susan BURNS, bond 26 May 1845;
 bdsm: Enos Burns.   [AB]
 John F. Stone & Susan J. BURNES, 29 May 1845. (RFC)   [B2]
STONE, L. M., & Maria A. McCLANAHAN, 15 Jan. 1835. (SJn)   [B2]
STONE, Moses, & Matilda ROBINSON, 16 Apr. 1835. (JMh)   [B2]
STONE, Robert, & Sarah WHALEY, bond 16 Sept. 1814;
 f/b: Wm. Whaley; bdsm: Robt. Stone, Wm. Whaley.   [AB]
 Robert Stone & Sarah Whaley, 18 Sept. 1814.   [JA,S1]
STONE, Samuel, & Ann LANE, bond 8 Feb. 1821;
 bdsm: James Sudduth.   [AB]
 Samuel Stone & Ann Lane, 8 Feb. 1821.   [S1]
STONE, Valentine, & Lizzie NEAL, bond 16 July 1828;
 bdsm: Henry Neal.   [AB]
 Valentine Stone & Sisley Neal, 17 July 1828. (JEv)   [B2]
STONE, Wm., & Mary Ann McCORMICK, bond 27 Oct. 1846;
 bdsm: Samuel McCormick.   [AB]
 William Stone & Mary Ann McCormick, 29 Oct. 1846. (SJn)   [B2]
STONER, Peter S., & Mary F. PHELPS, bond 10 Oct. 1844.   [AB]
 Peter S. Stoner & Mary F. Phelps, 10 Oct. 1844. (JnSm)   [B2]
STOOPS, Wm., & Mary Ann McCLELLAN, bond 30 Nov. 1830;
 f/g: John Stoops; bdsm: Wm. M. Sudduth.   [AB]
 William Stoops & Mary Ann McCLELAN, 30 Nov. 1830. (JEv)   [B2]
STORM, William, & Patsey LAVIASTERS [Lamaster?], 10 Feb. 1820.   [S1]
STORM or Stone?, Wm., & Ann STEELE, bond 15 July 1828;
 bdsm: Thos. Barker.   [AB]
STORY, Lewis, & Margaret LYNAM, bond 1 Oct. 1838 [or 33?];
 f/g: Thomas Story; bdsm: Len Lynam.   [AB]
 Lewis Story & Margret Lynam, 2 Oct. 1833. (ALy)   [B2]
STORY, Lewis, & Mary EM[M]ONS, bond 7 July 1845;
 bdsm: Wm. Emmons.   [AB]
STOUT, Abner, & Harriet WHALEY, bond 1 Sept. 1828;

bdsm: John Price.	[AB]
Oliver H. Stout & Harriett Whaley, 4 Sept. 1828. (DWh)	[B2]
STUART, J. B., & Phebe MORRIS, 19 Feb. 1844. (RFC)	[B2]
SUDDUTH, Lewis E., & Caroline MOFFITT, 16 Sept. 1834. (DST)	[B2]
SUDDUTH, Wm., & Lucy LANE, bond 14 Oct. 1815;	
bdsm: Henry Lane, Wm. Sudduth.	[AB]
William Sudduth & Lucy LAIN, 1816.	[S1]
SUDDUTH, William H., & Philadelphia S. MOFFITT, no date [1834?]. (DST)	[B2]
SUMMERS, Charles, & Avrelia [Amelia?] WHALEY, bond 9 Nov. 1819;	
f/b: Wm. Whaley; bdsm: Charles Summers, Wm. Whaley.	[AB]
SUMMERS, Jesse, & Sally BROMMEN, bond 12 March 1824;	
bdsm: B. F. Johnson.	[AB]
SUMMERS, ?Thomas, & Margaret S. HAZELRIGG, bond 5 Jan. 1838;	
bdsm: Eli Hazelrigg.	[AB]
Thomas Summers & Margaret Hazelrigg, 9 Jan. 1838. (DST)	[B2]
[SUTLE?] Leetch or Suth?, Andrew, & Nancy CARPENTER, bond 27 Nov. 1849;	
bdsm: Sq. Carpenter.	[AB]
Andrew J. SUTLE & Nancy Carpenter, 28 Nov. 1849. (JHe)	[B2]
[SWANK?] Swarck, G. W., & Leeda JOHNSON, bond 24 July 1838;	
f/b: Isaac Johnson; bdsm: Samuel Myres.	[AB]
George SWANK & Leweda Johnson, 25 July 1838. (JGW)	[B2]
SWANK, George W., & Rebeca P. HIMER, 12 Oct. 1831. (JGW)	[B2]
SWARTS, Wm. A., & Frances Ann McCAUSLAND, 30 Dec. 1844. (WRg)	[B2]
SWEATMAN, Thomas, & Cardin YOUNG, bond 18 May 1831;	
bdsm: Sinnett Young.	[AB]
SWEATMAN, Wm., & Nancy SWEATMAN, bond 15 Oct. 1825;	
bdsm: Thos. Sweatman.	[AB]
William S. Sweatman & Nancy Sweatman, 16 Oct. 1825.	[S1]
[SWEATNAM?] Swatmon, John, & Eliza BAYLEY, bond 7 Apr. 1832;	
bdsm: Marvin Bailey.	[AB]
John B. SWEATNAM & Eliza BAILEY, 10 Apr. 1832. (SJn)	[B2]
SWENY, John, & Minerva METER, bond 6 Jan. 1834;	
bdsm: Thos. Meter.	[AB]
John SWINEY & Menerva Jane METEER, 9 Jan. 1833. (RTy)	[B2]
SWETMOR, Joseph, & Polly ATCHISON, bond 9 Jan. 1832;	
bdsm: Wm. Atchison.	[AB]
SWIM, Wm., & Lucinda DONITHAN, bond 7 Aug. 1838;	
f/b: Thos. D. Donithan; bdsm: Wm. Donithan.	[AB]
SWIN, Alexander, & Elizabeth HUNT, bond 12 Oct. 1829;	
bdsm: Anthony Mathew;	[AB]

Alexander SWIM & Elizabeth Hunt, 14 Oct. 1829. (JGW)   [B2]

SWIN, Asa, & Elizabeth PIPER, bond 15 June 1832;
     bdsm: Thomas McDeeter.   [AB]

Asa M. SWIM & Elizabeth Piper, 15 June 1837. (GWM)   [B2]

[SWINNEY] Swinez, Henry, & Lucinda DOUCHE, bond 24 Apr. 1828;
     bdsm: Mathew Doncho.   [AB]

Henry SWINNEY & Lucinda DONOHEW, 24 Apr. 1828. (JPk)   [B2]

SWINNEY, Thomas, & Elizabeth WISHARD, bond 16 June 1812;
     bdsm: Thos. Swinney, John Burton.   [AB]

Thomas Swinney or SWINNY & Elizabeth WISHART, 16 June 1812.   [JA,S1]

SWINY, Miles, & Polly BERRY, bond 8 March 1818;
     bdsm: Henry Berry.   [AB]

Miles SWANEY & Polly Berry, 9 March 1819. (JPH)   [TP,RS]

SWITIZER, John, & Mary Ann RANDOLPH, bond 25 Sept. 1827;
     f/g: Abraham Switzer; bdsm: Reuben Randolph.   [AB]

John SWITZER & Mary an Randolph, 27 Sept. 1827. (JnSm)   [B2]

SWITZER, Peter, & Magalane SMITH, bond 26 Nov. 1821;
     f/g: Abraham Switzer; bdsm: Michael Smith.   [AB]

Peter SWITZIER & Manellen Smith, 27 Nov. 1821.   [S1]

TABER, Duncan, & Amelia CANNON, bond 19 May 1825;
     bdsm: Jacob Sheller or Shuler.   [AB]

TABER, Wm. G., & Mary McINTIRE, bond 28 March 1848;
     bdsm: Thomas McIntire.   [AB]

TACKET, John C., & Mary SWETNAM, bond 5 Sept. 1846;
     bdsm: D. S. Thompson.   [AB]

John Tacket & Mary SWEETMAN, 6 Sept. 1846. (SKc)   [B2]

TACKETT, Barler, & Milly TACKETT, bond 13 Aug. 1827;
     bdsm: Baylis Tackett.   [AB]

Bayless Tackett & Milly Tackett, 14 Aug. 1827. (JVc)   [B2]

TACKETT, Charles, & Anna? RICE, bond 20 Dec. 1833;
     bdsm: Holman Rice.   [AB]

TACKETT, Francis, & Nancy WARREN, bond 15 Oct. 1847;
     bdsm: Wm. Warren.   [AB]

Francis M. TACKET & Nancy Warren or WARNER, 15 Oct. 1847. (SKc)   [B2]

TACKETT, John, & Elizabeth WILFISTIN, bond 29 Dec. 1837;
     bdsm: Frederick McIntosh.   [AB]

John TACKET & Elizabeth HELVENSTINE, 1 Jan. 1838. (JWR)   [B2]

TACKETT, Thomas, & Rebecca BEADLE, 10 Nov. 1844. (SKc)   [B2]

TACKETT, William, & Isabel DONALDSON, 6 May 1834;

bdsm: Alexander Donaldson. [AB]

    William J. TACKET & Isabel Donaldson, 8 Apr. 1834. (SJn) [B2]

TAILOR, William, & Polly JOSET, 2 Oct. 1835. (PHn) [B2]

TALLY, Samuel H., & Susan M. BROTHERS, 18 Dec. 1834. (JnSm) [B2]

TALOR, William P., & Mary H. MATIRE, 20 March 1848. (BBv) [B2]

TANNER, John, & Lucy YARBROUGH, bond 9 June 1812;

    bdsm: John Yarbrough. [AB]

    John Tanner & Lucy Yarbrough, 11 June 1812. [S1]

    John TURNER of Bath Co. & Lucy YARBOROUGH of Fleming Co. [JA]

TAP, John, & Deborah JACKSON, bond 10 Feb. 1832;

    bdsm: Morrison McCormick. [AB]

    John TAPP & Deborah Jackson, 12 Feb. 1832. (SMc) [B2]

[TAP?] Sapp, Nelson, & Nancy ?FIFHTBRICASTER, bond 10 June 1825;

    bdsm: W. B. Winn. [AB]

    Nelson TAP & Nancy FIGHTMASTER, 12 June 1828. (JPk) [B2]

TAPP, ?Harcus, & Pol(l)y Ann INGRAM, 13 March 1851. (WRg) [B2]

TAPP, James H., & Emily MANFIELD, bond 11 Aug. 1831 or 34;

    bdsm: John Dawson. [AB]

TAYLOR, Ben, & Sally P. STAMPER, bond 3 March 1827;

    bdsm: John Stamper. [AB]

    Benoni Taylor & Sarah P. Stamper, 6 March 1827. (JSt) [B2]

TAYLOR, F. Hizah, & Cassia WORKMAN, bond 2 Feb. 1846;

    bdsm: James Workman. [AB]

    Elijah A. Taylor & Casias C. Workman, 5 Feb. 1846. (BHr) [B2]

TAYLOR, Harrison, & Francis WILLHITE, 16 Oct. 1841. (SMc) [B2]

TAYLOR, John, & Polly NAYLOR, bond 5 Dec. 1838;

    bdsm: Benj. Northcutt. [AB]

    John Taylor & Polly NAILOR, 25 Dec. 1838. (BNc) [B2]

TAYLOR, Memory, & Eleanor BROWN, bond 11 Oct. 1827;

    bdsm: Joshua Power. [AB]

    Memory Taylor & Elenor Brown, 12 Oct. 1822. [S1]

TAYLOR, S. N., & L. LEDFORD, bond 16 Aug. 1828;

    f/b: James Ledford; bdsm: N. Ledford. [AB]

TAYLOR, Samuel, & Jane MICHEL, 26 Aug. 1835. (MGs) [B2]

TAYLOR, Solomon, & Sarah BRACKEN, bond 28 July 1823;

    f/b: James Bracken; bdsm: Robert Bracken. [AB]

    Solomon Taylor & Sarah Bracken, 11 Aug. 1823. [S1]

TAYLOR, Wilford, & Eliza Ann DUTY, bond 30 Apr. 1833;

    bdsm: Daniel Duty. [AB]

    Wilfred TAILOR & Eliza Ann Duty, 7 May 1833. (RTy) [B2]

TAYLOR, Wm., & Sally KENNARD, bond 3 Nov. 1814;
    bdsm: Wm. Taylor, James _____. [AB]
TEAL, Howard, & Mary COFER, bond 7 June 1849;
    bdsm: Harrison Cofer. [AB]
    Howard Teal & Ma(r)y Cofer, 7 June 1849. (WRg) [B2]
TEAL, John, & Barbary SHROPSHIRE, bond 5 Feb. 1848;
    bdsm: John Teal. [AB]
    John Teal & Barbary SOPSHER, 4 Feb. 1848. (SKc) [B2]
TECKUM, Isaac, & Fanny EMMONS, bond 11 July 1842;
    bdsm: F. Powell. [AB]
    Isaac TERHON & Frances Emmons, 18 July 1842. (ASd) [B2]
TEMPLEMAN, Eli, & Susan BUTLER, bond 8 Oct. 1846;
    bdsm: John Butler. [AB]
    Eli Templeman & Susan Butler or BULLER, 8 Oct. 1846. (SKc) [B2]
TEMPLEMAN, Ephriam, & Louinda VICE, bond 30 Aug. 1842;
    f/b & bdsm: Martin Vice. [AB]
TEMPLEMAN, Jesse, & Louina GREGORY, bond 13 Feb. 1842;
    f/b: Nathaniel Gregory; bdsm: Joseph Gregory. [AB]
[TEMPLEMAN] Temperance, Lewis, & Charlotte GREGORY, bond 20 Feb. 1815;
    bdsm: James Jamison, L. Temperance. [AB]
    Lewis TEMPLEMAN & Charlotte Gregory, 25 Feb. 1815. [S1]
    Lewis Templemon & Charlotte Gregory, 23 Feb. 1815. [JA]
TERRIL, Timothy & Nancy SEXTON, bond 11 Nov. 1819;
    bdsm: John Sexton. [AB]
    Timothy TEAREL & Nancy Sexton, 15 Nov. 1820. [S1]
THARP, Israel, & Avis JOHNSON, bond 4 or 5 March 1813;
    m/b: Hannah Atchison; bdsm: Israel Tharp, Henry Atchison. [KM]
    Israel THORP or Tharp & Aves Johnson, 5 March 1813. [JA,S1]
THATCHER, Haden, & Velinda NAYLOR, bond 10 Feb. 1820;
    bdsm: Wm. Vice. [AB]
    Haden Thatcher & Celinda VEALEY, 10 Feb. 1820. [S1]
THOMAS, Elzaph, & Bertha RALSTON, bond 1 Nov. 1830;
    f/b & bdsm: John Ralston. [AB]
THOMAS, Henry, & Mary BUCHANAN, bond 7 Feb. 1838;
    bdsm: James Buckanan. [AB]
THOMAS, James, & Catherine or Caty McVAY, bond 16 Apr. 1814;
    m/b: Sarah McVay; bdsm: Jas. Thomas, Larkin Thomas. [KM]
    James Thomas & Caty McVEY or McVee, 17 Apr. 1814. [JA,S1]
THOMAS, James, & Mary Ann CROW, bond 7 Nov. 1824;

bdsm: John Sorrell [Gorrell?].	[AB]
James Thomas & Mary Ann Crow, 7 Nov. 1824.	[S1]
THOMAS, James W., & Mary BARNES, 4 Feb. 1841. (JnSm)	[B2]
[THOMAS] Tommas, John, & Rebecca VIZ [Vice?], bond 3 May 1814;	
f/b: Wm. Viz; bdsm: John Thomas, Joseph Kennedy; mar. 3 May.	[KM]
John Thomas & Rebecca Viz, 3 May 1814.	[JA,S1]
THOMAS, John, Jr., & Elizabeth SIX, bond 11 Feb. 1829;	
bdsm: Jno. Yarbrough.	[AB]
John THOMASMAN & Eliza Six, 12 Feb. 1829. (PCy)	[B2]
THOMAS, Thomas J., & Ma(r)y Ann FLOOD, 10 June 1847. (BBv)	[B2]
THOMAS, Wm., & Hannah BUTCHER, 25 March 1817.	[JA]
William Thomas & Fannah Butcher	[S1]
THOMAS, Wm., & Cyntha GOODPASTURE, 6 Nov. 1828. (JPk)	[B2]
THOMAS, William, & Susan POWEL, 17 Dec. 1831. (RTh)	[B2]
THOMPSON, David, & Jemima SMITH, bond 20 Dec. 1824;	
bdsm: David Thompson, David McClain.	[AB]
David Thompson & Jemima Smith, 22 Dec. 1824.	[S1]
THOMPSON, David, & Nancy PARKS, bond 9 Apr. 1836;	
bdsm: Jonathan Otis.	[AB]
THOMPSON, David S., & Jeannette SWEATMAN, bond 7 Sept. 1842;	
bdsm: Filander Thompson.	[AB]
THOMPSON, George, & Nancy HASTY, bond 23 March 1824;	
bdsm: Wm. Ferguson.	[AB]
George Thompson & Nancy Hasty, 28 March 1824.	[S1]
THOMPSON, George, & Polly DO [ditto?], 21 Dec. 1826.	[B2]
THOMPSON, James J., & Elizabeth E. RICHARDS, bond 22 Sept. 1846;	
bdsm: Wm. M. Thompson.	[AB]
THOMPSON, John, & Polly RICHARDS, bond 3 Jan. 1821;	
bdsm: Wm. Richards.	[AB]
John Thompson & Polly Richards, 8 Feb. 1821.	[S1]
THOMPSON, Richard, & Polly ROABERRY, bond 30 Aug. 1819;	
bdsm: Alexander Barberry.	[AB]
Richard B. Thompson & Polly ROSEBERRY, 2 Sept. 1819.	[S1]
THOMPSON, Richard, & Mary Ann DUTY, bond 26 May 1845;	
bdsm: Daniel Duty.	[AB]
Richard Thompson & Mary Ann Duty, 5 May 1845. (ODB)	[B2]
THOMPSON, Wm., & Louisa KENNARD, bond 11 Sept. 1846;	
parent/b: Sinthy Kennard; bdsm: G. W. Warfield.	[AB]
THOMPSON, Wm., & Elizabeth GRIFFIN, bond 21 March 1848;	
f/b: Geo. Griffin; bdsm: James Williamson;	[AB]

William Thompson & Elizabeth Griffin, 22 March 1848. (WRg) [B2]

THOMPSON, William, & Emily M. OAKLEY, 11 Sept. 1851. (JHe) [B2]

TIDINGS, John W., & Rachael M. BARNES, 18 Dec. 1834. (WMc) [B2]

TINCHER, John S., & Elizabeth Jane WARNER, 2 Apr. 1850. (SKc) [B2]

TINDLE, Thomas W., & Susanna THOMAS, 17 Sept. 1818. [S1]

TIPTON, Robert, & Evlin PEROTT, bond 23 July 1845;
bdsm: Jas. Piratt. [AB]

TOLLIN, Geo. W., & Harriet GILL, bond 14 Jan. 1836;
bdsm: Wm. Fenwick. [AB]

George W. Tollin & Harriet Gill, 14 Jan. 1836. (JnSm) [B2]

TOMLINSON, Nathan, & Parthena FISENO[?], bond 10 July 1824;
bdsm: Robt. B. Croaks. [AB]

TONEY, Tarlton, & Melinda DUNCAN, 13 Nov. 1817. [S1]

TOY, Andrew J., & Amanda HATTON, bond 17 Dec. 1845;
f/b: Marcus Hatten; bdsm: Marcillis Hatten. [AB]

Andrew J. Toy & Amanda J. HATEN, 18 Dec. 1845. (SKc) [B2]

TOY, George, & Melvina NEWMAN, bond 6 Dec. 1837;
bdsm: B. F. Sudduth. [AB]

George Toy & Melvina NUMAN, 10 Dec. 1837. (JnSm) [B2]

[TOY, Joseph?] Craig, Jonathan, & Cynthia CRAIG, bond 25 Nov. 1847;
bdsm: Joseph ?Toy. [AB]

Joseph TOY & Cinthy Craig, 23 Nov. 1847. (SKc) [B2]

TOY, Patrick, & Sarah WARREN, 20 July 1851. (RRg) [B2]

TRAILER, Lowry, & Rhody BUTLER, bond 8 Feb. 1829;
bdsm: William Vice. [AB]

TRAILER, Philip, & Susan PURVIS, 17 Aug. 1851. (PCy) [B2]

TRAITON or Traton, Andrew, & Eliza PIDGETT, 21 Jan. 1841. (MGs) [B2]

[TRAVIS] Tronis?, Jeremiah, & Elizabeth RICE, bond 9 Feb. 1828;
bdsm: R. R. Rice. [AB]

Jeremiah TRAVIS & _____, 12 Feb. 1828. (SJk) [B2]

TRAYLOR, Andrew, & Delila TRAYLOR, bond 14 Jan. 1833;
bdsm: John Traylor. [AB]

Andrew Traylor & Delila Traylor, 5 Feb. 1833. (TIs) [B2]

TRAYLOR, David, & Elizabeth Ann GRAYSON, bond 12 June 1845;
bdsm: John Grayson. [AB]

TRAYLOR, G. W., & Arminta DODGES, bond 3 Dec. 1848;
bdsm: Wm. Dodger. [AB]

TRAYLOR, James, & Davey TRAYLOR, bond 14 Jan. 1825;
bdsm: John Traylor. [AB]

TRAYLOR, Joel, & Polly GRIMES, bond 27 Aug. 1831;
    bdsm: Saul Hicks. [AB]
    Joel Traylor & Polly Grimes, 28 Aug. 1831. (ALy) [B2]

TRAYLOR, John, & Sally TRAYLOR, bond 15 July 1811;
    f/b: Nicholas Traylor; bdsm: John Traylor, Ransom Traylor. [AB]
    John Traylor & Saley Traylor or TRAYLER, 18 July 1811. [S1,JA]

TRAYLOR, John, & Mary FLETCHER, Nov. 1845. (SKc) [B2]

TRAYLOR, Josiah, & Mary REED, 12 July 1839. (GFs) [B2]

TRAYLOR, Lawson, & Lucinda TRAYLOR, bond 2 Apr. 1819;
    parent/b & bdsm: Cary Traylor. [AB]

TRIBLE, Orson, & Nancy ?PARIDO, 28 Dec. 1844. (WRg) [B2]

TRIMBLE, Lewis, & Phebe RATCLIFF, 11 Feb. 1843. (JGW) [B2]

TRIPLETT, Francis, & Ann DICKENS, bond 14 Nov. 1829;
    bdsm: John Triplett. [AB]

TRIPLETT, Thomas, & Rebecca WAGSON, bond 12 Aug. 1815;
    parent/b: J. W. Wagan; bdsm: Thomas Fletcher. [AB]
    Thomas Triplett & Rebeccah WAGNER, 1816. [S1]

TRIPLETT, Wm., & Martha STELLE, bond 14 Dec. 1847;
    bdsm: Rich Richardt. [AB]

TRUIT, Daniel, & Elizabeth KIRK, bond 6 Nov. 1821;
    f/b: Mathew Kirk; bdsm: James Wilson. [AB]

TRUMBO, Andrew, & Jenny LOVENCY [Sorency], bond 28 Jan. 1819;
    bdsm: W. M. Sudduth. [AB]
    Andrew Trumob & Jenney SOUALEY, 28 Jan. 1819. [S1]

TRUMBO, Andrew, & Eliza TRIPLETT, bond 24 Oct. 1821;
    bdsm: Thomas Triplett. [AB]

TRUMBO, George, & Mary ROLLINS, bond 24 Apr. 1825 (or 28?);
    bdsm: Joseph Bryan. [AB]
    George Trumbo & Mary FORBUS, 24 Apr. 1828. (JnSm) [B2]

TRUMBO, Geo., & Olive MOORE, bond 11 Jan. 1847;
    bdsm: Silas Moore. [AB]
    George TRUMBOW & Olivine MOORES, 11 Jan. 1847. (BCs) [B2]

TRUMBO, Isaac, & Elizabeth ?KEITH, bond 29 Jan. 1821;
    bdsm: John Kieth. [AB]
    Isaac Trumbo & Elizabeth HEATHLY, 1 Feb. 1821. [S1]

TRUMBO, Jackson, & Polly YOUNG, bond 11 Nov. 1840;
    bdsm: John A. Trumbo. [AB]

TRUMBO, John, & Sarah MANLY, bond 12 Oct. 1833;
    bdsm: Lewis Perry; [AB]

John Trumbo & Sally Manly, 13 Oct. 1833. (JEv) [B2]

TRUMBO, John F., & Polly SWENCY [Sorency?], bond 20 Jan. 1827;
    bdsm: John ?Swency. [AB]

TRUMBO, John K., & Emily BROWNING, bond 20 Jan. 1845;
    bdsm: James F. Jones. [AB]
    John K. Trumbo & Emily Browning, 20 Jan. 1845. (SMc) [B2]

TRUMBO, Matoch, & Hannah TAYLOR, bond 29 Oct. 1821;
    f/g: Jacob Trumbo; bdsm: John Taylor. [AB]
    Monara Trumbo & Hannah Taylor, 1 Nov. 1821. [S1]

TRUMBO, Oliver, & Nancy MANLEY, bond 2 Nov. 1840;
    f/b & bdsm: James Manley. [AB]

TRUMBO, Wm. Andrew, & Louisa TRPTILL[?], 24 Oct. 1821. [S1]

TUCKER, Nathaniel, & Elizabeth HAWKINS, bond 16 March 1829;
    parent/b: C. Hawkins; bdsm: Valentine Hawkins. [AB]
    Nathaniel Tucker & Eliza Hawkins, 15 March 1829. (PHn) [B2]

TUNLY, John H., & Polly HENDRIX, 25 Sept. 1817. [S1]

TURLEY, William, & Betsey RIVELY, 1813. (LTu) [KM]
    William Turley & Betsey RINELY [S1]

TURNER, Jacob, & Elizabeth EDEN, bond 25 Aug. 1820;
    f/b & bdsm: Jacob Eden. [AB]
    Solomon Turner & Elizabeth Eden, 27 Aug. 1820. [S1]

TURNER, James, & Rebecca COOPER, bond 1 Jan. 1815;
    f/b: Adam Cooper; bdsm: James H. Cooper. [AB]
    James Turner & Rebecca Cooper, 2 Jan. 1816. [JA,S1]

TURNER, Jeremiah, & Patsey ANDERSON, bond 22 Jan. 1842;
    f/b: Ezekiel Anderson; bdsm: Wm. Turner. [AB]

TURNER, Wm., & Lucy HAM, bond 21 June 1842;
    bdsm: Wm. Sudduth. [AB]
    William Turner & Lucy Ham, 21 June 1842. (JnSm) [B2]

TYLER, John, & Louisa D. A. RAY, bond 26 March 1840;
    f/g: Joseph Tyler; f/b: John Ray; bdsm: Joel Wilhoit. [AB]
    John Tyler & Louisa D. A. Ray, 26 March 1840. (SMc) [B2]

TYLER, Joseph, & Elizabeth Ann GOSSITT, 22 Dec. 1842. (SJn) [B2]

TYLER, Preston, & Martha CASSITY, bond 8 July 1845;
    bdsm: James Becroft. [AB]

ULERY, David, & Delila SHROUT, bond 19 Dec. 1821;
    bdsm: John Shrout. [AB]
    David Ulery & Delila Shrout, 19 Dec. 1821. [S1]

ULERY, George, & Nancy BOYD, bond 17 Nov. 1825;
    bdsm: George Boyd. [AB]

ULERY, Henry, & Rachel BOYD, bond 1 Aug. 1827;
  bdsm: Joseph Boyd. [AB]
ULERY, Isaac, & Mary SETTERS, bond 13 Jan. 1848;
  bdsm: Park Fettlers. [AB]
  Isaac Ulery or ULY & Ma(r)y Setters, 13 Jan. 1848. (SKc) [B2]
ULERY, Joseph, & America BARBER, bond 15 Feb. 1840;
  f/b & bdsm: Thomas Barber. [AB]
ULERY, Lemuel, & Catharine BARBER, bond 9 Oct. 1848;
  bdsm: Thos. Barber. [AB]
  Samuel ULEY or Urley & Catharine Barber, 10 Oct. 1848. (SKc) [B2]
UNDERWOOD, James, & Elizabeth BURBRIDGE, 9 Oct. 1811. [S1]
UNDERWOOD, James, & Matilda SHUMATE, bond 12 Jan. 1824;
  bdsm: Wm. Shumate. [AB]
UNDERWOOD, Wm., & Jemima RICHARD, bond 26 May 1829;
  bdsm: Alfred Rice. [AB]
  Wm. Underwood & Jemima RICHARDS, 28 May 1829. (JHH) [B2]
UTTERBACK, Benjamin, & Laura HARVEY, bond 12 Oct. 1846 [48?];
  bdsm: George Harvey. [AB]
  B. F. Utterback & Luiza or Suza ?Harvey, 15 Oct. 1848. (TRk) [B2]
UTTERBACK, Harmon, & Jane McGINNIS, bond 5 Jan. 1824;
  bdsm: Wm. McGinnis. [AB]
  Thomas Utterback & Jane McGIVINS, 6 Jan. 1824. [S1]
UTTERBACK, John, & Debby FARROND, bond 24 Dec. 1816;
  bdsm: Zephriah Farrerd, J. Utterback. [AB]
  John Utterback & Debby FERNAND, 26 Dec. 1816. [JA,S1]
UTTERBACK, John, & Melinda DUTY, bond 14 July 1836;
  bdsm: Daniel Duty. [AB]
UTTERBACK, Wm., & Alabama A. SHARP, bond 7 Dec. 1845 (or 40?);
  m/b: Mary Sharp; bdsm: Wm. M. Sharp. [AB]
VANARSDALL, Wm., & Anna ARROSMITH, bond 4 Dec. 1848;
  f/b: Massey Arrosmith; bdsm: Thos. Arrosmith. [AB]
  William Vanarsdall & Ann AROWSMITH, 7 Dec. 1848. (PHn) [B2]
VANLANDINGHAM, Austin, & Rachel KINNAMAN, bond 30 Aug. 1847;
  bdsm: Uriam Gillet. [AB]
  Austin Vanlandingham & Rachel Kinnaman, 31 Aug. 1847. (DBk) [B2]
VANLANDINGHAM, James, & Elizabeth HUGHLEY, bond 29 May 1830;
  bdsm: G. W. Beshears. [AB]
  James Vanlandingham & Elizabeth HUSE, 30 May 1830. (ASh) [B2]
VANLANDINGHAM, James, & Elenor PERKINS, bond 11 Nov. 1836;

bdsm: Jonathan Denton. [AB]

VANLANDINGHAM, John, & Nancy VANLANDINGHAM, bond 16 Nov. 1816;
bdsm: John Vanlandingham. [AB]

John Vanlandingham & Nancy VANLANGHAM, 17 Nov. 1816 or 1817. [JA]

John Vanlandingham & Nancy Vanlandingham, 17 Nov. 1816. [S1]

VANLAND(ING)HAM, Joshua, & Eliz. ROSS, 11 Feb. 1829. (ALy) [B2]

VANLANDINGHAM, Madison, & Jemima TRUMBO, bond 16 Aug. 1847;
bdsm: Job F. Trumbo. [AB]

Matison Vanlandingham & Jemima H. Trumbo, 19 Aug. 1847. (DBk) [B2]

VANLANDINGHAM, Thomas, & Elizabeth KINCAID, bond 3 Sept. 1827;
m/b: Rebecah Kincaid; bdsm: Jeremiah Vanlandingham. [AB]

VANLANDINGHAM, Washington, & Harriet BARNBY, bond 2 Feb. 1827;
bdsm: Wm. Barnby. [AB]

VARNELL, Daniel, & Rachael MICHAEL, bond 4 Feb. 1819;
bdsm: Solomon Con. [AB]

Samuel VEWUEL & Rachel MICHALL, 4 Feb. 1819. [S1]

VICE, Aaron, & Elizabeth GRIFFIN, bond 7 July 1838;
bdsm: Matthias Griffin. [AB]

VICE, Aaron, & Ann FLETCHER, bond 3 Sept. 1845;
f/b: Wm. Fletcher; bdsm: Lymon Butcher. [AB]

VICE, Aaron, & Dorcus BOYD, bond 10 Dec. 1846;
bdsm: Washington Boyd. [AB]

Aaron VISE or Vice & Dorcas Boyd, 10 Dec. 1846. (BCs) [B2]

VICE, Alvin, & Kitty BUTLER, bond 31 Dec. 1828;
f/g: Henry Vice; bdsm: H. Vice. [AB]

Alvin Vice & Kitteiry? Butler, 1 Jan. 1829. (JVc) [B2]

[VICE?] Vise, Andrew, & Kitty FLETCHER, 5 Sept. 1845. (BCs) [B2]

VICE, Asbery, & Nancy KIBBLE, 27 Oct. 1835. (JVc) [B2]

VICE, Enoch, & Nancy? GILKSON, bond 7 May 1842;
bdsm: Anderson Lyson. [AB]

VICE, Enoch, & Frances TEMPLEMAN, bond 14 Oct. 1845;
bdsm: Ephriam Templeman. [AB]

Enoch G. Vice & Francis Templeman, 22 Oct. 1845. (SKc) [B2]

VICE, Greenberry, & Amelia CHEW, bond 21 May 1827;
bdsm: James Edward. [AB]

Greenbury Vice & Amelia G. Chew, 23 May 1827. [B2]

VICE, Gunnel S., & Elizabeth WILLIAMS, bond 18 Jan. 1836;
bdsm: Aaron B. Vice. [AB]

Gunnel Vice & Elizabeth Williams, 21 Jan. 1836. (ALy) [B2]

VICE, Harmon, & Nancy BAIRD, bond 4 ?June 1829;

f/b: George Baird; bdsm: Wm. Warkman. [AB]

Harrison VISE & Nancy BEARD, 7 June 1829. (PHn) [B2]

VICE, Herryman, & Emily VICE, 2 Feb. 1828. (JVc) [B2]

VICE, Hiram, & Margaret BRUMGEAR, bond 25 Sept. 1837;
   bdsm: Jefferson Brumgear. [AB]

VICE, Isaac, & Betsy VICE, bond 20 Oct. 1832;
   bdsm: Lawrence Vice. [AB]

Mr Vice & Elizabeth Vice, 21 Oct. 1832. (JVc) [B2]

VICE, Jefferson, & Rachel VICE, bond 6 June 1837;
   bdsm: Aron Vice. [AB]

Jefferson Vice & Rachael Vice, 6 June 1837. (JVc) [B2]

VICE, Jefferson, & Sarah ARNETT, bond 3 May 1842;
   bdsm: Ben Taylor. [AB]

VICE, John, & Margarett BUNGANER, 26 Sept. 1818. [S1]

VICE, John, & Nancy BUTLER, bond 23 Dec. 1828;
   bdsm: Lawrence Vice. [AB]

John Vice & Nancy Butler, 24 Dec. 1828. (JVc) [B2]

VICE, John, & C. Sandra TRAYLOR, bond 28 May 1838;
   bdsm: Reuben Traylor. [AB]

John VISE & Cossie Traylor, 29 May 1837. (JVc) [B2]

VICE, John, & Elenor BROMAGEN, 28 Nov. 1839. (SRg) [B2]

VICE, John, & Ann BARBER, bond 7 March 1840;
   f/b: Lewis Barber [Barbee?]; bdsm: Robert Riddle. [AB]

John Vice & Anna BARBEE, 8 March 1840. (SRg) [B2]

VICE, Lawrence, & Nancy ASBURN, 10 Nov. 1817. [S1]

VICE, Manning, & Sarah VICE, bond 21 July 1824;
   bdsm: Souen Vice. [AB]

VICE, Martin, & Gehasy BARBER, bond 18 July 1840;
   bdsm: John W. Bridges. [AB]

VICE, Minalds or Menaldo?, & Sorelda Ann WILLSON or Oakley?, bond 20 Aug. 1840;
   bdsm: Gunnell Vice. [AB]

Menaldo Vice & Sorelda Ann WILLIAMS, 3 Sept. 1840. (JVc) [B2]

VICE, Mourning, & Polly BRACKEN, 21 July 1824. [S1]

VICE, Nathan, & Winniford ROUT, 12 Aug. 1835. (AHu) [B2]

VICE, Presely, & Sally DEAKIN, bond 12 March 1827;
   f/b: Daniel Deakin; bdsm: Moses Deakin. [AB]

Presly Vice & Sally DUSKINS, 15 March 1827. (JEv) [B2]

VICE, Robert, & Mrs. Theo MILLER, bond 20 Apr. 1832;
   bdsm: Aaron Vice; [AB]

Robert Vice & Theodocia MILLAR, both of Bath Co., 3 Apr. 1832. (ALy) [B2]

VICE, Tralcott, & Nancy THOMPSON, bond 21 June 1833;
  bdsm: John Offill. [AB]

VICE, Westin, & Louann? VICE, 5 July 1826. [S1]

VICE, William, & Charlotte CLAVILL, bond 26 Dec. 1814;
  m/b: Elizabeth Clavill; bdsm: Wm. Vice, John Jones. [AB]

VICE, William, & Hanah NAYLOR, widow, bond 31 Oct. 1816;
  bdsm: John Jones, Wm. Vice. [AB]
  William Vice & Hannah Naylor, 28 Dec. 1816. [S1]
  William VIZE & Hanah Naylor, 31 Oct. 1816. [JA]

VICE, Wm., & Nancy MOCABEE, bond 15 March 1830;
  bdsm: Wm. Mocabee. [AB]
  William Vice & Nancy McBEE, 15 March 1830. (JVc) [B2]

VICE, Wm., & Rachel VICE, bond 2 Apr. 1832;
  bdsm: Isaac Vice. [AB]
  William Vice & Rachel _____, 3 Apr. 1832. (JVc) [B2]

VICE, Wm., & Edith [Eda] BUTLER, bond 8 July 1840;
  bdsm: David Hawkins. [AB]
  William Vice & Edith Butler, 12 July 1840. (SRg) [B2]

VICE, Wm. B., & Margaret WOODARD, 4 Feb. 1851. (JDy) [B2]

VICE, William M., & Malinda DEEN, 24 June 1835. (PHn) [B2]

VINCENT?, James S., & Elizabeth A. JONES, 21 Aug. 1850. (JHe) [B2]

VONNSBY, J. Henry, & Missouri FOCKE, 22 Apr. 1852. [S2]

WADE, F. A., & Louisa ROBERSON, 27 July 1843. (MGs) [B2]

WADE, Greenberry, & Mary KELSO, bond 22 May 1823;
  f/b: Walker Kelso; bdsm: James Wade. [AB]
  Greenberry Wade & Mary KILSO, 26 May 1823. [S1]

WADE, Wm., & Ruby BOLES, bond 2 Oct. 1823;
  bdsm: Henry Hopkins. [AB]
  William Wade & Katy BOLIN, 2 Oct. 1823. [S1]

WADLE, Alexander, & Ann SPENCE, bond 3 June 1834;
  bdsm: Wm. Spence. [AB]

WADDLE, James, & Julian POOR, bond 17 Nov. 1827;
  bdsm: James Wells. [AB]
  Joseph Waddle & Julian Poor, 25 Nov. 1827. (JPk) [B2]

WALKER, Adam R., & Malinda M. GRAHAM, bond 30 Dec. 1818;
  bdsm: W. M. Sudduth. [AB]
  R. Adam Walker & Melinda GRAYHAM, 31 Dec. 1818. [S1]

WALKER, Alexander, & Malinda CONN [Carr?], 2 June 1826. (JCr) [B2]

WALKER, Henry F., & Fanny B. CROOKS, 17 Sept. 1835. (DST) [B2]

WALKER, John M., & Lydia An MAXY, 14 March 1843. (GGd)   [B2]
WALKER, Joseph, & Elizabeth ENGLISH, bond 25 Sept. 1815;
   bdsm: Alexander Farris.   [AB]
   Joseph Walker & Elizabeth English, 1816.   [S1]
WALKER, Robert W., & Sarah BRADSHAW, 4 July 1844. (GGd)   [B2]
WALKER, Wm., & Charlotte LINEY, bond 31 Jan. 1821;
   bdsm: Geo. Liney.   [AB]
   William WACKER & Charlotte LINCY, 1 Feb. 1821.   [S1]
WALKER, Wm., & Lydia SANDERS or Landers, 19 Jan. 1826. (JtSm)   [B2]
WALLIN, Isaac, & Margaret MYERS, bond 16 June 1834;
   bdsm: Adam Myers.   [AB]
WALLS, Washington, & Nancy MOCKBEE, bond 7 March 1822;
   bdsm: Stephen Mockbee.   [AB]
   Washington Walls & Nancy MOCKEBA, 14 March 1822.   [S1]
WALLTON, Wm., & Juliah FITZGERALD, bond 22 March 1831;
   f/g: Wm. Wallton; bdsm: Simon Link.   [AB]
   Wm. WALTON, Jr., & Julia? Fitzgerald, 24 March 1831. (JGW)   [B2]
WALTERS, Jacob, & Polly McKINNEY, bond 13 Oct. 1812;
   bdsm: Jacob Walters, Jas. Ivans.   [AB]
   Jacob Walters & Polly McKinney / Polly W. Kinney, 15 Oct. 1812. [S1,JA]
WALTON, Greenberry, & Lucinda MYERS, bond 24 Oct. 1847;
   bdsm: John Lain.   [AB]
WALTON, Isaac, & Nancy LAFFERTY, bond 1 March 1811;
   f/b: Manuel Lafferty; bdsm: Isaac Walton, Wm. Youmans.   [AB]
WALTON, James, & Louisa SPENCE, bond 23 May 1829;
   f/g: William Walton; bdsm: William Spence.   [AB]
WALTON, James, & Malvina SEAL, 20 Apr. 1843. (WRg)   [B2]
WALTON, John, & Lydia DONATHAN, 2 Oct. 1844. (JGW)   [B2]
WALTON, Mark, & Elizabeth JONES, bond 11 June 1821;
   f/b & bdsm: John Jones.   [AB]
   Mark Walton & Elizabeth Jones, 14 June 1821.   [S1]
WALTRONS, Horace W., & Margaret F. MIRCHLEY, bond 10 Oct. 1842;
   bdsm: Marcus Gill.   [AB]
   Horace WATROWS & Polly Ann MERLEY, 13 Oct. 1842 (JGW);
   also: Horace WATRONS & Polly Ann MESKLY   [B2]
WARD, A. C., & Eliza A. PHELPS, 5 Oct. 1843. (SMc)   [B2]
WARD, R. G., & Ann Amelia BERRY, 9 July 1850. (GGd)   [B2]
WARDEN, William, & Catherine DAVIS, bond 25 Jan. 1812;
   f/b: Joseph Davis; bdsm: Ignatious Davis;   [AB]

William Warden & Katharine Davis, 26 Feb. 1812. [S1]

Wm. Warden & Katherin Davis, 16 Apr. 1812. [JA]

WARNER, Allen, & Vienna CLAYTON, bond 9 June 1838;
bdsm: Jonas Warner. [AB]

WARNER, Ben, & Betsey PHYMON, bond 22 July 1825;
bdsm: Samuel Sailor. [AB]

Benjamin Warner & Betsey F. HINER [P. Himer?], 24 July 1825. [S1]

WARNER, George, & Nancy TRUMBO, bond 20 Aug. 1816;
bdsm: John Trumbo. [AB]

WARNER, George, & Margaret MOORE, bond 24 Feb. 1830;
bdsm: George Feland. [AB]

WARNER, Henry Harrison, & Helen I. OAKLEY, bond 1 Nov. 1846;
bdsm: John Goodpaster, Sr. [AB]

H. H. Warner & E. J. Oakley, 1 Nov. 1846. (SMc) [B2]

WARNER, Jonas, & Elizabeth CLAYTON, 16 Apr. 1826. (AMx) [B2]

WARNER, Robert, & Polly FITZGERAL, 25 Dec. 1817. [S1]

WARNER, William, & Mary TRIPLETT, bond 30 Dec. 1818;
f/b: Thomas Triplett; bdsm: James Triplett. [AB]

WARREN, J. K., & Mary M. LIGHT, bond 30 May 1847;
f/g: John B. Warren; f/b: Jonathan Light; bdsm: Tinah? Williamson. [AB]

J. R. Warren or WARNER & Mary M. Light, 30 May 1847. (SKc) [B2]

WARREN, James, & Jane JONES, bond 12 Feb. 1820;
bdsm: John B. Warner. [AB]

James WARRAN & Jacies Jones, 13 Feb. 1820. [S1]

WARREN, James, & Elizabeth ?COATIGAN [Costigan?], bond 31 Oct. 1831;
bdsm: John Wells. [AB]

WARREN, Robert, & Sally WARD, bond 7 Dec. 1836;
bdsm: B. F. Suddith. [AB]

WARREN, Thomas, & Martha Jane WRIGHT, bond 23 July 1846;
bdsm: Ambrose Wright. [AB]

Thomas Warren & Martha Wright, 23 July 1846. (SKc) [B2]

WARREN, Wm., & Elizabeth KINCAID, bond 31 July 1821;
m/b: Abigail Kincaid; bdsm: John Warren. [AB]

William Warren & Elizabeth KINCAIDE, 2 Aug. 1821. [S1]

WARREN, William, & Mary ?BARBER, 5 Oct. 1851. (SKc) [B2]

WATSON, William Henry, & Mary Ann Pater BLACKBARN, 2 Feb. 1841. (SMc)
[B2]

WEBSTER, Francis M., & Ann Eliza SURENNY, 13 March 1843. (GGd) [B2]

WEBSTER, John B., & Susan WELLS, bond 13 Oct. 1849;

bdsm: Thos. Wells.	[AB]
John ?B. Webster & Susan WILLS, 14 Oct. 1849. (SKc)	[B2]
WEBSTER, Samuel, & Anna ROBINS, bond 11 July 1821;	
f/b: James Robins; bdsm: John Robins.	[AB]
Samuel Webster & Anna Robins, 12 July 1821.	[S1]
WEDGER, John, & Louisa LEE, bond 1 June 1849;	
bdsm: Wm. Baxter.	[AB]
WELCH, George, & Polly CHOAT, bond 20 Dec. 1821;	
bdsm: Augustin Choat.	[AB]
George Welch & Patsy Choat, 24 Dec. 1822.	[S1]
WELCH, Wm., & Matilda WELLS, bond 20 June 1848;	
bdsm: James Wells.	[AB]
Wm. Welch & Matilda WELLSE, 20 June 1848. (SKc)	[B2]
WELL, Thomas, & Amanda WARREN, 26 March 1826. (JPk)	[B2]
WELLS, Alexander, & Grace GOODAN, bond 7 Nov. 1836;	
f/b: Daniel Goodan; bdsm: W. S. Williams.	[AB]
WELLS, Alford M., & Elizabeth MARKWELL, 25 Sept. 1850. (SKc)	[B2]
WELLS, Ben, & Eady POOR, bond 30 Oct. 1827;	
bdsm: Moses Poor.	[AB]
Benjamin Wells & Cady Poor, 31 Oct. 1827. (JPk)	[B2]
WELLS, Ben, & Mary Jane WRIGHT, bond 4 Sept. 1848;	
bdsm: Fleming Wright.	[AB]
Benjamin WELLSE or Wells & Mary Jane Wright, 1 Sept. 1848. (SKc)	[B2]
WELLS, Benjamin, & Elizabeth WADLE, bond 31 May 1834;	
bdsm: Joseph Wadle.	[AB]
WELLS, Edmund, & Jane KINCAID, bond 25 Oct. 1845;	
bdsm: James Sudduth.	[AB]
Edmond Wells & Jane KINCADE, 25 Oct. 1845. (SKc)	[B2]
WELLS, Edmund, & Emaline BOYD, bond 28 Apr. 1849;	
bdsm: J. H. Lee.	[AB]
WELLS, Edward, & Mary Ann PARKER, bond 31 Dec. 1823;	
bdsm: Edmond Parker.	[AB]
Edmond Wells & Marian Parker, 1 Jan. 1824.	[S1]
WELLS, George, & Sally MOORE, bond 21 Apr. 1820;	
f/b: Jacob Moore; bdsm: H. Watson.	[AB]
George WILLS & Sally Moore, 21 Apr. 1820.	[S1]
WELLS, James, & Polly BECRAFT, bond 3 Jan. 1824;	
bdsm: Wm. Becraft.	[AB]
James Wells & Polly Becraft, 11 Jan. 1824.	[S1]
WELLS, James or Jones, & Rebecca McWORTHY, bond 8 June 1842;	

bdsm: Mason R. Tate. [AB]

James WALLS & Rebecca McWorthy, 10 June 1842. (WRg) [B2]

WELLS or Wills, Jeramiah, & Elizabeth ?KARH, 13 Jan. 1851. (BBv) [B2]

WELLS, John W., & Caroline TINDLE, bond 17 May 1838;
bdsm: Joseph Thomas. [AB]

John W. Wells & Caroline Tindle, 17 May 1838. (JnSm) [B2]

WELLS, Richard, & Sally SMITH, bond 21 Dec. 1825;
f/b: Wm. Smith; bdsm: Joseph Wells. [AB]

Richard WELL & Sally Smith, 22 Dec. 1825. (JPk) [B2]

WELLS, Robert, & Corthina WEBSTER, bond 12 Jan. 1846;
bdsm: Samuel Webster. [AB]

Robert Wells & Parthena Webster, 20 Jan. 1846. (SKc) [B2]

WEST, Walton, & Eliza SORRELL, bond 27 Aug. 1842;
bdsm: John Sorrell. [AB]

WESTCOAT, Timothy, & Polly MANLEY, 16 Sept. 1844. (BCs) [B2]

WHALEY, Charles, & Amanda B. HILL, bond 10 Feb. 1827;
f/b: Thos. Hill; bdsm: Joshua Barnes. [AB]

Chas. Whaley & Amanda B. Hill, 12 ___ 1827. (RTy) [B2]

WHALEY, Charles, & Sarah NEWLAND, bond 1 Oct. 1849;
f/g: James Whaley; parent/b: A. N. Newland; bdsm: T. Snelling. [AB]

WHALEY, George W., & Maria WHALEY, bond 2 June 1845;
bdsm: James Wholey. [AB]

George Washington Whaley & Maria Whaley, 4 June 1845. (SJn) [B2]

WHALEY, Harrison, & Fanny STONE, bond 22 Sept. 1845;
bdsm: John Stone. [AB]

Harrison Whaley & Fanny Stone, 25 Sept. 1845. (SJn) [B2]

WHALEY, James, & Peggy CANNON, bond 22 Apr. 1820;
f/g: Vincent Whaley; bdsm: Charles Summers. [AB]

WHALEY, James, & Mary WHEALLAN, bond 6 June 1834;
bdsm: Samuel Jones. [AB]

WHALEY, James, & Jane McALISTER, bond 10 Sept. 1847;
f/g: John Whaley; bdsm: Sam Lemaster. [AB]

James Whaley & Jane McCALLISTER, 14 Sept. 1847. (GWB) [B2]

WHAL(E)Y, James, & Catharine McALISTER, 2 March 1852. (LGH) [B2]

WHALEY, Vincent, & Agnes CANNON, bond 25 May 1812;
bdsm: Vincent Whaley, Wm. Whaley. [AB]

WHITE, Archibald, & Eliza STEARMAN, bond 28 Dec. 1829;
bdsm: Robt. Stearmon. [AB]

WHITE, Augustin, & Peggy McCLAIN, bond 14 Apr. 1821;

bdsm: Joseph Donahue.	[AB]
WHITE, James, & Frances PAYNT, 15 Jan. 1835. (JRW)	[B2]
WHITE, Robert, & Edith GOODAN, bond 1 June 1834;	
bdsm: James Newcom.	[AB]
Robert White & Editha Goodan, 5 June 1834. (JFY)	[B2]
WHITE, Samuel, & Elizabeth BUTLER, bond 19 Aug. 1824;	
f/b: John Butler; bdsm: Austin Oakley.	[AB]
Samuel White & Elizabeth Butler, 20 Aug. 1824.	[S1]
WHITE, Wm., & Latitia JACKS, bond 26 Jan. 1816.	[AB]
William White & Tabitha Jacks, 9 Jan. 1816.	[JA,S1]
WHITNEY, Elijah, & Gelania JONES, bond Aug. 1832;	
consent/b: James Jones; bdsm: Thos. Gooch.	[AB]
WHIT(T)INGTON, Charles, & [Mrs.] Hetty LONSDALE, bond 9 Dec. 1821;	
bdsm: Wm. Sudduth.	[AB]
Charles Whillington & Hetty Saundale [sic], 10 Nov. 1822.	[S1]
WHITTINGTON, Charles, & Susan TINDELL, bond 21 Apr. 1836;	
bdsm: Thos. D. Owings.	[AB]
Charles Whittington & Susan Tindell, 21 Apr. 1836. (JnSm)	[B2]
WICKLIFF, Robert, & Louisa MORROW, bond 3 June 1829;	
f/b & bdsm: Robert Morrow.	[AB]
WIGGINTON, ?Worcly, & Sintha BENSON or Bennon, bond 9 June 1825;	
f/b: James Benson; bdsm: Peter Wiggington.	[AB]
WIGINGTON, John F., & Maranda BENSON, 11 Sept. 1851. (SRg?)	[B2]
WILBORN, Isaac F., & Essa (Eliza?) ROZOR, 5 Dec. 1843. (SMc)	[B2]
WILEY or Wyley, John, & Polly BARRY, bond 9 March 1811;	
bdsm: Jo Wiley, Joseph Smith.	[AB]
WILHITE, James, & Permelia JACKSON, bond 2 June 1839;	
bdsm: Wm. Wilhite.	[AB]
WILKERSON, Abiram, & Maria ANDERSON, 14 July 1818.	[S1]
WILLIAMS, Charles, & Sarah MYNER or Mynes, 14 Aug. 1817.	[S1,JA]
WILLIAMS, Charles E., & Loucan B. MORROW, bond 13 Oct. 1834;	
f/b: Robert Morrow; bdsm: Alexander Barnes.	[AB]
WILLIAMS, D. B., & Rebecca ULERY, bond 22 Aug. 1848;	
bdsm: Isaac Ulery.	[AB]
D. B. Williams & Rebecca Ulery, 22 Aug. 1848. (SKc)	[B2]
WILLIAMS, Eli, & Elizabeth SAPP, bond 14 Jan. 1832;	
bdsm: Joseph Sapp.	[AB]
Eli Williams & Elizabeth Sapp, Jan. 1832. (ALy)	[B2]
WILLIAMS, Francis P., & Amelia GERAN (or Green?), 13 Dec. 1837. (PCy)	[B2]
WILLIAMS, James, & Joanna NOE, bond 15 May 1829;	

bdsm: Thornton Huffner.	[AB]
James Willson [sic] & Joanna Noe, 15 May 1828. (JnSm)	[B2]
WILLIAMS, John, & L. C. MORROW, bond 27 Aug. 1831;	
f/b: Robert Morrow; bdsm: Thomas Barnes.	[AB]
John Williams & L. C. Morrow, 30 Aug. 1831. (JnSm)	[B2]
WILLIAMS, John W., & Elizabeth JOHNSON, 30 July 1835. (JGW)	[B2]
WILLIAMS, Jonathan, & Almira POORE, bond 21 May 1833;	
bdsm: Moses Poore.	[AB]
Jonathan Williams & Almira POOR, 24 May 1838. (JnSm)	[B2]
WILLIAMS, Mardesai [Mordecai?], & Margaret DUNCAN, 10 Oct. 1817.	[S1]
WILLIAMS, Phillip, & Eliza MOORE, bond 13 March 1837;	
bdsm: Geo. Feland.	[AB]
Phillip Williams & Eliza Moore, 16 March 1837. (TIs)	[B2]
WILLIAMS, Rason, & Harriet RIGHT [Wright?], bond 26 Oct. 1833;	
bdsm: Flem Right.	[AB]
WILLIAMS, Reason, & Francis RICE, bond 18 Feb. 1845;	
bdsm: Holman Rice, Jr.	[AB]
Reason Williams & Francis Rice, 18 Feb. 1845. (SKc)	[B2]
WILLIAM(S), Samuel, & Patsy HUGHART, bond 10 Oct. 1816;	
bdsm: Wm. Sweatman.	[AB]
Sam'l Williams & Patsy Hughart or HOGHANT, 22 Oct. 1816.	[JA,S1]
WILLIAMS, Thos., & May JOHNSON, bond 12 March 1849;	
bdsm: Howard Tebe.	[AB]
Thomas Williams & Ma(r)y Johnson, 12 March 1849. (WRg)	[B2]
WILLIAMS, Whitten, & Sally GREER, 15 March 1818.	[S1]
WILLIAMSON, Absolem, & July Ann EPPERSON, 10 Apr. 1843. (WRg)	[B2]
WILLIAMSON, David, & Sally GRIFFIN, bond 22 May 1821;	
bdsm: Wm. Griffin.	[AB]
David Williamson & Sally Griffin, 22 May 1821.	[S1]
WILLIAMSON, James M., & Ardona STORMS, 25 Sept. 1851. (JHe)	[B2]
WILLIAMSON, L., & Margaret McCARTY, bond 5 June 1847;	
bdsm: Sam McCarty.	[AB]
S. Williamson & Margarett McWORTHY, 10 June 1847. (SKc)	[B2]
WILLS, Aaron, & Rhoda NORRIS, bond 14 May 1823;	
bdsm: John Norris.	[AB]
Aaron Wills & Roda Norris, 18 May 1823.	[S1]
WILLS, Alfred, & Sarah A. NORIS, 10 Sept. 1851. (BBv)	[B2]
WILLS, David, & Ruth McCARTY, bond 5 March 1840;	
bdsm: James Roberson.	[AB]

WILLS, Richard, & Julina McCARTY, bond 6 Aug. 1848;
  f/b: Sam McCarty; bdsm: A. Wills.   [AB]
  Richard Wills & Julian McWORTHY, 6 Aug. 1848. (SKc)   [B2]
WILLS, Sam or ?Jam, & Marthy CORDE, 3 Jan. 1837. (PHn)   [B2]
WILLS, William, & El(i)za STONE, 11 Sept. 1850. (SJn)   [B2]
WILLSON, David, & Elizabeth JONES, bond 6 Jan. 1827;
  bdsm: Lee Wilson.   [AB]
  David WILSON & Eliz. Jones, 6 Jan. 1827. (AMx)   [B2]
WILLSON, David, & Mary HERNDON, bond 22 Aug. 1846;
  parent/b: T. K. Herndon; bdsm: Thos. Matthews.   [AB]
  David WILSON & Mary ?HERNDAN, 25 Aug. 1846. (RFC)   [B2]
WILLSON, James, & Sally HUGHES, bond 11 Sept. 1832;
  f/g & bdsm: David Willson.   [AB]
WILLSON, Jesse, & Julian PRATHER, bond 18 May 1833;
  f/b: Jeremiah Prather; bdsm: Ambrose Jones.   [AB]
  Jesse WILSON & Juliann PRAETER, 19 May 1833. (ASh)   [B2]
WILLSON, Jesse, & Matilda VICE, bond 8 Jan. 1842;
  f/b & bdsm: John Vice.   [AB]
  Jesse WILSON & Matilda Vice, 11 Jan. 1842. (JVc)   [B2]
WILLSON, Joseph, & Nancy JACKS, bond 1 Nov. 1831;
  bdsm: Abraham Shank.   [AB]
  Joseph WILSON & Nancy Jacks, 1 Nov. 1831. (ASh)   [B2]
WILLSON, Lueny, & Theodia EVAN, bond 8 June 1848;
  bdsm: J. F. Horn (or Hooe?).   [AB]
WILLSON, Robert, & Eliza Jane KINCAID, bond 25 March 1833;
  bdsm: Andrew Kincaid.   [AB]
  Robert L. Willson or WILLIAMS & Eliza Jane Kincaid, 28 March 1833. (DWh)
                                                                       [B2]
WILLSON, Samuel, & Elizabeth ROGERS, bond 20 Apr. 1814;
  bdsm: Samuel Wilson, James Rogers.   [AB]
  Samuel WILSON & Elizabeth Rogers, 21 Apr. 1814. (JPH)   [TP,RS]
WILLSON, Shelton, & Louisa FIELDER, bond 8 June 1848;
  f/g: Ptolemy Wilson; bdsm: Ben Staten.   [AB]
WILLSON, Soloman, & Polly FOOT, bond 1 May 1816;
  bdsm: John Wilson, S. Willson.   [AB]
WILLSON, W., & A. JONES, 3 July 1828.   [S1]
WILSON, Abner, & Margaret TIPTON, bond 18 June 1819;
  bdsm: Jeremiah Wilson.   [AB]
WILSON, Abner, & Polly McTER, 4 Nov. 1826. (AMx)   [B2]
WILSON, Harvey, & Margaret LOVENCY (Lane? Lawrence?), bond 10 May 1838;

f/g: Lewis Wilson. [AB]

Henery T. WETSON & Margaret SORENCY, 17 May 1838. (DST) [B2]

WILSON, Henry, & Mary BENSON, 26 Oct. 1844. (BCs) [B2]

WILSON, Henry F., Jr., & Mary GOODLOE, bond 1 March 1848;
bdsm: Harrison Gill. [AB]

WILSON, Jacob, & Frances HART, bond 25 Apr. 1828;
bdsm: Thos. Hart. [AB]

Jacob Wilson & Fannie Hart, 27 Apr. 1828. (JEv) [B2]

WILSON, James, & Elizabeth POWER, bond 23 Jan. 1837;
f/g: Uriah Wilson; bdsm: George Power. [AB]

WILSON, James, & Oaly An GOULDER, bond 4 Sept. 1846;
bdsm: Joseph Self. [AB]

James Wilson & Polly Ann ?GNALDIN, 4 Sept. 1845. (SMc) [B2]

WILSON, James R., & Hannah BAILEY, bond 8 Oct. 1838;
bdsm: H. C. Renfro. [AB]

James R. Wilson & Hannah Bailey, 14 Oct. 1838. (SJn) [B2]

WILSON, John, & Meninda HEEGER, bond 17 Aug. 1833;
bdsm: Polly Butcher. [AB]

WILSON, John, & Ann PETTETT, 23 March 1851. (JDy) [B2]

WILSON, John, & Eliza Jane ?COFSER [Coffer?], 13 Jan. 1852. (WRg) [B2]

WILSON, Joseph, & Louisa LINNEY, bond 5 Nov. 1827;
bdsm: Geo. Linney. [AB]

Joseph WILLSON & Louisa Linney, 6 Nov. 1827. (JnSm) [B2]

WILSON, Mathew, & Mary WHALEY, 27 May 1841. (MGs) [B2]

WILSON, Matthew, & Margurite DOWNING, bond 9 Jan. 1819. [AB]

WILSON, Michel, & Mary Ann YOUNG, bond 1 Feb. 1834;
bdsm: Joseph Bondurant. [AB]

WILSON, Omar, & Ellen RATLIFF, bond 6 May 1845;
f/b: Caleb Ratliff; bdsm: David Wilson. [AB]

Omer Wilson & Ellen Ratliff, 7 May 1845. (SJn) [B2]

WILSON, Reuben, & Maria DURATT, bond 14 Dec. 1847;
bdsm: Jonathan Crouch. [AB]

Ruben WILLSON or Wilson & Marian PERSAUL, 15 Dec. 1847. (JGW) [S1]

WILSON, Wm., & Ann OAKLEY, bond 3 Feb. 1824;
f/b: Edmund Oakley; bdsm: Cary Oakley. [AB]

WILSON, Wm., & Littilba[?] STATEN, bond 1 March 1834;
f/b: James Staten; bdsm: James Sorrell. [AB]

William WILLSON & Tillitha STATON, 2 March 1834. (TIs) [B2]

WILSON, William, & Rachael BOGGS, bond 18 Dec. 1846;

bdsm: Wm. Rogers. [AB]

    William Wilson & Rachal Boggs, 7 Dec. 1846. (WRg) [B2]

WINBERELY, Thomas, & Sophia BARNS, bond 18 Oct. 182;

    bdsm: Nell Barns. [AB]

    Thomas WIMBERLY & Sophiah Barns, 18 Oct. 1815. [JA]

    2 Jan. 1816 [S1]

WITHERS, Richard E., & Ailcy Ann BOYD, bond 12 Nov. 1846;

    m/g: Mary Withers; bdsm: Andrew Boyd. [AB]

    Richard E. Withers & Acley Ann Boyd, 24 Sept. 1847. (MGs) [B2]

WOOD, George R., & Celia (or Cetia?) MACKEY, 21 June 1851. (RFC) [B2]

WOOD, John, & Ruthy McGAHEE, bond 31 Aug. 1813;

    f/b: Barna McGehee. [KM]

    Jno. WOODLAND, Jr., & Ruthy McGEHE, 21 Sept. 1813. [JA]

    John Woodland, Jr., & Ruthy McGUBE, 2 Sept. 1813. [S1]

WOOD, Joseph, & Sarah WALLS, bond 11 June 1825;

    bdsm: Washington Walls. [AB]

WOOD, Samuel H., & Minerva DAVIS, bond 3 June 1840;

    m/b: Elizabeth Davis; bdsm: Edmond Wells. [AB]

    Samuel H. Wood & Minerva Davis, 4 June 1840. (FBN) [B2]

WOOD, William, & Nice INGRAM, 17 Sept. 1818. [S1]

WOOD, William H., & Emelia JONES, 7 June 1826. (JGW) [B2]

WOODARD, John, & Sarah Ann ANDERSON, 27 Aug. 1843. (LCb) [B2]

WOODARD, Turner, & Nevira MITCHELL, bond 15 Feb. 1833;

    bdsm: James Mitchell. [AB]

    Turner Woodard & Merinda Mitchell, 17 Feb. 1833. (SJn) [B2]

WOODARD, Wm., & Jane ANDERSON, bond 21 Aug. 1834;

    f/b: Ezekiel Anderson; bdsm: Collerd Anderson. [AB]

WOODLAND, Fielder, & Nancy GRAHAM, bond 30 July 1825;

    bdsm: Lewis Riddle. [AB]

[WOODLAND?] Woodlang, James, & Peggy BAY, bond 29 Oct. 1812;

    bdsm: James & John Woodland; mar. 3 Nov. [KM]

    James WOODLAND & Peggy DAY, 3 Nov. 1812. [S1]

WOODWARD, Mitchell D., & Emily St. Hubert WOOD, bond 22 March 1830;

    bdsm: John B. Warren. [AB]

    Mitchel Woodward & Em. St. Aubert Wood, 25 March 1830. (SJk) [B2]

WORFORD, James H., & Elisabeth AMOS, 3 Nov. 1851. (LGH) [B2]

WORKMAN, James, & Rebecca HAWKINS, bond 11 Oct. 1824;

    bdsm: Valentine Hawkins. [AB]

    James Workman & Rebecca R. Hawkins, 14 Oct. 1824. [S1]

WORKMAN, Samuel, & Betsy OCKERMAN, bond 16 Aug. 1813;

f/b: Daniel Ockerman. [AB]

    Samuel Workman & Betsey Ockerman, 1813. (LTu) [KM]

WORKMAN, William, & Elizabeth RALLS, 21 Jan. 1841. (PHn) [B2]

WREN, Enoch, & Harriet TRIPLETT, bond 11 Feb. 1833;

    bdsm: Wm. P. Warder. [AB]

    Enoch Wren & Harriette TRIPLITT, 14 Feb. 1833. (RTy) [B2]

WREN, John R., & Henrietta BYRAM, bond 25 Aug. 1847;

    bdsm: I. Byram. [AB]

    John Wren & Harriett BYRAN, 26 Aug. 1847. (RFC) [B2]

WREN, Thomas, & Jane TRIPLETT, bond 19 July 1830;

    bdsm: Thomas Triplett. [AB]

    Thomas S. Wren & Jane Triplett, 20 July 1830. (MJm) [B2]

WRENCHY?, Simpson, & Sarah Ann HARDIN, 7 Nov. 1850. (TDL) [B2]

WRIGHT, Ambrose, & Catharine WRIGHT, bond 1 May 1848;

    f/b: Ben Wright; bdsm: R. Wright. [AB]

WRIGHT, Ambrose, & Barby SHROUT, bond 28 March 1849;

    bdsm: John Shrout. [AB]

    Ambros R. Wright & Barbary Shrout, 28 March 1849. (SKc) [B2]

WRIGHT, Ambrose L., & Catharine MOORE, 13 July 1839. (EBr) [B2]

WRIGHT, B. L., & Martha CLAYTON, bond 4 June 1846;

    bdsm: Charles Clayton. [AB]

    B. J. Wright & Nurtilia? Clayton, 4 June 1846. (BBv) [B2]

WRIGHT, Benjamin, & Susan WRIGHT, bond 13 Apr. 1846;

    bdsm: Samuel Hart. [AB]

    Benjamin WRITES & Susan HART, 15 Apr. 1846. (SKc) [B2]

WRIGHT, Callen N., & Elizabeth JOHNSON, 28 Oct. 1850. (SKc) [B2]

WRIGHT, Gabriel P., & Mildred A. WREN, bond 4 March 1838;

    bdsm: Ambrose Wright. [AB]

WRIGHT, Hodel, & Amanda BOYD, bond 11 Feb. 1833;

    f/b: Spencer Boyd; bdsm: James Johnson. [AB]

    Noble RIGHT & Amanda Boyd, 12 Feb. 1833. (JPk) [B2]

[WRIGHT] Right, John, & Nancy ATHERSON, bond 11 Jan. 1821;

    bdsm: John Atherson. [AB]

    John WRIGHT & Nancy ATKINSON, 11 Jan. 1821. [S1]

WRIGHT, L., & Lucretia CLAYTON, 27 Apr. 1850. (BBv) [B2]

WRIGHT, W. S., & Emily GILL, bond 10 Aug. 1838;

    f/b: Samuel Gill; bdsm: B. F. Sudduth. [AB]

    W. L. Wright & Emila Gill, 10 Aug. 1838. (JGW) [B2]

YARBER, Alfred, & Rebecca CLAYTON, bond 23 June 1848;

f/b: Geo. B. Clayton; bdsm: Silas Davis. [AB]

YARBROUGH, John, & Sally RICE, bond 21 Dec. 1822;
   bdsm: John Bailey. [AB]
   John Yarbrough & Sally Rice, 22 Dec. 1822. [S1]

[YARBROUGH] Yarbaugh, Randle, & Ann GRIFFIN, bond 16 March 1833;
   bdsm: Geo. Dawson. [AB]
   Randle YARBROUGH & Ann Griffin, 16 March 1837. (JnSm) [B2]

YARBROUGH, Thomas, & Betsy GRAHAM, bond 27 Dec. 1823;
   bdsm: Lewis Ridder. [AB]
   Thomas Yarbrough & Betsy Graham, 1 Jan. 1824. [S1]

YARBROUGH, Wm., & Debey CLAYTON, bond 24 Nov. 1822;
   bdsm: Jeremiah Power or Pever. [AB]
   William YARBOROUGH & Dobby Clayton, 25 Nov. 1822. [S1]

YOCUM, Abel, & Amilda J. HINDS, 5 Oct. 1850. (JHn)
   groom also listed as Able Yocom, bride as Amelda [B2]

YOREL or Yarel?, Figah S., & Marky SCOOT (Scott?), 12 Dec. 1850. (PHn) [B2]

YOUNG, Charles, & Mary FREEMAN, bond 28 Aug. 1833;
   f/g: Sinnett Young; f/b: Humphrey Freeman; bdsm: Thos. Freeman. [AB]

YOUNG, Daniel, & Sally ?SAMART, 1813. (LTu) [KM]
   Daniel Young & Sally SMART [JA,S1]

YOUNG, David B., & Sindy NELSON, bond 1 March 1825;
   bdsm: James Cook. [AB]

YOUNG, David B., & Lucinda HARDMIN, 12 May 1843. (RTh) [B2]

YOUNG, Edwin, & Sarah BAILEY, bond 11 Sept. 1838;
   bdsm: Ben F. Webb. [AB]
   Edwin Young & Sarah BAILY, 11 Sept. 1838. (JnSm) [B2]

YOUNG, Harrison, & Nancy ROTHWELL, bond 22 Feb. 1838;
   bdsm: Thomas Rothwell. [AB]

YOUNG, James F., & Marinda BURIDGE, bond 3 Oct. 1848;
   bdsm: W. Allen. [AB]

YOUNG, James M., & Kitty Ann YOUNG, bond 9 June 1830;
   f/b: John Young; bdsm: Thos. Sudduth. [AB]
   James Young & Catharine Young, 10 June 1830. (WWh) [B2]

YOUNG, John, & Paulina ?GLOUERSMART, bond 8 Apr. 1828;
   bdsm: Edward Smart. [AB]

YOUNG, John, & Tabitha YOUNG, bond 10 Dec. 1832;
   bdsm: Joseph Bondurant. [AB]

YOUNG, Lewis, & Emily THOMPSON, bond 3 Aug. 1847;
   bdsm: George Thompson. [AB]

YOUNG, Reuben, & Nancy WARNER, bond 20 Aug. 1825;
    bdsm: Jacob Warner. [AB]
YOUNG, Reuben, & Mildred CARRINGTON, bond 19 June 1847;
    bdsm: Timothy Carrington. [AB]
YOUNG, Samuel, & Margaret HIGGINS, bond 11 Dec. 1825;
    bdsm: Thomas Trimble. [AB]
    Samuel Young & Margaret Higgins, 14 Dec. 1821. [S1]
YOUNG, Sinnett, & Vernetta ARNOLD, bond 15 July 1845;
    bdsm: Wm. Arnold. [AB]
YOUNG, Thos., & Elizabeth YOUNG, bond 17 May 1815;
    bdsm: James Young. [AB]
    Thomas Young & Elizabeth Young or TANNY, 18 May 1815. [JA,S1]
YOUNG, William, & Nancy SNELLING, 1816. [S1]
YOUNG, Wm., & Martha TRUMBO, bond 22 Apr. 1829;
    bdsm: Wm. Matthews. [AB]
    William Young & Martha Trumbo, 22 Apr. 1829. (ALy) [B2]
YOUNG, Wm., & Liza LEDFORD, bond 10 Aug. 1829;
    f/b: James Ledford; bdsm: Nathaniel Ledford. [AB]
YOURMAN?, John, & Fanny HOUZE, bond 28 July 1819;
    bdsm: John House. [AB]
    John YOUMAN & Fanny FOWES, 20 March 1820. [S1]
ZIMMERMAN, R. F. D., & Lucinda ATCHISON, bond 31 July 1849;
    bdsm: Wm. Atchison. [AB]
    R. S. D. Zimmerman & Lucinda Atchison, 2 Aug. 1849. (WMV) [B2]

APPENDIX

Marriages performed by Rev. Joseph P. Howe, 1795-1826,
  in present-day Bath and Montgomery counties, KY

After 1795, the Rev. Joseph Price Howe was Presbyterian minister of Springfield Church in present-day Bath County, Kentucky, and of Little Mountain Church in Mt. Sterling, Montgomery County, Kentucky. Howe recorded all the marriages he performed between 1795 and 1826; the original of this record is preserved at the Presbyterian Historical Society in Philadelphia. Howe's book provides the most complete surviving record of marriages in early Montgomery County, and many marriages for families living in the area that became Bath County in 1811.

The following appendix compares the two known transcriptions of Howe's marriage book, both of which follow Howe's chronological order rather than alphabetizing his records. Some of the earliest marriages were also recorded in Bourbon and Clark counties, before Montgomery was formed in 1797. From 1811 onward, some of Howe's marriages also appear among Bath County marriage bonds and returns.

Sources for J. P. Howe's marriages:

[RS]   Robert Stuart Sanders, "An Historical Sketch of Springfield Presbyterian Church, Bath County, Kentucky," Frankfort, KY, 1954. Includes a transcription of the marriage book kept by Rev. Joseph Price Howe, 1795-1826.

[TP]   Anonymous typescript of J. P. Howe's marriages, bound at Kentucky Historical Society Library with Burns's Bath County marriage bonds (no date). Includes the statement: "Copied from photostats made from the original manuscript in the Presbyterian Historical Society, Philadelphia, Pa."

[Bo]   Nina M. Visscher, "Marriage Records of Bourbon County, 1786-1800," in Kentucky Marriage Records: from the Register of the Kentucky Historical Society, Baltimore, Genealogical Publishing, 1983.

[Ck]   Mrs. Julia (W. B.) Ardery, "Clark County Marriages" (1793-97), in *Kentucky Records, Volume I*, Lexington, 1926.

ALEXANDER, John C., & Polly KELSOE, 11 Dec. 1817. [TP]
   John C. Alexander & Polly KELSEE [RS]
ALISON, James, & Naomi HARDWICK, 3 Aug. 1820. [TP,RS]
ALLEN, Douglas, & Ann ALISON, 9 Dec. 1819. [TP,RS]
ALLEN, James, & Sarah JONES, 30 Sept. 1813. [TP,RS]
ALLEN, William, & Catherine JONES, 22 Dec. 1808. [TP,RS]
ANDERSON, _____, & _____ ANDERSON, "Licence fr.clk.c." 27 June 1810. [TP,RS]
ANDERSON, David, & Martha GLOVER, 5 Sept. 1810. [TP,RS]
ANDERSON, James, & Nancy HARMON, 9 Jan. 1823. [TP]
   James Anderson & Nancy HARMAN [RS]
ANDERSON, Robert, & Sally JONES, 5 March 1805. [TP,RS]
ANDERSON, William, & Polly Graham ROBISON, 31 Dec. 1812. [TP,RS]
ARD, John, & Deborah ST. DRESKIE, 7 July 1795. [TP,RS]
   John Ard & Deborah ST. DUSKEY, 7 July 1795. [Ck]
ARMSTRONG, Samuel, & Polly RICE, 14 March 1815. [RS]
   _____ Armstrong & Polly Rice [TP]
ARNETT, John, & Rebeckah WHITCRAFT, 1 Nov. 1798. [TP,RS]
ARRASMITH, Alexander, & Jane GRAY, 23 Oct. 1817. [TP,RS]
BAKER, Joseph, & Susanna BALLARD, 30 Oct. 1809. [TP,RS]
BARCLEY, Edward, & Polly SHANKLIN, 10 May 1821. [TP]
   Edward BARCLAY & Polly Shanklin [RS]
BARKLEY, Lazarus, & Lavina SHANKLIN, 27 March 1817. [TP]
   Lazarus Barkley & Levina Shanklin [RS]
BARNES, Thomas C., & Maranda MORROW, 1 Nov. 1821. [TP,RS]
[see Bath Co., KY, marriage bonds]
BARR, John, & Margaret LEMON, 19 Dec. 1796. [TP,RS]
   John Barr & Margaret Lemon, 1796. [Ck]
BARR, John, & Martha CALDWELL, 17 Dec. 1801. [TP,RS]
BECRAFT, James, & Fannie OKELEY, 3 Feb. 1803. [TP,RS]
BERRY, Francis, & Phebe COONS, 16 Sept. 1812. [TP]
   Francis BARRY & Phebe Coons [RS]
BERRY, John, & Polly COONS, 27 Feb. 1817. [TP,RS]
BERRY, Samuel K., & Susannah LANE, 18 March 1813. [TP,RS]
BERRY, William, & Sarah HILL, 22 Dec. 1802. [TP,RS]
BIRCH, Weston F., & Harriette CAMPBELL, 19 Sept. 1826. [TP]
   Weston F. Birch & Harrietta Campbell [RS]
BLACK, Alexander, & Eliza Bell HENDERSON, 11 Sept. 1822. [TP,RS]
BLACK, Ezekiel, & Mary Douglass McCLURE, 12 Sept. 1805. [TP]
   Ezekiel Black & Mary Douglas McClure [RS]

BLACK, John, & Nancy B. CROOKS, 19 Dec. 1822. [TP,RS]
BLACK, William, & Isabella King HENDERSON, 10 Jan. 1811. [TP,RS]
BLAIR, William, & Jane DOWNEY, 25 March 1811. [TP,RS]
BOYD, John, & Dorcas HENDRIX, 3 Dec. 1795. [TP,RS]
    John Boyd & Dorcus Hendrix [Ck]
BOYD, Joseph, & Anna KING, 25 Jan. 1821. [TP,RS]
    [see Bath Co., KY, marriage bonds]
BOYD, Richard, & Polly DOWNIE, 31 March 1796. [TP,RS]
    Richard Boyd & Polly Downie, 3 March 1796. [Ck]
BOYD, Robert, & Margaret RALSTON, 1 March 1821. [TP,RS]
BOYD, Thomas, & Lucy McINTIRE, 31 Oct. 1811. [TP,RS]
    [see Bath Co., KY, marriage bonds]
BOYD, Thomas, & Ann DAVIS, 7 Jan. 1823. [TP,RS]
BOYD, William, & Sally ROGERS, 26 Sept. 1822. [TP,RS]
    [see Bath Co., KY, marriage bonds]
BRACKEN, Matthew, & Nancy ROGERS, 23 Feb. 1797. [TP,RS]
    Mathew Bracken & Nancy Rogers, 23 Feb. 1797. [Ck]
BRACKEN, Robert, & Eliz. MAPPIN, 9 March 1797. [TP,RS]
    Robert Bracken & Elizabeth Mappin, March 1797 [Bo]
BRACKEN, Theophilus, & Mary KINCAID, 16 Jan. 1800. [TP,RS]
BRADLEY, Elisha, & Betsey STEELE, 2 Oct. 1810. [TP,RS]
BRADSHAW, David, & Mary CROOKS, 27 Feb. 1800. [TP,RS]
BRADSHAW, John, & Polly NEWTON, 1 Apr. 1813. [TP]
    1 Aug. 1813 [RS]
BRECKENRIDGE, Alexander, & Anne BRECKENRIDGE, 30 Sept. 1802. [TP,RS]
BRIDGES, George, & Rebekah LOCKRIDGE, 24 Apr. 1817. [TP,RS]
BRIDGES, James, & Peggy LOCKRIDGE, 11 March 1819. [TP,RS]
BRIDGES, William, & Isabella K. LOCKRIDGE, 4 July 1815. [TP,RS]
BRIGHT, Wm., & Sarah ?EASTON, 9 July 1801. [TP]
    William Bright & Sarah EASTEN [RS]
BRINDLEE, Wm., & Nancy LAUNSDALE, 27 Dec. 1796. [TP,RS]
    Wm. BRINDLE & Nancy LONSDALE, 27 Dec. 1796. [Ck]
BRINIGAR, Benjamin, & Malinda SHANKLIN, 15 Feb. 1821. [TP,RS]
    [see Bath Co., KY, marriage bonds]
BRINTON, John, & Elizabeth HAWKINS, 16 Feb. 1804. [TP,RS]
BROWN, Daniel, & Sarah HARRA, 26 Dec. 1797. [TP,RS]
BROWN, Lanville, & Peggy OLIVER, 7 Feb. 1822. [TP,RS]
BROWN, William B., & Mary P. FARROW, 21 Aug. 1823. [TP,RS]
BRYANT, Charles, & Nancy WOODWARD, 26 Jan. 1815. [TP,RS]

BURBRIDGE, Joseph Howe, & Elizabeth UNDERWOOD, 6 June 1822.   [TP,RS]
  [see Bath Co., KY, marriage bonds]
BURBRIDGE, Robert, & July RICHARDS, 25 May 1803.   [TP,RS]
BURNS, Ignatius, & Malinda W. HOWE, 10 Jan. 1822.   [TP]
  Ignatius BYRNS & Malinda W. Howe   [RS]
BURNS, James, of Bourbon County, & Rebecca TROTTER, 22 Apr. 1813.   [RS]
  John Burns (Bourbon Co.) & Rebecca Trotter
BURNS, John, & Polly WHITECRAFT, 27 June 1811.   [TP,RS]
  [see Bath Co., KY, marriage bonds]
BUTCHER, Isaac B., & Elizabeth YOCUM, 22 May 1817.   [TP,RS]
CALDWELL, James, & Margaret ROBINSON, 2 Feb. 1804.   [TP,RS]
CALDWELL, James M., & Nancy SAMPLE, 11 Sept. 1823.   [TP]
  11 Sept. 1828 [sic]   [RS]
CALDWELL, John, & Mary KINCAID, 13 March 1800.   [TP,RS]
CALDWELL, Robert, & Amelia MELOAN, 22 March 1804.   [TP,RS]
CALDWELL, Thomas, & Eleanor BOYD, 29 June 1813.   [TP,RS]
CALDWELL, William, & Polly PARKS, spinster, 2 Aug. 1804.   [TP,RS]
CAMPBELL, Robert, & Elizabeth GROOVER, 14 Sept. 1815.   [TP,RS]
CAMPBELL, William, & Sarah CAMPBELL, 18 Sept. 1800.   [TP,RS]
CANTRALL, William, & Deborah METTS, 7 June 1804.   [TP,RS]
CANTRELL, Joshua, & Rachel McCOLLOM, 16 Apr. 1799.   [TP,RS]
CANTRILL, William, & Nancy McCOLLOM, 1 Nov. 1798.   [TP,RS]
CANTRILL, Zebulon, & Sally McCOLLAM, 31 Aug. 1797.   [TP,RS]
CARR, Samuel, & Margaret HARBERSON, 27 May 1806.   [TP,RS]
CARTMELL, Thomas, & Patsey McDANOLS, 2 Jan. 1810.   [TP]
  Thomas Cartmell & Patsey McDANIELS   [RS]
CASSADY, James, & Elizabeth CAMPBELL, 7 Jan. 1800.   [TP,RS]
CASSIDY, Alexander, & Eliza D. GROVES, 26 Feb. 1824.   [TP,RS]
CHAMBERS, William, & Rebecca GILL, 22 March 1814.   [TP,RS]
  [see Bath Co., KY, marriage bonds]
CLARK, William, & Polly STEVENSON, 14 March 1820.   [TP,RS]
CLYCE[?], William, & Polly WYATT, 5 March 1819.   [TP,RS]
COCHRAN, William, & Peggy REYNOLDS, 30 Jan. 1804.   [TP,RS]
COFER, George, & Nancy ERVIN, 6 Jan. 1815.   [TP,RS]
COLEMAN, John, & Sally BUTLER, 25 Apr. 1799.   [TP,RS]
COLLINS, James, & Elizabeth PECK, 22 May 1816;   [TP,RS]
  "married at once" with John Marshall & Mary Peck.   [TP]
CONELY, Arthur, & Jane STEEL, 2 March 1815.   [TP,RS]
CONLEY, Alexander, & Eliza STEEL, 5 Sept. 1811.   [TP,RS]
CONNELLEY, Gilmore, & Jane LONG, 29 Dec. 1825.   [TP,RS]

CONNELLY, Robert, & Margaret DAVIS, 24 Apr. 1806. [TP,RS]

CONNERS, Matthew, & Betsy SHAVER, 28 Jan. 1798. [RS]

    Matthew CONNERA & Betsy Shaver [TP]

COOK, Abraham, & Tursey HAMILTON, 8 March 1815. [TP,RS]

    [see Bath Co., KY, marriage bonds]

COOK, George, & Jemima LANE, 6 Oct. 1812. [TP,RS]

COOKE, Joseph, & Sally WOODARD, 3 Dec. 1816. [TP,RS]

COOKE, Peter, & Martha CALDWELL, 17 March 1808. [TP,RS]

COONS, Elijah, & Sally BLACK, 16 Jan. 1823. [TP,RS]

COONS, Jacob, & Matilda Jane HOWE, 8 Nov. 1820. [TP,RS]

COOPER, William, & Rachel CRANE, 2 March 1820. [TP,RS]

COUCHMAN, George, & Polly STEEL, 10 Dec. 1807. [TP]

    George Couchman & Polly STEELE [RS]

COVINGTON, Coleman, & Matilda DUNCAN, 12 Apr. 1822. [TP,RS]

    [see Bath Co., KY, marriage bonds]

CRANE, A. M., & Rebekah MAFFETT:

    "I was to have married [them] on the 21st of December [1826] but could not on
    Account of having as an Agent to attend to the Collection & Sale of certain Negroes
    willed by Uncle John Dunlap to the Children of Isabel & Jane Howe, the Sale of wch.
    amounted to 8.5.66$." [TP,RS]

    [see Bath Co., KY, marriage bonds]

CROCKETT, John, & Jenny CARTMEL, 17 Apr. 1800. [TP,RS]

CROOKS, Robert B., & Betsey F. GRAHAM, 20 Feb. 1816. [TP,RS]

CROOKS, Uzal, & Margaret CROOKS, 26 June 1800. [TP,RS]

CROUCH, Jonathan, & Susannah CASSIDY, 15 Feb. 1809. [TP,RS]

CUMMINS, William, & Anna Maria LINDSEY, 7 Aug. 1817. [TP,RS]

CURRY, Henry, & Nancy SHIELDS, 1 May 1806. [TP,RS]

DABNEY, William, & Elizabeth MEANS, 24 Dec. 1818. [TP,RS]

DARNALL, Ezekiel, & Rheuhaina CAYWOOD, 24 Sept. 1817. [TP,RS]

DAVIS, Alfa [Asa?], & Phebe WILLIAMS, 24 May 1798. [TP,RS]

DAVIS, Harrison, & Patsey CROCKETT, 30 Aug. 1798. [TP,RS]

DAVIS, John, & Amy MCBEE (Mcbee), 24 March 1808. [TP,RS]

DAVIS, John, & Heathy DAVIS, 9 March 1809. [TP,RS]

DAVIS, John, & Selene McDOUGLE, 27 May 1817. [TP,RS]

DAVIS, Wm., & Sarah DUNCAN, 27 Dec. 1798. [TP,RS]

DAYS, Anthony, & Nancy SHELBY, 16 Nov. 1809. [TP,RS]

DEAN, Edward, & Betsey CROOKS, 22 Sept. 1803. [TP,RS]

DICKEY, Robert, & Maria FLETCHER, 5 Jan. 1818. [TP,RS]

DIVINE, Nathan, & Betsy ERWIN, 1 June 1812: "Monday morning at one o'cl." [TP,RS]

DONNALDSON, Robert, & Isabella CONNELEY, 14 Sept. 1820.   [TP,RS]

DOWNEY, Samuel, & Maryann ROBINSON, 1 Dec. 1803.   [TP,RS]

DOWNING, Andrew, & Eunice COCHRAN, 2 Feb. 1797.   [TP,RS]

    Andrew Downing & Emma COCHRON   [Ck]

DRYSDALE, John, & Martha McGLAUGHLIN, 15 Feb. 1809.   [TP]

    John Drysdale & Martha McCLAUGHIN   [RS]

DUFF, Daniel, & Susanna SADDLER, 23 June 1809.   [TP,RS]

DUNLAVY, Daniel, & Martha YOCUM, 4 Feb. 1802.   [TP,RS]

DUNN, William, & Susannah DUNIGAN, 28 Dec. 1818.   [RS]

    William Dunn & Susannah DUNIGA_, 29 Dec. 1818.   [TP]

ELLIOTTE, Hamilton, & Elizabeth HOPKINS, 18 Dec. 1800.   [TP,RS]

ELLIS, Charles, & Sally SIMPSON, 6 May 1807.   [TP,RS]

ELY, Benjamin, & Nelly BOYLES, 3 Sept. 1811.   [TP,RS]

ERVIN, Jas., & Nelly MAFFETT, 15 June 1810.   [TP,RS]

EVANS, Robert, & Jane HOWE, 6 Jan. 1803.   [TP,RS]

EVINS, Francis, & Catherine HAMILTON, 31 Jan. 1799.   [TP,RS]

FARROW, Perygin, & Isabella MALOAN, 23 Apr. 1811.   [TP,RS]

FICKLIN, William, & Fanny WALKER, 2 Feb. 1815.   [TP,RS]

FINDLEY, John, & _____ YORK, 7 Oct. 1812.   [TP,RS]

FLEMING, William, & Betsey LAMASTERS, 11 March 1802.   [TP]

    William Fleming & Betsey LaMasters   [RS]

FLETCHER, Thos., & Nancy McELHANNY, 15 Jan. 1801.   [TP,RS]

FLETCHER, Col. Thomas, & Margaret G. BARTLETT, 13 Aug. 1818.   [RS]

    13 Aug. 1818   [TP]

    [see Bath Co., KY, marriage returns]

FORD, Robert, & Nancy YARBROUGH, 6 Apr. 1810.   [TP,RS]

FORD, Samuel, & Mary YATES, 30 May 1811.   [TP,RS]

FORGEY, James, & Peggy ROGERS, 23 Feb. 1797.   [TP,RS]

    James Forgey & Peggy Rogers, 23 Feb. 1797.   [Ck]

FOSTER, James, & Drusilla YOUNG, 3 Sept. 1811.   [TP,RS]

FRAME, James, & Elizabeth ROGERS, 10 Dec. 1801.   [TP,RS]

FRAZER, Alexander, & Polly KING, 13 Sept. 1798.   [TP,RS]

FRAZER, James, & Rachel DALE, 14 Oct. 1817.   [TP,RS]

GARRETT, Peter R., & Jane SIMPSON, 1 June 1816.   [TP,RS]

GARRISON, Jesse, & Polly SEE, 17 Sept. 1811.   [TP,RS]

GILKEY, William, & Polly METEER, 29 Dec. 1803.   [TP,RS]

GILL, John, & Eliz.(abeth) C. ALEXANDER, 20 Aug. 1811.   [TP,RS]

GILMAN, Matthew, & Sarah PHILLIPS, 9 Aug. 1798.   [TP,RS]

GLEN, Witchill, & Sally COX, 8 Oct. 1818.   [TP]

    Whitchill Glen & Sally Cox   [RS]

GLOVER, Jesse, & Eliza ANDERSON, 25 Jan. 1816. [TP,RS]

GONDY, Samuel, & Isabella CONNELLY, 1 Apr. 1806. [TP,RS]

GRAHAM, Joseph, & Nancy Ralston ELLISON, 24 Nov. 1808. [TP]

    Joseph Graham & Nancy Ralston ELLISTON [RS]

GRAVES, Thomas, & Nancy GALLAWAY, 28 Dec. 1820. [TP,RS]

    [see Bath Co., KY, marriage bonds]

GRAY, Jonathan or Jonothan, & Eliza WILSON, 3 May 1809. [TP,RS]

GROVES, John, & Elizabeth ROBINSON, 24 May 1803. [RS]

    John Groves & Elizabeth Ribinson [sic] [TP]

HAMILTON, Abner, & Elizabeth ELLIOTT, 2 Jan. 1812. [RS]

    2 Jan. 1811 [sic? betw. entries for Dec. 1811 & Jan. 1812] [TP]

HAMILTON, Archibald, & Rebeckah BERRY, 1 March 1804. [TP,RS]

HAMMOND, William, & Priscilla JONES, 24 Dec. 1812. [TP]

    William HAMMONS & Priscilla Jones [RS]

HARNEY, Samuel A., & Betsey DALZELL, 30 Dec. 1806. [TP,RS]

HARRISON, Joseph, & Eliza B. HOWE, 26 March 1818. [TP,RS]

HARROW, Robt., & Jane HARROW, 21 Apr. 1812. [RS]

    Robt. Harrow & Jane HARROR [TP]

HARROW, William, & Peggy HARROW, 1 Jan. 1811. [RS]

    1 Jan. 1810 [sic? betw. Dec. 1810 & Jan. 1811 entries] [TP]

HAYDON, William C., & Eliza SIMPSON, 16 Aug. 1813. [TP,RS]

HAZELRIGG, Eli, & Rebeckah FLETCHER, 1 Jan. 1801. [TP,RS]

HEFFLIN, John, & Prudence LAMBERT, 9 Jan. 1812. [TP,RS]

HENDERSON, John, & Betsey CRAWFORD, 24 Nov. 1803. [TP,RS]

HENDRIX, Jacob, & Caty THOMSON, 30 Apr. 1797. [TP]

    20 Apr. 1797 [RS]

HENDRIX, Moses, & Franky HENRY [Honey], 22 Dec. 1801. [TP,RS]

    [1800? out of sequence, betw. Dec. 1800 & Jan. 1801 entries]

HENRY, Thomas, & Eliz.(abeth) BIGGS, 18 July 1799. [TP,RS]

HICKMAN, Daniel, & Sally YOUNG, 28 Sept. 1801. [TP,RS]

HILL, Thomas, & Jane METEER, 6 March 1811. [TP,RS]

HIND, John, & Peggy McMILLAN, 21 Dec. 1815. [TP,RS]

HINES, John, ploughboy, & Susan LEECH, spinster, 24 Aug. 1820:

    "married Thursday night." [TP,RS]

HOPKINS, Francis, & Catherine ELLIOTTE, 27 Feb. 1800. [TP,RS]

HOPKINS, William, & Polly LEWIS, 23 Oct. 1810. [TP,RS]

HOWE, David, & Sally HOWE, 23 Feb. 1804. [TP,RS]

HOWE, Isaac P., & Jane BOYD, 11 June 1812. [TP,RS]

HOWE, Robt., & Rebekah WOODS, 28 June 1799. [TP,RS]

HOWE, William, & Ann WHITCRAFT, 26 Feb. 1807. [TP,RS]
HUFF, William, & Elizabeth LOVE, 22 July 1802. [TP,RS]
HUGHES, John, & Polly PATTERSON, 9 Nov. 1809. [TP,RS]
HUMPHREYS, Orsen, & Isabella KEITH, 5 Sept. 1797. [TP,RS]
HUNTER, Benjamin, & Margaret MONTGOMERY, 5 Jan. 1802. [TP,RS]
HUTTON, Alexander, & Polly or Polley YARDLEY, 24 May 1798. [TP,RS]
ILES, Thos., & Polly WHEELER, 20 Nov. 1810. [TP,RS]
IRVINE, Elias, & Mathew[?] EATON, 2 Aug. 1811. [TP,RS]
JACKSON, Wingate, & Polly BURBRIDGE, 4 Dec. 1804. [TP]
    Wingate Jackson & Polly BURGRIDGE, 13 Dec. 1804. [RS]
JAMES, Archer, & Jane GRAY, 13 Dec. 1804. [TP,RS]
JAMES, David, & Polly CRAIG, 10 Oct. 1810. [TP]
    18 Oct. 1810. [RS]
JAMESON, David, & Elizabeth HARTGROVE, 25 Nov. 1817. [TP,RS]
JAMISON, John, & Martha HENDERSON, 20 Dec. 1821. [TP,RS]
JEFFRIES, Enoch, & Nancy WILSON, 26 May 1819. [TP,RS]
JOHNSON, Nicholas, & Polly TRIMBLE, 14 Nov. 1805. [TP,RS]
JOHNSTON, James, & Ann KINCAID, 10 Sept. 1801. [TP,RS]
JONES, James, & Lydia B. RAWLS, 2 Sept. 1813. [TP,RS]
    [see Bath Co., KY, marriage bonds]
JONES, Silas, & Lucinda COOKE, 7 Feb. 1819. [TP,RS]
JONES, Thomas, & Fanny MILLER, 4 Feb. 1813. [TP,RS]
KELSO, George, & Celia CALDWELL, 23 Sept. 1817. [TP,RS]
KELSO, Robert, & Gala UNDERWOOD, 4 Apr. 1816. [TP,RS]
    [see Bath Co., KY, marriage bonds]
KINCAID, Andrew, & Ann Patterson CALDWELL, 13 Aug. 1807. [TP,RS]
KINCAID, Joseph, & Nancy ROGERS, 12 Sept. 1822. [TP,RS]
    [see Bath Co., KY, marriage bonds]
KINCAID, Thomas, & Mary BRACKEN, 13 March 1800. [TP,RS]
KINCAID, Thomas, & Abigail HIRONS, 22 Sept. 1802. [TP]
    21 Sept. 1802 [RS]
KINIARD, George, & Johannah Morris BALDWIN, 23 Nov. 1802. [TP]
    George KINAIRD & Johannah Morris Baldwin [RS]
KIRK, John, & Sally FERIS, 4 Feb. 1812. [TP,RS]
    [see Bath Co., KY, marriage bonds]
KIRK, Thomas, & _____ LEMASTERS, 28 July 1812. [TP]
    Thomas Kirk & _____ Lemasters, 28 June 1812. [RS]
    [see Bath Co., KY, marriage bonds]
KNOX, Thomas, & Jane TREADAWAY, 16 Nov. 1808. [TP]
    Thomas Knox & Jane TREADAWAY, 14 Nov. 1808. [RS]

LANCASTER, Abraham, & Susanna ARNETTE, 29 Sept. 1801.   [TP,RS]

LANCASTER, John, & Chrystena DECKER, 10 Jan. 1799.   [TP,RS]

LANCASTER, Joseph, & Rachel FLETCHER, 15 March 1798.   [TP,RS]

LANCASTER, Thos., & Catherine DECKARD, 1 Jan. 1801.   [TP,RS]

LANE, Hugh, & Louisa P. GRAHAM, 28 Jan. 1824.   [TP,RS]

LANGSTON, Isaac, & Sarah PATTON, 6 Dec. 1798.   [TP,RS]

LEMASTERS, Benjamin, & Betsey FREEMAN, 2 July 1818.   [TP]
    Benjamin LeMasters & Betsey Freeman   [RS]

LEMASTERS, Richard, & Polly KIRK, 3 Aug. 1812.   [TP]
    Richard LeMasters & Polly Kirk   [RS]

LOCKRIDGE, James, & Rachel JONES, 17 May 1814.   [TP,RS]
    [see Bath Co., KY, marriage bonds]

LOCKRIDGE, John, & Margaret KILLOUGH, 3 Sept. 1811.   [TP,RS]

LOCKRIDGE, Robert, & Betsey [?]MATOUN, 23 Oct. 1810.   [TP,RS]

LOGAN, Samuel, & Margaret W. CONELLY, 17 Nov. 1814.   [TP]
    Samuel Logan & Margaret W. CONNELLY   [SR]

LONG, Robt., & Polly CALDWELL, 3 Jan. 1811.   [TP,RS]

LOVE, Joseph, & Nellie HUFF, 13 Jan. 1803.   [TP,RS]

LYKINS, William, & Rebekah COFFEE, 18 Jan. 1816.   [TP,RS]
    [see Bath Co., KY, marriage returns]

MALOANE, Andrew, & Polly LONG, 21 Dec. 1815.   [TP,RS]

MALONE, Stephen, & Polly YONGUE [Young?], 9 Dec. 1802.   [TP,RS]

MALONE, Thos., & Milly HIGGINS, 19 Apr. 1810.   [TP,RS]

MANLEY, Samuel, & Anna RICHART, 9 Apr. 1811.   [TP,RS]
    [see Bath Co., KY, marriage bonds]

MARSHALL, John, & Mary PECK, 22 May 1816;
    "married at once" with James Collins & Elizabeth Peck.   [TP]
    John Marshall & Mary Peck, no date.   [RS]

MATHERS, Saml., & Levisy ROGERS, 1 Jan. 1807.   [TP,RS]

MAVICK, Samuel, & Peggy GARRISON, 21 Nov. 1799.   [TP,RS]

McANULTY, James, & Margaret WILEY, 21 July 1808.   [TP,RS]

McCARLEY, John, & Betsy or Betsey PATTON, 25 Sept. 1798.   [TP,RS]

McCEARLY, Thomas, & Peggy PATTON, 25 July 1799.   [TP,RS]

McCLINTICK, Richard, & Charity MONTGOMERY, 14 Jan. 1812.   [TP,RS]

McCOLLOM, John, & Sarah SMITH, 2 July 1801.   [TP,RS]

McCOLLUM, Patrick, & Elizabeth SAINT DRESKIE, 5 May 1795.   [TP]
    7 May 1795   [RS]

McCORMICK, Adam, & Dolly HOPKINS, 16 May 1799.   [TP,RS]

McCORMICK, Wm., & Jane McCANN, 9 Feb. 1796.   [TP,RS]

McDANNOLD, Alexander, & Kitty TAPP, 16 Feb. 1815.   [TP,RS]

McGARY, Robert, & Patsey MONTGOMERY, 15 Jan. 1799.   [TP,RS]

McGUIRE, Holliday, & Sally LAFTLY, 13 June 1816.   [TP,RS]

McILVAINE, James, & Fanny MOORE, 27 July 1809.   [TP]

    James McILVANS & Fanny Moore   [RS]

McINTIRE, William, & Rachel STEPHEN, 10 March 1808.   [TP,RS]

McNAB, Andrew, & Delilah CASSIDY, 22 Feb. 1810.   [TP,RS]

McNAB, John C., & Jane CLUBB, 16 Aug. 1825.   [TP,RS]

    [see Bath Co., KY, marriage bonds]

McNEALL, James, & Matilda DARREL, 25 Jan. 1811.   [TP,RS]

MEANS, Jas., & Elizabeth WYATT, 11 Feb. 1813.   [TP,RS]

MEANS, William, & Sary EVINES, 6 Oct. 1808.   [TP,RS]

MENEFEE, Richard, & Polly LANSDALE, 2 Sept. 1802.   [RS]

    Richard Menefee & Polly Landdale [sic]   [TP]

METEER, Thomas, & Elizabeth HILL, 4 Dec. 1804.   [TP,RS]

MILLER, James, & Sally OKIM[?], 21 Dec. 1809.   [TP,RS]

MILLER, William, & Casandra ROSS, 30 Sept. 1813.   [TP,RS]

    [see Bath Co., KY, marriage bonds]

MILNER, John, & Polly GALLOWAY, 27 Sept. 1804.   [TP,RS]

MITCHELL, Mathew, & Martha CALDWELL, 4 Feb. 1802.   [TP,RS]

MITCHELL, Thomas, & Rebeccah MITCHEL, 19 Sept. 1805.   [TP]

    Thomas Mitchell & Rebeccah MITCHELL   [RS]

MONTGOMERY, Isaac, & Patsey McCLURE, 18 Dec. 1799.   [TP,RS]

MONTGOMERY, Joseph, & Nancy DAVIS, 30 Aug. 1797.   [TP,RS]

MONTGOMERY, Patrick, & Nancy HADDEN, 6 July 1797.   [TP,RS]

MOOR, James, & Mary C. DEAN, 19 Dec. 1811.   [TP,RS]

    [see Bath Co., KY, marriage bonds]

MOORE, John, & Polly FULTON, 4 Aug. 1807.   [TP,RS]

MYERS, William, & Susannah BECRAFT, 10 Feb. 1805.   [TP,RS]

MYERS, William, & Polly RICHART, 5 March 1818.   [TP,RS]

NAYLOR, Samuel, & Eliz.(abeth) ATCHISON, 1 Nov. 1798.   [TP,RS]

NELSON, James, & Frances DAVIS, 27 Feb. 1809.   [TP,RS]

NELSON, James I., & Mary YEATES, 21 Oct. 1819.   [TP,RS]

NEWTON, Levi, & Susannah JONES, 6 Dec. 1814.   [TP,RS]

NORTHCUT, John, & Jane TRIMBLE, 16 May 1811.   [TP,RS]

OAKLEY, John, & Eleanor OAKLEY, 6 July 1815.   [TP,RS]

OLSOP, John, & Ellener WREN, 23 Jan. 1800.   [TP]

    John OLSOY & Ellener Wren   [RS]

PATTERSON, Charles, & Jenny CONNOLY, 1 Apr. 1806.   [TP,RS]

PATTERSON, Thomas, & Matty WAILKES, 9 Jan. 1798. [TP,RS]

PATTON, Jas., & Polly HANSFORD, 16 Dec. 1806. [TP,RS]

PECK, George, & Nancy BARKER, 15 March 1796. [TP,RS]

    George Peck & Nancy Barker, 15 March 1796 [Ck]

PEEBELS, Thos., & Polly SIMPSON, 13 Aug. 1801. [TP]

    Thomas PEEBELE & Polly Simpson [RS]

PLANCK, Jacob C., & Mary ROGERS, 27 Sept. 1826. [TP,RS]

POSEBROUGH, James, & Rebeckah LOVE, 31 Aug. 1797. [TP,RS]

POWEL, Chas., & Marry HARRAH, 5 Feb. 1801. [TP,RS]

POWELL, Joseph, & Sally ALKIRE, 4 Oct. 1804. [TP,RS]

POWELL, Nathan, & Nancy BYRNS, 14 March 1822. [TP,RS]

    [see Bath Co., KY, marriage bonds]

PRATHER, Newman, & Polly McCLENNEGER, 28 July 1823:

    "married at Jones Henderson's." [TP,RS]

PRICHATT, Andrew, & Phebe LEMASTERS, 29 Dec. 1803. [TP,RS]

RABOURN, David, & Sara HENSON, 28 March 1811. [TP,RS]

RAINEY, William, & Reuhamah LINDSEY, 29 Oct. 1818. [TP,RS]

RALSTON, Andrew, & Rhoda ATKINSON, 22 Dec. 1808. [TP,RS]

RALSTON, Andrew, & Patsey NEALEY, 27 Nov. 1817. [TP,RS]

RALSTON, John, & Sarah BLACK, 7 Nov. 1815. [TP,RS]

RAMSEY, Samuel, & Isabella KING, 3 Dec. 1801. [TP,RS]

RAMSEY, William, & Rachel WHITESETT, 13 Sept. 1804. [TP]

    William Ramsey & Rachel WHITSETT [RS]

RAYNOLDS, John, & Mary B. NOLAND, 23 Nov. 1811. [TP]

    John REYNOLDS & Mary B. Noland [RS]

REED, Samuel, & Elizabeth PATTERSON, June 1795. [TP,RS]

REES, John, & Polly GATSON, 4 May 1802. [TP]

    John REESE & Polly Gatson [RS]

REID, Daniel, & Polly WAYNE, 18 May 1821. [TP,RS]

RHEA, William, & Polly McVICKER, 2 March 1807. [TP,RS]

RICE, Jonathan, & Elizabeth HIGEN, 18 May 1820. [TP,RS]

RICHARDS, Wm., & Mary GRANT, 10 May 1798. [TP,RS]

RICHART, Duncan O., & Patsey SHARP, 31 Aug. 1813. [TP,RS]

    [see Bath Co., KY, marriage bonds]

RIGGS, Isaac, & Hannah COLLIER, 6 Nov. 1800. [TP,RS]

RIGGS, James, & Caty HATHAWAY, 22 Dec. 1796. [TP,RS]

    James Riggs & Caty Hathaway, 22 Dec. 1796. [Ck]

RIGGS, John, & Darky HATHAWAY, 27 Aug. 1801. [TP,RS]

RINGO, Cornelius, & Nancy FRAZER, 26 Oct. 1797. [TP,RS]

RINGO, Peter, & Peggy HENDERSON, 6 Oct. 1813. [TP,RS]
  following the above entry: "263 couples" [TP]
ROBERTS, Jesse, & Dorcas DANNOLS, 13 Nov. 1809. [TP]
  Jesse Roberts & Corcas Dannols [RS]
ROBERTSON, Emirey, & Susannah LIVINGSTONE, 13 March 1800. [TP]
  Eiry Robertson & Susannah Livingstone [RS]
ROBINSON, John, & Sarah BROWN, 10 Dec. 1795. [TP,RS]
  John Robinson & Sara Brown, 31 Dec. 1795. [Bo]
ROBINSON, John, & Nancy HERR, 8 March 1821. [TP,RS]
ROBINSON, Samuel, & Jane RICHEY, 19 Nov. 1811. [TP,RS]
  [see Bath Co., KY, marriage bonds]
ROBINSON, William, & Mary A. HILL, 17 Dec. 1795. [TP,RS]
  Wm. Robinson & Mary Anne Hill, Dec. 1796. [Bo]
RODGERS, Saml., & Sarah MAPPIN, 14 May 1801. [TP,RS]
ROUTT, George, & Catherine HENDRIX, 28 Dec. 1797. [TP,RS]
SANDUSKY, Eli, & Peggy McCOLLUM, 7 Apr. 1796. [TP,RS]
  Eli ST. DUSKEY & Margaret McCALLUM, 7 Apr. 1796. [Ck]
SEE, Wm., & Betsy OXYER, 3 June 1805. [TP,RS]
SHARP, Moses, & Delpha HAMPTON, 25 Oct. 1825. [TP,RS]
SHARP, William B., & Maria S. CALDWELL, 15 Feb. 1825. [TP,RS]
SHELING, David, & Betsey MARSHALL, 18 Jan. 1810. [TP,RS]
SHUTS, John, & Susanna GRIFFIN, 5 March 1807. [TP,RS]
SIMPSON, James, & Polly CAMPBELL, 19 Apr. 1796. [TP,RS]
  James Simpson & Polly Campbell, 21 Apr. 1796 [Bo]
SINCLAIR, George, & Peggy TRIMBLE, 27 Apr. 1815. [TP,RS]
SLAVENS, Stewart, & Polly RIGGS, 28 Nov. 1816. [TP,RS]
SLAVINS, Dr. John, & Sophia A. GRAHAM, 18 Apr. 1821. [TP]
  Doct. John SALVINS & Sophia A. Graham [RS]
SMART, William, & Ann GLOVER, 3 Apr. 1817. [TP,RS]
SMATHERS, Andrew, & Elizabeth BRISTOL, 30 Apr. 1807. [TP,RS]
SMITH, Lane, & Amy L. THOMAS, 27 July 1813. [TP,RS]
SORRENEY [Sorency], David, & Susye BROWN, 28 June 1798. [TP,RS]
STEEL, Jacob, & Debby OWINGS, 20 March 1817. [TP,RS]
STEELE, Samuel, & Jane TRIMBLE, 24 Oct. 1811. [TP,RS]
STEELE, Thos., & Catherine Temple McCLURE, 12 Feb. 1801. [TP,RS]
STEPHENSON, John, & Catherine HOLT, 4 Sept. 1823. [TP,RS]
STEVENS, John, & Polly TRIMBLE, 2 Nov. 1808. [TP,RS]
STEVENSON, Samuel, & Mary Ann FRY, 14 Aug. 1823. [TP,RS]
STEWART, John, & Rachel WOOLSEY, 22 Oct. 1801. [TP,RS]

STEWART, Thomas, & Margaret LONG, 23 Aug. 1803.   [TP,RS]

STORY, John, & Polly STEWART, 1 Jan. 1822.   [TP,RS]

SWANEY, Miles, & Polly BERRY, 9 March 1819.   [TP,RS]

    [see Bath Co., KY, marriage bonds]

TAYLOR, Charles, & Polly ARNETT, 4 Dec. 1817.   [TP,RS]

THOMPSON, Hugh D., & Rebeccah GILKEY, 13 March 1810.   [TP,RS]

THOMPSON, James, & Elizabeth YEATES, 14 Oct. 1817.   [TP,RS]

TINKER, Anderson, & Elizabeth HEDRICK, 11 Dec. 1800.   [TP,RS]

TIPTON, Solomon, & Margaret BRADSHAW, 16 March 1809.   [TP,RS]

TITSWORTH, Abraham, & Silome BARNS, 12 Sept. 1797.   [TP,RS]

TITSWORTH, James, & Jenne WICK, Aug. 1796.   [TP,RS]

TODD, John, & Margaret COOKE, 7 Nov. 1808.   [TP,RS]

TODD, John, & Sally SIMS, 15 Sept. 1812.   [TP,RS]

TODD, Joseph, & Catherine FERGUSON, 13 Sept. 1810.   [TP,RS]

TRIMBLE, David, & Polly ZELFROW, 19 Aug. 1802.   [TP,RS]

TRIMBLE, Hugh, & Elenor CALDWELL, 12 Aug. 1802.   [RS]

    Hugh TREMBLE & Elenor Caldwell   [TP]

TRIMBLE, Hugh, & Nancy NORTHCUTT, 19 Feb. 1811.   [RS]

    Hugh TRIMBEL & Nancy NORTHCUT   [TP]

TRIMBLE, Robert, & Elizabeth YOUNG, 24 Nov. 1814.   [TP,RS]

TRUMBO, Jacob, & Elizabeth DOWNEY, 22 Nov. 1798.   [TP,RS]

TRUSSELL, Nehemiah & Eliz. RICHARDSON, 15 July 1802.   [TP]

    Nehmiah Trussell & Elizabeth Richardson   [RS]

VERSITHE, John, & Polly LOVE, 19 Sept. 1805.   [TP,RS]

VICE, Enoch, & Elizabeth TUCKER, 8 Oct. 1801.   [TP,RS]

VILEY, Samuel, & Jane ROBINSON, 29 Aug. 1816.   [TP,RS]

WADE, Samuel, & Polly LONG, 5 Oct. 1826.   [TP,RS]

WALKER, Jas. E., & Mary Ann FERRIS, 17 March 1807.   [TP,RS]

WALL, Zachariah, & Thompy OSBURN, 5 Jan. 1825.   [TP]

    Zechariah Wall & Thompy Osburn   [RS]

WARD, Joseph, & Fanny THOMAS, 23 Oct. 1817.   [TP,RS]

WARRICK, Jacob, & Jane MONTGOMERY, 10 March 1796.   [TP,RS]

    Jacob WARRIK & Jane Montgomery, 10 March 1796.   [Ck]

WATSON, Hezekiah, & Polly CARTWELL, 17 Apr. 1800.   [TP,RS]

WEAVER, George, & Bridget DOUGHERTY, 6 Feb. 1797.   [TP,RS]

    George Weaver & Bridget DOHERTIE, 6 Feb. 1797.   [Ck]

WELLS, John, & Hannah LIVINGSTONE, 29 Aug. 1799.   [TP]

    John Wells & Hannah LEVINGSTONE   [RS]

WHITECRAFT, Cleanthus, & Jane McCALISTER, 24 March 1818.   [TP,RS]

WHITECRAFT, John, & Rachel ARNETT, 7 Nov. 1816.   [TP]
    John WHITESCRAFT & Rachel Arnett   [RS]
WIGHT, Alexander, & Sarah RAMY, 13 Aug. 1818.   [TP,RS]
WILEY, Hugh, & Elizabeth STEVENSON, 26 Apr. 1804.   [TP,RS]
WILEY, John, & Sarah LEIPER, 2 July 1807.   [TP,RS]
WILKERSON, Joshua, & Lucinda DICKEY, 23 Jan. 1816.   [TP,RS]
WILLIAMS, Daniel, & Eleanor DAVIS, 3 June 1819.   [TP,RS]
WILLIAMS, James, & Hannah MAPPIN, 11 May 1797.   [TP,RS]
WILLIAMS, Thomas, & Rachel LANSDALE, 28 Feb. 1805.   [TP,RS]
WILLIAMSON, Jesse, & Elizabeth HALL, 25 Feb. 1811.   [TP,RS]
WILLIS, Thomas, & Nancy HIGGINS, 24 Dec. 1808.   [TP]
WILSON, John, & Catherine RINGO, 17 Aug. 1815.   [TP,RS]
WILSON, James, & Elener McCLURE, 9 Sept. 1806.   [TP,RS]
WILSON, Samuel, & Elizabeth ROGERS, 21 Apr. 1814.   [TP,RS]
    [see Bath Co., KY, marriage bonds]
WISE, Richard, & Patsey GILMORE, 29 March 1821.   [TP,RS]
WOODROOF, David, & Naomi BEVERLY, 28 Aug. 1800.   [TP,RS]
WOODS, Saml., & Anna PURVIANCE, Sept. 1796.   [TP,RS]
    Samuel WOOD & Anne Purviance, 8 Sept. 1796.   [Bo]
WYATT, Anthony, & Polly SMITH, 9 May 1816.   [TP,RS]
WYATT, Emmanuel, & Susanna REDD, 8 March 1804.   [TP,RS]
YARDLEY, Joseph, & Catherine BALDRIDGE, 23 July 1801.   [TP,RS]
YOCUM, George, & Christina SMITH, 24 Oct. 1811.   [TP,RS]
YOUNG, Daniel, & Polly McILHANY, 1 Nov. 1804.   [TP,RS]
YOUNG, Samuel, & Nancy TRIMBLE, 25 Dec. 1810.   [TP,RS]
YOUNG, Sinnet, & Hannah YOUNG, 16 Apr. 1818.   [RS]
    Sinnet Young & _____ Young   [TP]

CROSS-INDEX

ABBOT(T) / ABBET Nancy 8
  Wm. D. 75
ACKERMAN Mabela 12 Peter
  127
ADAMS Amanda 28 Caleb 3
  Christeena 46 Christiana 128
  Elizabeth 5 42 65 Hannah 13
  James 90 128 John 13 128
  Larkin 42 Martha 35 Nancy 10
  90 Polly 108 Richard 35 Susan
  W. 1 Thomas 1 Wm. 28 46
ALEXANDER Cynthia 91
  Elizabeth 73 169 Hirman 73
  Hugh 46 60 101 Jane 101
  Margaret 31 Peggy 60 Robert 31
  Sarah 29 Sharlot 46 Thomas 29
  60 91 Wm. 101
ALFREY Abram 2 Adam 2
  Elizabeth 104 Fielding 104 John
  2 82 104 Rachel 104
ALKIRE Sally 174
ALLEN Daniel 95 F. W. 112
  George 95 John 4 85 111 Louisa
  95 Lucy 4 Nancy 85 W. 162
  William 73
ALLEY Delila 46
ALLINDEN / ALENDEN Malinda
  76
ALLINGTON (see Ellington)
ALLISON / ALISON Ann 165
  James 55 Ruth Ann 55
AMOS Elisabeth 160 Mary Jane 7
  Polly 29 Wm. 7
ANDERSON Asinah 26 Cassy 38
  Cobert 3 Collerd 160 Daniel 51
  Eliza 39 98 170 Ezekiel 147 160
  Fanny 72 Jane 160 Julian 108
  Leah 52 Maria 156 Mary 2
  Patsey 147 Polly 50 Richard 72
  Sanford 98 Sarah 3 Sarah A. 55
  160 Swafford 123 W. M. 50
  Wm. 52 55 109 ____ 165
ARGO Nancy 113 Turnell 113

ARMITAGE Hester 81 James 25
  Wm. 81
ARMSTRONG Jane 83 John 78
  Polly 112
ARNETT Clenthus 42 Margaret
  24 Mary 85 Polly 176 Rachel
  177 Sally 34 Sarah 150 Susanna
  172 Thomas 34 51 86
ARNOLD Fentan 12 Lucy O. 118
  Thos. 8 Vernetta 163 Wm. 163
ARRO(W)SMITH / ARRASMITH
  / AROSMITH Abner 66 Anna 70
  148 Catharine 133 Eladia 129
  Elizabeth 132 Kizzy 131 Mary
  105 Massey 148 Nancy 66 68
  Thos. 148 Wesley 22 Wm. 60
  105
ASBURY Heziah 62
ASHLEY / ASHBY Ellen 62 M. I.
  62 Peggy 124 Peter 124
ATCHISON / ETCHISON Dolly
  68 Elizabeth 33 124 125 129 173
  Elizah 47 Hannah 143 Henry
  143 James 60 Jesse 5 91 97
  John 6 Lucinda 163 Margaret 38
  135 Mary Ann 58 Maryan 38
  Minerva 132 Polly 50 140 Sarah
  8 60 97 Silas 5 76 129 Thomas 5
  35 Wm. 68 132 140 163
ATHA / ATHE / ATHY Jane 16
  Lucinda 89 Matilda 103 Sarah
  102 Walter 6
?ATHERSON John 161 Nancy
  161
ATKINS / ADKINS Dudley 33
  Eber 79 Francis 33 Martha 78
  Nancy 54 Sally 83 Thomas 33
  54
ATKINSON Caroline 58 John 58
  61 161 Nancy 161 Rhoda 174
  Susan 61
AULLICK Geo. 4
A(U)SBURN Nancy 150 Susan
  78 Wm. 78
AUSTIN Martha 51

179

BADGER Eliza 6 Mary A. 13
BADGESON Hetty 55
BAGBY Robert 10
BAILEY / BA(Y)LEY Absolom 6
  Alson 7 Carie 40 Charles 30
  David 7 69 90 125 Elijah 95
  Eliza 140 Elizabeth 5 59 Hannah
  79 159 John 29 40 125 162 L.
  69 Lorency 99 Louisa 30 Lucy 1
  34 Mary A. 134 Marvin 140
  Nancy 30 79 Polly 5 Robert 120
  Robertta 120 Sally Ann 120
  Sarah 162 Wm. 1 34 79 103 119
?BAINBRIDGE John 116
BAIRD / BEARD Angeline 66
  Ann Gelina 66 Archibald 29
  Elizabeth 21 66 74 100 117
  George 23 150 H. 7 63 Hardon
  100 Henry 122 John 21
  Margarett 114 Mary 23 Nancy
  149 150 Philadelphia 62 63 Polly
  109 Ratliff 63 117 Samuel 66
  109 114 Wm. 96
BAKER Edwin 122 Peggy 122
  Rezin 122
BALDRIDGE Catherine 177
BALDWIN Johannah Morris 171
BALER Robert 70
BALL / BOW Margaret 75
BALLA George 21 Lewie 21
  Mary 32 ·
BALLARD Susannah 165
?BALTER (see Baxter)
?BANTA / BONTY Ann 2
  Elizabeth 130 Mary Ann 32
BARBEE Anna 150 Lewis 150
  Lucy 17 Robert 8 17
BARBER America 148 Ann 150
  Catharine 42 148 Ed 8 Elizabeth
  42 Gehasy 150 Harriet 92 John
  42 60 Landon 70 Lewis 150
  Louisa F. 91 Lucinda 16 Mary
  153 Minerva J. 70 Nancy 75
  Polley 105 Priscilla 40 Robert 17
  Thomas 75 148

?BARBERRY (see Roseberry)
BARDOLPH Elizabeth 62
BARKER Elizabeth 42 Nancy 174
  Thomas 109 139
BARKLEY Edward 39 Robt. 17
BARN(A)BY / ?BARBABY Eliza
  23 Harriet 129 Swan 127 Wm.
  127 149
BARNES / BARNS Alexander 156
  Alvisa 9 Dorothy 30 Eliza 111
  Elizabeth 93 94 131 Henrietta 98
  Hyram 89 Joshua 98 128 155
  Martha Ann 116 Mary 144
  Matilda 5 Nell 160 Patience 20
  Permelia 117 Polly 121 Rachel
  74 145 Robt. 16 Sarah 31
  Silome 176 Sophia 160 Thomas
  30 74 157 Tushatha 20 William 9
  30 121
BARNETT / BARNAT Eliza 23
  Nancy 1 Pauline 128 Sarah 40
?BARNSON Malon 17
BARTLETT Margaret G. 51 169
BARTLEY Charles 103
BAS(H)FORD Elizabeth 95 John
  9 95 Nancy 44
BASHAW / BESHAW Emily 13
  Jane 106 Polly 38
BATTAIL(L)E Louisa 126 Wm.
  126
BAXTER Jane 26 Wm. 27 32 127
  154
BAY Peggy 160
BEADLE Rebecca 141
BEAL Betsey 57 Jane 114 John
  114
BEAN Betsey 130 Jane 114
BECK Eady 55
BECKNER Caroline 104 Peter
  104
BECRAFT / BECROFT Anna 48
  Ben 48 Hetty 14 James 57 147
  Margaret 75 Polly 154 Susannah
  173 Wm. 48 154
BEDELL / BID(D)ELL Deborah 22

Elizabeth 118 Huldah 30 John
125 Samuel 118 125
BEDFORD Eliza 134
BELL Betsy 57
BELLOWS / ?BALLOW Catherine
15 Thos. 59
BENSON James 45 156 James,
Jr. 45 Lucinda 45 Lucretia 3
Maranda 156 Mary 159 Sintha
156
BERDEN Polly 77
BERRY / BARRY Ann Amelia 152
Elizabeth 61 73 Geo. 11 Henry
141 James 135 Jesse 61 John L.
32 Joseph 32 73 Mary Jane 32
Polly 141 156 176 Rebeckah 170
Wm. 88
BESHEARS G. W. 148
BETT John F. 13
BEVERLY Naomi 177
BIGGS Elizabeth 170
BIRSON James 71
BIVIN Sarah A. 75
BLACK M. L. 29 Sally 168
Sarah 174
BLACKBURN / BLACKBARN
Mary Ann Pater 153 Polly 131
BLAIR Elizabeth 59 Martha 81
BLAKE Geo. 67 Henry 12
Margaret 67 68
BLEVINS / BLEVENS Catharine
118 Hannah 47 James 12 48 118
Jane 11 Solman 120
?BOACHEN Abigail 55
BOAT Margaret 74
BOAZ Asher 71 Austin 13
BOGIE Mary 64
BOGGS Rachael 159 160
BOLES / BOLIN Katy 151 Ruby
151
BOMAN / BOWAN Parmelia 60
BONDURANT Joseph 11 159 162
BOOK Frederick 6 12
BOON / BOONES Alexander 113
Eliza 56 Lucinda 22 Marthew

112 Nancy 81 Wm. 9
BOTTS Ben 33 107 Eliza 107
Emily 56 F. 13 George Ann 2
Jefferson 110 John 49 Margaret
49 Nancy 14 41 Robert 14 Sally
57 Thomas 41 57 Wm. 2
BOW / BON Margaret 75
BOYD Acley Ann 160 Amanda
161 Andrew 160 Betsy 69 C. B.
56 D. B. 49 77 101 Dorcas 14
96 149 Eleanor 167 Elizabeth 7
41 49 65 72 80 Emaline 154
Emily 79 George 60 72 147 J.
132 Jane 170 John 15 Joseph
148 Louisana 101 Lucy 94
Lydia 121 Malinda 30 60 Nancy
14 49 138 147 Narcissa 125
Polly 96 Rachel 148 Rolling 65
Spencer 12 31 79 80 92 101 161
Washington 149 Wm. 41 96 124
138
BOYLES Nelly 169
BRACKEN Elizabeth 70 James 9
70 142 Jane 14 15 76 Mary 171
Nancy 14 Polly 9 150 Robert 70
142 Sarah 131 142 Theophilus
76
BRADLEY Alexander 119 Eliser
105 Elisha 16 Elizabeth 16
Margaret 119 Martha 119 120
Mary 120 N. E. 92
BRADSHAW David 64 98 121
Elizabeth 34 Jas. F. 82 Louisa
Ann 64 Lucinda 121 Margaret
176 Marilla Jane 118 Minerva J.
82 Nancy 137 Polly W. 126
Sarah 152 Thos. 118 131
BRAMBLET / BRAMELL Delila
Ann 6 Henry 16
BRECKINRIDGE /
BRACKENRIDGE Anne 166
Mary 138
BRENT John L. 80
BRETON Susanna 75
BRIDGES Hiram 14 77 91 John

W. 150 Mae 91 Permelia 77
BRIGHT Hinson 17
BRINTON / BRINSON Betsy 69
BRISTO(W) / BRISTOL Elizabeth
175 John 123 Margaret 119
Mattea 92 Sally 123
BROCK Tarlton 18 46
BROMAGEN / BROMIGAN /
BROMAGER / BROMMEN
Allen 70 Catharine 40 Elenor 150
Jeremiah 102 Lydia 51 Margaret
43 70 Martha 18 Sally 123 140
Siddy 51 Thos. 51
BROMER / BRAMER Ganter 96
Robert 96
BROOK Wilton 90
BROTHERS Elizabeth S. 128
Susan M. 142
BROUCH Mary 118
BROWN Alexander 19 Betsey
127 Caleb 87 Cassey 90 Casus
34 Clarinda 103 Copy 105
Eleanor 142 Eliza 103 Elizabeth
28 54 Geo. 28 James 28 Jane 96
Jemima 64 John F. 66 Maria 34
Mathew 103 Nancy 25 87 Nancy
Jane 66 Peggy 28 Polly 19 105
Richard 103 115 Sally 81 Sarah
175 Susan 115 137 Susye 175
Walker 106 Wm. 105
BROWNING Emily 147
BRUCE / ?BANCE Eliza 131
James 14 131 Mary Ann 14
Nancy 81
BRUMGEAR / BRUNGER /
BURGEAR Allen 75 Jefferson
150 Margaret 150 Melissa 119
Sam 119
BRYAN(T) (see also Byram)
Joseph 146 Mary 108 118
Rachel 48
BUCHANAN Fielden 69 James
143 Mary 143
BUCKLEY Wm. 46
BUCKNER Wm. 11

BUDLE (see Bedell)
BUNGANER (see also Garner)
Margarett 150
BURBRIDGE Elizabeth 148 John
20 50 Marinda 162 Patsy 100
Polly 171 Robt. 20
BURCH David 106 Hannah 106
John 9 107 Nancy 9 Sarah 107
BURKE Elizabeth 20
BURNETT / BURNITT Claburn
90 Polly 139 Wm. 139
BURN(E)S / BYRNS Adam 20
Barbara 120 Dennis 113 Eliza
131 Eliza Jane 116 Elizabeth 130
Emerk 45 Enoch 113 119 Enos
21 139 James 21 John 9 Julian
119 Kerin 46 Kern H. 45 Maria
84 Mary Ann 21 Nancy 113 174
Nicholas 90 Rice 22 66 Susan 66
104 139 Wm. 117
BURTON John 141
BUSBY / BUSBE(Y) / BUSLEY
Amanda 23 Elizabeth 63 Isaac
110 Jackson 60 James 63 82
John 23 135 Malinda 110 135
Marandy 51 Minerva Ann 60
BUTCHER H. M. 81 Hannah 144
Isaac B. 167 Lymon 149 Polly
159 Sarah 57 132
BUTLER Abegail 65 Alpheus 65
105 Ann 137 Artimecia 124
Betsy 78 Delila 104 138 Dorcas
22 Eda 151 Elizabeth 15 156
Emily 101 John 22 137 143 156
Katharine 4 Kitty 149 Malinda
44 Matilda 54 Nancy 150
Nathan 4 15 65 99 Rachel 99
Rhody 145 Sally 167 Sarah 53
Susan 143 Wm. 101
BYRAM / BYROM / BYRAN
Henrietta 161 I. 161 Malilda 1
Mary 80 108 Nancy 109 Ruth 65
109 Thomas 109
CALDWELL / COLDWELL Ann
Patterson 171 Celia 171 Elenor

176 Elizabeth 86 95 Ephraim 86
James 68 82 John 32 Juirley 118
Lura 68 Maria S. 175 Martha
165 168 173 Polly 172 Robt.
137 Walter 689 127 Wm. 59 82
CALK Benj. 127
CALL Elizabeth 19 Hamilton 19
CALVERT (see Colbert)
CAMPBELL Alexander 23
Elizabeth 167 Harriette 165 Jane
72 Margaret 58 Polly 175 Sarah
167
CAMPLIN Elizabeth 132
CAN(N) (see also Carr) Alvin 35
Jane 16 21 Julian 130 Susannah
21
CANNINGS / COMINGS Mary
137
CANNON Agnes 12 155 Amelia
141 Esther 37 Geo. 12 Malinda
11 Nancy 51 98 Newble 37
Newton 24 Noble 65 Nubald 12
Peggy 155 Sally 65
CANTERBURY Asa 2
CANTRELL Christopher 20 Phebe
20
?CARAH / CONAH Polly 58 59
CARE Hannah 63
CAR(E)Y Mary 117 Sally 44
CARNES Elizabeth F. 124
CARPENTER Cythia 56 Margaret
56 Nancy 140 Squire 25 140
CARR (see also Kerr) Alvin 28
Ann 59 Eliza 26 Hullerry 114
Julian 130 Levina 130 Malinda
151
CARRINGTON Elizabeth 65
Mildred 163 Susan 27 Timothy
27 65 163
CARROL / CARRELL / CORRELL
Honor 34 James 134 Rachel 134
Rutha Ann 134
CARSLEY Joseph 10
CARTER Anna 123 David 26
Elijah 28 Joseph 26 97 123

Virginia 97
CARTMILL / CARTMELL /
CARTMEAL Amanda 38
Andrew 28 125 David M. 120
Frances 112 Harrison 28 Jas. H.
26 Jenny 168 John 61 Lucinda
125 Maremy 73 Martha 120
Mary 37 61 120 122 Nancy 28 70
Polly 176 Thos. 26 37 38 70 73
W. 112 Wm. 22 Zebulen 122
CARTSILL Rudd 125 Sally 125
CARTWELL (see Cartmill)
CARTWRIGHT (see Cutright)
CASE Nancy 81
CASEY Geo. 128
CASH Joseph 126
CASSITY / CASITY / CAS(S)IDY
Alexander 87 Amanda M. 49
Anne 38 David 27 Delilah 173
Elizabeth 3 68 82 107 Emily 82
Esther 97 Fielding 80 Francis
123 G. W. 27 Henry 3 46 112
Hester 97 J. A. 72 Jacob 28 38
82 137 Jesse 27 John 2
Jonathan 2 49 Lucinda 123 Lydia
62 Madeson 107 Martha 147
Mary E. 27 Mary Jane 74 Nancy
38 Patsy 87 Polly 46 137 Rachel
2 Reuben 96 Ruth 112 Stephen
97 Susan 59 Susannah 168
Wm. 28
CATES Polly 35
CATLETT Ann 41
CA(Y)WOOD / KAYWOOD Asa
119 Matilda 95 96 Rheuhaina
168 Thomas 96
CHANDLER Allen 117 Eliza 36
Elizabeth 17 Fanny 36 Mary Jane
71
CHAPMAN Robt. O. 94
CHARNOWIF Margaret 28
CHASTAIN Elizabeth 80 Judith
85 Magdalen 26 Martin 110
Ramey 80 Silas 26 85 110
CHEATHAM Judith 86 Martha

Ann 115
CHEN / CAHEN Peggy 46
  Samuel 46
CHERRY John 90
CHEW Amelia 149
CHILDERS / CHILDRES Phebe
  90 Sarah 90
CHILES Henry 75 139
CHIPMAN Darper 17 Joseph 66
  Margarett 17 Martha 17 Paris 54
  Perry 17 Sally 54
CHOAT / CHOTE / SHOAT
  Augustine 88 154 Augustus 56
  Austin 47 107 130 H. W. 56
  Margarett 47 Maria A. W. 55
  Mary 88 Maryariah 47 Patsy 154
  Polly 88 154
?CHORAY Sarah 12
CHURCH Isiah 76 Lemensey 76
  Louisa 76 Thomas 29 76
CLARK C. 29 Eleda Araminta
  129 Elijah 129 Essina 23 John 5
  52 60 64 73 Mary 64 Nancy 51
  Robert 127 Thomas 23
CLAVILL / CLOVILL Charlotte
  151 Eli 93 Elizabeth 151 Polly
  93
CLA(Y)TON Catherine 69 Charles
  5 15 94 161 Debey 162 Elizabeth
  75 153 Geo. B. 29 162 Joseph
  75 Lawrence 5 Lucinda 29
  Lucretia 5 161 Martha 103 161
  Mary 79 Melvina 5 Nurtilia 161
  Polly 90 Rebecca 25 161
  Robertta 90 Sarah 103 Sylvia 70
  Vienna 153 Vilinda 15 Wm. B.
  103
CLEM / CLEMON Lucinda 26
  Nancy 80
CLINE Doll 30 Elizabeth 30
  James 30 John 30 Martha 132
  Mary Ann 30 100 Samuel 30
CLOW Martha 130
CLUBB Jane 97 98 173
?CLUMMEN Mason 112

COB / CAB Nancy 36
COCHRAN Eunice 169
COFFER(S) / COFER / COPHER
  Cintha 106 Eliza Jane 159
  Ezekiel 34 Harrison 143 Henry
  116 Jane 61 96 Jesse 15 Joyce
  15 Lonizy 15 Mary 143 Polly
  102 Reuben 96 106
COFFEE Rebekah 88 172
COGER(S) Elizabeth 9 Isaac 21
COG(G)SWELL Elizabeth 41 86
  George Ann 128 Jeddiah 41
  Isaac 117 128 John 44 Lydia 41
  Yedariah 31 Zilphia 44
COLBERT / CALVERT Elizabeth
  119 Harriet 108 James 31 Jesse
  119
COL(E)MAN / COALMAN Eliza
  138 F. O. 138 Geo. 50 67 111
  131 Jesse B. 32 Lucy 108
COLGLAZIER / CELELASURE /
  COLGLAZLER David 131
  Elizabeth 131
COLLIER Hannah 174
COLLINS Amy 131 Bohannon 71
  120 Elisha 133 Elizabeth 102
  Hiram 13 James 172 Joseph 32
  Josiah 102 Lydia 30 Mary Ann
  32 Pauline 102 Pollina 120 Will
  102 Willis 32 120
COLLIVER / COLIVER Jane 22
  Joseph 22 Lydia J. 22
CON(N) (see also Can, Carr)
  Malinda 151 Solomon 149
CONNEL Susan 125
CONNELLY Isabella 169 170
  Jenny 173 Margaret W. 172
CONNER Elizabeth 49
CONYERS Enoch 132 Isaac 3 40
  81 John 70 Kiziah 132 Margaret
  70 Martha 81 Sarah 40
  Susannah 3
COOK Abraham 45 Abram 52
  Amanda 45 George Ann 52 Ibby
  Jane 52 James 33 162 Lucinda

184

171 Margaret 176 Mary A. 100
Matilda 88
COON(S) / KOONS / FOONS
Emily 7 John 89 Phebe 165
Polly 89 165 Thomas 7
COOPER Adam 58 147 Challis 30
Elizabeth 70 James H. 147 John
115 Leander 129 Margaret 50 58
Nancy 129 Pattsy 8 Rebecca 147
CORBIN Lavina 92 Louina 92
Lucy 105 Margaret 119 Sally 53
Zachariah 43 92 119
CORDE Marthy 158
?CORDURANT (see Bondurant)
CORY James 27 Zerilda 123
COSHOW / COSHAW /
CUSHAW Elizabeth 19 John 6
19 24 35 Lucy 6 Nancy 24
Patsey 23 Polly 35 Sarah 6
COSTIGAN / COATIGAN Ann 52
Elizabeth 92 153 Nancy 64 Sarah
92 Wm. 114
?COURA M. L. 40
COVINGTON Coleman 45
COWAN David 106
COX Agness Fay 33 James 35
John 71 Mary Jane 71 Sally 169
Solomon 35
COYLE George 36 69 91 James
35 76 83 Joseph 23 113
Margaret 23 Martha 113 Mary
Ann 69
CRAIG Ann 135 Betsy 11
Cynthia 145 David 109 Elizabeth
29 75 78 79 108 Jacob 16 29 114
Jonathan 145 Joshua 91
Margaret 115 Mary 91 Nancy
109 Peter 11 Polly 171 Robert
36
CRAIN / CRANE James 36
Rachel 168 Samuel 37
CRANDLE Easter 115 Esther 114
J. 114
CRAVER / GROVER Geo. 101
Lydia B. 91 Sarah Ann 101

CRAWFORD Betsey 170
Christana 37 Joseph 37
?CRAYE Lanny 71
CRAYCRAFT / CRACRAFT Alis
Ann 107 Betsey 62 Elizabeth 37
John 107 Mary 107 128 Nancy
105 125 Polly 66 Sarah 103
Thomas 128 131 Wm. 35 105
CREE Sarah 115
CROCKETT John 20 John A. 95
Margaret 87 Maryann 87 Patsey
168 Polly 26 Robert 26
CRONE(R) / CRONOR Dorothy
E. 102 Lincoln 33 Mary 101
CROOKS / CROAKS Arzel 12
Betsy 168 Eliza 83 Elizabeth 24
125 Fanny B. 151 John 24 80
Magaret 168 Mary 166 Nancy B.
12 166 Rebecca 79 Robert 3
Robt. B. 145 William 79
CROUCH Ann 115 Cauner 57
Cintha 53 Cuthbert 97 David 57
Elizabeth 36 54 Garner 57
Gounee 57 Isaac 9 28 36 53 110
James 53 110 Jesse 109 John
110 Jonathan 9 49 159 Judith 97
Minerva 110 Nancy 9 Sally 28
Wm. 10 97
CROW Ann 57 James 29 Mary
Ann 143 144 Polly 118
CRUMP Eliz. 73 Maryan 73
Melvin 72 Richard 38
CRUTCHFIELD Zopher 39
CUNNINGHAM / CUMINGHAM
Elizabeth 31 Jane 59 John 59
Rachel 35
CUPS David 129 Hester 122
CURRY Elizabeth 78
CUTRIGHT / CURTRIGHT
Arnolds 6 Elizabeth 127 James
17 John 39 Peter 27
DAIL(E)Y Amanda 72 Elizabeth
39 Lucy 34 Mary 46 Ralph 72
Sarah 39
DALE Frances 18 Jane 11 Rachel
169 Thomas 43

185

DALZELL Betsey 170
DANBY / DANDY Wm. 11 68
DANIEL / DANNOLS Dorcas 175
  Travis 5 99
?DAPUY R. 39
DARBEY James 40 Milly 40
DARNAL(L) / DARNELL /
  DARNOLD Anne 119 David 16
  70 81 85 Elish 132 Elizabeth 85
  Elliott 16 Fanny 16 Nancy 81
  Ruth 70 Susan 122
DARREL Matilda 173
DAUGHERTY / DOUGHERTY
  Bridget 176 Elizabeth 66 John 66
  67 Katherine 35 Margaret 66
  Samuel 35
DAVIS Allen 33 Almira 57 Ann
  31 166 Betsy 40 Catherine 152
  153 David 41 67 Eleanor 177
  Elizabeth 89 160 Frances 173 H.
  11 Harriet 84 Heathy 168
  Ignatius 106 153 Jane 103 104
  135 Jesse 93 103 John 28
  Jonathan 89 Joseph 153 Lydiann
  34 Margaret 168 Mary 40
  Minerva 160 Nancy 65 90 173
  Nell 33 Polly 130 Sally 93 Sally
  Ann 22 Sarah 67 106 Silas 162
  Thomas 84
DAWSON Geo. 162 John 142
  Mary A. 50
DAY Jacob 41 James 41
  Katharine 109 Peggy 160 Peter
  41
DEAKIN / DUSKINS Daniel 150
  Moses 150 Sally 150
DEAN / DEEN Daniel 101
  Deborah 77 Louisa 39 Malinda
  151 Margaret 4 Mariah 42 Mary
  C. 101 173 Nancy 65 Polly 65
  ____ 41
DECKARD / DECKER Catherine
  172 Chrystena 172
DELAY John 118 Sally 7
DENBY Milieson 43

DENNIS Hannah 124 Jesse 42 51
  Mary 51 Thomas 51
DENTON Celia 110 Elinor 72
  Elizabeth 124 Jane 118 John 42
  Jonathan 149 Reuben 34 42 52
  72 Wm. 118 124
DICKEN(S) Ann 146 Jesse 53
  Sarah 53
DICKEY Lucinda 177
DILLON Laticha 36
DIXEN / DISCON Henry 117
  Sarah 117
DO (ditto?) Catherine 116 Polly
  144 Sally 5
DODGES / DODGER Arminta 145
  Wm. 145
DOGGET(T) Arthur 15 Elizabeth
  15 Elizabeth Martha 102 Franky
  32 Henry 34 Nancy 34 Polly
  132 Richard 132 Sarah 32
  Thomas 15
DOLAND Mary 122
DOLEMAN John 43
DONAHUE / DONOHEW Joseph
  39 156 Lucinda 141 Matthew 79
  141 Sally 79
DONALDSON Alexander 19 43
  142 Barbary 43 F. 43 Elizabeth
  19 87 Isabel 141 142 James 68
  87 114 Mary Jane 19 Wm. 19
DONATHAN / DONITHAN Elijah
  43 Elizabeth 103 Lucinda 140
  Lydia 152 Nancy 118 Thomas
  103 118 Thos. D. 140 Wm. 140
?DOODLAR Mary M. 50
?DOUCHE / DONCHO (see
  Donahue)
DOWNEY / DOWNIE Elizabeth
  176 Jane 166 Polly 166
DOWNING Celice 113 Cidney
  113 Margurite 159
DOWNS / DOWNES Eliza Jane
  102 Milly Jane 137 Robt. 121
  Wm. 102 137
DOYLE John 35 54 Matilda 35

?DRAIN Robert 36
DRESKIN Isaac 114 Paulina 114
DUCKWORTH Alfred F. 45 Ane
  Elisa 1 John 44 95 102 Sam 65
DUNCAN Eliza 115 Elizabeth 89
  Henry 34 Margaret 157 Matilda
  34 35 168 Melinda 145 Sarah
  168 Wm. 89
DUN(A)WAY John 83 Joseph 45
DUNIGAN Susannah 169
DUNLAP / DONGLAP John 44
  168
?DURATT Maria 159
DUREAL Eliz. 26 James 26
DURHAM John 45
DUTY D. D. 117 Daniel 21 35
  142 144 148 David 1 Eliza Ann
  142 Elizabeth 21 Jane 1 134
  John 71 135 July 71 Margarett
  101 Mary Ann 135 144 Melinda
  148 Nancy 35
EASTON Elizabeth 46 Sarah 166
EATON Charles 46 Hannah 62
  Jeremiah 88 109 Mathew 171
  Nancy 88 Rachel 47
EDEN / EADEN Elizabeth 147
  Jacob 147 Jeremiah 93 John 45
  Mary 93 Sarah 45
EDWARD(S) Eliza Ann 19 Hester
  Ann 129 James 149 Joseph 19
  Margaret 88 Owen 129
ELEGE Charity 126
ELLINGTON David 27 Elizabeth
  27 104 Isaac 27
ELLIOTT Betsey 86 Catherine
  170 Elizabeth 61 170 James 61
  126 Lucinda 126
ELLIS / ELIS Jane 3 17 John 17
  Owen 3
ELLIS(T)ON James 12 Nancy
  Ralston 170
EMMETT Alexander 66 68 Jane
  66
EMMONS Elizabeth 138 Frances
  143 James 103 Mary 139 Nancy

41 Sally 113 Stoker 113 Wm.
  139
?EMSIGM Sarah 89
ENGLAND Aaron 74 David 7 89
  102 Jesse 6 69 Lucy 22 79
  Malvina 102 Melvina 103 Martha
  6 Nancy 69 Polly 7 Sally 24 25
  Stephen 25
ENGLISH Elizabeth 46 152 John
  22 47 Maratha 47 Rhoda 22 102
  Rhody 101
EPPERSON Elizabeth 56 Hannah
  77 James 48 July Ann 157 Mary
  48 Nancy 74 Peter 56 64 Polly
  64 76 Robert 74 77
ERINGAN Patrick 58
ERVIN Susannah 58
ERWIN Betsy 168
EVANS / EVINS / EVAN / EVENS
  / IVANS Catherine 47 Caty 7
  Dan 7 Even 40 Francis 4 81
  James 47 97 152 John 21 Mariah
  7 80 81 Nancy 45 Permelia 4
  Polly 97 Sally 21 113 Theodia
  158
EVINES Sary 173
EWING / EWIN / EUIN Caty 6
  Joshua 129 Mary 53 Permelia 4
  Putman 53
FANNIN(G) / FANNON Achillas
  49 Akalis 47 Atkin 25 John 67
  Letty 67 Nancy 74
?FARLOW Siddy 12
FARMER Achellas 49
FAR(R)IS / FER(R)IS Alexander
  152 Mary Ann 176 Michael 49
  Sally 83 171
FARROND / FERNAND Debby
  148 Zephriah 148
FARROW Mary P. 166
FATHERGILL Eliza 53 John 119
  Polly 119 Rachel 132
FAWSIT Elizabeth 95
?FENTON (see Sexton)
FENWICK Izabel 109 Joseph 41

Wm. 145
FERGUSON / FURGERSON
  Catherine 176 Cynthia 83 84
  Frances 8 Mary 16 Peggy 128
  Polly 42 Susan 64 Tom 8 V. 8
  Wm. 144
FERRELL Thos. 26
FERRIS Mary Ann 176
FICKLIN Allen 25 Charles 28 48
  John 49 Mariah 64 Melinna 28
  Meranda 64 Nancy 48 Susan 49
  Thomas 32
FIELD Skidmore 123
FIELDER / FIELDIN America 93
  July an 92 Patsey 139 Sarah F.
  133 Wm. 93 133
FIGHTMASTER Frederick 107
  Hannah 107 Nancy 142 Sally 11
FILSON / FELSAN Narcissa 50
?FISENO Parthena 145
FITZGERALD / ?FITZGOOD
  Hester 129 130 Julia 152 Polly
  153 Thos. 87
FLEMING Hannah 53 Patsy 63
  Poly 63 Wm. 63 78
FLETCHER Ann 149 Betsy 27
  David W. 39 115 Eda 86 Eliza
  66 92 Elizabeth 27 99 Feilding
  99 Franky 52 Jacob 52 67 83
  Jane 83 Kitty 149 Margaret 126
  Margaret Ann 22 Maria 168
  Mary 146 Rachel 172 Rebeckah
  170 Thomas 69 74 88 146
  William 22 149
FLOOD Mary Ann 144
FLORAH / FLOROUGH Nancy
  99
FOCKE Missouri 151
FOLAND / FELAND / FILAND
  George 8 10 111 153 157
  Katharine 8 Rebecca 10 111
FOONS (see Coons)
FOOT Polly 158
FORBUS Mary 146
FORD Robert 79

FORRAN Jeremiah 51
FORSYTHE Abraham 48 Hetty
  48 James 86
FORT / FONT Peggy 71 Peter 71
FORTUNE Levi 75 Lewis 2
FOSTER David F. 10 Lot 52
  Nancy 37 Sally 72
FOUCH Evin 6 Matilda 4 Wm. 4
FOUTY Henry 49
FOWLER Robert 108
FRANKLIN Betsey 58 George
  108 Sarah 108
FRAZ(I)ER / FRASURE Disey
  133 Dr. 52 118 Emily 136 John
  52 136 Lucinda 118 Matilda 47
  Nancy 174 Wm. 32 136
FREELAND Adaline 97 Catherine
  116 James 12 Jonah 57 Liddy
  12 Nancy 42 Robert 40 42 44 98
  116 Ruth 74 Sarah 17
FREEMAN Betsey 172 Cadmun 6
  Humphrey 162 John 114
  Julyann 117 Mary 162 Sally 24
  Thos. 162 Wm. 117
?FRIER / FRYERS (see Frazier,
  Searcy)
FROME / FRAME Malinda 74
  Wm. 12 68 74
FRY Ann C. 69 Mary Ann 175
FUGATE Grizzy 115 Rachel 90
  Reuben 90 115 131 Ruth 138
FULTON Polly 173
GADD Edwin Frederick 56
GAINES Mary B. 87
GALDEN / GNALDIN /
  GOULDER Eliza 114 Polly Ann
  159
GALLOWAY John 53 Nancy 58
  170 Polly 173 Robert 58
GALVIN Christopher 38
GARNER / GARONER Aaron 10
  31 Andrew 78 Elizabeth 78
  Jacob 129 Jane B. 87 Jean 24
  Nancy 87 Sally B. 129
GARRARD Nathaniel 17

GARRET(T) Ana Eliza 127
Debera 88 Flemming 98 Julia
Ann 98
GARRISON Peggy 172
GATSON Polly 174
GEORGE Bailey 54 130 Eliza 130
Elizabeth 43 Harriet 130 Henry
43 Jane 73 Leuce 130 Levina
130 Wm. 73
?GERAN Amelia 156
GIBSON / GIPSON Betsy 52
Elizabeth 123
GILES James 42
GILKEY Rebeccah 176
GILKINSON / GILKSON Sarah
44 Nancy 149
GILL Cassy 125 Cinthia 52 Eliza
112 Elizabeth 9 Emily 161
Harriet 145 Harrison 159 July
Ann 50 Marcus 152 Mossalite 26
Peter R. 28 50 62 Rebecca 28
167 Samuel 5 9 73 112 161
Sarah 43 Susan 117
GILLASPIE / GALASBY /
GLASPA Ann 111 Francis 134
Hannah 134 Jane 55 Rebecca
115
GILLET Uriam 148
GILLIS Eleanor 135
GILLON Reuben 47
GILMORE / GILLMORE Mathew
10 Patsey 177 Paulina 125
Nancy J. M. 62 Sally 10
?GILTKENS Nancy 96
GILVIN Joseph 55 Minerva 45
GININS Jas. 8
GINN Lucy Wyatt 55
GINTER Betsey 9 Elizabeth 107
John 9 Lydia 138
GITTER Samuel P. 127
GLOVER Ann 175 Creed 123
Martha 165 Mary W. 123
GOANS / JOANS Leuiez 21
GOFF / LOFF Jacob 74
GOOCH Thos. 156

GOODAN / GOODIN Bradford 57
Daniel 154 Edith 156 Grace 92
154 Levi 57
?GOODBE Mary 50
GOODLOW / GOODLOE Charlott
131 Francis 32 Julieth 50
Margaret 111 Mary 159 Nancey
George 105
?GOODMAN L. 57
GOODPASTER /
GOODPASTURE Ann 106 B.
93 Barford 37 Cinthia 20
Cornelius 57 Cyntha 144
Deborah 110 Elizabeth 44 Hardin
56 J. P. 82 Jacob 20 James 44
John 110 John, Sr. 153 Joseph
56 107 Latisa 79 Lemantha 82
Mary 57 Mebule 30 Nancy 38
Neale 106 Noah 38 Polly 56 107
Rhoda 56 Sally 129 Samuel 56
Susan 12
GOODWIN / GOODING Elenor
121 Frances 32
GOOLSBERRY / GOODBERRY
Caty 12
GORE Dulcina 11 Fanny 10 John
11 Nancy 33
GORREL(L) Elizabeth 32 Frances
58 John 32 144 Mary 39 Polly
32 Thomas 39 Wm. D. 32
GOSSETT / GOSSITT Elizabeth
Ann 147 Sarah Jane 79
?GOV Lucinda 59
GRAHAM Betsy 162 168 Fanny
3 James 84 139 Louisa P. 84
172 Malinda 151 Nancy 102 160
Sally 61 Sophia 139 175
GRANT Jailey 71 Janey 71 Mary
174
GRAY / GREY Anna 17 Catharine
138 Elisha 138 Elizabeth 1 Isaac
23 105 Jane 165 171 Joseph 1
17 Louisa ana 106 Louissiana
105 Mary 23 _____ 23
GRAYSON Elizabeth Ann 145

John 43 58 145 Marcby 74 Polly
129
GREEN Amelia 156 Anah 99
   Fielding 1 16 Goldsberry 59
   Nancy 16 Ona 99 Polly 59
   Thos. 16 Winny 88 Z. 88
GREER Elizabeth 48 Sally 157
GREGG John 59
GREGORY / GRIGORY Charlotte
   103 143 Dicey 78 Elizabeth 112
   Elizah 78 Inonna 18 John 103
   Joseph 143 Louina 143 Mahaly
   14 Malinda 124 Nancy 35
   Nathaniel 18 143 Sharlah 4
   Trenella 122 Wm. 4 8 23 125
GRIFFIN Andrew 60 Ann 162
   Eliza 74 Elizabeth 144 145 149
   Geo. 144 Matthias 27 149 Sally
   157 Susanna 175 Wm. 55 115
   157
GRIMES / GRIMS Artimila 26
   Delila 24 Edward 26 Nancy 45
   Polly 146 Rachel 28 Wm. 24 28
GRIMSLEY Gabriel 121 Mary
   Jane 47
GROOMS James M. 60
GROOVER Elizabeth 167
GROVES / GRAVES Ben 108
   Eliza D. 167 Mary L. 77 Wm. E.
   62 Willis 77
GUDGEL(L) Allen 45 95 Andrew
   45 115 Elizabeth 45 Joseph 45
   100 Mary E. 39 Polly 45
   Rebecca 100 Sally 63 Terissa 95
   Thomas 63 99
GUNN Melissa C. 113
HADDEN Nancy 173
HAGGAN John 68
HALL Elizabeth 19 177 Jane 68
   Rachel 137 Seny 133 Susan 136
HALSEY / HOLSEY Mary Ann 27
HAM Lucy 147
HAMILTON Catherine 169 Ester
   48 Jane 25 Luncey 33 Malinda
   110 Samuel 25 Saul 110 Tursey

33 168 Wm. 110
HAMMOND Edward 130
HAMPTON Delpha 175
HANKS Seby 98
HANLEY John 67
HANNAHS / HANERS Kisei 12
   Sarah 103
HANSFORD Polly 174
HARAMON / HARRIMAN (see
   Horseman)
HARBERSON Margaret 167
HARDIN Elizabeth 20 Emily 3
   Jane 7 John B. 3 Joseph 3
   Lewis 10 62 Manly 102 Melah
   13 Nicely 3 Presly 10 20 Sally
   10 Sarah Ann 161 Wm. 51
HARDMIN Lucinda 162
HARMON / HARMAN /
   HANNON Anna 74 Elizabeth 75
   George 74 Jacob 63 John 75
   Michael 3 Nancy 165 Polly 115
   Rachell 3
HARPER Emily 18 Geo. 68
   Georgeann 68 James 63 John 18
   43 91 106 Maria 17 Melinda 106
   Nancy 43 Sally 91 Wm. 32
HARRA(H) Mary 174 Sarah 166
HARRISON Albert 84 Philip 63
HARROW Jane 170 Peggy 170
HART / HEART David 66 72
   Eliza 68 Eliza A. 65 Frances 159
   Henry 134 Honor 25 John 69
   Mahala 101 Margaret 135 Mary
   Ann 92 Polly 1 Rebecca 67
   Robt. T. 77 Samuel 79 161
   Susan 161 Thos. 159 Wm. L. 10
HARTGROVE Elizabeth 171
HARTY / HEARTY Elizabeth 46
   M. 64
HARVEY George 148 Laura 148
   Luiza 148
??HASSIE / HES Sou(e) 2
HASTY Elizabeth 46 54 Meredith
   92 Nancy 55 144 Wm. 54
HATHAWAY Caty 174 Darky

174

HATTEN Amanda 65 Marcillus
65 Marcus 65
HAWKINS C. 147 David 53 133
151 Elizabeth 147 166 Elvira I.
105 Emma 82 Harry 32 James
116 James F. 130 John 82 116
117 Malinda 53 Maranda 114
Martha 117 Mary 43 64 Mary
Ann 82 Moses 9 Nancy Ann 91
Rebecca 160 Thomas 77 91
Valentine 147 160
HAZEL John 57
HAZELRIGG Caroline 117 Eli
102 122 140 Izza 113 J. H. 65
James 37 James A. 26 James G.
103 John 13 John F. 122
Joshua 113 Margaret S. 140
Mary 122 Nancy 9 Perlina 103
Sally 13 Wm. 21
HAYDON Robt. 30 31
HEATE Thatcher 48
HEATH(LY) (see Keith[ley])
HEATON Benj. 82 Polly 82
HEDGES James 54 John H. 54
Lucinda 54 Mary Jane 54 Robert
66
HEDRICK Amanda I. 123
Elizabeth 176 J. C. 123 John 5
Margaret 5
HEEGER Meninda 159
HEFFLIN Lucia 60
HEGGARD (see also Hughart)
Jane 59
HELPHINSTINE /
HELVENSTINE Elizabeth 141
John 96 Rebecca 96
HENDERSON Elenor 74 Eliza
Bell 165 Isabella King 166 Jones
174 Martha 171 Peggy 175
Rebecca 26
HENDRIX / HENDRICKS Anne
37 Catherine 175 Dorcas 166
Elizabeth 8 Icy 41 J. H. 35 Jane
95 John 14 Kerenhappuch 67

Lucinda 96 Maranda 125 Martha
5 Minerva 16 Nancy F. 57 Peter
57 67 95 96 Philip 37 Polly 14
147 Rebecca 26 Susan 22
Theophilus 14 16 38 41 125
Yourath 41
HENRY Elender 137 Franky 170
Jacob 137 Lane D. 116 Mary D.
116
HENSL(E)Y John 8 27 Nancy 71
HENSON Sara 174
HERNDON Levi 39 Maria 2
Mary 158 T. K. 158
HERR Nancy 175
HIAT Hester Ann 90
?HICKLIN (see Ficklin)
HICKMAN Martha 117 Wm. 117
HICKS Madlin 61 Saul 146
Thomas 78
HIGEN Elizabeth 174
HIGGINS / HOGGINS C. Y. 111
Elizabeth 13 128 Ellinor 111
Margaret 71 163 Milly 172
Nancy 177 Polly 13
HILEY / HEILY Ala Ann 9 Nancy
111 Sarah 118 Wm. 118
HILL Amanda B. 155 Berrilla N.
83 Elizabeth 98 173 Mary Ann
175 Sarah 165 Thos. 155
HIMER / HYMER / HINER
Amarinda 39 Betsey 153 C. B.
132 Caroline P. 38 Katherine P.
132 Lidia 99 Rebeca P. 38
HINES / HINDS Amilda J. 162
Elizabeth 19 Hannah 20 John
131 Nancy 56 Rebecca 131
Sally 32
?HINGS Wm. 74
HINKLE Sarah 103
HIRONS Abigail 171
HITEN / HYTEN Rebecca 57
HOIKINSON Mary Ann 82
HOLLIDAY Charles 68
HOLT Catherine 175 Mahala 137
Rachel 137

HON Anna 11 Prudence 68
HONAKER / HARNAKER
  Margarett 64 Martin 64 P. J. 64
  Polly 87 Wm. 91
HONEY Franky 170
?HOOD Ganlda 118 Patsey 2
?HOOPER Patsey 8
HOPKINS Ann 96 Daisy 58
  Dolly 172 Elizabeth 36 169
  Emily E. 58 60 F. 36 Francis 69
  84 96 97 126 Henry 151 Joseph
  131 Kenin 53 Margaret 68 Mary
  52 101 Wm. 60
HOPPER Elizabeth 34 Katherine
  69 Levi 34
HORD / HERD Mary 128
HORN J. F. 158
HORNBACK A. 132 Abraham 15
  81 Abram 74 78 Atevura 85
  Catherine 125 David 4 Dorothy
  15 F. 70 Isaac 85 Jacob 70
  John 12 70 Keziah 4 Martha 15
  Mary Ann 78
HORSEMAN / HARAMON Ann
  Matilda 132 Elizabeth 69 Hannah
  91 Matilda 35 Milly 36
HOSTETLER Elizabeth 117 118
  Solmon 118
HOUSE / HOUZE Alinina 60
  David 41 Eveline 41 Fanny 163
  John 163 Margaret 82 Minerva
  58 Sarah 24 Wm. 24
HOVERMILL Dilila 100 Elizabeth
  104
HOWARD Eli 48 84 James 103
  Joseph 28 103 Lydia 84 Nancy
  71 R. T. 64 Sarah 103 Sophia
  48
HOW(E) Anna 11 Eliza B. 170
  Isabel 168 Jane 168 169 Malinda
  W. 167 Matilda Jane 168 Peter
  11 Sally 18 170
HOWELL Dolly 1 Patsy 2 Wm. 2
HUBLE Hariet N. 17
HUFF Nellie 172

HUFFMAN / HUFFNER
  Thornton 157
HUGHART / HUGHARD /
  HOGHANT James 39 Julia 80
  Mary 39 Patsy 157
HUGHES / HUGH(S) / HUSE
  Alexander 2 Betsy 4 Catharine
  65 Cytha 137 F. 72 Elizabeth
  130 148 James 72 John 64 65
  130 John S. 13 137 Liverzy 72
  Lucy 116 Mildred 137 Nancy 2 8
  Polly 13 Reuben 4 62 67 107
  Sally 158 Wm. 34
?HUGHLEY Elizabeth 148
?HUGIN J. P. 62
HULS(E) Paul 39 Rosy 39 40
HUMPHREY Peter 104
HUNT Ab 88 Abraham 72 Berry
  73 David 64 Dester 126 E. J. J.
  8 Elizabeth 71 140 141 Emil 25
  Foster 3 Henry 101 Hester 123
  Hiram 71 Isa 110 Jeremiah 72
  126 John 1 72 Lewis 3 72 Lyra
  3 Mahala 101 Nancy 126 Phebe
  76 Polly 1 92 Reuben 92
  Richard 72 Saley 72 Sarah 88
  Seth 23 Thomas 1 Wilson 123
IGO Comfort 63 N. 63
ILES Elizabeth 96 Minerva 98
  Thos. 5 96
INGRAM / INGRAHAM /
  INGHAM Abraham 55 Castriva
  42 Comfort 29 124 Mary 134
  Nancy 121 Nica 63 Nice 160
  Phebe An 73 Polly 37 44 Polly
  Ann 142 Rachel 8 Sary 121
  Sytha 55 Thomas 44 72 73 124
  Unica 63
IRVIN Nancy 167
JACK(S) Anna 85 John 114
  Latitia 156 Margaret 30 Nancy
  156 Tabitha 156
JACKSON Alfred 76 Allen 65 74
  Ann 60 Deborah 142 Drucilla 62
  Eliza 73 Elizabeth 83 97 Geo. 92
  97 Isaac 73 James 99 110 Jane

92 Jemima 52 Jeremiah 124
John 62 Josemia 53 Joseph 63
Lena 132 Lewis 38 126 Malinda
115 Malvina 115 Margaret 73
Michal 97 Nancy 25 55 63
Permelia 156 Polly 14 Samuel 14
63 75 Sarah Ann 64 Thomas 65
83 Wm. 14

JAMES Elizabeth 10 Margaret 30
Thomas 89

JAMISON James 143 Lucy 123
Wm. 123

JOHNSON Alizanna 91 Anderson
2 Angelina 18 Arman 76 Arnold
129 Avis 143 B. F. 17 140
Berea 29 Biney 115 Cassandria
85 Caty 110 David 31 Elizabeth
16 132 157 161 Isaac 76 85 126
140 James 2 64 74 95 161 Jane
46 Jefferson 133 John 127 131
Levi 18 134 Leweda 140
Lucinda 31 126 Lucy 115
Margaret 70 Mary 157 Mary Jane
85 Nancy 5 76 131 Patsey 2
Polly 133 Richard 29 Robert 76
Sally 54 134 Sarah 36 Thomas
77 131 Vianns 20

JOHNSTON Alizanna 91
Angeline 18 David 27 Lucinda
31 126 Jacob 76 John 76 Robert
22 Sarah Ann 104 Susan 27
Thomas 77

JONES A. 158 Abraham 40 108
Ailsy 87 Amanda 14 Ambrose 85
158 Amelia 128 Amos 60 Ann
D. 60 Armida R. 59 Ben T. 80
Benj. 87 Carolinah 107
Catherine 163 Charles 22 25 94
135 Eliza 110 Eliza Ann 7 Eliza
Jane 85 Elizabeth 57 78 79 151
152 158 Emelia 160 Fanny 10 25
Frances 78 Francis 79 Franklin
77 Gelania 156 Hannah 19
Harriet R. 6 James 47 78 156
James F. 116 147 Jane 69 153

John 14 75 77 79 87 121 137 151
152 Jones 78 Joseph 70 Josiah
44 Leticha 37 Lucinda 25 Lydea
Ann 78 Lydia L. 14 Magdaline
57 Margaret 77 Martha Ann 44
89 Martin 79 Mary 29 37 83
Mary Ann Levina 87 Mathews 65
Molly Ann 105 Nancy 121
Oliver 87 Patsey 94 Polly 10 62
70 73 77 Priscilla 170 Rachel 87
172 Reuben 15 Sally 25 163
Samuel 76 124 155 Sarah 4 163
Susan America 60 Susannah 173
Susen 105 Thomas 10 14 70 77
89 121 Wm. 78

JOSET Polly 142

JOUETT John 138 Polly 138

KAR(R)ICK / KER(R)ICK
Elizabeth 18 Evelina 80 Hugh 81
93 106 John 94 Maud 93 Nancy
94 106

KEITH Couth 98 Elizabeth 146
Isabella 171 John 146 Rebecca
98

KEITHLEY Jane 77 John 77 109
Elizabeth 146

KELSO Isabella 94 Jane 48
Joseph 80 Mary 108 151 Polly
165 Rebecca 12 Walker 94 151
Wm. 12

KENAILL Elizabeth 122

KENDALL / KENDLE / KINDLE /
KINDALL Banford 83 James
Harvey 82 Jude 128 Nancy 95
Ramison 65 Sandford 95 Tuthila
Jane 54

KENNARD / KINARD Louisa
144 Sally 143 Sinthy 144
Sythania 25

KENNEDY / KANADAY /
CANNADY / KINNADA
Elizabeth 125 Joseph 144
Margaret 57 Sarah 51

KENNY / KINNEY James 81
Polly W. 127

?KENSEY Elisha 81
KENT Susan 38
KERNS Elizabeth 4 Levi 33
  Lucindah 4 Malinda 40 Nancy 33
  Nancy Ann 80 Sally Ann 121
  Susan 78 Tilman 4 33 81 121
KERR / ?KARH (see also Carr)
  Elizabeth 155 John 104 Peggy
  104 Samuel 76 104 110
KERREY John 113
KIBBLE Nancy 149
KIGGINS / KYGINS Asamith
  115 Elizabeth 128 Ellinder 111
  Susannah 55
KILLOUGH Margaret 172
KIMBROUGH Elizabeth 8 W. 8
KINCADE / KINCAID /
  KINGCADE Abigail 109 153
  Andrew 158 Ann 171 Archibald
  99 128 David 47 Eliza Jane 158
  Elizabeth 19 149 153 G. 50 Geo.
  19 103 Jane 83 154 John 16 21
  116 Joseph 23 Julia 128 Jully
  A. 23 Louisa Ann 69 Margarett
  111 Mary 166 167 Narcissa 21
  Patsey 36 Rebecca 35 116 149
  Rodah 16 Samuel 123
KINDER Esther 45 Vira 4
KING Anna 14 166 Elijah 14
  Eleanor 86 Ellen 86 Isabella 174
  Jesse 6 14 John 86 Mary 10
  Polly 169 Sally 6
KINNAMAN / KINIMON Nancy
  124 Rachel 148
KIRK Cassy 13 Elizabeth 146
  Mathew 146 Polly 172 Rachel 36
  Wm. 19 36
KNOX F. 54 Geo. 83 108 James
  41 Mary Jane 41
?LACNAW Maria 43
LADDERS / SODERS Henry 88
  99 Rosanna 99 Sarah 88
LAFFERTY Manuel 152 Nancy
  152 Sally 24
LAFTLY Sally 173

LAMBERT Prudence 170
?LAMEMAN Michael 86
LANCASTER Jos. 99 Katharine
  67 92 Louisa 2 Matilda 51 52
  Minerva 109 Nancy 10 11 Polly
  40 Rebecca 124 Thomas 109 124
LANDESS / LANDELSS Deavna
  22 Henry 22
?LANDERS Lydia 152
LANE / LAIN Ann 139 Dilly 89
  Elizabeth 84 Jemima 168 John
  85 152 Lewis 88 Lucy 88 117
  140 Margaret 159 Mary Ann 63
  Mary Virginia 101 Rebecca 124
  Robert 63 Robt. G. 63 Sam 117
  Susannah 165 Thos. 88 W. N.
  84 Wm. 6 89 Wm. S. 38
LANSDALE / LONSDALE
  Elizabeth 46 Hetty 156 Martha
  73 Nancy 166 Polly 173 Rachel
  177 William 74
LANSDOWN Geo. 68 98 116
LATHRAM / LATHROM Anthony
  87 Charity 86 George 125
  Nancy 125
LAW (see also Low) Benj. 16
  Elizabeth 84 Giny 16
LAWRENCE Jacob 125 Margaret
  159
LAWSON / LOSSON Polly 73
  Travis 73
LAYMON John 137
LEACH / LEECH Elizabeth 108
  James 41 John 85 Lucy Ann 41
  Susan 170
LEAVY Susan 70
LEDFORD / LEAFORD Hestar 86
  James 11 26 61 112 142 163
  John 10 L. 142 Liza 163 Mahala
  61 Malinda 10 Margaret 35 N.
  142 Nathaniel 163 Philadelphia
  112 Polly 11 Susannah 26
LEDINGZ Rebecca 1
LEE Eliza 70 J. H. 154 Louisa
  154 Missouri 98 Sullda 32

194

Susannah 86 Wm. 22 86
LEGGET / LIGGETT Susan 72
LEIPER Sarah 177
LEMASTER(S) Ben 24 Betsey
  169 Carsanna 83 171 Elijah 13
  M. 86 Patsey 109 139 Phebe 174
  Richard 83 86 Sam 155
LEMON Agnes 68 Jacob 68
  Margaret 165
?LENTON / LEXTON (see Sexton)
?LEONEY / LEANSCY (see
  Searcy)
?LETT John 127
LEWIS Polly 170
LEYETT David 48
LIGGETT / LEGGET Susan 72
LIGHT Jonathan 153 Mary M.
  153
LIGHTFOOT C. 131 Frances 131
  Martha A. 131
LINCH / LINCOLN / LYNCH
  Daniel 20 35 Geo. 35 Matilda
  131 Nancy 20 Peggy 35 82
LINDSEY Anna Maria 168
  Rheuhamah 174
LINE Samuel 79
LINEY / LINNEY Charlotte 152
  Elizabeth 19 Geo. 19 152 159
  Louisa 159
LINK Simon 152
LINTON Mary 44 Thomas 53
LINVILL(E) Elisha 87 Martha 18
LINZLIN Elizabeth 82
LITRO Almira 99
?LITTER (see also Sett, Setter)
  John 63
LIVINGSTONE Hannah 176
  Susannah 175
LOCK(E) Elizabeth 108 James 24
  128 Mariah P. 135 Meromes 107
  Rebecca 24 Richard 108 135
  Wm. 108 135
LOCKRIDGE D. 84 Isabella K.
  166 Peggy 166 Rebekah 166
LOGAN Mary 36 Wm. 36

?LOMAS Richard 24
LONG Jane 167 John 88
  Margaret 176 May 15 Polly 172
  176
LOR(V)ENCY / LOVEVEY (see
  Sorency)
LOVE (see also Lane) Ann 8 C.
  G. 84 Elizabeth 171 Hugh 9
  John 85 Lucy 117 Polly 176
  Rebecca 124 Rebeckah 174 W.
  N. 8 Wm. 84 Wm. S. 85
LOW(E) (also see Law) Gracy 16
  Isaac 20 84 Polly 20 Roda 49
  Samuel 49 William 85
LOWRY Delila 127 Mary 47
  Moses 11 Peggy 11
LOY Andrew 80 Catharine 80
  Geo. C. 80
LUTTRELL Andrew 25 107 Judy
  Ann 25
LYLEY Cassandra 113
LYNAM / LYMAN / LYRAM /
  LYSOM Absolom 23 Anderson
  149 Artemicea 59 Elizabeth 23
  Hester Ann 52 Len 139 Margaret
  139 Rachel 119 Richard 23 31
  52 Sally 120 Sally Lane 23
LYONS Elizabeth 73 Mahaley 61
  Margaret 22 Nancy 54 Noah 54
  Samuel 87
MABEL John W. 29 Nancy 29
MACKEY Celia 160
MAGAN John D. 50
MAHONY / MAHANY /
  MALEOND John 89 Malinda 70
  71
MALOAN / MELOAN Amelia 167
  Isabella 169
?MALY John 102
MANFIELD Emily 142 Thos. 136
MANIER / MANNEAR (see
  Minnear)
MANIS / MANNUS Henry 108 J.
  P. 118 Polly 118
MANL(E)Y Cobbert 55 David 90

Ezekiel 93 James 90 147 James
R. 104 116 Lydia 32 Nancy 147
Polly 155 Sally 147 Samuel 8
Sarah 146 Unice 116
MANNON / MAN(N)IN /
MANSON John 125 Lucinda
125 Meredith 91 Polly 46
?MANNY Francis 69
MAPPIN / MAUPIN / MOPPIN
Abigal 86 Elizabeth 67 166
Hannah 177 Jane 86 John 50
Malinda 82 Martha 42 Polly 67
Rebecca 113 Sally 116 Sarah 50
175 Wm. 19 82
?MARKER Wm. 70
MARKHAM Margaret 139 Wm.
139
MARKLAND Elizabeth 49
Fourtlan 5 Margaret 5 Sally 70
MARKWELL Abel 92 Elizabeth
154 Mary Jane 92
MARSH Nicholas 47
MARSHAL(L) Betsey 175 Jane
110 John 167
MARTIN Amanda 68 Anny 49
Betsy 49 Elizabeth 96 James 5
102 Louisa 28 Polly 23 109
Wm. 31 49 68 102 109
MARVEL Nancy Jane 31
MASON Lydiann 19 Peter 19
MATEER / METEER / ME(E)TER /
McTER / MATIRE Adalelle 37
Eliza 53 Emily Ann 95 Jane 170
Mary H. 142 Minerva 140 Polly
158 169 Sally 113 Therman 37
Thos. 140
MATOUN Betsey 172
MATTHEW(S) / MATHEWS
Anthony 140 Thos. 158 Wm.
163
MAURY Elizabeth 105 Matthew
105 Sarah Ann Slaughter 11
MAXEY / MAXY Anna 110 Asa
110 Lydia An 152 Rhoday 108
MAZE / MAYS / MACE Betey 83

Hugh 75 James 59 John 42 89
Margaret 43 Thomas 59
McAL(L)ISTER / McCALLISTER /
McOLISTER Catherine 155
Charles 72 Jane 155 176 Mark
20 Mouier 105 Sally 46
McBEAN Betsy 130
McBEE / MAC(K)BEE (see
Mockbee)
McCANN Jane 172
McCARD / McCORD Drusilla 100
Wm. H. 93
McCARNISH / McCORNISH
Adam 89 Margaret 89
McCART John 112 Sally 112
McCARTHA Malinda 136
McCARTY Amanda 80 Augustin
94 Catherine 134 Elizabeth 34
Hannah 94 106 James 136
Jerusha 99 John 99 Julina 158
Leah 114 Margaret 157 Nancy
38 Phebe 94 133 Rene 9 Ruth
157 Sally 136 Sam 157 158
Thomas 133
McCAUSLAND Frances Ann 140
McCILVAIN Hannah 89
McCLAIN / McCLANE / McLAIN
Angeline 96 Betsey 134 David
44 144 Edany 133 Elizabeth 39
71 73 990 Franky 92 Genela 81
James 73 92 100 106 122 137
Janella 93 John 44 71 84 93 94
Martha 25 Mary Ann 137
Melinda 136 Nancy 129 Peggy
155 Petty 122 Polly 22 Prissilla
122 Rachel 44 106 Rebecca 20
Sally 51 136 Solman 99
Susannah 58 Wm. 86
McCLAN(N)AHAN /
McCLANIHAN Anna 68 Gincey
31 James 90 Lucinda 90 Maria
A. 139 Susan 49 Susannah 17
McCLARIN Rebecca 16
McCLELLAN / McCLELLEN
Mary Ann 139 Susan 48

McCLENNEGER Polly 174
McCLESE Catherine 124
McCLINE Peggy 92
McCLURE Agness 71 Catherine
  Temple 175 Elener 177 Jane 12
  71 Mary Douglas 165 Patsey 173
  Susanna 49 Thomas 71
McCOLLOM Nancy 167 Peggy
  175 Rachel 167 Sally 167
McCORMICK Cythian 44 Eliza
  Ann 55 Elizabeth Jane 27 Jane
  62 Mary Ann 139 Morrison 142
  Nancy Ann 27 Reuben 27 95
  Samuel 27 44 139 Wm. 55 62
McCOY Elizabeth 123 James 114
McCULLOUGH / McCOLLOUGH
  / McCULLY / McCULLA(H)
  Betsy 135 Eliza 133 Elizabeth 72
  Hetty 107 Jas. 72 Lydia 67
  Melinda 62 Polly 136
McDAN(I)EL Daniel 96 Patsey
  167 Permela 78 Sally 117 124
McDAVID Margaret 64
McDEETER Thomas 141
McDONALD / McDONEL Enoch
  30 John 114 Rebecca 97 Susan
  122
McDOUGLE Selene 168
McDOWDLE / McDOUDALE /
  McDOYLE Elizabeth 67 Polly 67
McDOWEL(L) Nancy 18
McFARLAND / McFARLING
  Eliza 65 Margaret 10 131 Sarah
  11
McFERRAN Thomas 67
McFETERS Tely Ann 91
McGAHEE / McGEHE Barna 160
  Ruthy 160
?McGILL Susan 117
McGIN Polly 17
McGINNIS James 53 Jane 148
  Milton 132 Nancy 132 Sarah 53
  Wm. 96 148
McGLOCKLIN / McGLAUGHLIN
  John 94 Martha 169 Patsy 55

McGLOTHIN Elizabeth 55 John
  M. 30 Margaret 30
McGOWAN / MAGOWAN /
  McGOWIN Charlotte 69
  Cynthaana 34 Eliza 86 Francis
  13 John D. 34 63 Louisa 40
  Miranna 34
McHENRY Maranda 4 Polly 62
McILHENNY James 61 138 John
  51 Margaret 51 Nancy 20 169
  Polly 62 74 76 177 Virlinda 95
McINTIRE Abigail 76 Alexander
  15 Drucilla 61 Elizabeth 47 John
  123 Lucretia 123 Lucy 15 166
  Mary 141 Thomas 106 141 U.
  S. 114
McINTOSH Elizabeth 33
  Frederick 33 141
McKEE Lavina 99
McKINNAN Solomon 67
McKINNEY Polly 152 Sally 59
  Sarah 59 Virginia 26
McLAUGHLIN / McLAUGHTIN
  John 136 Polly 101
McMILLAN Peggy 170
McNAB(B) Abner 25 Andrew 98
  Delilah 27 Eliza 48 James 48
  John 97 Nancy 98 Patsy 25
  Stephen 98
McNULTY Robert 93
McPHERSON Betsy 114 Jesse
  114 Stephen 98 Thomas 96
McQUADY / McQUIDDY Polly 97
McVEY / McVAY Catherine 143
  Jane 130 Sarah 143
McVICKER Polly 174
McWORTHY Julian 158
  Margarett 157 Rebecca 154 155
MEANNOR Tarlton 125
MEANS Elizabeth 168
MENIFEE / MENFEE Alfred 116
  Mary 84 85
MERIS / MENIS / ?MEFRIS
  Joseph 35 Levina 95
MERLEY / MIRCHLEY /

?MOXLEY (see Manley)
MULBERRY Celia 69 Fanny 36
 John 36 69 Mary 69
MULHOLN Wm. 71
MULLIN(S) Delila 43 James 44
MUN(N)S / MUNN / MURR
 David 40 Kesiah 40 John 8 55
 119 128 Polly 8 131 Rebecca 71
 Wm. 131
MURPHY Leah 109 Linly 114
 Sealy 113 Zepha 114
MYERS / MYRES / MEYERS
 Adam 152 Cena 29 Christopher
 104 Eliza 42 Elizabeth 31 48
 Henry 33 100 104 121 John 74
 Joseph 48 130 Julian 14
 Katharine 19 Lucinda 152
 Mahala 100 Margaret 152 Martha
 74 Mary Adaline 121 Mary Ann
 135 Milton 34 Polly 33 34 49
 Rebecca 130 Sam 19 48 104 140
 Solomon 14 Suzy 31
MYNHE(I)R / MYNER (see also
 Minnear) Joseph 104 Sarah 85
 156 Wm. 18 44
NARBRY Anna 105
NAYLOR / NAILOR Delila 104
 Hanah 151 Ignatius 67 70 Nancy
 67 Paul 53 Polly 142 Velinda
 143 Wm. 67
NEAL Henry 81 139 John 10 73
 81 Lizzie 139 Mary 81 Meca 10
 Meed 10 Nancy 81 Sisley 139
NEALEY / NEABY Jude 77
 Juliett 76 Patsey 174
?NEAT (see West)
NELSON Cyntha 134 Elvira J.
 130 Emily 109 James 22 Jane
 22 Jesse P. 3 Joseph 33 Sindy
 162 Suphia 33
NESBIT(T) / NEASBET Andrew
 112 Elizabeth 96 Grizella 31
 Hugh 31 Jane 41 105 112 John
 41 49 96 112 L. M. 74 Sally 49
NESTER Andrew 138 Malinda

126
NEWCOM James 156
NEWLAND A. N. 155 Elizabeth
 132 Sarah 155
NEWMAN Melvina 145
NEWTON Polly 166
NICHOLAS Emily 104 Isaac 124
 Malvina 117 Mary 85
NICHOLS / NICKOLS Emily 104
 Melinda 94
NICKLSON / NICOSON Ann 112
NIXON B. D. 69
NOE / NOAH Addaline 106
 Amanda 113 Geo. 113 James 6
 James S. 87 Joanna 156 157
 Joseph 113 Sophiah 71 Susan
 124
NOLAND Mary B. 174 Rubel 123
NORMAN Margaret 31 Thomas
 31
NORRIS / NORIS Ann 10 David
 93 106 128 John 9 20 93 94 106
 128 157 Malvina 94 Nancy 128
 Polly 128 Rhoda 157 Sarah A.
 157 William 106
NORTHCUTT Benj. 142 Nancy
 176
OAKLEY / OACLY / OKELEY A.
 47 Ann 159 Austin 107 129 156
 Cary 159 Ch. 31 Christopher 52
 E. 107 E. J. 153 Edmund 159
 Eleanor 173 Elizabeth 52 Emily
 M. 145 F. 89 Fannie 165 Helen
 I. 153 John P. 52 Malinda 94
 Mariah 107 Minerva 47 Nancy
 52 75 Polly 55 Prior 96 Rachel
 96 Sorelda Ann 145 Wm. 51
OCKERMAN Anna 100 Betsey
 160 161 Daniel 84 100 161
 Perline 126 Sarah 84
OFFICERA / OFFICULA Chithy
 123
OFFILL John 151
?OKIM Sally 173
OLIVER Peggy 166
OSBURN (see also Ausburn)

199

Thompy 176
OTIS Jonathan 144
OWINGS Ann E. 91 Casandrid
137 Debby 175 Eli 71 Elihu 58
60 87 George 130 Julian 58
Marcy H. 61 Matilda 87 Melinda
37 Menerva 60 Nancy 71 Rachel
109 127 Richard 108 Samuel 58
60 Thos. D. 156
OXYER Betsy 175
PAGET / PIDGETT Eliza 145
Robb 108
PAINTER / PANTHER Isabel 4
James 108 Polly 1 Solomon 4
?PARIDO Nancy 146
PARKER Edmond 154 Ethel 108
Joel 109 110 John 62 Mary Ann
154 Myran 37
PARK(S) Artaniss 4 Elizabeth 64
Geo. 4 Margaret 76 Nancy 144
Polly 167 Susannah 47
PARMER / PALMER Daniel 75
Elizabeth 75
PARRIS / PERRIS John 111 Obe
109 Thomas 111
PARSONS Edward 60 James 109
PATRICK Alcy 104 Alley 49
Betsy 113 Elizabeth 47 Enoch 49
Herod 24 49 91 Jane 47
Jeremiah 109 Margaret 104
Nancy 18 Noah 81 Rachel S. 24
Samuel 127 Susan R. 38
PAT(T)ERSON Elizabeth 174
Polly 31 171 Robert 39
PATTON Betsy 172 Peggy 172
Sarah 171
PAXTON Archibald 77
PAYNE / PAYNT Ann M. 106
Clarrisa M. 14 Frances 156
Henretta 57 John 57 67 Lucilla
67 Lucinda 57 Susan 70
PAYTON Wm. 110
PEARSALL / PIERSALL /
PEARCEALL / PERSAUL
Elizabeth 54 Frances 38 Marian

159 Nancy 78 Pheby 3 Samuel
113 Thornton 38
PECK Elizabeth 167 172 Mary
167 172
PEEBLE(S) / PEPLES Adalia 87
Alecia 87 Jane 17 John 17
Margaret 92 Wm. 17
PEN Rebecca 56 Samuel 56
PENDLETON Clarissa 81 Fanny
10 Heacher 48 Lucy 48 Martha
81 Mary 38 Patsy 38 Rice 10 38
Thacker 38 81 W. 110
PENIX / PENIC Betsy 99 John
99 Patty 23
PERATT / PIRATT Betsy 56
Delila 27 Elizabeth 57 Evlin 145
James 57 145 Valentine 110
PERGRAM / PURGRAM Emily
18 95 James 2 10 39 42 John 10
18 Mary 39 Narcissa 2 Rachel
10 Robert C. 111 Sally 42
PERKINS Ed 42 Elenor 148
Elizabeth 14 15 42 Jane 42 Sally
A. 127 Susannah 15 Thos. 127
PERRY America 52 Ben 111
Juison 52 111 Lewis 111 146
PERVIS (see Purvis)
PETTIT Ann 159 Asa 72
Elizabeth 105 Jesse 38 Matthew
136
PEV(E)LER / PEVILER / PEBLER
/ PERLLER David 126 Daniel 27
Magerne 2 Margaret 92 93 Sibby
93
PHELP(S) Amanda 30 Eliza A.
152 Elizabeth 34 Kirziah 51
Mary F. 139 Nancy B. 107 Wm.
30 112
PHIL(L)IPS / PHILPS Elizabeth
34 Jos. H. 32 Lorenzo 56 Lucy
6 Nimwood 112 Sally 116
Sarah 169 Wm. 6
PICKLEHIMER (see also Himer)
Polly Ann 99
PIERCE / PEARCE Charles 18

105 John 100 John S. 116
Martha 32 Mary Ann 51 Nancy
Ann 105 Sarah 18
PIPER Elizabeth 141
PLATT Ann 108 Hetty 108
PLEAK Emily 121
POOR Almira 157 Cady 154
Eady 154 Elener 113 Julian 151
Moses 154 157 Wm. 113
PORTER (see also Prater)
Archibald 114 Catherine 36
Elizabeth 50 Isaac C. 114 John
109 Lucinda 98 Thomas 36 98
POWEL(L) Ashford 138 F. 143
Isaac 17 Susan 144
POWER Elizabeth 43 95 96 159
Elinor 113 Elleanor 32 George
61 159 James 113 Jeremiah 43
162 Joshua 14 142 Mary Jane
124 Mary M. 60 Sally 43 111
Wm. 43
PRATER / PRATOR Elizabeth 88
91 Sally 104 Wm. 104
PRATHER Eli 35 Elizabeth 72
Henry 114 Jeremiah 72 158
Julian 158 Mary 72 Sally 3
Susannah 126
PRATT(S) Henry 37 James 110
John 110 William 115
PRESLEY / PERLEY Jane 46
PRICE John 140 Joshua 97
PRINCE John 115
PROCTOR / PROCTER Ann 45
James B. 45 Jeremiah 45 135
Syntha 45
PURGRAM / PURGRON (see
Pergram)
PURVIANCE Anna 177
PURVIS / PERVIS Ann 111
Betsey 118 Catherine 41
Cynthiana 115 Eleanor 97 Geo.
59 Hetty 134 Jane 135 John 135
136 Kate 134 Milly 59 135
Susan 145 Thomas 97 115 118
134 Wm. 135

QUILLIN Jesse 35 73 Polly 27
RABURN / RAIBORN Angelina
119 Julyan 61 Margaret 20
Seldon 20
RAFFERTY Abner 128
RAGLAND Eliza 26 James 55
Nancy 28 Polly 91 Raney 91
Wm. M. 115 131
RAIMEY / RAM(E)Y Able 35
Acho 80 Archabell 82 Elizabeth
80 Hester 35 Rachel 82 Ruth 4
Sarah 177
RAINEY / RANEY James 132
James S. 116 Mary D. 116
RAIN(E) / RONE Paulina 120
Thomas 67 Wm. 120
RALLS / RAWLS / ROLLS
Elizabeth 161 Geo. 16 George
W. 105 138 John 24 Lydia B. 78
138 171 Lucinda 138 Marian 79
Mary Ann 79 Nancy 21 Nancy
Ann 105 Nathan 116 Nathaniel
R. 78 79 Susan 53 Susannah
138 Valentine 138
RALSTON / ROLSTON /
ROSTON Bertha 143 John 65 77
126 135 143 Margaret 166
Nancy 135 Patsey 126 Polly 65
W. D. 23
RANDOLPH Eliza Ann 122
Elizabeth 62 Emily 30 Evelery 30
James 30 80 122 Lucy 80 Mary
Ann 141 Nancy 26 Reuben 141
?RASSMORE Joseph 46
?RATLAND Tudor 115
RATLIFF / RATCLIFF Caleb 18
56 58 100 159 Coleman 78 80
Eliza 80 Ellen 159 Emily 18
Henry 80 Joann Francis 58
Katharine 128 Kesiah 37 Nancy
100 Phebe 146 Rich I. 58
Sanford 18 Susan 56
RAY John 147 Louisa D. A. 147
RAZOR / ROZER / ROZOR
Charlotte 31 Essa 156 Geo. 115

Jennett 31 Wm. 124
REDD Susanna 177
REED / READ(E) Dolly 24 Eliza
  Jane 126 Elizabeth 55 130 Henry
  30 116 Jane 89 Julia Ann 90
  Mary 146 Nancy 135 136 Sally
  89 Wm. 24 55 135
REEVES Isable 120 Mahala 120
RENDALL Frances 62
RENFRO Emaline 47
RENER Nancy 127
?RERNLEY W. W. 128
REYNOLDS Peggy 167
RHUE Abraham 119
RIADON / RHIDON / RHEDON
  Geo. 122 Martha 122 Sarah 122
RICE Alfred 148 Anna 141 Eli
  128 Eliza 97 132 Elizabeth 145
  Francis 157 Henry 57 Holman
  88 141 Holman, Jr. 53 157 Jane
  88 89 Jefferson 120 John 83
  Levina 89 Martha 128 Melvina
  38 Nelson 37 P. 40 Palmer 88
  Peggy 8 Polly 37 164 R. R. 145
  Rachall 31 Sally 40 162 Sarah 38
  Wm. 120
RICHARD(S) Betsey 129
  Elizabeth 93 104 144 Elza 119
  Frances A. 120 J. H. 127 J. N.
  37 James 119 Jane Nelley 98
  Jemima 148 John 75 122 John
  W. 91 July 167 Malinda 119
  Margaret 28 119 Nancy 27 119
  Patsy 106 Peggy 1 Phebe 129
  Philey 128 Polly 144 R. 129
  Robert 98 Sarah Jane 127 Thos.
  53 W. 92 William 119 144
RICHARDSON Elizabeth 93 176
  Josiah 121
RICHAR(D)T Anne 90 172
  Duncan 90 122 Eliza B. 123
  James 8 90 Jane 122 Lydia 8
  Polly 173 Rich. 146
?RICHEY Jane 122 175
RICHISON Naomy 94

RICKETTS Eliza 50 Reuben 50
RIDDLE Lewis 160 162 Robert
  121 150
RIGGS Polly 175
RINGO Catherine 177
RIVELY / RINELY Betsey 147
ROB(B)INS Anna 154 James 77
  120 154 John 154 Margaret 120
  Rebecca 77
ROBERTS Amelica 65 America
  65 Caty 93 Ellen 18 John 93
  Mare 28 Nancy 28
ROBERTSON / ROBERSON
  Elizabeth 17 63 119 Ellen 18
  James 157 John 39 122 Jones
  122 Katherine 106 Kesiah 3 L.
  R. 3 Lawson 17 Louinda 128
  Louisa 151 Lucy Ann 39 Mary
  86 Patsy 88 Peggy 117 Richard
  39 63 128 Sylvester 123 Wm. 63
ROBISON Abby 12 Sally Graham
  165
ROBINSON Ally 12 Caty 93
  Elizabeth 63 170 Jane 176 Patsy
  88 Lawson 117 Margaret 117
  167 Maryann 169 Matilda 139
  Sally 122 Sally Jane 106
ROE Abigail 66 Abrget 66 C. T.
  119 Ellen 126 Frances 69
  Gehazi 6 Jahazah 6 James 6 69
  Salem 66 69
ROGAN / ROGEN(S) Betsy 77
  Jane 65 T. J. 1
ROGERS / RODGERS Alford 123
  Alfred 59 Betsey 77 Caroline 62
  Elizabeth 51 158 169 177
  Fletcher 51 James 5 15 65 158
  Jane 65 John 51 77 Levisy 172
  Margaret 51 59 132 133 Martha
  F. 132 Mary 75 174 Nancy 82
  166 171 Peggy 169 Polly 5
  Sackett 132 Sally 15 166 Samuel
  82 86 Selah 6 Sibellar 17
  Stephen 17 Susannah 10 52
  William 62 92 123 127 133 160

202

ROLLINS Mary 146
ROMINS Wm. 23
?RONE (see Rain)
ROSEBERRY / ROSEBURY
  Alexander 10 144 Malinda 10
  Polly 144
ROSS Casandra 99 173 Cordelia
  M. 108 Eliz. 149 James 108
  Malinda G. 28 Phillip 28 Richard
  86 Samuel 108
ROTHWELL Margaret 8 Nancy
  162 Solomon 2 Thomas 162
ROUT(T) George 91 124 Lucy 91
  Winneford 150
RUDDER / RUDDEN Ed 7 125
  Lucy 6 Nancy 7 47
RUNNELS / RUMMELLE
  Elizabeth 100 Sally 100 Susanna
  100
RUSSELL Morgan 41 Robert 41
RYAN / RYON Maria E. 110
  Melinda Ann 61 Moses 61 Wm.
  32
SAD(D)LER Druslia 136 Geo.
  112 Susanna 169
?SAENWON Maria 43
SAILOR / SAILER Delilah 3
  Elizabeth 112 Frederick 52 John
  3 11 112 Louisa 104 Mary 52
  Nancy 11 Samuel 153 Wm. 52
  86
SAMPLE Hannah B. 23 Nancy
  167
SAMPSON Agella 12
SANDERS / SAUNDERS Henry
  72 L. A. 112 Louisana 38 Lucy
  47 Lydia 152 Oliver 38 47 127
  Polly 82 Robert 82 Sophia 127
SANDERSON L. F. 112
SANDUSKY / ST. DUSKIE / ST.
  DRESKIE Deborah 165
  Elizabeth 172
SANFORD Agustin 68 John 62
SAP(P) (see also Tap) Barbary 29
  Daniel 126 Elizabeth 156 Jacob

29 Joseph 156 Mary 110 Nelson
  142 Thomas 100
SCOT(T) / SCATT / SCOOT Ann
  92 Easter Ann 22 Edward 127
  Elias 18 Eliza 54 Elizabeth 26
  Harry 50 Jane 15 Jefferson 127
  John 34 92 Maria 50 54 Marky
  162 Robert 26
SEAL Malvina 152
?SEARCY / SWICEY ?James 16
  Rebecca 16
SEE Missouri 98 Polly 169
SEIRS Samuel 126
SELF(E) Joseph 9 159 Martha 9
?SELTON / SERTON (see Sexton)
SETT John 86 98
SETTER(S) Abigail 29 Mary 148
  Park 148
SEXTON Anne 35 Ben 68 Benj.
  38 Bry 88 Comfort 97 John 97
  143 July 68 Malvina 127 Mary
  Ann 88 Nancy 136 143 Rebecca
  6 Sally Ann 6 Syntha Ann 89
  Wm. 6 29 88
?SHAIN Lucinda 59
SHANK Abraham 158
SHANKLIN Andrew 8 17 Lavina
  165 Malinda 17 166 Polly 8 165
SHARP Alabama A. 148 Ann 54
  Ann Eliza 33 Elizabeth 131
  Judith 39 Julia Ann 97 Margaret
  32 Mary 39 44 45 148 Moore 54
  Moses 67 Nancy 112 Patsey 30
  121 174 Polly 19 Polly Ann 131
  Richard 121 Susan 67 Wm. M.
  148
SHAVER Betsey 168
SHEANT John 124
SHELTON Thos. 135
SHEWBERT Susannah 90
SHIELDS / SHEALS Hannah 47
  James 36 Nancy 169
SHIPMAN (see Chipman)
SHORTRIDGE Chas. 40 52
SHROPSHIRE / SOPSHER

Barbary 143 Elizabeth 68 James
68 110 Mary 110 Nancy 94
Sarah Ann 16 Wm. 94
SHROUT / SROUT Barbary 161
Casper 127 Delila 147 Eliza 120
Elizabeth 68 127 Genela 129
Issac 40 120 Jehu 129 John 129
147 161 Mary 63 Noah 129
Polly 40 Rachel 20 Susan 98
SHUAR Nancy 71
SHULER / SHELLER Jacob 141
SHULTZ / SHOALTZ / SHOOTS
Catharine 108 Elizabeth 62 110
Henry 130 John 108 110 129
Phebe 60 Sally 110
SHUMATE Ann 46 Bailey 130
Eliza 119 Matilda 148 Wm. 148
SIMPSON Eliza 170 Frances J.
130 Jane 169 Mary 2 Polly 174
Sally 169
SIMS Elenor Miner 56 Joe 56
Sally 176
SINCLAIR Francis 85 Patsey 13
Susannah 43 Thomas 13
SIX Catherine 11 Elizabeth 144
John 11 Phiber 105 Rebecca 32
105
SLAUGHTER Mary 19 20
SMALL Catharine 1 Geo. 82 Jas.
51 Jesse 130 Polly 82 Thomas 1
37
SMALLWOOD Bean 42 114
Beave 53 Ben 129 Katharine 53
Lydia 42 Sarah 129 Wm. 120
SMART / ?GLOUERSMART
Edward 162 Paulina 162 Sally
162 W. N. 132
SMITH Betsy 134 Christina 177
Eliza 37 Eliza Ann 53 Elizabeth
85 Fanny 74 Franky 73 Hestty
123 Hetty 124 Jemima 144 John
9 83 86 Joseph 76 156 Lucy 82
Magalane 141 Mariah M. 86
Matilda 102 Michael 85 101 102
141 Nancy 13 57 94 Peggy 102

Polly 1 58 76 86 87 102 129 177
Sally 2 155 Sarah 172 Susanna
101 Virginia 30 Wm. 123 155
Y. 86
SMOOT Eliza Ann 123 Louisa 43
Mary 22 Polly 88
SMOTHERS / SMITHERS /
SMATHERS Emaline N. 11
Joseph 18 66 86 Mary 18
Philadelphia 86 Sarah 66
SNEDEGAR / SNEDIGER /
SNEDAKER Angelina 65 C. 47
Elizabeth 46 96 Isaac 1 Mary 1
Matilda 52 Robert 65 Susanna 44
Wm. 65 _____ 121
SNEDDLY JulyAnn 33
SNELLING Benjamin 27 42 77 92
111 Elizabeth 80 111 F. T. 19
Hannah 77 Lucinda 92 Mary 103
Nancy 163 Polly 87 111 T. 155
Thornton 132 Wm. P. 87
SODERS (see Ladders)
?SOESBY Sally 41
SORENCY / SWENCY /
SURENNY Ann Eliza 153
Artimisia 105 David 105 Jamima
61 Jenny 146 John 105 147
Margaret 158 159 Nancy 112
Polly 147 Silas 112
SORREL(L) / SORELL Elisha 133
134 135 Eliza 155 Elizabeth 76
93 107 133 Febe 106 Frances
135 James 58 67 133 134 159
James, Sr. 133 Jean 93 John 133
136 144 155 Joseph 40 107 133
Joshua 93 94 133 Mallellda 50
Margaret 67 115 Mary Ann 93
134 Matilda 50 Milly 40 Racheal
76 Thomas 39 61 Wm. 50 133
SPARKS Eliza 116 Polly 19
SPENCE / SPENCER Aaron 135
Ann 151 Elizabeth 60 131 John
36 Jonathan 135 Letty 72 Lewis
31 Livia 29 Louisa 152 Mariah
106 Martha 93 Mary 123 Mason

136 More 134 Nancy 64 Phebe
31 Sarah 34 Thos. 64 101 Wm.
72 97 151 152
SPOON Margaret 33
SPRATT Martha 95 Solmon 95
SQUIRES Nancy 7
STAFFORD / SAFFORD Eliza 21
STAMPER Elisabeth 83 John 142
Mariah 128 Rebeckah 108
Richard 86 Sarah P. 142
Washington 135
STANDCRIFF Jas. 115 Mary 115
STATON / STATEN Amanda 134
Ben 158 Elizabeth 95 James 94
159 John 136 Julian 73 Lucretia
121 Margaret 133 Martha 43
Mary 94 Nancy 131 Polly 127
Reuben 95 127 133 Sally 64 95
109 Samuel 73 Thomas 95
Tillitha 159 Wm. 43 134 136
Wm., Sr. 136
STAUSBERRY Rachel 113
STAVER / STOVER Michel 108
STEARMAN Eliza 155 Martha
133 Robt. 133 155
STEEL(E) Ann 99 139 Betsey 166
Colgate 100 Eliza 167 Jacob 21
101 132 Jane 167 Margaritte 101
Maria 21 Nancy 21 Perry S. 9
Polly 168 Polly Ann 89
Prudence 63 Riley 61 Robert 12
Samuel 137 Solomon 102
Theophilus 24
?STELLE Jacob 132 Martha 146
STEPHENS / STEVENS Emily
138 John 138 Lucy 116 Milly
138 Nancy 33 Tabiltha 12 Polly
119 Rachel 173 Sally 83 W. O.
33 Wm. 119 138
?STEPLEN / STEPEN(A)
Elizabeth 78 Polly 119 Wm. 78
120
STEVENSON / STEPHENSON
Elizabeth 177 Polly 75 167 Mary
100

STEWART / STURT / STEMORT
Elizabeth 103 Mitchell 138 Polly
176 Serena 127 Verva 127
STICKLER Phebe 9
STILLWELL John 138
STITH James 138
STONE Ann 7 Caroline 14 100
Charles 66 101 139 Eliza 158
Elizabeth B. 121 Fanny 155
Gary 66 James F. 21 53 John
155 Johnson 66 Margaret 65 66
Maria 7 Mary Ann 101 Matilda
138 Nancy 99 116 Robert 100
Samuel 7 116 Susan 66
Valentine 138 Wm. 139
STONECLIFT James 120
STONER G. W. 54 Mary Ann 54
STOOPS Anna 20 John 139
STORM(S) Ardona 157 Wm. 89
108
STORY Lewis 47 Thomas 139
STREET Jane 64 Milly Jane 64
STULL James 8
SUDDUTH / SUDOUTH /
SUDITH Benj. F. 1 2 36 57 109
117 123 135 145 161 Eleanor 84
James 6 18 37 48 63 64 79 80 86
101 106 107 114 124 138 139
154 Lewis 40 84 Margaret 104
Thos. 162 W. S. 1 W. T. 15
Wm. 40 84 96 104 106 147 156
Wm. M. 3 11 55 58 65 66 71 84
101 122 139 146 151
SUMMERS Charles 155 James 69
Sary 16
SUTTELL (see Luttrell)
SWE(A)TNAM / SWE(A)TMAN
Elizabeth 74 Jeanette 144 John 7
Joseph 48 114 Mary 141 Nancy
140 Thos. 140 Trinvilla 7 Wm.
74 157
SWIN / SWIM Alexander 73
Polly 44
SWINEY / SWINNEY Caroline 97
Elizabeth 98 Emily 84 John 140

Miles 84 97
SWITZER / SWARTZER /
  SWISHER Abraham 34 43 116
  141 Eliza 116 Louisa 34 Mary
  103 Polly 43
SYLCOX Ewell 105
TABER(T) Jesse 31 Queen 87
TACK Mary 133
TACKET(T) Archibald 26 Baylis
  80 141 Eliza 43 Fanny 74 Lucy
  80 Mildred 26 Milly 141 Nancy
  8 51 Rebecca 83 Wm. 8
?TANNY Elizabeth 163
TANT Jesse 19
TAP(P) (see also Sap) Elizabeth
  121 Emily 50 Isaac 126 Jane
  121 Kitty 173 Lucinda 126 N.
  50 Nelson 126 Wm. I. 65
TATE Mason R. 155
TAYLOR / TAILOR Agnes 33 B.
  85 Ben 150 Benoni 68 Betsey
  85 Charles 62 Frances 11 Geo.
  W. 126 Hannah 147 John 33 85
  112 147 Juan 52 Julian 83
  Malisa L. 68 Norman 81 Sarah
  E. 62 Solomon 121 Wesley 83
TEAL / TEEL / ?TEBE (see also
  Seal) Dye 89 127 Elizabeth 129
  Howard 157
TEMPLEMAN Cynthian 23
  Ephraim 23 59 149 Frances 149
  Jesse 59 Lewis 59 Louisa 123
  Mahala 59 Mary 23 S. 123
TERHON Isaac 143
TERRELL Timothy 136
THATCHER Hoden 122 Mariah
  122
THOMAS Amy L. 175 Cynthia
  115 Elizabeth 41 88 Fanny 176
  Geo. 26 Gillian 134 Isaac 52 134
  136 Jackin 8 James W. 42 Jane
  22 Joseph 155 Larkin 75 143
  Nancy 33 Sally 136 Samuel 75
  Sarah 75 Susannah 52 145 Wm.
  22

THOMPSON / TOM(P)SON
  Betsey 7 78 Caty 170 D. S. 141
  Eliza 48 Elizabeth 65 Emily 102
  162 Filander 144 George 162
  Jane 2 107 Joseph 8 48 Lucretia
  136 Margaret 48 Martha 116
  Mary 2 Nancy 107 151 Patsy 30
  114 Polly 83 118 Sareney 74
  Wm. 25 114 118 Wm. M. 144
?TILLET Hiram 111
TINCHER Francis 127 John 62
  Martha Ann 72 Sally 16 127
  Wm. 39 127
TINDLE / TINDELL Caroline 155
  Susan 156
TIPTON Elizabeth J. 56 Joshua
  56 Margaret 158 Mayor D. 138
  Mitchel 138 Nancy 138 Sarah
  138
TOL(L)Y / ?SALLY Clabourn 79
  George 88 Patsy 79 80
TOMLINSON Archibald 3 James
  121 Martha Ann 121 Mary 75
  Sarah 3
TOULSON Bernit 23 Sally 23
TOWNSEND Emily 136 Wm.
  137
TRAYLOR / TRAILOR / TRAILER
  Agnes 22 Armon 70 C. Sandra
  150 Cary 33 45 146 Cawood 52
  Davey 145 David 71 Delila 145
  Elizabeth 22 Epsey 116 Joel 133
  John 54 70 83 134 145 Luann 97
  Lucinda 146 Mary 61 83 Matilda
  1 Minty 45 Nicholas 133 146
  Peggy 133 Polly 96 136 Ransom
  146 Sally 146
TREADWAY Jane 171
TRIB(B)LE Frances 38 108
TRIMBLE Jane 173 175 Nancy
  177 Peggy 175 Polly 171 175
  Thomas 163
TRIPLETT Eliza 146 Harriet 161
  James 153 Jane 161 John 146
  Mary 153 Sarah E. 24 Thomas
  99 146 153 161

206

?TROUTT (see Shrout)
TROTTER Rebecca 167
?TRPTILL Louisa 147
TRUETT Nancy 61
TRUMBO Andrew 18 78 Betty 75
  Cholloth 111 David 85 Deborah
  78 Dorothy 28 Elizabeth 27 111
  Elizabeth Jane 54 Eunice 92 F.,
  Jr. 27 George 36 92 Harriet 124
  Isaac 132 Jacob 48 124 131 147
  Jemima 149 Job. F. 149 John 27
  28 56 75 78 111 132 153 John A.
  146 John F. 4 John L. 111
  Lydia 131 M. A. 2 46 M. F. 15
  Malissa 15 Margaret 107 132
  Martha 163 Mary Jane 5 Nancy
  153 Peggy 48 132 Rachel 56
  Ruth 27 S. M. 30 54 Sally 132
  Sarah A. 2
TUCKER Elizabeth 176
TURLEY Wm. 104
TURNER Ann E. 43 J. F., Jr. 32
  John 142 John F. 39 43 131
  Larkin 71 Patricia 57 Phebe 134
  Wm. 147
TYDINGS John W. 137
TYLER Joseph 147
ULERY / ULLERY David 129
  Isaac 156 Rebecca 156
UNDERWOOD Ann 20 Elizabeth
  20 166 Gala 80 171 John 80
  Margaret 41 Milly 130 Reuben
  60 93 130 Wm. 41
UTTERBACK John 51 Polly 41
  Winnefied 130
?VAN Alfred 54
VANARSDALL Carnelius 111
  Mary E. 120 Sarah 113 114
VANLANDINGHAM Jeremiah
  149 Nancy 149 Susan 84
  Susannah 37
VANNATTON Lucinda 30
VANSCHOCK Rachel 45
VANULE / VANUELLS Caty Ann
  79 Daniel 79

VEALEY Celinda 143
VICE / VISE Aaron 14 46 149 150
  Betsy 150 Eliza 40 Elizabeth 3
  14 Elvira 18 Emily 150 Fanny
  15 Franky 81 Greenberry 42 63
  Gunnell 150 Henry 149 Huldah
  62 Isaac 151 James 7 John 15
  158 Joseph 63 Lawrence 62 150
  Louann 151 Louinda 143 M. B.
  43 Manning 130 Margaret 43
  Maria Elizabeth 113 Martin 143
  Matilda 158 Nancy 15 46 Nancy
  Ann 42 Rachel 150 151 Rebecca
  144 Robt. 15 Roberta 51 Sally
  63 Sarah 81 150 Souen 150
  Wm. 40 81 104 143 145
VINKIRK / VINCERK Debby 10
  Henry 10
?VIOSON William 106
WADE Dolly 84 Elizann 88 F.F.
  15 James 13 84 151 Peggy 13
  Polly 84 Samuel 88
WADLE Elizabeth 154 Joseph 154
WAG(A)NER / WAGAN /
  WAGSON J. W. 146 John 118
  Rebecca 146
WAILKES Matty 173
WAITT Elizabeth 127
WALKER Betsey 12 Elizabeth C.
  98 Fanny 169 James 44 83
  Joseph 14 98 Lucinda 68
  Malinda 61 84 Narcissa 44 Polly
  11
WALLS / WATTS Delila 85
  Genetta 46 James 155 Reuben 46
  Sarah 160 Washington 160
  Zachariah 85
WALTON / WALLTON Andrew
  43 Sarah 55 Wm. 55 87 90 105
  152
WARD Nancy 71 Sally 153 Wm.
  29 94 134
WARDER Wm. P. 161
WARFIELD Betsey 87 88 Calib
  88 G. W. 144 Providence 115

WARNER (see also Warren)
David 58 Elizabeth Jane 145
George Ann 125 Hatty 75 Hetty
84 J. R. 153 Jacob 84 163 John
B. 153 Jonas 90 153 Joseph 199
Margaret 4 54 Martha 6 84
Nancy 110 141 163 Polly 111
Salley 89 Serilda 32 Wm. 32
WARREN (see also Warner)
Amanda 154 Elizabeth 58
Elizabeth Jane 64 James 34 52 92
John 58 111 153 John B. 27 53
56 93 129 153 160 Martha 6
Mary 56 Nancy 53 141 Polly
111 Rebecky 36 Sarah 90 145
Wm. 6 141
?WASSON George C. 91
WATKINS Arminea 132
WATROWS / WATRONS Horace
152
WATSON H. 154
WAYNE Polly 174
WEBB B. A. 86 Ben F. 21 31
162 G. M. 21 Margaret 21
WEBSTER Charlotte 125
Corthina 155 F. M. 97 Parthena
155 Samuel 120 155
WELCH Geo. 73 Harriet 26 John
26 Martha 99 Polly 99 Sarah
124 Thos. 26
WELLS Ben 36 Cynthia Anna 114
Ed 51 Edmond 28 160 Edward
52 James 35 151 154 John 151
Joseph 56 155 L. 100 Matilda
154 Susan 56 153 Thos. 154
WEST Bailasy 83 Barbary 82
Walter 76
WHALEY Amelia 140 Charles 71
113 137 Elizabeth 116 117
Harriet 139 140 James 912 117
155 John 155 Johnson 70 Jon
69 Julia 106 107 Maria 155
Mary 159 Sarah 17 139 Sarah
Jane 71 Vincent 34 155 Wm.
139 140 155

WHEALLAN Mary 155
WHEELER Eliza 6 Polly 171
WHITE Aursted 117 Celice 44
Cely 40 Eliza 28 Elizabeth 12
Frederick 48 James 12 John M.
28 Polly 114 Wm. 85
WHIT(E)CRAFT / WHITECROFT
Ann 171 C. 46 Jane 1 John 21
53 63 Nancy 72 Polly 21 167
Rebeckah 165 Sally Lyde 63
WHIT(E)SETT Rachel 174
WHITLEROPH John 112
WHIT(T)INGTON / WHITTEN
C. 98 Charles 46 78 Mahala 35
WICK Jenne 176
WICKLIFFE Hutchis 56
WIGGIN(G)TON Mary 25 Peter
156
WIGLE Thos. 125
WILEY Jo 156 Margaret 172
WILHITE / WILLHITE /
WILHOIT Catherine 64 Francis
142 Joel 147 Nancy 13 Wm.
156
WILLIAMS Aaron 124 Ann 93
Anna 138 Betsy 61 Cynthia 77
Elizabeth 126 149 Hester A. R. 7
James 61 71 76 77 John 93 130
Joseph 31 46 64 73 126
Katherine G. 73 Kiziah 109
.Lucy 29 Malinda 76 Martha D.
126 Mary 45 Mary Ann 124
Nancy 114 Phebe 168 Phillip 25
Polly 48 Rebecca R. 72 Robert
L. 158 Samuel 1 Sorelda Ann
150 Thomas 104 133 W. S. 154
WILLIAMSON Catharine 135
David 26 75 James 144 Martha
Ann 75 Tinah 153 Wm. 114
WILLS (see also Wells) A. 158
Elizabeth 66 George 154
Jeramiah 155 Joseph 56 Susan
154
WILSON / WILLSON Arsenath 29
Catharine 114 Charles 46 David

www.ingramcontent.com/pod-product-compliance
Lightning Source LLC
Chambersburg PA
CBHW080237270326

41926CB00020B/4272